EMERGENCE AND EMPIRE

Emergence and Empire

Innis, Complexity, and the Trajectory of History

JOHN BONNETT

McGill-Queen's University Press
Montreal & Kingston • London • Ithaca

ISBN 978-0-7735-4202-0 (cloth)
ISBN 978-0-7735-4203-7 (paper)
ISBN 978-0-7735-8911-7 (ePDF)
ISBN 978-0-7735-8912-4 (ePUB)

Legal deposit third quarter 2013
Bibliothèque nationale du Québec

Printed in Canada on acid-free paper that is 100% ancient forest free (100% post-consumer recycled), processed chlorine free.

McGill-Queen's University Press acknowledges the support of the Canada Council for the Arts for our publishing program. We also acknowledge the financial support of the Government of Canada through the Canada Book Fund for our publishing activities.

Library and Archives Canada Cataloguing in Publication

Bonnett, John, 1965–, author
Emergence and empire : Innis, complexity, and the trajectory of history / John Bonnett.

Includes bibliographical references and index.
Issued in print and electronic formats.
ISBN 978-0-7735-4202-0 (bound). – ISBN 978-0-7735-4203-7 (pbk.). – ISBN 978-0-7735-8911-7 (ePDF). – ISBN 978-0-7735-8912-4 (ePUB)

1. Innis, Harold A., 1894–1952 – Criticism and interpretation. 2. History – Philosophy. I. Title.

HB121.I6B65 2013 330.092 C2013-903791-8
C2013-903792-6

This book was typeset by True to Type in 10.5/13 Sabon

Contents

Acknowledgments

Harold Innis once wrote that "'the sediment of experience' provides the basis for scientific investigation." But as I look at a now happily completed manuscript on a crisp, autumn morning here in Ontario, I find myself gratefully aware that the matter of that sediment is much more than the material and manuscript traces that Innis referred to in his article. My name appears at the front of this book, but no book is ever the product of a single voice. Its sediment derives from the faith of family and friends who express confidence that you will finish what you start, even when you have a hard time believing it yourself. It is also the product of conversations with colleagues who help you clarify a thought, smooth distressing syntax, or correct an error that never should have made it into the manuscript in the first place. And it is the product of friends who opened their homes on research trips, and archivists who steer you in directions you never would have thought to go on your own. The sediment of this book is formed from the network of relationships that helped build it. To those of you who played a role in its composition – all of you, named and unnamed – please accept a gratitude that is far deeper and more heartfelt that I can express.

I would first like to mention Chad Gaffield. As I write, I remember the first conversation I ever had with him about the project that eventually became this book. At the time, I hadn't the first clue what this book would be. I asked Chad for an idea, and to his credit he refused to give me one. He knew that doctoral work that means anything – and more to the point reaches completion – is largely self-conceived and self-generated. Thankfully, I was soon able to locate a topic that I came to care deeply about: the writings of Harold Adams Innis. Once

I crossed that threshold, Chad offered his complete and generous support, support that has been unstinting as I have widened my research interests to include new domains such as the digital humanities. Thanks Chad. I say to you now something I once said in 2001: you are one of the finest exemplars of the oral tradition that I know.

I would also like to thank the many readers and peer-reviewers who commented on the materials and drafts that eventually made their way into this manuscript. I am particularly indebted to my friend and colleague Steven High for his extensive comments and his constant encouragement. He has elevated the material presented here. He has elevated the work of all who have had the privilege of working with him. I am also deeply indebted to Janet Ajzenstat, Lee Bonnett, Alicia Colson, Nicki Darbyson, Donald Davis, Gerald Friesen, Paul Heyer, Eda Kranakis, Jane McLeod, Douglas Moggach, John Robson, David Schimmelpenninck van der Oye, and Elizabeth Vlossak for their comments and criticisms. Where this book has been improved, it is to their credit. Where it remains in error, the responsibility of course is entirely my own.

I would also like to thank colleagues and friends at the Institute for Information Technology at the National Research Council for their comments, and for exposing me to trends in information management that I would never have encountered in an archive or in the Innis literature. They have accused me of changing in small measure the way they think. They should know they have changed in large measure the way I think. Their imprint is on this manuscript as well, particularly in the sections devoted to visualization. I am particularly grateful to Martin Brooks, Michael Lehane, Steve Marsh, John Meech, and Arnold Cantwell Smith for their comments and encouragement.

On a personal note, I would like to thank my friends Robert Neufeld and the late Liz Combes. While I was reviewing the Innis Papers at the University of Toronto, they opened their home to me, providing not only their hospitality but also the far more valuable gift of their friendship. I would also like to thank my friend and mentor Brian Villa, who continued to exercise an influence over me long after he was my MA supervisor. He taught me much about the historian's craft in the decade that I was privileged to know him. The lesson I prized most, though, was the one that he embodied rather than stated; namely, that when the past is approached with flexibility in conception, and dignity in exposition, there is joy in execution. Thanks, Brian. I would also like to thank friends and colleagues in Columbia,

South Carolina, who were a source of encouragement to me while I was completing the final version of this manuscript. I am particularly grateful to David Miller and Jennifer Guiliano at the University of South Carolina, who made it possible for me to spend a stimulating and productive year in Columbia. I am also grateful to Bob and Felicia Best, Jeff and Pam Debessonet, Dan and Jean Dix, Carlos and Ruth Iglesias, and Don and Donna Vroblesky for their interest in the book and their encouragement while I was in South Carolina. My deepest thanks to you all.

I am also happy to acknowledge the institutional support I received during the research and composition of this work, and in particular the financial support of the Social Sciences and Humanities Research Council, the Canada Research Chair Foundation, and funding from the province of Ontario via an Ontario Graduate Scholarship. I am also deeply indebted to archival personnel at the University of Toronto Archives and the MIT archives, and in particular to Harold Averill, who was always ready to share his deep knowledge of the Innis papers with me.

And finally, I would like to thank my parents, Lee and Shirley Bonnett. They have given me more than they know. They were a never-ending source of encouragement and support to me in the years I devoted to this project. Their presence fills these pages, and for that reason I dedicate this work to them. Thanks, Mom and Dad.

EMERGENCE AND EMPIRE

Introduction

A prophet is not without honour, save in his own country, and in his own house.

Matthew 13:57

Harold Innis would have resisted identification with the above epigram, for he was many things. He was modest. He was hard working. He was brilliant, ribald, and a scamp.[1] But he was not pretentious, and would have disavowed any claim of divine inspiration. A former Baptist, he would have greeted comparison of this nature with a mixture of displeasure and derisive laughter. Still, there is much to commend in Christ's description of the prophet when considering the career of Harold Adams Innis. Like most prophets, Innis had much to say that was important to the past, present, and future of his country. And like most prophets, he has often been misunderstood. He never spoke in parables, but his prose had a similar effect on his audience. Although praised by Marshall McLuhan as ideogrammatic, his writings were derided by other scholars as an abomination of the English language, with a penchant for snatching obscurity out of the jaws of clarity.[2] A 1947 review in *The Economist* ruefully noted: "Incoherence, indeed, is Professor Innes' [sic] besetting sin."[3]

Since his death in 1952, Innis has paid a posthumous price for this sin. He is now an obscure figure in Canada, known only to a cross-section of academics and graduate students. In a 2000 *Maclean's* survey of Canadians who inspired the world, his name was nowhere to be found. The omission is not surprising: Harold Innis is an awful read. When it comes to Canadian theorists of communication, it is McLuhan, not Innis, who has received popular global approbation.[4] Within the academy, however, Innis remains a respected figure, albeit one in whom scholars have learned to hate the sin and love the sinner. Judith Stamps notes of her initial encounter with Innis: "it was the strangest text I had ever seen. I could only vaguely make out its meaning, but I had the sense of being in contact with something profound."[5] In a recent historiographical essay, Charles Acland and William Buxton suggest that similar insights have stimulated a renewed scholarly interest in Innis's writings: "There is something about his work – its intellectual breadth and theoretical shifts – that lends itself handily to reinterpretation."[6] There is a sense, then – almost a statement of faith – among Canadian scholars that Innis is among the most profound thinkers Canada has ever produced. In an era when globalization and new communication technologies are transforming and tasking us, Innis still has much to impart. Canadians would do well to become better acquainted with him.

But for all the approbation, there still remains the matter of Innis's "besetting sin." Acland and Buxton note that scholarly interest has also been tinged by frustration, the kind that initiates feel before a prophet who simply refuses to get to the point. Hugh Aitken perhaps best voiced this sentiment, which he experienced as a student of Innis at the University of Toronto: "To be taught by Innis and to learn from Innis called for an act of faith. You had to believe that there was something really important there. Grains of doubt crept in from time to time – can anyone honestly deny it? Perhaps the Emperor had no new clothes after all."[7] But in Acland and Buxton's judgment, most scholars continue to see him as fully clothed, since for the past thirty years his name has continued "to come up, showing that there is a consensus that he initiated something important, though the consensus-makers may not be sure what."[8]

Innis interpreters have faced a challenge, then, in recommending his writings to scholars within Canada and without. Aside from agreeing that Innis initiated something important and that his early and late writings share a common framework, scholars have been unable to point to a consensus on the nature of this framework. Consequently, scholars have also failed to reach agreement on his place in Canadian letters or, to the extent that they have considered the matter, in the broader fields of international economic and cultural historiography.[9] Furthermore, Acland and Buxton suggest that, for many Canadian interpreters, initial interest and confusion have recently deteriorated into a state of disaffection: "The demonstration of high regard for Innis' work sometimes has the same enthusiasm as an obligation to visit a relative one doesn't really like."[10]

I propose, however, that the writings of Harold Innis deserve a renewed place of prominence in scholars' social calendars. There is in them a coherence, a unity of purpose that has not yet been properly demonstrated in the literature. The entirety of his work – staples and media studies alike – can and should be viewed as a sustained exploration of change, and more specifically the variant of change that governs human history. The overarching purpose of Innis's career was to demonstrate that the patterns of Canadian economic and global history should be identified with the characteristics of emergent change. Societies are systems, governed by rules that pertain to emergent systems. Innis's aim was to demonstrate to his contemporaries that cultures which historically had operated within the constraints of these rules, through default or design, had prospered and endured. By contrast, cultures that had violated these strictures had not. Instead, they collapsed.

Harold Adams Innis was born in Otterville, Ontario, in 1894. Raised in a poor, devoutly Baptist farming family, he was nevertheless encouraged to develop his aptitude for learning and scholarship, despite his family's material privation. Throughout his life, Innis seemed to live with a characteristic wilfulness. In life, it propelled him to produce a remarkable corpus of work devoted to the history of Canadian extractive industries, be it fur, cod, or wheat, and his own take on the history of Western Civilization, based on communication media and the oral tradition. On the eve of death, his wilfulness motivated him to deny the existence of the cancer that would prematurely end his life in 1952, to the distress of his family and friends.[11] But in youth, Innis's determination enabled him to overcome his and his family's limited means. Starting in a one-room school house, through a combination of hard work and talent, he advanced to high school, and then McMaster University in 1913.[12]

Innis rarely had trouble discerning what he wanted out of life. Overall, it was a trait that stimulated great achievement. In a minority of instances, it propelled him to commit acts of great folly. Innis's biographer Donald Creighton reports that Innis, upon beginning his first term at McMaster University, quickly realized his financial resources were barely sufficient to maintain a subsistent standard of living. Rather than ask his parents for financial assistance, he subjected himself to a regime of stringent penury, arriving home in Otterville for Christmas emaciated and ready to end his university career. His family prevailed upon him to continue, this time with help from home. Overall, though, his determination to learn stood him in good stead at McMaster, and he enjoyed a successful university career from the winter term of 1914 until his graduation in 1916. Michael Gauvreau suggests that it was during his time there that Innis became exposed to the questions and concepts that would preoccupy him for the remainder of his career. The central question of his communication studies – "Why do we attend to the things to which we attend?" – was first posed to him by his philosophy professor at McMaster, James Ten Broeke.[13]

After graduating, Innis joined the Canadian Army, and philosophical concerns gave way to the more pressing problems of staying alive as an artillery spotter in the First World War. According to Creighton: "The war was the second great influence in his life ... With little preparation and with almost no appreciation of what was involved, he was suddenly caught up in a life of fast movement, and violent activity, and deadly peril."[14] Life at McMaster had taught him that Western culture was subject to inquiry; life as a soldier would teach him that it was subject to catastrophe. Innis was circumspect about the horrors he witnessed at the front, but even a cursory review of his later writings shows that they affected him deeply. In his last decade he would interpret the First and Second World Wars as symptomatic of a civilization in decline.[15]

In July 1917, at Vimy Ridge, Innis was injured in the leg and removed to Britain for treatment. During his convalescence, he made the shift from soldier to graduate student, beginning research for a dissertation on the problems associated with repatriating Canadian soldiers after the war. On his return to Canada in April 1918, he was discharged from the army and completed the requirements for his Master's degree the same month. The next fall, Innis entered the PhD program in Economics at the University of Chicago. There, he completed a thesis devoted to the history of the Canadian Pacific Railway. And there, he focused on a third insight regarding human cultures: not only were they subject to critical inquiry, and subject to collapse, but societies were also subject to a specific form of change. Introduced to the writings of Thorstein Veblen, Innis, as we see in chapter 2, would employ them in the 1920s to argue for the reconstitution of economic theory. Economists could no longer rely on the mechanical constructs of change embedded in classical economics, he said. Economic systems were not static entities. They emerged; they evolved; they transformed themselves. As arenas of change, they were more akin to biological than physical systems, displaying patterns of change found in embryology and ecology.[16]

After completion of his doctorate in 1920, Innis accepted a position with the Department of Political Economy at the University of Toronto. During his tenure there as a scholar, professor, and administrator, he distinguished himself as one of the most prolific scholars in the history of Canadian letters. In 1930 and 1940 respectively, he published *The Fur Trade* and *The Cod Fisheries*, the works that would distinguish him in the field of economic historiography. In both, he would advance the staple hypothesis, the proposition that the constitutions of Canada's social, economic, and political structures were derivatives of the initiating stage of European economic activity in each region. If the culture of the Maritimes differed from that of Central Canada, it was because the inhabitants of that region had historically extracted a different commodity, or staple, from the environment.[17]

In the early 1940s Innis's career took a radical turn. With the publication of *Political Economy in the Modern State*, his emphasis shifted from economic systems to the more multi-dimensional arena of cultural systems. His object in making the shift was to identify the core problem of the West. In the first half of the twentieth century, the peace of Europe and North America had collapsed twice, and Innis proposed to explain why. His solution was as surprising as it was simple: cultures became dysfunctional because they failed in the fundamental task of information management. For Innis, information was a tool to stimulate creativity. When cultures lost control of the information circulating within them, they invariably became rigid or unstable in their thinking, and often turned to violence prior to their collapse.[18]

The question of information management would also preoccupy Innis in his most famous communications studies, *Empire and Communications* (1950) and *The Bias of Communication* (1952). In each, Innis proposed to study the history of Western civilization, from ancient Egypt to the present, in parallel with the history of communications technology. He would also reiterate that a culture's success was predicated on its success in managing information. And he would argue that a culture's adoption of a new communication technology had an important consequence: the culture's assumption of a new cultural bias, one directed toward the dimension of space, time, or in very rare instances, space-time.[19]

By the time Innis completed his first communication anthology in the mid-1940s, he had already distinguished himself as a scholar who had a great deal to say to Canada, the United States and Europe, having published scores of articles in addition to his major staple studies. And for the most part, he earned the respect of his colleagues – even if they did not agree with him, even if they failed to completely understand him. This respect was subsequently transformed into recognition, through promotion, and through honours. In 1937 Innis was appointed chair of the Department of Political Economy, and in 1947 he became dean of the University of Toronto's Graduate School. Academic honours soon followed. Innis was made president of the Royal Society of Canada in 1947, and president of the American Economics Association in 1951. He served on royal commissions and funding bodies such as the Rockefeller Foundation; he received honorary doctorates, and was invited to lecture at Oxford in 1948 and the Collège de France in 1951. And then – in his prime – Innis stopped. After suffering persistent back pains in the winter of 1952, he learned he had terminal cancer. He succumbed the following November. Eric Havelock would perceptively characterize his premature death as a disaster in the history of human letters.[20]

In the sixty years since Innis's death, scholars have continued their efforts to understand him and, as we have seen, have emerged in the twenty-first century with the uneasy sense of having had little success. At base, they have had two goals: to demonstrate that Innis's early and late works are unified within a single framework, and to unearth the identity of that framework. The supposition of this study is that Innis's work – early and late – was an attempt to characterize human society as an emergent system. As such, the disparate sub-systems of society, be they economic, be they cultural, were subject to the forms of change associated with emergent systems. The basis for this supposition stems from a statement made by W.T. Easterbrook shortly after Innis's death, that Innis had "throughout remained a disciple of Adam Smith and no name appears more frequently in his observations on economics past and present."[21] Robert Babe has recently noted as well that Smith's "influence on Innis was probably much greater than is generally recognized."[22]

Smith's writings had a specific significance for Innis. Citing Alfred Marshall, he describes them as "architectonic," offering "the great concept of society as a whole." Smith's ideas, he argues, were distinguished by their suggestion that societies and economic phenomena "were manifestations of an underlying order in nature governed by natural forces." These insights into natural law were sufficiently powerful, in Innis's estimation, that they influenced the subsequent development of biology and the social sciences. Darwin's theory of natural selection in turn traced an intellectual lineage back to the writings of Smith, while the economics of Thorstein Veblen stemmed from ideas first voiced in *The Wealth of Nations*. In short, Innis identified Smith with the genesis of an emergent construct of change.[23]

Aside from Innis's acknowledgment of his intellectual debt to Smith, the suggestion that his writings are informed by an emergent or ecological conception of change also stems from numerous statements to that effect in the literature. Innis interpreters such as Vincent di Norcia, Paul Heyer, Barrington Nevitt, William Melody, David Crowley, James Carey, Judith Stamps, Ian Parker, and Cole Harris have all noted Innis's appeals to ecological constructs of change.[24] While all have made valuable contributions by highlighting this dimension of Innis's thought, they have nevertheless suffered from a difficulty that stems from the peculiar nature of Innis's prose. As Ian Parker observes, Innis's writings are grounded "in detailed historical study of particular systems … As a result, notwithstanding some passages that appear to summarize aspects of his theoretical position, most of his analytical framework is *only* available in *implicit* form and can only be extracted and rendered *explicit* through an extended inductive process involving a period of intensive absorption in his work."[25]

Parker's observation suggests that, given the nature of the material, it is difficult if not impossible for interpreters to make affirmative statements about Innis's views regarding change within the span of a periodical article. An effective understanding of the worldview that is embedded in Innis's early and late writings can only be reached in a monograph-length study, a format that allows for the in-depth examination and interpretation that Innis's thought requires. Such a genre also permits extensive quotations from each work, in order to make explicit the common framework embedded in his disparate studies.

To date, no such study has appeared in the literature, and it is this gap that this study seeks to fill. While a few monographs devoted to Innis's writings have appeared in the past twenty years, none have addressed this topic specifically. Arthur Kroker focuses on Innis's thoughts about the social and political effects of technology, while Judith Stamps emphasizes his work on epistemology. Graeme Patterson's study does address Innis's views on historical change, specifically the role of formal cause, but the focus of his attention is Canadian historiography, not Innis.[26] Although J. Alexander Watson offers an interpretation of Innis's construct of change in his recent *Marginal Man*, his reading suffers from an important limitation: it is not based on a sustained reading of Innis's economic writings. This shortcoming makes it difficult for the reader to assess the validity of his interpretation, particularly his claim that there is a conceptual divide between Innis's early and late work.[27] Given Parker's observation about Innis's writings, then, it may be suggested that many of the characterizations of Innis's construct of historical change are based more on assertion than demonstration. The assessments are not necessarily wrong, but the literature requires the benefit of a more substantial evidentiary base before an emergent construct, or any construct of change for that matter, can be assumed. That is the primary task of this study.

A second task, addressed in the first chapter, is to provide as precise a definition of change as possible, be it the mechanical change that informed classical economics or the emergent change that Innis instilled in his own writings. More specifically, I propose a definition of emergent change consistent with the one used by scientists in the interdisciplinary science of complexity. I also offer a description of Innis's intellectual context. The construct of emergent change consists of several constituent concepts, and Innis's access to them, singly and in conjunction, can be demonstrated through a reading of two economists whose influence he cited: Thorstein Veblen and Alfred Marshall.

Researchers in the science of complexity study *complex adaptive systems* and suggest that they are ubiquitous both in nature and in human society, including the economy. They are governed by emergent change and share several common features. They are composed of numerous agents, which interact one with another. By virtue of their interaction, the agents self-organize into systems – systems that display emergent structures or properties that persist over time. Complex adaptive systems are also distinguished by the governance of *formal and final cause.* In the case of formal cause, once a system emerges, it begins to regulate the behaviour of its agents or constituents, assigning specific tasks to specific agents. A bee in isolation, for example, can potentially perform a variety of roles, from reproduction to construction. But once it is embedded in a colony, *formal cause* operates to limit its activities. If it becomes a labourer, it will not reproduce. Complex systems illustrate the governance of *final cause* in that they display behaviour that can be construed as purposive. Such systems are not passive conduits for matter and energy. Rather, they operate much like economies, interacting actively with their environments and appropriating materials to maintain their existence.

As the succeeding chapters reveal, the template of change associated with complex adaptive systems proves extremely useful for unearthing the construct of change embedded in Innis's writings. It enables us to measure Innis's knowledge of the characteristics of emergent change and self-organizing systems, and in conclusion to reach an evaluation of its extent. The answer offered in retrospect will be the same as the one offered in prospect: Innis knew a great deal.

Innis's first major books, *A History of the Canadian Pacific Railway* and *The Fur Trade in Canada*, are the focus of the second chapter. In these works, Innis took his first concrete steps to initiate a research agenda that was conceived at McMaster, elaborated at the University of Chicago, and finally given expression in an important article, "The Work of Thorstein Veblen." In that essay, Innis made clear his opposition to the dominance of mechanical constructs of change in economic analysis, and wrote of the need to appropriate alternative models from disciplines such as biology. As a young economist, Innis believed the discipline needed to be reconstituted, and he pressed his young peers to take up the challenge.[28] His study of the CPR is of interest because it gives a foretaste of what he would later express in the Veblen essay. It was his first attempt to incorporate Veblen's evolutionary economics into Canadian economic history. It is also important because it indicates that Innis formulated much of the research agenda he would later undertake as an economic historian while he was still a graduate student at the University of Chicago. The preface and conclusion of the book both anticipate his interest in change and the studies in staples industries that he would pursue from 1920 to 1940.

As a study of economic change, however, Innis viewed his first monograph as something of a failure, and it was not until the publication of *The Fur Trade in Canada* in 1930 that Innis produced a study that met the expectations he had set for himself. There he would provide an evolutionary history of Canadian institutions that demonstrated their emergence as a result of agent interaction with other agents, with the environment, and Europe. And there, he would also emphasize that the attributes of Canada's institutions – like complex adaptive systems – persisted through time, and were governed by formal cause. To understand the internal organization of Canada's economy in the 1930s, Innis argued, one had to study its origins in the 1630s. Chapter 3, through a study of *The Cod Fisheries*, examines an attribute of emergent systems that Innis highlighted in his disparate studies of the Atlantic fisheries: *increasing returns*. In complex adaptive systems, the behaviour of the agents that constitute them is regulated by *positive feedback*. If a constituent agent acts in a way that enhances the survival of the system, it receives rewards. If it performs in such a way that it decreases the system's fitness, its share of resources is diminished, and at times the agent is even expelled. The same principle holds with respect to a system's interaction with its immediate environment. When it acts in a way that is adaptive, it receives resources – or positive feedback – from the environment. When it does not, the system perishes.

In economics, positive feedback is referred to as increasing returns. As we see in chapters 3 and 5, the concept played a central role not only in Innis's economic histories, where he showed it to have been instrumental in enabling England to defeat France for hegemony over North America, but also in his later communication studies. To understand Innis's ideas on how communication technologies affect a culture's disposition toward change, one needs an understanding of the economics of increasing returns. To elucidate this concept, chapter 3 summarizes the writings of one of its leading exponents, economist W. Brian Arthur, and continues with a reading of "The Rise and Fall of the Spanish Fishery," "The Economic History of the Maritimes," and *The Cod Fisheries*.

Innis's first communications anthology, *Political Economy in the Modern State*, is the focus of the fourth chapter. Part political treatise and part jeremiad, the anthology was intended as a prescription for cultural renewal. In addressing the problem of information management, Innis touched on another characteristic of change associated with complex adaptive systems: namely, that their capacity to emerge and adapt is determined by crucial inputs called *control parameters*. *Political Economy* suggests that, in the history of the West, the quantity of circulating information was an important control parameter that governed the emergence of new social, cultural, and economic patterns, and their subsequent adaptation. While analyzing emergent systems, Innis also came to understand a fundamental point that would later be articulated by contemporary proponents of the science of complexity: systems can only change when they are governed by the right balance between freedom and constraint; and that balance is determined by the control parameter of circulating information. For Innis, the issue of information overload was crucially important. It explained what he saw as the cultural decline of the nineteenth century; and it explained the onset of the First and Second World Wars.

The fifth chapter offers an interpretation of the two best known and widely cited books of Innis's corpus: *Empire and Communications* and *The Bias of Communication*. In both, Innis painted the history of the West as a history of constructs of change, constructs stabilized and de-stabilized by the emergence of new communication technologies in the form of script, physical media, or genres of speech. He laid particular stress on the latter, or as he referred to it, the oral tradition, since it represented the communication environment most conducive to creative thought and cultural adaptation. It also points to Innis's belief that cognitive structures are themselves emergent systems, subject to the governance of formal cause.

Chapter 5 also shows that Innis did not hold a position commonly ascribed to him; namely, the supposition that certain media invariably predispose cultures to embrace a bias toward space or time. Innis did not see a linear relationship between the physical properties of any given medium and a particular construct of change. In his narratives, not every culture using papyrus, for example, retained a bias toward space. In ancient Israel, the prophets employed papyrus to champion a worldview predisposed toward time, while in ancient Rome papyrus supported a cultural disposition toward space. The relationship that Innis drew between agents and media was far more complex than is traditionally assumed in the literature. It was a relationship that emphasized contingency. It was a relationship that emphasized human freedom. But most of all, it was a relationship governed by the regulation of emergent change.

The final chapter moves from a study of the substance of Innis's corpus to a consideration of its significance, with the simple purpose of arguing that Harold Innis was a prescient thinker. Whether one considers his thoughts on what we would refer to today as information cascades, his promotion of information visualization, or even his writings promoting an Idealist interpretation of history, his works, all told, have a remarkably contemporary feel to them. Innis's ideas are important because they anticipated many of the practices and concerns that scholars today are adopting and promoting. They are also significant because they show an Innis who refused to be bound by the intellectual fashion of his time, particularly in its shift away from Idealism. He may have been right to do so. Innis pressed his colleagues to retain insights from Plato and Kant in their reading of history, and in our final chapter we see how some scholars – particularly in the sciences – are reaching conclusions very similar to his.

Harold Innis ended his career much as he began it. He considered it vital that cultures understand the regime of change in which they operate. Such had been his concern in the staples studies. In *The Cod Fisheries* in particular, he stressed the importance of agents, their ability to self-organize, and the importance of increasing returns in mediating the fortunes of the European empires occupying the perimeter of the North Atlantic. In his staple and communication studies, Innis would also emphasize the importance of balance between liberty and constraint. Maintenance of a proper balance would enable Canada's institutions to emerge and thrive. It was a neglect of proper balance that had precipitated the catastrophes of the First and Second World Wars, catastrophes that Innis was by no means certain the West could avoid repeating in the second half of the twentieth century. In early study and late Innis would also emphasize the importance of formal and final cause, suggesting that both forms of causation allowed room for the individual and collective creativity he desperately wanted to nourish. Innis's purpose throughout was to illustrate the constraints imposed by emergent change, the dangers they imposed, and the opportunities they wrought. Let us see how.

1

Constructs of Change

Let us start by reiterating the fundamental argument of this book: Harold Innis's writings enjoy an underlying coherence; they can and should be characterized as a sustained meditation on the nature of emergent change. It is all very well to make such a statement; it is quite another to demonstrate its purchase. And here, our friend Innis, Harold the Obscure, offers little help. If we are to make any sense of his writings, we need to work around his penchant for concrete description and explore the constructs of change that concerned him. More specifically, we must consider a precise description of mechanical change, the construct he resisted, and a precise description of emergent change, the construct he embraced.

Before reading Innis himself, we also need to place him in his intellectual context, to demonstrate his access to the concepts associated with emergent change. That placement, I suggest, can be obtained in two ways. The first is to use a contemporary formulation of emergent change: the *complex adaptive system*. Coined by the science of complexity, the construct offers a number of advantages for interpreters seeking to identify Innis with a concept of self-organizing change. To start, it offers a far more systematic expression of the concept than formulations extant in Innis's time, such as those offered by C. Lloyd Morgan and Samuel Alexander.[1]

In this construct, important phenomena are not only described but are characterized by concepts such as self-organization, the edge-of-chaos, positive feedback, and formal and final cause. Further, the constituents of complex adaptive systems are not discussed in dispersed sections of voluminous tracts. They are, rather, presented as a unified set of propositions that describe the operation and adaptation of emergent systems. Put simply, the construct provides a concrete list of elements to search for as we follow Ian Parker's call to translate Innis's analytical framework from its implicit to an explicit form. The concept is also important because it provides a contemporary measure of Innis's knowledge of the dynamics of emergent change. Researchers in the science of complexity hold that complex adaptive systems appear everywhere in nature, in contexts ranging from cellular biology to human economy; and furthermore, that the defining features of such systems cannot be derived in their totality from examination of any one type of system. A feature obvious in one context may be hidden in another. The formulations offered, therefore, stem from the study of systems in multiple human and natural contexts. They offer a measure that rests on an empirical breadth and depth that differentiates them from earlier constructs of emergent change, and which in turn suggests that Innis knew much about the dynamics of emergent change.

Innis's writings can also be situated in their context by reading him in relation to economists he deemed important. Over the course of his career Innis placed his work in relation to a number of economists, including Adam Smith, Norman S.B. Gras, and George Unwin. But aside from Adam Smith, there is one economist who is widely acknowledged in the Innis literature as being central in the formation of Innis's thought: Thorstein Veblen. Veblen was a pioneer in the field of evolutionary economics and a leading figure in the field of institutional economics. His preoccupation, like Innis's, was change, at the institutional and individual level. Innis was exposed to his writings while at the University of Chicago. As someone who was seeking a coherent way to explain the history and trajectory of Canadian institutions, Innis quickly grasped the significance of Veblen's writings, to the extent that he joined a discussion group dedicated to Veblen during his time at Chicago. The force of Veblen's ideas was such that, almost a decade after he completed his dissertation, Innis wrote a programmatic essay calling on young economists to apply and extend them.

Veblen is important for our purposes because through him we can demonstrate Innis's exposure to the concepts associated with emergent change, singly, and in conjunction. While Veblen was not as systematic as contemporary researchers in his exposition of emergent change, his writings nevertheless presented a complex of ideas that young scholars such as Innis could find and use. The purpose of this chapter is to show that those concepts were available for appropriation and, in turn, to demonstrate that there is a remarkable coherence between, on the one hand, the writings of Veblen and Innis and, on the other, the writings of philosophers and scientists interested in complex adaptive systems and emergent change.

I

The first concept of change that concerns us – mechanical change – was derived from seventeenth-century physics, specifically from the celestial mechanics of Sir Isaac Newton. Newton envisaged the universe as being housed in a three-dimensional Euclidean space. Space and time were viewed as separate dimensions, and each was seen as an independent, neutral medium. Neither dimension was constituted by the objects within it; both were considered logically prior to them.[2] All objects in space were thought to be governed by an independent, homogeneous set of laws. No provision was made for separate layers of organization governed by distinct sets of laws, as would pertain today, for example, in physics, where the movements of planetary bodies are described by celestial mechanics, while the movements of subatomic particles are described by quantum mechanics. After Newton demonstrated that gravitation is susceptible to mathematical expression, and that his formulae described the movement of both terrestrial and celestial objects, scholars in the sciences and philosophy embraced his vision of a cosmos governed by universal laws that operate independent of time.[3]

Newton's was a vision that privileged Aristotle's concept of efficient cause at the expense of formal, final, and material variants of causation. Efficient cause was identified with external forces acting on inert objects. One example was gravity, a force that determined the positions of bodies in space. Newton's view of matter was atomistic. Matter was in essence immutable, subject only to the push-pull of forces from the outside. The implication of that position was to consign purpose – final cause – to the wind. It also determined which attributes of matter were to be labelled primary, or important, and secondary, or trivial. Attributes associated with the internal properties of the object – such as mass – and not subject to context were labelled the "real" – or primary – qualities of matter. Those properties that were dependent on context, and that were seen as a function of its relations with other objects such as colour and temperature, were seen as secondary. Since the internal properties of matter were held to be constant regard-less of context, wholes were deemed to be qualitatively indistinguishable from their parts. Indeed, the very existence of aggregates was seen to derive from efficient cause; they were considered an epiphenomenon. There was no appeal to self-organization, no sense that a system might emerge and appropriate a part to either generate or retain its formal integrity. With nothing to qualitatively distinguish building blocks from their aggregates, formal cause was also removed from the explanatory framework of the sciences and modern philosophy.[4]

The consequent of a formulation based on efficient cause and the immutability of matter was twofold. First, time ceased to have directionality or meaning. Since the essential nature of every system was identified with its governing rules, and those rules never changed, there was nothing of importance to distinguish Time A from Time B. The only way to distinguish temporal events was to track the changing position of objects within a system, positions that were determined by its covering laws. Since all systems were by definition closed, no variable, such as a change in the system's content, or an unexpected intrusion by the outside environment, could prevent an observer from predicting or retrodicting distinctions in the system's state, past or present.[5] By virtue of this construct, time became a secondary category. As Floyd Merrell notes, matter "thus became indifferent to the lapse of time, and time became a mere accident, a succession of instants totally independent of material attributes. Hence this quantitative and qualitative immutability of matter was counterpart to the homogeneous, but unrelated flow of time."[6]

The second consequent of Newton's formulation is that it erased any possibility of accounting for human agency. By divorcing celestial mechanics from time, Newton undercut any basis for asserting that time was unidirectional. If one were to film the orbit of Saturn for two millennia, and then play it backward, the formula a physicist would use to describe its trajectory would be the same. Purposive behaviour, by contrast, is not as easily detached from a directional sense of time. The philosopher Alicia Juarrero notes: "Newton's heirs dealt the final blow to Aristotle's concept of final cause by dismissing as illusory the apparent unidirectionality displayed both in the development of organic forms and by the aimed-for goal-directedness of voluntary, intentional behavior. In doing so, the one-way reaching out of *orexis* (from soul to world), which accounted for the purposiveness of action, became a problem in need of an explanation, as did the vector-like quality of action itself. If real things (atomic particles), were unaffected by time and context, an object's interactions with its environment and the unique trajectory it traced through time and space also became secondary, 'accidental' properties of no account to what really makes a thing the kind of thing it is and no other."[7]

II

In contrast to the closed systems described by Newtonian mechanics, complex adaptive systems are characterized as environments produced by virtue of the interactions of agents within systems. Whereas Newtonian mechanics assumed a universal covering law that determined the movement and relationship among its constituents in perpetuity, the relationships among components in complex systems do not remain fixed. There is no Clockmaker. Control is highly dispersed among the system's agents. If the system demonstrates any coherence, it is a result of the competition and cooperation of the actors involved. Complex adaptive systems are ubiquitous in the natural world. The economy, too, is an example of such a system. Its agents are individuals, participant corporations, and states. The brain is also a complex adaptive system, with individual neurons acting as agents.[8]

An important by-product of systems with agents acting in parallel is that they display emergent properties. Previously uncorrelated particles – aggregates – undergo a *bifurcation* (also called a *phase transition*), in which they interconnect and form an orderly arrangement, a system. The difference between an aggregate and a system is akin to the difference between a sandpile and an ant colony. Aside from number and spatial proximity, there is nothing that inherently distinguishes the properties of a sandpile from an individual grain of sand. In complex adaptive systems by contrast, the whole is more than the sum of its parts. An ant colony, for example, can display a range of behaviour that an ant in isolation cannot. As the number of ants, and the number of interactions between ants, increases, the repertoire of skills, or behavioural competence, of the colony also increases.[9]

Complex adaptive systems are also characterized by patterns that persist through time, or display *differential persistence*. A system's identity rests in the emergent pattern, not the identity of its constituent agents. The human body, for example, is a complex system. Its constituent agents – human cells – are routinely replaced, and yet the pattern defining the individual remains. A standing wave is a second example of differential persistence. The pattern remains, despite the continuous turnover of water molecules.[10] Since adaptation is a continuous process, complex adaptive systems can also display multiple levels of organization. In such a circumstance, a system at one level of organization will fill the role of agent in the next. Cells, for example, recombine with other cells to form an organ. Organs combine to form an organism.[11] And as Juarrero observes, each sequence of a self-organizing system is distinguished by increasing complexity, and "a progressive differentiation into a highly articulated, multilevel hierarchy in which new, functionally defined individuals or components emerge … A system emerges when previously uncorrelated particles or sequences or processes suddenly become coordinated and interconnected. In subsequent steps of an evolutionary sequence, components and processes are correlated and interconnected differently – in an even more complexly differentiated hierarchy. What makes each step of a self-organized process new is that its components are systematically interrelated in qualitatively novel ways."[12]

Since each step of self-organization is precipitated by a contingent event, complex adaptive systems have their own unique history. They become individuated over time as the complexity of each level of organization, and the number of levels of organization, increases.[13] The historical context of the system is important not only for explaining emergence, but also the function of its constituents. Multi-functionality in biological systems provides one example. A set of three bones used to provide a flexible linkage in the gill arch of a fish later came to have different applications in a reptile's jaw and the inner ear of a mammal.[14]

The development of complex systems cannot be described by the linear mathematical equations employed in Newtonian mechanics. Rather, as John Holland explains, while interactions in at least some emergent systems can be described in terms of invariant laws, the trajectory of the system is subject to constant change, and is more susceptible to the narrative mode of explanation employed by historians: "The definition of the generated system, although it determines all the rest, is no more than a simply described starting point; subsequent activities can be determined only by extended examination and experiment."[15]

Complex adaptive systems are also distinguished insofar as they are systems out of equilibrium. Contrary to expectations associated with Newtonian mechanics, which identified non-equilibrium as a disruption of a system's order, research by Ilya Prigogine, Stuart Kauffman, Chris Langton, and others suggests that non-equilibrium is a *source* of order, albeit a non-linear one. A linear process is akin to a machine. Move a lever and the machine moves; change the input of a system governed by a linear function, and the system changes as you adjust the input. Matters are less straightforward in non-linear systems. One can change the value of the *control parameter* – the input – for a period of time and observe no discernible change in the behaviour of the given system. As the input continues, however, the system will suddenly reach a bifurcation point, one in which the system self-organizes into a coherent structure, commonly referred to as a dissipative structure. Dissipative structures can be seen as an evolutionary adaptation. By virtue of their formation, they dissipate the non-equilibrium that has built up in the system, and are consequently better adapted to new conditions set by the control parameter.[16]

The Bénard cell is a classic example of a dissipative structure. To start, imagine a pot of water at room temperature. It is at equilibrium. The water's temperature is the same regardless of where it is measured within the pot. Once heat is applied, however, the scenario changes. As the control parameter rises, the system initially attempts to maintain equilibrium – a mean temperature – through negative feedback. The system attempts to prevent the emergence of a temperature gradient by the use of conduction. As the temperature continues rising, the system shifts further away from equilibrium, to a point where maintenance of a thermal mean is no longer a viable mode of organization. At that juncture, the system shifts from a static to a dynamic form of organization. Instead of suppressing thermal fluctuations around a mean temperature, the system begins to reinforce them through positive feedback, leading to the emergence of a convection current, or Bénard cell.

Anyone who has poured cream into coffee will recognize the hexagonal pattern of a Bénard cell. Water molecules in a glass of water behave in an uncorrelated fashion; they demonstrate spatial symmetry. Water molecules in a swirling cup of coffee, by contrast, organize themselves into macroscopic patterns; they behave in a correlated fashion.[17] When Bénard cells emerge, non-equilibrium is reduced as the "complicatedness of millions of independent molecules of water bouncing helter-skelter into each other" becomes streamlined "into the complexly organized, macroscopic, dynamic process structure of a Bénard cell," thereby facilitating the dissipation of the critical temperature gradient that had built up.[18] This strategy should be familiar to anyone who, about to get into a bath, has discovered that the water in the tub is too hot. Filling the tub with cool water is only a partial solution, since one half of the tub will subsequently contain water that is too cold, while the remaining half remains too hot. The entry of the cool water into the tub, however, does introduce non-equilibrium into the system; there is now a temperature gradient. Non-equilibrium is reduced – a comfortable overall temperature is obtained – by artificially introducing a convection current. The bather stirs the water in a circular fashion before plunging in.

While the emergence of macroscopic structures is a common feature of complex systems, a second common characteristic is that they appear only in association with a finite range of values for the control parameter. Kauffman's work with genetic circuits serves as a notable example. In the early 1960s, Kauffman came across François Jacob and Jacques Monod's path-breaking research into genetic circuitry. In their papers, the two demonstrated that the cell contains a number of regulatory genes that routinely activate and deactivate one another. In essence, they are switches in a biochemical computer. As a basis of orderly behaviour, genetic circuits appeared to be the likely basis of cell differentiation – the reason that one cell becomes a brain cell and another a liver cell. Kauffman's innovation was to suggest that the cell's computer did not carry out its instructions in a linear fashion, as an IBM mainframe would, but rather in parallel. The process was not one in which Gene A would activate Gene B, leading in turn to the activation of Gene C, and so on.[19]

Instead, Kauffman argued that since more than one regulatory gene was likely to be active at any time, cells were likely to be differentiated by self-consistent, self-organized sets of active genes. While Kauffman was able to construct computer models that supported his contention that regulatory genes formed self-organizing networks, he also discovered that emergence only occurred within certain constraints. The control parameter in this case was the number of connections between genes. If there were too few, most of the switches settled into a pattern of simultaneously switching on and off. If the switches had been light bulbs, the effect would have been akin to a strobe light. The effect was also analogous to the equilibrium of a pot of water at room temperature. In such a circumstance, when the control parameter is too low, the system goes into stasis. It is stable.

By contrast, when Kauffman created too many connections between his simulated genes, the sequence of switches continued firing, never settling into a stable pattern, like an array of lights in which members switch on and off in a random fashion. The system went into a state of flux and became unstable. In such a scenario, the effect was similar to turning up the heat higher than the point where the pot's water moved beyond the relative stability of convection currents to the turbulence of boiling. Only when Kauffman limited the number of connections to two did his genetic networks begin to display emergent behaviour.[20]

Mitchell Waldrop observes that the above pattern – stasis, bifurcation, turbulence – is a pattern that researchers have noted in a variety of complex systems.[21] Chris Langton, for example, found a similar "edge of chaos" pattern in cellular automata, a mathematical construct used to model physical and chemical processes, and which he used to explore how life might have emerged in the distant past. A part of the answer, Langton suggests, may rest in a balance between order and disorder. As Waldrop notes: "More precisely, [Langton is] saying that you should look at systems in terms of how they behave instead of how they're made. And when you do, he says, then what you find are the two extremes of *order* and *chaos*. It's a lot like the difference between solids, where the atoms are locked into place, and fluids, where the atoms tumble over one another at random. But right in between the two extremes ... at a kind of abstract phase transition called 'the edge of chaos,' you also find *complexity*: a class of behaviour in which the components of the system never quite lock into place, yet never quite dissolve into turbulence, either."[22]

By virtue of their ability to maintain a peculiar tension between order and chaos – to adapt – complex adaptive systems reside in a state that is meta-stable. In so doing, they also display a resiliency that stable systems cannot match. While stable systems display the same flexibility in organizing subsystems as complex systems, they are generally unable to withstand the introduction of heterogeneous elements, or fluctuations in their environment. The Great Lakes constitute a stable eco-system, but many indigenous fish stocks were unable to withstand the entry of the lamprey into their immediate environment. Resilient systems, Juarrero writes, are able to absorb changes and still maintain their integrity: "Resilient systems are able to modify their specific structure so as to ensure the adaptability and survival of their overall organization … Complex systems are usually more resilient than simple ones, with complex open systems that interact with their environment exhibiting the highest degree of resilience."[23]

Finally, complex adaptive systems are distinguished because they are governed by formal and final cause. Stated another way, emergent systems seek to maintain their integrity and do so by regulating the behaviour of their subsystems and interacting with their environment in a way that can be construed as purposive. Autocatalytic sets provide a straightforward example of the role played by formal cause. They are a second construct of Kauffman, who used them to explore the conditions surrounding the origin of life. Kauffman's interest in the topic was prompted in the late 1960s by his dissatisfaction with the then-prevailing view held by biologists. While Harold Urey and Stanley Miller had demonstrated how simple molecular building blocks of life might have emerged spontaneously, through the interaction of lightning with the constituent gases of earth's early atmosphere, no biologist had taken the next step and demonstrated how amino acids and sugars might have combined to produce an organism. Most assumed that DNA was the product of random chance, a fortuitous combination of chemicals in a primitive pond.

Kauffman chose to challenge the assumed process – random combination – and the assumed requisite outcome – the formation of DNA. In his eyes, the mathematical odds of producing even a simple protein through random chance were prohibitive, requiring a period of time larger than the age of the universe. He also resisted the notion that life was dependent on a complex mechanism such as DNA. He set out to find a way in which a self-replicating system might have started, a system that would have served as a building block for life and have emerged from simple chemical reactions.[24] Kauffman's line of reasoning was as follows. In the primitive pond alluded to above it is likely that some random reactions took place between amino acids and sugars, thereby producing molecules with short chains and branches capable of further linkage with other molecules. Some of these molecules operated as catalysts, molecules that promote the combination of other molecules, and their transformation through chemical reaction into different molecules. Catalysts facilitate chemical reactions between molecules at a rate far exceeding the rate that would take place in the constituent molecules in isolation. Kauffman envisioned a situation in which a molecule A would serve as a catalyst leading to the formation of molecule B. Molecule B in turn would have a catalytic effect on the production of molecule C. If enough molecules were located in the primeval pond, the process would continue until a molecule Z catalyzed the creation of A, thereby closing the loop of interactions between constituent molecules.

At such a juncture, Kauffman reasoned, the system begins to display lifelike properties. It grows, incorporating molecules from outside the system. It acquires something akin to a metabolism: outside molecules are taken in and transformed into molecules useful to the set. The central point is that once the system attains closure it ceases to be a passive conduit for energy and materials from the environment. Rather, components from the outside are *selected* on the basis of their capacity to contribute to the integrity of the whole.[25] The system also assumes a regulatory role over its constituent processes, akin to an organism's physiology. It regulates the rate of its constituent chemical reactions to ensure the continued existence of the set by controlling the intake of requisite materials and energy. By virtue of its capacity to select, an autocatalytic set is more accurately described as a product of formal cause. It is not the passive recipient of matter and energy, a scenario consistent with efficient cause. Rather, it selects from the environment what it needs to maintain the integrity of the set: formal cause.[26]

The role of final cause – or purpose – can be demonstrated on two levels. The first is that the behaviour of autocatalytic sets in particular and complex adaptive systems in general is asymmetrical, tending toward the "goal" of greater organizational complexity and greater competence in the face of threats from the environment. On a second level, complex, emergent systems possess a capacity akin to the competence that humans display when they employ mental schemas, the capacity to model the world, thereby facilitating prediction of future consequences based on a specified action.[27] The schemas of complex systems are not passive. They activate when systems confront situations specified by their schema. They are subject to testing, refinement, and rearrangement as the system gains experience. According to John Holland, the capacities of organized systems to predict and model are qualities that predate the existence of the brain as an organ and the later emergence of consciousness. Few would construe bacteria as an entity with consciousness, and yet their behaviour reveals a model with suppositions about their surrounding world. Bacteria contain enzyme systems that lead them to swim toward stronger concentrations of glucose. The presence of the enzymes suggests two important suppositions about the immediate environment: one, that chemicals diffuse away from their source; and two, that the further chemicals travel, the more their concentration declines. The two observations are sufficient to form a prediction. If a bacterium follows the gradient in the direction of higher concentration, it will locate food.[28]

In complex adaptive systems, formal and final cause can be identified with each other, since both refer to the system's role as an active agent that exploits matter and energy from its environment in order to maintain its formal integrity. The system, by regulating the behaviour of its constituent parts to maintain its existence, demonstrates the purpose associated with final cause, and the distributed whole associated with formal cause. The same system reveals the governance of a distributed whole when it interacts with the environment, by replacing constituents, and adding new ones to heighten its behavioural competence. And in so doing, it simultaneously reveals the presence of a final cause through its use of a schema or model of the environment to differentiate the fitness of one constituent over another in meeting the system's needs.[29]

III

As an instrument for interpreting Innis, then, the construct of the *complex adaptive system* points to six distinct characteristics to search for in our reading of his writings:

- Interacting agents
- Emergent properties
- Meta-stable systems at the edge of chaos, governed by a control parameter
- Differential persistence
- The governance of formal cause
- The governance of final cause

It is a compelling construct, but for an interpreter seeking to use it to read Innis's writings it also presents an important problem: it was first formulated in the 1980s, well after Innis's death in 1952. How might it be applied so that it does not present an anachronistic and retrospective reading of Innis? Here we would do well to take the straightforward step of reading what Innis had to say on the topic of change and, in turn, the writings of Thorstein Veblen, whom Innis identified as instrumental in shaping his own thinking about change. We would also do well to consult Veblen's writings directly, most notably the essays that Innis cited from *The Place of Science in Modern Civilization*. There, we will be able to determine if Innis had access to the array of concepts associated with the *complex adaptive system*.

In 1929 Innis published "The Work of Thorstein Veblen." Veblen had died that year and had left a reputation badly in need of repair. He was a brilliant man, but for many of his contemporaries he had also been a difficult man. He was not easy to like. He had had a sharp tongue and a difficult personality, and, by the standards of the time, had led a scandalous personal life. Innis's purpose in his retrospective was to restore the reputation of the person he believed to be "the most important economist to come out of America."[30] Innis argued that Veblen had been unfairly categorized as a "satirist with barbed phrases" in the wake of scholarly and public exposure to his book *The Theory of the Leisure Class*. True, he had skewered the spending habits of America's elite with phrases such as "conspicuous consumption," but his significance as an economist rested on the far more positive contribution he had made as an economic theorist.[31] Innis was drawn to Veblen because of his commonality with Adam Smith, namely "his attention to current events and his interests in dynamics."[32]

By extension, Innis writes, Veblen's work was distinguished by its "onslaught on static economics," the supposition that economic systems were characterized by stability. The standard classical economic doctrine of the time – typified by the writings of Alfred Marshall and others – argued that perturbations in economic systems were not seeds of growth. Rather, they were anomalies to be corrected by negative feedback processes. Once these mechanisms had completed their work, the system was restored to its original harmony. The problem with such assumptions, Veblen complained, was that they could not account for institutional growth and decay. Economics had become little more than the practice of taxonomy, the classification of static forms.

By contrast, Veblen pressed for an economics that addressed questions routinely faced in the biological sciences; namely, the problems of emergent form and systemic change. According to Innis, "Veblen attempted the study of the embryology, morphology, physiology, ecology, and aetiology of economics."[33] His method of modelling the dynamics of economic systems was to study the time series of price data, and the relation of those data with "the state of the industrial arts – on the introduction of railroads, the ocean steamship, and agricultural machinery." Veblen's studies of the dynamics of the wheat market and business cycles, Innis argued, emerged as "models for the work of later economists in analysing the relationship of complex factors."[34] It was a method that Innis would later apply and advocate in his own writings, particularly in his studies of media and communication.

Innis was also drawn to Veblen's work because of the latter's insistence that human purpose was an important constituent in economic change. One of Veblen's most important contributions in *The Theory of the Leisure Class* had been his attack on marginal utility theory, according to which a commodity's value derives solely from objective or environmental factors such as production costs. Veblen maintained that subjective factors – the individual's desire for social status, for example – also played a role in the adjudication of value.[35] For Innis, human purpose was important because it had a direct bearing on the construct of change that one could apply to explain alterations in individual and collective ascriptions of value. To insist on the importance of the individual was to admit the presence of the contingent event, and consequently on the need for a dynamic form of change. *The Theory of the Leisure Class* and Veblen's collective work illustrated for Innis "a clash between the viewpoint of the German historical school with its stress on the evolution of institutions and the classic theory."[36]

Innis was also taken with Veblen's assertion that throughout history the structure of economic systems had had a direct bearing on the preconceptions that economists brought to bear in analyzing them. Such had been the case in the early nineteenth century; a new economics emerged in conjunction with the handicraft system. Such had also been the case in the industrial era. In reviews and articles, Veblen "traced the effects of industrialism on economic theory."[37] Its cumulative effect, Veblen argued, would be to shift economists' attention from static systems to the dynamics of economic systems. While Veblen endorsed the shift, he also perceived an attendant danger, namely that analysts would move from one theoretical extreme – an emphasis on static form – to another – a recurring assumption on the part of scientists and economists that systems were always in motion and never at rest. Indeed, in his article "The Evolution of the Scientific Point of View" he voiced the concern that chemists would forgo the notion that matter had any intrinsic stability at all.[38]

For this reason, Veblen insisted that economists maintain an awareness of the constitution of their surrounding environments and of their inner mental constructs. For Innis, Veblen was conspicuous in his attempts "to maintain an unbiased approach." Veblen's interest in anthropology and his wit protected him "from absorption into the partialities of modern movements. His anxiety has always been to detect trends and to escape their effects." At base, Innis noted, Veblen felt it important in the analysis of institutions to "resort to words and concepts that express the thoughts of the men whose habits of thought constitute the institution in question."[39]

In Innis's estimation, the force of Veblen's ideas in the preceding three decades had been such that "the most virile of the younger economists [had] been strongly influenced by his work."[40] It was a group whose ranks Innis plainly aspired to join, not only by promoting Veblen's work, but also by forwarding a research agenda that drew inspiration from Veblen. His work had proven significant, Innis argued, not only because it challenged economists' preconceptions and pressed them to explore the implications of the industrial revolution, but also because it identified the chief handicap compromising economic theory: "In the perennial struggle between standardization and dynamic growth, between static theory and dynamic history, between Frankenstein's monster and Frankenstein, between mechanization and the instinct of workmanship, Veblen has waged a constructive warfare of emancipation against the tendency toward standardized static economics which becomes so dangerous on a continent with ever increasing numbers of students clamouring for textbooks on final economic theory."[41]

Innis considered it important for economists to continue Veblen's efforts to achieve "a closer synthesis between economic history and economic theory," and to do so in two ways. First, he pressed economic historians to continue their inquiries, such as those undertaken by Charles Fay, George Unwin, and Norman S.B. Gras, into the conditions underlying the origin and growth of institutions. Second, he urged his colleagues to build on Veblen's efforts to "outline the economics of dynamic change," and particularly one subset of that dynamic: the theory of cyclonics.[42] Veblen realized that the characteristics of economic change in newly developing countries were different from those of their more highly industrialized counterparts. According to Innis, Veblen's insight into the cyclonics – as opposed to the general dynamics – of economic change was a result of his personal experience of life in the United States, where he "actually lived through one of the economic storms of new countries."[43] While the characteristics of new and developed countries differed, Innis believed their attributes could be partly or completely harmonized under a single framework.[44] But such unification would only occur if the economics of developing countries were subjected to future study: "The conflict between the economics of a long and highly industrialized country such as England and the economics of the recently industrialized new and borrowing countries will become less severe as the study of cyclonics is worked out and incorporated in a general survey of the effects of the industrial revolution such as Veblen has begun and such as will be worked out and revised by later students."[45]

For Innis's interpreters, his reading of Veblen in the end proves to be both a situation and a direction. Through Veblen, Innis situated his past, present, and future work in relation to the intellectual context of his time. He outlined the crucial problems facing the discipline of economics as he understood them. He stated his theoretical preferences and outlined the program of work that he believed economists should pursue in future. Innis's reading is also a direction, since it refers readers to the specific works by Veblen that he knew and endorsed. If we are to learn more about the construct of change that engaged Innis, we will need to accept that direction, since Innis did not present a high-resolution portrait of it. We see little of Veblen's appropriation of concepts such as self-organization, and nothing at all of his use of other important features of emergent change. They are nevertheless present. A survey of the essays Innis cited from Veblen's *The Place of Science in Modern Civilization* can demonstrate Innis's exposure to all of the features of emergent change we have identified here, a construct Veblen would variously refer to as evolutionary change or genetic change.

IV

Veblen's writings on economics can be characterized as a reaction to the two "canons of truth" that he maintained had governed economics in the first half of the nineteenth century. The first was the construct of human behaviour favoured by hedonistic and associationist schools of psychology. The second proposed that history was governed by a "meliorative trend," a law of progress designed to push individuals and cultures to the optimal end that could be obtained for the domains with which they concerned themselves. It was a philosophy of history that posited that things always turned out for the best.[46]

Veblen was adamantly opposed to the first proposition and partially opposed to the second. His opposition to the first stemmed from his reaction to the efforts of the hedonist school to reduce the human actor to terms consistent with mechanical change. In the hedonistic construct, the agent was divorced from history and from any contemporary human context. The individual was an anonymous actor characterized by one essential, primary property – a desire to enhance pleasure, or profit, and avoid pain, or pecuniary loss. In this construct, humans exercised no agency and initiated no relationship with a counterpart. They formed homogeneous aggregates, not systems, and therefore could not be characterized as possessing qualities that could be categorized as secondary properties.

According to that proposition, Veblen complained, the human actor could at best be taken as little more than "an intermediate term in a causal sequence of which the initial and the terminal members are sensuous impressions and the details of conduct."[47] In the hedonist schema, humans were little more than inert matter, buffeted by forces in the environment in which they were situated: "The hedonistic conception of man is that of a lightning calculator of pleasures and pains, who oscillates like a homogeneous globule of desire of happiness under the impulse of stimuli that shift him about the area, but leave him intact. He has neither antecedent or consequent. He is an isolated, definitive human datum, in stable equilibrium except for the buffets of the impinging forces that displace him in one direction or another ... Spiritually, the hedonistic man is not a prime mover. He is not the seat of a process of living, except in the sense that he is subject to a series of permutations enforced upon him by circumstances external and alien to him."[48]

Veblen's opposition to the second canon governing nineteenth-century economics was less forceful because it was tied to the emergent construct of change that he sought to recommend. He was not opposed to the notion that economic systems moved in a particular direction and settled from time to time into periods of relative stability. He objected to the notion that when an economic system stabilized, it always selected the optimal choice available to sustain human welfare, and that history was locked into a trajectory that would culminate in the best of all possible worlds. Veblen opposed the law of progress because there was no self-evident definition of what constituted an optimal outcome for any given situation, or a self-evident constitution for the best possible world that would be realized at the end of history. All too often, visions of the "best" and the "optimal" were derivative of nothing more than the individual, institutional, and cultural assumptions of the economists who formulated them.[49] And even if one accepted a given end as optimal, Veblen noted, economists were foregoing their faith in optimal outcomes because the systems they studied were not performing according to expectation. Empirically, the canon failed to pass muster.[50]

The canon, however, while containing objectionable assumptions about the nature and direction of history, also contained a promising construct of change, and much of Veblen's work as an economist would be devoted to extricating the latter from the former. The second major premise of nineteenth-century economics, Veblen wrote, "fell into shape as a belief in an organic or quasi-organic (physiological) life process on the part of the economic community or of the nation; and this belief carried with it something of a constraining sense of self-realising cycles of growth, maturity and decay in the life history of nations or communities."[51] The significance of this construct was that it defined the worldview not only of a significant portion of practising economists, but also, in the wake of Darwin, of a significant portion of practising scientists, in disciplines ranging from biology to inorganic chemistry.[52] Science had become concerned with process, a process "which is taken as a sequence of cumulative change, realized to be self-continuing or self-propagating, and to have no final term."[53]

Veblen had three reasons for promoting a construct of change based on self-organization. First of all, he believed that formulations positing static economic systems did violence to reality as he understood it. Second, he observed that a construct based on self-organization had become the dominant construct of the modern era. "The social and political sciences must follow the drift" toward the new construct of change," he counselled, "for they are already caught in it."[54] And finally, Veblen promoted "genetic change," or the "evolutionary method," as he variously called the new construct, because it was the only formulation that could account for the increasing complexity of economic systems over time.

Veblen laid particular stress on this point. Economists had traditionally perceived economic systems in the same way that biologists had perceived natural forms – as fixed entities immune to the influence of natural history. Since time was an irrelevant consideration for them, there was no reason to consider the possibility that some process, or some mechanism, might have mediated the relationship between an organism living in the present and an ancestor living in the past. Both organisms were qualitatively the same. For this reason, in the traditional view, the only task remaining to science was to determine the relationship of extant forms with each other. The proper task of science, and by extension economics, was the classification of forms based on an ontology established by convention and observation; the proper task of the sciences was taxonomy.

Or so it was thought, until natural philosophers and political economists observed that the organisms and systems that concerned them were not fixed but had, over time, evolved. They had become more complex, with respect to their internal constitutions, and to the number and variety of tasks they were able to perform. For Veblen, this realization forced biology and other sciences to accept a central conclusion: "There is no ultimate term, and no definitive solution except in terms of further action." Form was not fixed, and for this reason scientists in biology and other domains had no choice but to concern themselves with active processes as opposed to taxonomy. Contemporary theory was "always a theory of genetic succession of phenomena, and the relations determined and elaborated into a body of doctrine are always genetic relations."[55] For reasons stemming from extant economic doctrine, from their own observations, and from the cultural authority of modern science, economists were also by now endeavouring "to make the science a genetic account of the economic life process."[56]

And in many cases they were not succeeding. Much of Veblen's writings promoting genetic change was also devoted to showing how nineteenth-century economic doctrine hindered economists from effectively explaining the emergence of increasingly complex economic systems and practices. Put simply, canon one – hedonism – undercut economists' efforts to appropriate the salvageable portions of canon two – emergent, genetic change. The writings of John Bates Clark, a contemporary of Veblen, typified this concern. Veblen considered Clark the finest exemplar of economics informed by hedonistic principles. Clark's acumen was such that he acknowledged the need to account for process in economics. And his writings, at first glance, came across as works of genetic history. Repeatedly, the economist had emphasized the need for studies of industry that started with a simple scheme out of which more complex forms had developed: "It looks as if the intended line of approach to the modern situation might be such as an evolutionist would choose, who would set out with showing what forces are at work in the primitive economic community, and then trace the cumulative growth and complication of these factors as they presently take form in the institutions of a later phase of the development."[57]

Such may have been Clark's aspiration. But Veblen argued that no economist, regardless of his stated aspiration, could meet such a promise if his underlying suppositions would not support it. In the end, Clark identified historical economics with "statics," a term from physics that is used to "designate the theory of bodies at rest or of forces in equilibrium." He proposed to subsume economic history under a fixed, immutable set of laws, an idea which, as we have seen, is consistent with the construct of mechanical change. In Veblen's estimation, however, there was too much in extant economic doctrine "to which the analogy of bodies at rest or of forces in equilibrium [did] not apply."[58] Hedonistic economics could not "approach questions of the class which occupy the modern sciences," questions relating to the emergence, evolution, and increasing complexity of economic systems or, in Veblen's words, "questions of genesis, growth, variation, process (in short, questions of a dynamic import)."[59]

Hedonism's interest was restricted to a "mechanically limited range of phenomena." Its account of growth, therefore, never extended beyond the formation and extension of aggregates: "Hedonistic economics does not, and cannot, deal with phenomena of growth except so far as growth is taken in the quantitative sense of a variation in magnitude, bulk, mass, number, frequency." Such an emphasis, however, was beside the point, since it did nothing to explain the growing complexity and qualitative transformation of the systems under study: "Quantitative variation alone does not give rise to cumulative change, which proceeds on changes in kind."[60]

Having fulfilled his first purpose, to undermine the canons of nineteenth-century economics, and his second, demonstrating that Clark, Alfred Marshall, and other important contemporaries were practically if not rhetorically ignoring the fact of self-organization and heightened complexity in the systems that concerned them, Veblen turned his attention to his third and most important task: providing a detailed description of the constituents of emergent change. As Veblen scholar Geoffrey Hodgson notes, the American political economist never did so in a systematic way.[61] But despite the lack of a concise expression of the construct, Veblen's writings nevertheless consistently point to the concepts associated with emergent change: active agents and final cause, interaction and emergence, differential persistence and formal cause, and meta-stability.

Active Agents and Final Cause

Veblen began his defence of the action of human agency and his assertion that human agents were the driving force of economic change by noting that the psychological premises underlying economics were "no longer so neat and succinct" as they had been in the days of Jeremy Bentham and James Mill, two important political economists of the early nineteenth century. The default assumption of classical political economy had been to impute teleology – the exercise of agency to achieve a pre-defined end – to non-human phenomena and to human action only at the collective level. Individuals were not construed as agents committing purposive acts.[62]

The problem with these core assumptions, derived from hedonistic and associationist psychology, was that they flew in the face of recent developments in psychology, science, and economics. Mid-nineteenth-century psychology insisted that individual purposive activity could be discerned at every turn. Contemporary science asserted that teleological activity, by contrast, could not be detected in nature or at the social level of human organization. And even if it could, its presence was not central to understanding the operation of a given system under observation.[63]

In economics, new tenets – which Veblen referred to as the New Hedonism and the New Associationism – informed the metaphysical assumptions of mid-century economists such as John Stuart Mill, John Elliott Cairnes, and William Stanley Jevons. Mill refined Bentham's utilitarian economics, and in particular the appeal to the simple opposition between pleasure and pain, by introducing distinctions between different forms of pleasure as the impetus for conduct. New Associationism was also forcing economists to reconsider long-standing assumptions about how agents perceived stimuli, derived ideas from stimuli, and took consequent action. Associationist psychology had traditionally argued that human reaction to stimuli or extant ideas was prompted by their contiguity, or proximity. The traditional formulation had until then demanded neither a construction of stimuli nor an exercise in volition from the human observer, but simply an acceptance of the new array, the new contiguity, of environmental forces that were neither controlled nor initiated by the observing agent.[64]

New Associationism, by contrast, demanded something more. It argued that the ground of connection between ideas and stimuli was "similarity." The significance of this innovation, Veblen argued, was that economists could no longer characterize human observation "as a purely mechanical process, a concatenation of items simply." The concept of "similarity" presupposed the presence of a mind capable of making comparisons between one impression and another: "It implies some degree of constructive work on the part of the perceiving subject. The perceiver is thereby construed to be an agent in the work of perception; therefore, he must be possessed of a point of view and an end dominating the perceptive process."[65] Veblen further argued that a similar implication followed from the qualitative distinctions associated with the New Hedonism: the act of distinction implies a spiritual, teleological process on the part of the perceiving or discretionary agent.[66]

While asserting the existence and impact of human autonomy, Veblen did not intend to diminish the corresponding import of the environment as a variable explaining human conduct. His purpose, rather, was to suggest that contemporary psychology offered a different way to conceive the relationship between agent and environment, a conception that pointed to the import of cognitive schemas, and a conception that pointed to the import of final cause. In Veblen's understanding, the new psychology did not "conceive the organism as a causal hiatus." The "reflex arc," the causal sequence between the impact and the response, he said, is continuous. But in contrast to past formulations, which conceived the reflex arc "in terms of spiritual substance transmitting a shock," modern formulations of human response were framed in terms of cognitive schemas. They were "stated in terms of tropism ... imputing to the organism a habit of life and a self-directing and selective attention in meeting the complex of forces that make up its environment. The selective play of this tropismatic complex that constitutes the organism's habit of life under the impact of the forces of the environment counts as discretion."[67]

Interaction and Emergence

Veblen described the origins and constitution of the human schema, the tropismatic complex, in terms that are consistent with the *complex adaptive system*. Schemas, he wrote, are composed of multiple components – habits, conventions – that are assembled into a larger whole. This whole is not fixed. It is a property arising from the interaction between individuals and their environment, and, by extension, human collectivities and their environments. The process of interaction and emergence continues throughout the life of the given individual or community. The human actor, Veblen writes, is "a coherent structure of propensities and habits which seeks realization in an unfolding capacity." The unfolding – or emergence – of a schema is prompted by the individual's interaction with its constituents, and with the environment. In addition to referring to a schema as a tropismatic complex, Veblen also referred to it as temperament. The temperament, he argued, is the product of the interaction between the individual's life experience and inherited cultural traits, "cumulatively wrought out under a given body of traditions, conventionalities, and material circumstances; and [affords] the point of departure for the next step in the process."[68] In its economic dimension, the schema "of the individual is a cumulative process of adaptation of means to ends that cumulatively change as the process goes on, both the agent and his environment being at any given point the outcome of the last process. His methods of life today are enforced upon him by his habits of life carried over from yesterday and by the circumstances left as the mechanical residue of yesterday."[69]

Veblen emphasized the import of emergence for explaining not only the origin and evolution of individual traits but also collective phenomena such as the attribution of value. In the wake of Bentham, Veblen writes, economics became "substantially a theory of value. This is altogether the dominant feature of the body of the doctrines: the rest follows from, or is adapted to, this central discipline."[70] The shortcoming of the utilitarian economics represented by Bentham was that it presented a theory of value in which the human actor counted for little. Individual decision-making was reduced to the hedonistic formulation of pleasure and pain, and purchasers, by extension, became sensitive to only one thing: price. The decision to purchase a commodity was nothing more than an assessment of the pleasure it would bring and whether that pleasure outweighed the pain that would be inflicted by its price.[71]

The difficulty with such a formulation, Veblen stated, was that it denied any social dimension to the attribution of value. Populations were treated as aggregates: "Society, in the utilitarian philosophy, is the algebraic sum of the individuals; and the interest of the society is the sum of the interests of the individuals."[72] In addition to removing human interaction as a basis for value, utilitarian economics also, through its appropriation of the hedonistic construction of the agent, removed human distinction. The result of this decision, Veblen argued, was that it encouraged Adam Smith and the utilitarian economists who succeeded him to tie human consumption patterns to nothing more than price. The cost of such a decision was to induce generations of economists to ignore an "entire range of phenomena comprised under the head of consumption."[73] With individual and social inputs removed from consideration, Veblen argued, value was wrongly construed as deriving solely from the costs associated with production. Economic laws – including those pertaining to the attribution of value – were conceived as nothing more than the "algebraic relations subsisting between the various elements of wealth and investment, – capital, labor, land, supply and demand of one and the other, profits, interest, wages."[74]

Veblen believed that better constructs of value were available, and he commended particularly the Natural Theory of Value proposed by Cairnes. The Irish economist's work was distinguished in Veblen's eyes by its recognition that value was an emergent property of systems composed of heterogeneous agents. It was not the mechanical outcome of a system proceeding to a "teleologically or hedonistically defensible consummation."[75] More specifically, Cairnes's work was marked by two innovations. His first contribution was to recognize a second source of value and the implication it presented for the trajectory of economic systems. Value, for Cairnes, was more than the product of the market signal of price; it resulted also from the social location of the potential customer. In Cairnes's doctrine, Veblen writes, "there are determinable variations in the alacrity with which different classes or communities respond to the pecuniary stimulus."[76]

The restoration of heterogeneity and agency to the human actor had an important implication for Veblen; namely, that economic systems did not proceed to one single, pre-determined outcome. They could and did move to one of multiple potential outcomes: "It follows that an unguided response even to the mere quantitative pecuniary stimuli may take different directions, and so may result in activities of widely differing outcome." It also followed that since a given system could proceed to one of multiple alternatives, it would not always select the outcome that all or a majority of its participants deemed optimal: "Therefore, the outcome of activity set up even by the normal pecuniary stimuli may take a form that may or may not be serviceable to the community."[77]

Cairnes's second innovation, Veblen writes, was the mirror of the one proposed by John Stuart Mill. Instead of proposing that agent decision-making with respect to production and acquisition was informed by varying degrees of pleasure, Cairnes proposed that it was informed by varying degrees of discomfort. As was the case with Mill, and with Cairnes's own appeal to heterogeneity, Cairnes's innovation on the concept of pain introduced the possibility of agency and individual choice in the context of an evolving, economic system. The ultimate significance of this innovation was to suggest that value was the emergent property of agent interaction. In Cairnes's construct, different people accorded different value to the same item.[78] Value became the outcome not only of production costs but also of interaction – bargaining – between producers and consumers: "The point of departure is taken from the range of market values and the process of bargaining by which these values are determined. This latter is taken to be a process of discrimination between various kinds and degrees of discomfort, and the average or consistent outcome of such a process of bargaining constitutes normal value."[79]

As Veblen characterizes him, Cairnes understood value to be the product of agent interaction, an emergent property of a self-organizing system: "In all this the proximate causes at work in the determination of values are plainly taken account of more adequately than in earlier cost-of-production doctrines; but they are taken account of with a view of explaining the mutual adjustment and interrelation of elements in a system rather than to explain either a developmental sequence or the working out of a foreordained end."[80]

Differential Persistence and Formal Cause

In addition to emphasizing the importance of agency and final cause, interaction, and emergent properties, Veblen also pointed to constituents in his construct of change that markedly resemble the concepts of formal cause and differential persistence. These constituents appeared in discussions in which Veblen treated with greater specificity the origin, operation, and transformation of schemas at the individual and cultural level. All were informed by a first, simple proposition regarding human schemas, namely that "habits of thought are an outcome of habits of life."[81] Human beings, Veblen argued, are analogical beings. They routinely use constructs and practices from one domain of activity to structure and interpret phenomena in another.

This proposition applied with particular force when considering cultural constructs of the natural world. In Veblen's interpretation of history, the earliest human cultures appealed to a domain of practice – the procurement and production of necessities for sustenance, including food, clothing, and tools – to inform their understanding of natural change. This was the domain, he believed, that dominated an agent's attention in the course of a day. It was also the domain in which a sequence of change was most likely to present itself to an individual for observation. Since the earliest humans had no access to industrial infrastructure and workflows, they were not exposed to analogues suggesting the use of impersonal, mechanical constructs of change to govern their interpretation of nature. Acquisition and production were tied to the individual's exercise of will and subsequent application of force to meet his or her stated purpose.

By extension, the concept of sequence became associated with the concept of volition. When human-induced sequences, such as the transformation of raw material into a tool, were seen to stem from individual purpose, it was not a huge leap to assume that naturally induced sequences were also prompted by an agent. This agent could be nature itself, or some deity or group of deities: "The inscrutable movements of the seasons and of the natural forces are apprehended as actions guided by discretion, will power, or propensity looking to an end, much as human actions are. The processes of inanimate nature are agencies, whose habits of life are to be learned."[82] While asserting that human beings were analogical beings, Veblen was also careful to dissociate himself from any hint of economic or technological determinism. Individual and social schemas, he wrote, are not unitary structures derived solely or predominantly from economic activity. Human thought stems not only from economic practice but also from social, civic, military, and religious practices. Each domain contributes constructs that inform individual and collective thought, and "between them they commonly take up by far the larger share of it."[83]

Human thought, then, was the product of human practice. It was not a unitary structure; it was a complex. This realization then raised an important question for Veblen: what was the relationship between the constituents that informed human thought? Did they operate in isolation? Or did they have some bearing on the operation of their counterparts? In Veblen's estimation, the latter was the correct answer. Human activity could not be isolated into distinct categories; nor could the constructs stemming from human activity. Human schemas were properly characterized as distributed wholes, in which the modification of one constituent, or the addition of another, served to alter the constitution or behaviour of some or all of the system's remaining counterparts. Veblen's description of the operation of human schemas, in other words, was markedly similar to the concept of formal cause.[84]

Veblen emphasized the distributed nature of individual and cultural thought in his article "Why is Economics not an Evolutionary Science?" in which he offered an extended discussion of the relationship between economic activity and its wider cultural setting. The impact of economic activity, Veblen argued, was pervasive. Its influence on "the cultural structure at all points" was so extensive "that all institutions may be said to be in some measure economic institutions." This was so because each action stems from "the entire organic complex of habits of thought that have been shaped" by prior acts. Every act, every thought, has been shaped by what transpired before it, and impinges on the acts and thoughts that follow, regardless of the domain in which they are performed. Everything is connected: "The economic interest does not act in isolation, for it is but one of several vaguely isolable interests on which the complex of teleological activity carried out by the individual proceeds." In every expression of the will, in each act designed to perform a certain end, the individual enters into "each successive action as a whole although the specific end sought in a given action may be sought avowedly on the basis of a particular interest; as e.g. the economic, aesthetic, sexual, humanitarian, devotional interests. *Since each of these passably isolable interests is a propensity of the organic agent man, with his complex of habits of thought, the expression of each is affected by habits of life formed under the guidance of all the rest* [emphasis mine]."[85]

Veblen also characterized schemas at the cultural level as a complex that constituted "a more or less congruous and balanced whole."[86] But cultural schemas also have a second feature, the retention of constructs that have been formulated in the past: they are not derived solely from the experience of contemporaries. They retain constituents that persist through history and are, as Veblen writes, more or less congruous with those of their counterparts. Some will contain assumptions that harmonize well with constituents that precede and succeed them; others will not. In the end, the important thing for Veblen was that cultural constructs had proven remarkably robust over time. True, they were subject to formal cause. And, like the three-boned apparatus we saw in our previous section, their function was dependent on the systemic context in which they were situated. But in the end, cultural constructs had shown themselves to be extraordinarily persistent, or, in contemporary parlance, to display differential persistence.

"The Place of Science in Modern Civilization" is an article that Innis did not cite. He was likely acquainted with it, however, given his familiarity with the remaining articles in the anthology of the same name, and his general familiarity with Veblen's corpus. The article is worth examining because it concisely highlights two important features of Veblen's thought: that history is composed of stages, and that formulations conceived in one stage will survive into those that follow. In his construct of world history, Veblen pointed to three stages. The first consisted of the earliest, pre-agricultural societies. In Veblen's view, cultures at this stage were largely benign. They were egalitarian and for the most part did not engage in armed conflict with their neighbours. This first age of history, Veblen asserts, was the savage stage of history.

It was followed by the move to agriculture, and the emergence of a second stage: the barbarian. This phase was characterized by the use of hierarchical social structures to govern society and apply force against neighbours and competitors. Medieval Europe, he said, was the most recent and most distinct example of barbarian culture. The modern era – Veblen's final stage – emerged in the eighteenth and nineteenth centuries, with the rise of industrialization, and the West's growing commitment to rest explanation on empirical evidence and efficient cause. Veblen was equivocal in his characterization of modernity. He detected the beginnings of a shift toward more egalitarian social structures, and a diminishing commitment to religious faith. But he also felt it was far too early to make any definitive statements on the characteristics of modern life. This was in part due to the persistence of constructs and practices from the near and distant past; it was possible that their influence would contain any challenge posed by constructs emerging in the Modern Era, but it was too early to say.[87]

What Veblen *was* willing to say was that constructs and habits from the past – particularly the savage stage of history – had shown themselves to be both resilient and persistent. In the present, constructs of early history were constituents of a larger cultural construct that also included schemas from higher barbarian cultures. The entire ensemble, in turn, was required to adapt to modern circumstance. "By force of the protracted discipline" of the savage stage of human culture, Veblen writes, "the human nature of civilized mankind is still substantially the human nature of savage man. The ancient equipment of congenital aptitudes and propensities stands over substantially unchanged, though overlaid with barbarian traditions and conventionalities and readjusted by habituation to the exigencies of civilised life."[88]

Veblen also emphasized the impact of differential persistence in the final instalment of "The Preconceptions of Economic Science," another article that Innis did cite. There, he further emphasized that the constituents of thought – in this case the metaphysical constructs associated with political economy – took on new roles and new expressions as they were subsumed into new intellectual contexts. The canons of scientific and economic thought, Veblen argued, "are of the nature of habits of thought, and habit does not break with the past, nor do the hereditary aptitudes that find expression in habit vary gratuitously with the mere lapse of time." In cultural and institutional settings, whether in law, commerce, science, or other domains, people are by nature conservative. They accept the prevailing grounds of knowledge, the prevailing metaphysics, generally without question, until experience forces communities of practice to question, criticize, and reformulate them. Even then, the process of change is slow, since conventions of thought have historically been subject to natural selection and adaptation: "The underlying metaphysics of scientific research and purpose, therefore, changes gradually and, of course, incompletely, much as is the case with the metaphysics underlying the common law and the schedule of civil rights. As in the legal framework the now avowedly useless and meaningless preconceptions of status and caste and precedent are even yet at the most metamorphosed and obsolescent rather than overpassed ... so in the science the living generation has not seen an abrupt and traceless disappearance of the metaphysics that fixed the point of view of the early classical political economy."[89]

By way of example, Veblen pointed to the persistence of the concept of teleology in economics, the assumption that economic systems move to a fixed outcome, the best one available for a given society. As we have seen, Veblen did not much care for the concept, because of its benign assumption about the behaviour of economic systems, which he felt were unwarranted, and because it encouraged economists to appropriate static constructs of economic systems. Despite its defects, Veblen believed the doctrine still retained some practical value. With respect to the history of economic thought, the doctrine showed the persistence of constructs through time. With respect to the behaviour of economic systems, the concept highlighted an important trait: they were neither perpetually stable, nor perpetually in flux. In contemporary parlance, Veblen believed economic systems to be meta-stable.

Scientists and economists before Darwin, Veblen writes, were not primarily concerned with the location and formulation of physical law. Their task, at least in their own eyes, was a deeper one – the detection of natural law. Natural law was fundamentally different from physical law; it was not an empirically derived description of phenomena governed by mechanical change. Rather, to them, "the great law of the order of nature [was] of the character of a propensity working to an end."[90] The problem with this emphasis, Veblen observed, was that it induced economists to fixate on systems in equilibrium. The object of attention was the consummation point of emergence, not the process of emergence itself. Systems, practically if not rhetorically, were deemed to be stable, and "natural laws" were devised to explain their operation: "These natural laws were of the nature of rules of the game of causation. They formulated the immutable relations in which things 'naturally' stood to one another before causal disturbance took place between them, the orderly unfolding of the complement of causes involved in the transition over this interval of transient activity, and the settled relations that would supervene when the disturbance had passed and the transition from cause to effect had been consummated."[91]

In the wake of Darwin, science shifted its attention from states of equilibrium to "the interval of instability between initial cause and definitive effect," or in more modern terms, to periods in a system's history when it experienced bifurcation and self-organization.[92] While he in general approved the shift in emphasis, Veblen also perceived a danger; namely, that science and economics would limit their focus to process and neglect the fact of stasis in natural, economic, and cultural history. Constructs emerging from contemporary practice and observation were leading researchers to subsume all phenomena under a "highly impersonal interpretation of phenomena in terms of consecutive change," and to completely ignore preceding modes of thought. As we have seen, Veblen also worried that even physicists and chemists were in danger of losing a conception of stable substance, given the current penchant to interpret all data from the standpoint of consecutive change.[93]

Veblen was not so inclined. His writings indicate respect for the work and formulations of contemporaries such as Clark and Marshall, even when he was in fundamental disagreement with them. This respect was due to a simple realization: no formulation, not even his, could hope to encapsulate all the phenomena that concerned economists. The formulations of static, classical economics merited respect because they represented important features of economic behaviour. Veblen extended this respect not only to his contemporaries but also to his predecessors in economics, particularly in their treatments of the concept of teleology. He did so because he agreed with a central tenet of the concept: systems from time to time come to rest; they are meta-stable. And he did so because his predecessors, from the Physiocrats and Smith to Cairnes, had seen value in the concept. It described an essential characteristic of economic behaviour that more recent formulations did not treat. And he did so, further, because his predecessors had over time removed objectionable features from the concept. The construct of teleology remained. But in the modern context it was denuded of any concept of God or providence. It was also stripped of any sense that the final point of a phase of self-organization was the best point that could be obtained. The concept had been adapted to new circumstances and, in our terminology, had displayed differential persistence.

Veblen expressed his interest in teleology and meta-stability first by a penetrating reading of Smith's doctrine of the Invisible Hand, and second by a negative formulation touching on the stability of economic systems. The doctrine of the Invisible Hand was significant, Veblen asserted, because it referred to behaviour that could not be reduced to mechanical forms of change. In essence, the doctrine referred to the tendency of systems to move toward a given end: "The scheme as a whole is guided by the end to be reached, but the sequence of events through which the end is reached is a causal sequence which is not broken into episodically."[94] Veblen identified the "sequence of events," the characteristic that impelled systems to move to a given end, with the term "mechanism." But in Smith's doctrine, "mechanism" had a specific connotation. It was, Veblen writes, an ingenious combination of "forces and motives capable of accomplishing an ordained result."[95]

In any understanding of Smith's teleological mechanism, Veblen argued, it was essential to differentiate between forces that supported the system in its movement toward its final state from forces that were random and mechanical: "The sequence of events, including human motives and human conduct, is a causal sequence; but it is also something more, or rather, there is also another element of continuity besides that of brute cause and effect present in the step-by-step process whereby the natural course of things reaches its final term."[96] The presence of a third element supporting the continuity and given trajectory of a system, in addition to human action and efficient cause, was evident for two reasons. First, Smith observed that it was possible to divert a system from a direct progression toward its given, optimal end. His construction of "the natural course of things" did not mean a necessary course of things, in the sense of their being causally determined by a mechanical construct of change. If such had been the intent of his construct, then "no divergence of events from the natural or legitimate course of things would be possible."[97] Second, Smith observed that when a conjunction of forces, effected by human volition, an act of nature, or both, caused systems to veer from their appointed path, the same systems "would right themselves if interference with the natural course ceases." By contrast, "in the case of a causal sequence simply" – in systems governed by efficient cause – the cessation of aberrant actions would "not leave the outcome the same as if no interference had taken place. This recuperative power of nature is of an extra-mechanical character. The continuity of sequence by force of which the natural course of things prevails is, therefore, not of the nature of cause and effect, since it bridges intervals and interruptions in the causal sequence."[98]

Systems, then, had a direction, and over the course of time reached a point of rest. If we are to identify Smith's reading of natural and economic history with Veblen, however, we are presented with an important problem. At one juncture, in a passage discussing self-organization, Veblen seems to oppose the possibility of a system reaching a final term. At a second, in his reading of Smith, he seems to accept it. The discrepancy can be resolved by considering Veblen's definition of the concept "final term." The problem is significant because its resolution provides a way to establish that the concepts of meta-stability and differential persistence were constituents of Veblen's thought. In Veblen's writings, "final term" had two connotations. The first was a stable state, a fixed terminus point that concluded a sequence of change, after which no further modification of a system's constituents or operation could be anticipated. Veblen did not endorse this option, and neither did his contemporaries, though many used it as a working assumption to generate the doctrine and equations associated with classical economics. While resisting a static conception of economic systems, he also resisted its opposite extreme. Many in the modern sciences had recently "gone so far," he observed, as to embrace a construct of emergent change that had no final term.[99]

Veblen's writings suggest that he took a stance between the two extremes, a position that in substance is markedly similar to the concept of meta-stability. He further believed that it was the position of most researchers in the modern sciences. The metaphysics and practices of modern science, he writes, could not be identified with "the nature of taxonomy simply." Its inquiries also touched on process, and any inquiries on an object of interest could only come to rest provisionally, "when it has disposed of its facts in terms of process. But modern scientific inquiry in any case comes to rest only provisionally; because its prime postulate is that of consecutive change, and consecutive change can, of course, not come to rest except provisionally."[100]

"Final term" in its second connotation referred to the belief that systems move toward an optimal end, "the settled course of material facts tending beneficently to the highest welfare of the human race." This was the stated belief of the Physiocrat school of economics, Smith, and others.[101] As we have seen, it was not Veblen's belief. But as we have also seen, Veblen did subscribe to a modified form of teleology, one that posited that natural and economic systems, for a time, enjoy a degree of stability. By extension, he believed that economic doctrines built on taxonomy had validity, since economic systems, institutions, and practices were sufficiently stable that they could, for a time, be classified. But for our purposes, this second connotation also illustrates a second point: Veblen's belief that constructs persist –

or display differential persistence – even when subsumed into new cultural or schematic contexts.

Veblen described, and endorsed, recent innovations in the concept of teleology that had rid it of its objectionable features, innovations that in his terminology had "metamorphosed" the concept and which were prompted by shifts in the underlying assumptions and attending data of the economic discipline. He believed that schemas emerging from industrial practice had induced British culture, and by extension British economics, to minimize the importance of an overriding agency in the operation of nature, and emphasize the importance of impersonal, mechanical causes. Even in Smith's economics, the doctrine of the Invisible Hand did not rely on a "meddling providence." God set the mechanism of history in place, and then left well enough alone.[102]

While Smith's work was an improvement, in Veblen's view, it was Cairnes who produced a teleological doctrine that met the demands of the prevailing metaphysics and empirical experience: "What may be done in economic science of the taxonomic kind is shown at its best in Cairnes's work."[103] Cairnes's work was an exemplar because, in appealing to natural law – the tendency of systems to move in a specific direction – it did so in a way in which "the metaphysics underlying this appeal to normality" was "so far removed from the ancient ground of the beneficent 'order of nature' as to have become at least nominally impersonal and to proceed without a constant regard to the humanitarian bearing of the 'tendencies' which it formulates." God, and any other imputation of personality, was left out, and so was any assumption of an optimal direction to economic life: "It is a natural law which, in the guise of 'controlling principle,' exercises a constraining surveillance over the trend of things; but it is no longer conceived to exercise its constraint in the interest of ulterior human purposes. The element of beneficence has been well-nigh eliminated, and the system is formulated in terms of the system itself. Economics as it left Cairnes's hand, so far as his theoretical work is concerned, comes near being taxonomy for taxonomy's sake."[104]

V*****

In their sum, then, Veblen's writings suggest that Harold Innis would not have found the *complex adaptive system* a particularly novel construct. Its core concepts – active agents, interaction, self-organization, differential persistence, meta-stability, and formal and final cause – are all there. They were part and parcel of the economic discourse of Innis's time. They may have had different names, but the substance and significance of each concept was known to Innis.[105] Our challenge now is to see how and when he applied them in his major works: *The Fur Trade*, *The Cod Fisheries*, *Political Economy in the Modern State*, *Empire and Communications*, and *The Bias of Communication*. And as we conduct that survey, we will notice several important things about Innis's works. Most are data dumps. Innis was never shy about exposing his readers to the primary and secondary sources he appropriated. Most reveal a pen that is not particularly distinguished. Innis was never in danger of winning his generation's version of the Man Booker prize. But all – in their substance and in their narrative – reveal an underlying picture: a scholar deeply committed to demonstrating that human systems, be they economic or cultural, are governed by a regime of change defined by emergent properties, differential persistence, and formal and final cause.

2

The Fur Trade

I

Harold Innis's economic histories are in major need of reappraisal. In the United States, Britain, and other north-Atlantic coastal countries, there is now an established movement among scholars, particularly those studying the eighteenth century, to recast national narratives as part of the much larger history of the North Atlantic Basin. In their reasoning, the North Atlantic had by the eighteenth century emerged into a coherent whole, thanks to the substantial political, cultural, and commercial ties linking both sides of the Atlantic. They further assert that these networks almost certainly had a bearing on the internal political, social, and economic development of its participants. Stated simply, proponents of the "New British History" in the United Kingdom and "Atlantic History" in the United States argue that to properly understand events that transpired within, one must relate them to historic trends that transpired without.[1]

Canadian historians should welcome these developments, if only because they reinforce lines of inquiry already present in the Canadian literature for some time. Since the 1930s the importance of the North Atlantic triangle has been a defining characteristic of the writings of earlier historian colleagues, especially Arthur Lower, John Bartlet Brebner, and of course Harold Innis.[2] There is every reason to expect that Canada, by virtue of its history and geography, will be an important contributor to the international effort to create a historiography of the North Atlantic Basin. But first, Canadian scholars would do well to reconsider the significance of contributions already in hand, particularly those of Harold Innis.

The central problem facing Canadian scholars in this arena is that, while a rich literature devoted to the interpretation of Innis exists, there is little consensus on the exact nature of his contribution to Canadian historiography, empirically or conceptually. In a recent historiographical essay, William Buxton and Charles Acland observed that within Canada, while there is respect for Innis as an "eminent scholar," there is also "some degree of bewilderment about his actual contribution." Although his writings are widely recognized as significant, there remains "some confusion about how [his] legacy can be best appropriated."[3] Current portraits of Innis are diffuse, ambivalent, and in their totality do not constitute a strong endorsement of his work in the field of Atlantic historiography – or any other historiography for that matter. Canadian historians face a quandary. If we are to introduce Innis to our colleagues abroad, on what basis do we recommend him?[4]

I propose that much of the esteem that Canadian scholars initially awarded Innis's work can be retrieved with a sharper understanding of his construction of change. In this chapter and the next, I commend Innis's work as pioneering both from the standpoint of method – the interpolation of Canadian within Atlantic history – and also from the standpoint of interpretation. Innis was a pioneer because he interpreted Canada as an economic system that displayed emergent properties and differential persistence, and was governed by formal and final cause. It is a view that is finding favour among some current proponents of Atlantic history.[5]

A reading along these lines has the potential also to clarify a perennial question in the Innis literature: how did Innis characterize the international economy that governed Canada's development? In writings devoted to Innis's studies of staple industries, three fault lines have traditionally divided scholars: two empirical and centring on the process of growth within Canada; one conceptual and centring on the nature of the economy outside Canada. The first division relates to Innis's interpretation of individual staple industries, particularly the fur trade.[6] The second and related division is over his characterization of Canadian economic development. Several scholars have charged that his focus on extractive industries was too narrow, and that in concentrating on a single economic sector at a time he missed essential features of the economy that shared responsibility for promoting economic growth.[7]

While this study cannot contribute to the first two points of contention, it can speak to Innis's characterization of the international economy. In 1963 Mel Watkins published the "Staple Theory of Growth," the now-classic proposition that staple-producing countries are governed by a normative principle of growth that distinguishes them from their counterparts, since their economic growth is stimulated by the export of primary products. The difficulty with this scenario, argued Watkins, is that staple products have historically proven to be poor mechanisms for generating the "spread effects" – the economic spin-offs – that could engender a diversified economy. Canada, since it lacked the requisite transport infrastructure, processing industries capable of adding value to staple exports, or manufacturing industries to provide consumer goods to workers in the primary sector, was unable to transform itself into a diversified economy, which in this formulation meant an economy with a substantial manufacturing base.

Because of the weak spread effects associated with commodity exports, Canada and other countries fell into what Watkins referred to as the "Staple Trap," engendered in part by perpetual debt and in part by the designs of its respective imperial centres. Watkins, and other proponents of the new Canadian Political Economy in the 1970s and 1980s, complained that commodity extraction kept Canadian producers in a perpetual state of dependence on foreign capital markets. Profits were continuously used to retire debts acquired from building transport infrastructure, a perpetual need in a staple economy, and Canadian firms were never able to divert capital toward the construction of an industrial base. The country was locked into the role of staple producer, and its specialization did not arise from the governance of abstract market forces. Instead, it was assigned its role by its respective imperial centres, which determined the location of investment, international monetary policy, and rules of individual trade. This was also a nationalist plaint: Canada's economy was organized not by the designs of its own inhabitants but by decisions made in Britain and then the United States.[8]

In making his formulation, Watkins claimed inspiration from Innis, and it is on this point that controversy arose. Critics charged that Innis's narratives could not be translated into a normative theory of development, as Watkins had attempted to do.[9] Other interpreters thought Watkins's theory had so oversimplified Innis's writings – omitting factors such as culture – that it bore no relationship to the original.[10] Historians charged that the contention by Watkins and proponents of dependency theory – that the Canadian periphery had enjoyed no agency in its relationships with its respective Imperial centres – found support neither in the historical record nor in Innis's histories. The relationship, they said, was more properly characterized by appeals to organic or ecological metaphors; in other words by interaction, not domination.[11]

Still, for all the criticism, some interpreters continue to identify Innis's writings with the tenets outlined by Watkins. In a 1981 article, James Carey argued that Innis moved beyond "the organic metaphors that so often led the Chicago scholars [of the Chicago School of Communication] astray and masked the facts of history ... Even if society were like an organism, there would be some controlling element, some centralized brain in the body, some region and group that would collect the power necessary to direct the nerves of communication and the arteries of transportation."[12]

The disparate opinions in the literature suggest the need to ask the following questions of Innis in our reading of *The Fur Trade* and *The Cod Fisheries*. Did Innis ascribe agency to Canada and other peripheral agents operating outside the imperial centre? In other words, did he see their relationship as one of dependence or interdependence? Did he see the imperial centre as a unified agent, or was the picture more complex? Did he see the economic specialization of his subjects – including imperial centres – solely as the product of design, or also as the product of market forces? And finally, did Innis see Canada's outcome as pre-ordained by virtue of its status as a colony; or was it a historically contingent outcome?

Since a reading of *The Fur Trade* in isolation will not answer all these questions, I address them in detail at the end of the following chapter, after looking at *The Cod Fisheries* as well. While *The Fur Trade* is devoted primarily to the development of Canada's economy, it says comparatively little about the historical constitution and capabilities of imperial economies such as Britain, France, or Spain. Conversely, while *The Cod Fisheries* addresses mainly the evolution of the North Atlantic economy, it also makes important statements about the regime of change governing the evolution of the Canadian economy that did not appear in *The Fur Trade*. In short, to determine if Innis was a proponent of a normative theory of economic development, or was, by contrast, an advocate of a theory appealing to historical contingency, a sustained reading of both studies is needed.

Governing both works was the intellectual agenda Innis set for himself at the start of his career in his first published work, *A History of the Canadian Pacific Railway*, an adaptation of his PhD thesis first published in 1923. That agenda is important because it suggests that Innis, from the start, endorsed a construct of change that contrasts with the one formulated by Watkins and conforms with the one proposed by Thorstein Veblen. This first work is also important because it indicates that Innis, by 1923, had formulated or nearly formulated the research agenda that would preoccupy him for the next seventeen years. In *The Fur Trade: An Introduction to Canadian Economic History*, Innis would promote a construct that emphasized the impact of historical contingency, rather than appealing to a normative theory of growth. And he would construct a narrative that emphasized the importance of emergent change, and the governance of formal and final cause.

II

In 1923, in the preface of his first book, Innis stated a grand ambition. Introducing his history of Canada's first trans-continental railway, he proposed "to trace the history of the *Canadian Pacific Railway* from an evolutionary and scientific point of view."[13] Innis was signalling his intent to follow the intellectual agenda set by Thorstein Veblen, at the same time making a commitment to present a narrative that affirmed the importance of dynamic change and human purpose in the unfolding of the historical process. By 1930, however, Innis had concluded that his first work had been a failure, acknowledging in *The Fur Trade* his sense of the "incompleteness of that volume."[14]

Why did Innis feel this way? What obligations did he assume for himself when he undertook to study Canada's past from an evolutionary perspective? The question is worth pursuing because it presupposes that Innis's earliest histories were informed by two concepts: the first – in the parlance of his time – was formal cause; the second – in the parlance of *our* time – was *differential persistence*. Through Darwin and Veblen, Innis was exposed to both concepts, and acquired the means, conceptual and rhetorical, to generate a persuasive explanation for the patterns embedded in Canada's economy, past and present. In the course of his career as an economic historian, starting with *A History of the Canadian Pacific Railway*, Innis would draw on both concepts.

To begin, consider Darwin's theory of natural selection. Darwin's theory forever changed the discipline of biology because, by providing a mechanism to explain the evolution of animate forms, or species, over time, it undermined the idea that natural kinds are eternal. In the history of any ecosystem, Darwin argued, certain species survived because they demonstrated a degree of "fitness" that distinguished them from their competitors. Stated another way, some organisms had historically proven more successful in extracting needed resources from the environment, whereas their less fit counterparts generally passed into extinction. Since the characteristics of a given ecological system determined the success of one species over another, fitness was construed not as a primary property of the organism, but rather as a secondary property, a product of its interaction with the environment. The ecosystem emerged as the agent of selection.[15]

Darwin further argued that a given species, by virtue of its selection by the environment, enters into a systemic relationship with its surrounding niche. That relationship enables selected organisms to survive and reproduce, but it also determines the future characteristics that the species will exhibit. An organism is distinguished from its counterparts by its interaction with its environment. Two animals of the same genotype, or genetic makeup, can display different visible properties and behaviour, or phenotypes, depending on the ecosystem in which they are embedded. A hare in one niche will tend to have brown fur, because that colour increases, or has increased, its chances of survival. In a different habitat, a similar hare will be white.

For Darwin, the importance of this insight was that the process of interaction and selection was continuous, and cumulative in its effect. As a result of a species' interaction with the environment, some members of its population are randomly subjected to mutations in their genetic makeup. Thanks to the mutation, they are born with a different phenotype, which alternately heightens or reduces their chances for survival. Mutations that are adaptive spread through the population. Its carriers enjoy greater success in accumulating resources, and are therefore selected by the environment for survival and reproduction. Over time, Darwin believed, the process of random mutation and selection resulted in species change. Surviving members of an ecosystem were therefore no longer mere variants, descendants whose traits fell within the potential range of characteristics displayed by their progenitors. Rather, the surviving members emerged as qualitatively different, a new genotype.[16]

While it was a powerful interpretation of natural history, Darwin's theory presented difficulties for those who sought to harmonize it with the accepted form of scientific explanation, namely reference to efficient cause. The theory of natural selection did not cohere with a construction of change in which external force is seen to govern the actions of a system's passive constituents, with no effect on their internal organization. As Alicia Juarrero argues: "With all causes reduced to efficient cause, the manner of causality whereby the selective pressures of the environment cause species to evolve into truly new forms became a problem in need of solution. ... How external to an organism is the niche in which it is located if, over time, features of that environment contribute to specifying the very primary properties of that kind of living thing? An organism's primary properties are, according to evolutionary theory, both a record of past environments and a conjecture about the current one. The overall species-niche super-system determines the traits that individual organisms will exhibit."[17]

Ernst Cassirer notes that evolutionary theory was not the only discipline in biology that faced the problem of explaining how a larger distributed whole regulated the properties of its constituent parts. In the late eighteenth century the philosopher Immanuel Kant was also concerned about the characterization of animate form as "a unified self-contained structure," a whole "so formed that it determines the properties of its various parts." He had realized that, once a whole is formed, its constituents cease to be an aggregate and became a system, an active agent whose self-regulation and purposive interaction with the environment cannot be accounted for by the principles of efficient cause. He proposed instead "the principle of formal purposiveness," a formulation strikingly similar to the concepts of formal and final cause. The purpose for the "principle of purposive combinations and forms in nature," Kant said, was to provide one more means to "bring the appearances under rules, where the laws of mechanical causality do not suffice."[18]

Innis, by appealing to an evolutionary framework in his history of the CPR, was committing himself to a history that highlighted the same set of problems as the biological sciences faced. To start, his framework required that he establish the presence of a distinct ecology that would account for the internal organization of the CPR. His personal mandate was also to produce a history that showed the company as an organism functioning in an ecosystem constituted by North America's topography and the North Atlantic economy. He was also committing himself to a history in which a distributed whole – "a railway-niche super-system" – was seen to govern the internal organization of its constituent parts, a dynamic that Alicia Juarrero suggests has "a strong echo of Aristotle's concept of formal cause."[19]

Perhaps most important, he planned a history in which the internal organization of the CPR, and the schema of its agents, would be seen as products not only of its present interaction with the environment but also of past interactions conducted by itself and the institutions from which it could claim descent. Such was the counsel of Darwin. And such was the counsel of Veblen, who, it will be recalled, argued that the individual agent – and by extension the individual institution – can be characterized as "a cumulative process of adaptation of means to ends that cumulatively change as the process goes on." The primary properties of the agent and his environment are "at any given point the outcome of the last process. His methods of life today are enforced upon him by his habits of life carried over from yesterday and by the circumstances left as the mechanical residue of yesterday."[20]

The problem is that, both narratively and empirically, Innis failed to deliver. In his conclusion to *A History of the Canadian Pacific Railway*, he realized the need to ground his history with a description of the activities of Canadian institutions that had preceded the CPR, noting their interactions with the environment, their internal organization, and the schema of their agents. Accordingly, on a general level, he noted that settlements in North America were marked by "the rapidity and directness with which institutions … were abandoned, or adjusted, or with which new institutions were created to meet effectively conditions imposed by a new environment." And with respect to New France, he observed that with "an increased knowledge of new conditions, with the necessary adaptability and with the more suitable environmental characteristics of Quebec in the St. Lawrence valley, this civilization gained a foothold on the eastern shores of the continent and grew steadily and persistently."[21] Unfortunately, after his brief narrative of the history of New France, his description of the evolution of Canadian institutions stopped. There is nothing in his account to link the emergence of New France with the institutional organization that would eventually be adopted by the Canadian Pacific Railway.

Instead, Innis turned to the schema that British settlers had developed in the American colonies, frameworks they brought to bear in their subsequent settlement of Canada and the construction of the Canadian Pacific Railway. British settlers had also made "adjustments essential to the existence and growth of settlement" in the colonies "further south along the Atlantic coast," but in a topography very different from New France. With limited access to the interior of the continent and the prospect of military invasion from a European competitor quite remote, British colonists abandoned the use of monopolies and other centralized institutions to organize commerce and government, and turned to extractive industries such as agriculture, fishing, and lumber. The outcome was a colony with agents characterized by a mindset of "enterprise, initiative and aggressiveness."[22]

By Innis's account, the American Revolution prompted United Empire Loyalists and other British settlers to focus their attention on territories to the north of Lake Ontario and Lake Erie. The cultural traits of the settlers – including their expectation of self-government – proved incompatible with the political culture of Quebec. In the Constitutional Act of 1791, a rough divide between English and French settlements was created by the British government through the establishment of Upper and Lower Canada. The schema of British settlers prompted change within Canada from the start, but according to Innis, it was just the beginning of a long process: "The loyalty to Great Britain characteristic of Upper Canada during this early period and the particular aggressiveness of this settlement were evident in later developments."[23]

One development was a continuous effort by Upper Canada to procure transport infrastructure to ensure the continuance of trade links within Canada and with the United States. In addition, the colony took steps to ensure that British possessions to the West, most notably British Columbia after the discovery of gold, were not incorporated into the United States. In Innis's narrative, these initiatives culminated in two significant events: Confederation in 1867 and, shortly thereafter, an agreement with British Columbia to construct a railway to ensure the colony's entry into Confederation. The latter undertaking, Innis wrote, was determined largely by "the acquisitiveness characteristic of eastern Canada."[24] The Canadian Pacific Railway was the outcome.

While Innis's narrative of British settlement in his history of the CPR was intriguing, from the standpoint of his own objectives it suffered from two major flaws. To start, as was the case with his writings on the organizational makeup of New France, Innis never developed his initial insight that British cultural traits in North America were the result of settler interaction with the environment. While he recorded the emergence of an entrepreneurial worldview in New England, he said nothing about its subsequent adaptation among the United Empire Loyalists after they came to Canada. Once again, he did not take a promising point of departure to its potential conclusion.

But at a fundamental level, Innis's account in its totality suffered from a more pressing problem. His account was little more than an assertion; it offered no empirical support to demonstrate the evolutionary nature of the CPR's past. While Innis brought forward evidence to document the CPR's history as a corporation, he did not provide material to indicate that it had operated in an ecology distinct from that of the United States. Nor did he show that the industry's internal organization was an adaptive response to that ecology, a response dictated by its descent from older Canadian institutions.

Innis was aware of these shortcomings. In his autobiography he wrote: "After the publication of my thesis I was compelled to think out my next fruitful line of study. I had enjoyed tremendously the instruments at Chicago and attempted to adapt and to use the various instruments with which I had become acquainted. I had a further uneasy feeling that my thesis was inadequate and indeed one or two reviews had pointed out this fact. I must, therefore, satisfy an uneasy conscience by continuing along lines which would offset its defects."[25] With this intention, Innis embarked on a study of commodities "and the marketing structure built up in relation" to specific commodities.[26] And in the ensuing two decades he produced a succession of histories devoted to Canada's staple industries. References in the book's conclusion to extractive industries on the Atlantic coast foreshadow studies of the timber trade,[27] Canada's wheat economy,[28] and most notably, *The Cod Fisheries*.[29] Mention of British Columbia's gold rush was in turn followed by a study of the province's mining industry in the mid-1930s.[30]

But in the short term, after his first study, Innis turned his attention to two areas. His studies in Chicago had stressed that in addition to the need to relate a firm's institutional structure to the physical characteristics of the commodity it sold, it was important to study the topography, or ecosystem in which it operated: "I realized that I must spend an enormous amount of time travelling about Canada and seeing at first hand its physical characteristics."[31] His purpose in making a trip of this nature was to establish first-hand what maps and documents often obscured; namely, that Canada contained a geographic coherence capable of sustaining a unified economic ecosystem.[32]

Innis's second new focus was the history of Canada's earliest staple industry: "My immediate task was that of offsetting the limitations of my thesis by attempting to show the inherent unity of Canada as it had developed before the railroad in relation to lakes and rivers. For this reason I concentrated in the beginning on the history of the fur trade as the oldest trade on the continent."[33] To write the evolutionary history of Canada's economic past that he sought, Innis's agenda required that he establish the presence of a unique ecosystem, and trace the internal organization of its institutions through time. Only then would he be able to write a convincing evolutionary history of the CPR, and only then would he be able to demonstrate the dynamics, and the forms of causation, that had governed Canada's economic past. It was this task that he undertook in *The Fur Trade: An Introduction to Canadian Economic History*.

III

Aside from his long-term commitment to describe the dynamics of economic change, Innis had two further objectives when he published *The Fur Trade* in 1930. The first was to establish the existence of a distinct economic ecology that could be correlated with Canada's topography and political boundaries, and which could be rhetorically employed to justify Canada's existence on ostensibly objective, rational grounds. Prior to *The Fur Trade*, these points had not been assumed in Canadian political economy. If anything, the bias of the discipline ran in the other direction, thanks to the writings of W.A. MacIntosh and other scholars. In MacIntosh's view, the natural flow of economic activity extended in a north-south direction because of constraints imposed by Canada's topography: the country was "a nation created in defiance of geography."[34]

In response, Innis argued that such assessments were based on examinations of the wrong history and the wrong topography. The river systems of Canada's Pre-Cambrian shield extended from east to west, and circumscribed the trading networks that dated back to the seventeenth century. The contours of those networks, he asserted, coincided with the present-day borders of the Dominion. Through an appeal to topography and history, Innis proposed in *The Fur Trade* to demonstrate that Canada "emerged not in spite of geography but because of it."[35] By appealing to a distinct economic ecology, he also hoped to explain the characteristics of important Canadian institutions such as the railway and banking industries. Their internal organizations – or genotypes – differed from those of their American counterparts. The United States had regional railways; Canada had national railways. Canada had national banks; the United States had local banks. Innis hoped to show that these differences stemmed from distinct histories and distinct ecologies.

Innis's second purpose was to demonstrate that the extent of the ecology within which Canada operated as an economic agent was much larger than scholars had traditionally supposed. Prior to the publication of *The Fur Trade*, Canadian historiography had generally reflected the tenets of the frontier hypothesis – the contention by American historian Frederick Jackson Turner that a distinct American culture had emerged in the nineteenth century thanks to the European settlers' protracted interaction with the environment. Adapting Turner's argument to Canada, Canadian historians argued that the characteristics of Canadian institutions were the product of interaction with their local environment.[36] In Innis's mind, however, Turner's argument overemphasized the impact of the indigenous environment, especially in the case of Canada, and underemphasized the connections that English, French, Dutch, and Spanish settlers had maintained with their respective homelands. Given that continuous interaction, the most the historian could claim was that Europeans modified their institutions and practices to meet the demands imposed by local conditions. But such modifications did not presuppose transformation. Canada and the United States remained part of the cultural discourse of the West, and were, in essence, part of a North Atlantic economic and cultural space, and European.[37]

Innis begins his narrative with the European and Aboriginal traders' selection of fur as the commodity to be extracted from the environment for the purpose of trade. The French chose fur by virtue of their need to secure European goods. The beaver pelt was attractive because it was readily obtained, susceptible to shipment by small boat, and capable of fulfilling a European demand for luxury goods while yielding a high profit. Aboriginals were agents in the selection process by virtue of their agreement to procure the furs and bring them to the French in New France.[38]

In Innis's account, the fur trade was subject to episodes of market disequilibrium from its beginning as a sustained enterprise in the seventeenth century. Initially, French traders operated in a market characterized by competition. The problem as Innis described it was that the environment was initially too competitive. Aboriginal traders were able negotiators and refused to bargain until a number of European traders were present. The price of European goods was driven down as natives bargained to attain the best price for their pelts. In French eyes, it was impossible for European traders to obtain a profit in such a highly competitive environment. In the face of market pressure, French traders self-organized into combinations that were later formalized under Samuel Champlain in 1613, and by the French government in the 1620s, in the form of charter monopolies:

> To the rendezvous was brought down each year what is called, in the parlance of economics, an inelastic supply of furs which was to be exchanged for an inelastic supply of European commodities. It was unprofitable for either party to return with the goods brought. Under competitive conditions the supply of European goods tended to be larger, furs were obtained at greater cost, and profits disappeared ... Through a gradual realization of the numerous difficulties of competition, Champlain was able to arrange monopoly control. Cooperation was apparently essential even under conditions of competition. Some of the traders joined forces with Champlain in his fight with the Iroquois in 1610. In 1611 a *patache* brought a supply of provisions to Lachine Rapids for all the competitors. These intangible forms of cooperation preceded the loose association of 1613 and the later monopolies. Undoubtedly the result was the first trust in North America, and the honor of being the first successful trust promoter must be given to Champlain.[39]

The tendency toward monopoly was reinforced in the 1660s as the French trading network with the Huron and other First Nations collapsed, as a consequence of war, disease, and the decimation of the local beaver populace. The French were forced to extend their commercial activities into the interior of the continent, and continued to rely on monopolies to regulate the market. According to Innis, the French had little choice, since only large firms could accumulate the capital necessary to sustain a large trading network and coordinate its activities. The monopolies established outposts and other infrastructure in the interior, hired traders, and ensured that food was available for them in the interior. In addition, monopolies were required because they provided the means to ship large quantities of furs to

Europe to meet costs, and to procure large quantities of French manufactured goods for use in the trade.[40]

The disequilibrium engendered by the collapse of the first trading network, however, brought about a second period of self-organization, and the establishment of forms of institutional organization that would persist through to the establishment of the Dominion. Innis writes that the reorganization of the French fur trade had three important consequences. First, it forced the Company of New France and succeeding monopolies in Quebec and Montreal to cede control of internal trade to independent traders resident in the interior. Competition with the English mandated the instigation of new trading contacts with natives in increasingly remote areas, contacts that could only be garnered by the willing cooperation of traders. Consequently, merchants were forced to relinquish a greater share of their profits to local traders, and to relinquish control over the terms of trade: "The result was essentially a type of organization in which profit sharing or partnership developed between the trader in the interior and the Montreal merchant."[41]

Alongside the reorganization of trade, the second important effect of the economic dislocation of the 1660s was the growing importance of final cause in the decision-making of the French. Recall from our previous chapter that one characteristic of self-organizing systems is that they are governed by schemas, which mediate their interactions with the environment and change as systems learn more about their respective environments. We should also note Robin Neill's contention that Innis's emphasis on values, or final cause, was a defining feature of his economics.[42] It was also a defining feature of his narration in *The Fur Trade*. In the wake of their reformation of the fur trade, Innis writes, French merchants and traders altered the European concept of monopoly to meet local conditions. The lessons they drew proved adaptive to their local environment, and persisted: "The period of development of the fur trade on a large scale as an independent industry witnessed the evolution of distinctive organizations. Typical European institutions of the period such as the monopoly were adapted and modified according to the demands of a new environment. The inherent dependence of the trade on its personnel and the increasing stress on this dependence with the exhaustion of the supply of beaver led to the development of an internal organization in which the individual traders took an increasingly important part ... The dominance of the local trader in internal organization was not carried to the external organization of the trade between Quebec and France."[43] The lessons drawn by the French regarding business organization were ones that in Innis's narrative would be adopted by British and Canadian policy makers after the fall of New France.

The final consequence of the trade's reorganization was a greater degree of state participation in the conduct of the trade, chiefly through mobilization of the colony's institutions to support the fur trade.[44] According to Innis, the changes were prompted in part by a desire to maintain revenue, and in part by economic processes – processes we can identify with formal cause. As discussed earlier, in systems governed by formal cause, the larger, distributed whole governs the behaviour of its constituent parts. Autocatalytic sets, for example, regulate the flow rates of their constituent processes to maintain their formal integrity. The earth and moon are governed by formal cause because the earth in isolation would display a different behavioural trait, namely no tidal patterns.[45] According to Innis, by the eighteenth century a similar dynamic had transformed the internal organization of both France and New France: "Commodities to exchange for furs were manufactured on a large scale, and served to stimulate the economic life of France. On the other hand fluctuations in the market for furs reacted on industrial life and affected her position. The economic and institutional life of Europe had reached a period of comparative adjustment and balance previous to the discovery of the New World. The economic and institutional life of France undoubtedly suffered material disarrangement through the importation of furs on a large scale from New France."[46]

Much of the fluctuation in the market was precipitated by English competition. As early as the 1630s, the internal organization of New France began adapting to the more competitive environment, with the French government instituting reforms to ensure the colony's continued ability to procure fur: "The energies of the colony were directed to defence against the inroads of the Iroquois and to the problem of keeping open the St. Lawrence and the Ottawa route ... To carry out these militaristic measures, the colony was subjected to a centralized policy in all its activities. Trade, agricultural development as in the seigniorial tenure, and even religious activities, as shown in the exclusion of the Huguenots and later control of the Jesuits, reflected the influence of centralized control."[47]

By devoting the majority of its human and financial capital to the fur trade, New France placed itself in a destructive cycle from which it never recovered. By the mid-eighteenth century, the fur trade had expanded from the St Lawrence drainage basin to the drainage basin of Hudson Bay. Acquisition and transport of furs had become expensive, and, as Innis recounts, the French were consistently outbid for their furs by English competitors in the south and north. Moreover, English manufactured products, especially woollen cloth, were superior to French products, and easier for natives with the best furs – those living near Hudson Bay – to acquire. While profits declined, costs rose as networks of military posts were constructed to prevent Indians from trading with the English. An increasing proportion of revenue from the fur trade had to be diverted to protect a dwindling source of revenue. It was a cycle that New France was never able to break, a cycle that consolidated its dependence on France for military protection and industrial products. Given such constraints, New France lost its dominance of the fur trade. And given the absence of a diversified economy, the colony was unable to attract migration or generate the resources required to ensure its survival.[48]

New France collapsed economically and then, with the Conquest, politically. After Britain's formal assumption of control of the colony in 1763, the fur trade fell into British hands. As Innis notes, because they faced the same constraints as the French, the British over the course of the next fifteen years "found it necessary to develop an organization which had features strikingly similar to those of the French *régime*."[49] Many of the reforms reflected French influence, suggesting again the importance of final cause in Innis's narrative. The reliance of new institutions on the expertise – and schemas – of individuals from old or defunct extractive industries is a theme that Innis would return to repeatedly in *The Fur Trade*.

In the case of the British this meant altering their approach and practices in fundamental ways. Prior to 1763 the British had relied on aboriginal traders to bring furs to outposts along Hudson Bay or in Albany, New York. Solicitation of trade and the maintenance of personal relationships with trading partners were not standard features of British practice. But, most notably in the case of the Northwest Company, which inherited the French trade routes in the St Lawrence Basin, British merchants learned from French *voyageurs* the importance of establishing working relationships with aboriginal suppliers. The British were no more able to compel trading partners to come to Montreal than the French had been.[50]

The British were also forced to change their schema regarding the internal organization of the trade. Facing restrictions on trade occasioned by the American Revolution, Montreal merchants were obliged to extend their commercial activities to the west. And there they in turn had to deal with the same constraints governing the trade that the French had met. According to Innis, "Methods of control and regulation adequate to the English trade were inadequate to the new demands."[51] Burdened by the challenges of servicing a constantly rising demand for European goods in the west, arranging for the shipment of furs to Europe, and installing depots to provide provisions for traders, the British had no choice but to cede control of commercial activity to traders in the interior. With respect to the French trade, Innis observed that it had "adapted to its specific geographic areas" and that its organization "persisted with unusual tenacity."[52] In his narrative of the British trade, Innis pointed to the emergence and persistence of the same pattern, both cognitively and organizationally: "The principle of the partnership was to persist as the dominant type of organization of the fur trade practically until the end of the nineteenth century. It was the device with which the trade could be prosecuted with great effectiveness over great distances in which the central authority could exercise no direct control over the individual trader."[53]

Aside from learning the need for distributed control within firms, the British also mirrored French practice by resorting to combinations between firms, in order to adapt to changing conditions in the ecological and economic environments of the time. Yet, despite the efforts of traders such as Alexander Mackenzie, the British trade never thrived under conditions of competition, even as it created an economic space that would eventually be transformed into the political space of Canada. Profits fell, and firms such as Mackenzie's XY Company eventually amalgamated with the dominant combine, the Northwest Company. Ultimately, the Northwest Company itself would amalgamate with the Hudson's Bay Company. In the parlance of *complex adaptive systems*, the characteristics of the British fur trade demonstrated differential persistence.[54]

As Canada's economy diversified and became more complex, the characteristics of the fur trade, Innis indicates, persisted and spread to other sectors. By the end of the eighteenth century, the fur trade had shifted west and north, necessitating the development of new lines of trade in the Canadas. By the start of the nineteenth century British North America had become immersed in an international economy that encouraged its continued specialization in staple products. As Innis describes it, especially in his account of economic change in Upper Canada, the effect of the North Atlantic economy was akin to formal cause. By means of trade, the colony interacted with Britain. Positive feedback in the form of profits led to the formation of a system, which in turn determined the internal organization of the two trading partners: "Energy has been directed toward the exploitation of staple products and the tendency has been cumulative. The raw material supplied to the mother country stimulated manufactures of the finished product and also of the products which were in demand in the colony. Large scale production of raw materials was encouraged by improvement of technique of production, of marketing, and of transport as well as by improvement in the manufacture of the finished product. As a consequence, energy in the colony was drawn into the production of the staple commodity both directly and indirectly."[55]

Under the influence of similar market conditions, Canadian institutions employed similar strategies to acquire needed capital, resources, and revenue. In Innis's mind, the coincidence in practice was no accident. Like Veblen, Innis believed that the structures and practices of institutions were persistent, or displayed differential persistence, and his narrative presented an argument strikingly similar in language and substance to that of Veblen to explain the persistence of institutional practices through time. Veblen's career was animated by a central purpose: to shift economists' attention from the dynamic of mechanical change to the dynamic of emergent change. His writings, however, also suggest a second fundamental purpose. Veblen believed that economists too often focused on the passive constituents of economic systems, namely industrial capital. While it was important, it was not, and never could be, the primary driver of economic change. If economists hoped to acquire a deeper understanding of the dynamics of a given economic system, they would need to turn their attention to its active constituent: the human agent.

For Veblen, this insight was crucial because of his belief that any expression of dynamics must rest on a formulation describing a continuous process, not a sequence of discrete points in time. Such a formulation could not be obtained by a focus on capital, technology, institutions, or infrastructure. All four, he argued, should be seen as "items in a process of cumulative change or as items in the scheme of life." For all intents and purposes, they were expressions of human thought: "These productive goods are facts of human knowledge, skill and predilection; that is to say, they are, substantially, prevalent habits of thought, and it is as such that they enter into the process of industrial development."[56]

Because productive goods and institutions are artifacts – expressions of human thought – Veblen considered them discrete events that could be situated in time but did not exhibit a relationship between instants in time. The continuity underlying "the economic life process," the relationship between past and present economic activity, would only be accounted for if economists turned their attention to the human agent. Only through reference to human activity could economists explain the fact of innovation and by extension, based on our review of Veblen's other writings on human schemas, the fact of persistence in human practice: "The changes that take place in the mechanical contrivances are an expression of changes in the human factor. Changes in the material facts breeds further change only through the human factor. It is in the human material that the continuity of development is to be looked for; and it is here, therefore, that the motor forces of the process of economic development must be studied if they are to be studied in action at all. Economic action must be the subject-matter of the science if the science is to fall into line as an evolutionary science."[57] Given his interest in Veblen, it is not a surprise, then, that Innis situated his history of Canadian institutions after the fur trade in a process of cumulative change, like Veblen; that he identified human activity as the basis for continuity in economic life, like Veblen; and that he emphasized the fact and import of persistence in human economic practice, again like Veblen.

In the wake of the eighteenth century, the fur trade's prominence in British North American economic life declined, "and the transport organization and personnel were shifted to the development of new lines of trade."[58] With them went the schema and practices of the fur trade. In response to the British shipbuilding industry's demand for forest products, the timber trade emerged as the dominant staple industry in Canada. As the beneficiary of the transport infrastructure developed by the fur trade, the timber industry was in turn a significant contributor to the economic development of Canada.

While the fur trade had carved out a significant economic space in the Canadas and to the west, it had not promoted the settlement necessary to translate both spaces into viable political entities; indeed, the trade presupposed vast tracts of unsettled territory. The timber trade, by contrast, had an inherent incentive to promote settlement to reduce its operating or overhead costs. While participant firms had an obvious source of cargo for ships heading to Europe, they had to deal with the problem of empty cargo holds for the return trip. Transporting migrants proved to be a good source of revenue. Increasing settlement led to the economic diversification of the two Canadas and, Innis remarked, to a new set of challenges for the colony's policy makers. While the timber trade was able to make use of the existing network of rivers, lakes, and rapids to transport logs to mills for processing prior to shipping them to Europe, producers of other commodities, such as wheat and potash, could not. What's more, the rudimentary transport infrastructure made it difficult for colonists to obtain imported manufactured goods.[59]

The growing need for transport infrastructure, and the emerging specialization in extractive industries, meant that the acquisition of foreign capital became a high priority for business leaders, and by extension for government policy makers in the two Canadas. That imperative, coupled with the boom-and-bust nature of staple markets, prompted the transformation, or self-organization, of the financial and constitutional structures of both colonies as Canadians sought to maximize their capacity to obtain capital from foreign markets. The ultimate outcome of the process, Innis argued, was Confederation, as Canadians increasingly looked to the state to underwrite foreign loans.[60]

It was in the financial sector, which had its roots in the fur trade, that the impetus toward centralization was initiated: "An extended financial organization under the fur trade was attested by the plans for the first establishment of a bank in Canada with the strong support of Phyn and Elice and the establishment of the Bank of Montreal in 1817 with John Gray, an old fur trader, as president."[61] The emerging financial sector shifted its focus to the newly dominant timber trade, entering into an association that would eventually transform it: "Canada's financial organization had been greatly strengthened through the strains incidental to the lumber industry. The crises in Great Britain and the United States in 1825–26, 1837, 1847, and 1857 had serious effects on construction industries and on the trade of a country interested in the export of lumber. The collapse of weaker banks in these periods contributed to the centralization of banking structure which became conspicuous in the period after Confederation. The fur trade and the lumber industry contributed the basic features essential to expansion after Confederation."[62]

Innis continues his analysis by suggesting that Canadian bankers, affected by market shocks similar to those experienced in the fur trade, resorted to the schemas and organizational forms that had proved adaptive in the fur trade. There was a parallel, he maintained, between the distributed control of the fur trade and the "branch bank system with headquarters in the east ... No such tendency toward unity of structure in institutions and toward centralized control as found in Canada can be observed in the United States."[63]

The need for capital for transportation infrastructure also twice prompted the reorganization of the Canadian state during the nineteenth century. The need for canals, Innis writes, stimulated the union of Upper and Lower Canada in 1840. But canals only proved a short-term expedient, as cold weather hindered their year-round use. Even prior to Confederation, railways emerged as a more flexible alternative, which in turn exercised a catalytic effect on Canada's economy and staple industries. By the 1860s the largest trees in the vicinity of easily accessible waterways had been cleared, and it had become more difficult for the industry to use waterways to acquire supplies and then transport materials to market. Railways facilitated the lumber industry's access to raw materials and its ability to ship them to market. They also eased the difficulty of transporting logs to sawmills for processing, and opened the mid-western American market to Canadian producers.[64]

The railway's success in transporting timber to new markets and bringing migrants to new settlements precipitated calls for expansion of existing networks, and eventually to the formation of the Dominion: "The lumber industry of eastern Canada was largely responsible directly and indirectly for the improvement of waterways and for the construction of railways prior to Confederation. Canal and railway construction was synonymous with heavy capital investment. Capital was obtained through private enterprise and substantial guarantees and aid from the imperial and colonial governments. Heavy expenditures involved the development of a strong centralized government in Canada."[65]

For Innis, the formation of the Dominion illustrated the importance of two particular recurring patterns in Canada's economic history. Large central organizations such as the Northwest Company had emerged in Canada because the environment within had not supported unregulated extraction of staples, while the environment without had refused to provide the capital that small-scale institutions needed. From an evolutionary standpoint, therefore, large-scale institutions with a limited degree of distributed control enjoyed a selective advantage. The second significant pattern was that institutions supporting the staples trade generally assumed the same form of organization that characterized the staples trade, usually because the same agents occupied roles in both the staple industry and the supporting institution.[66] This had been the case with Canada's financial institutions, and proved to be the case with the Dominion and its adoption of a federal form of government: "The British North America Act, like the Act of Union, has provided for a strong central government. The prairie provinces as producers of wheat were controlled from Montreal and Ottawa as they were controlled in the earlier period as producers of fur under the Northwest Company. With the United States residuary powers were left with the states whereas in Canada they remain with the federal government or rather with eastern Canada."[67]

Once his history of Canadian institutions was in place, with its emphasis on continuity with respect to agents, forms of organization, and schemas, Innis was in a better position to account for the internal organization – or genotype – of the Canadian Pacific Railway than in his earlier book devoted to the topic. In his estimation, the large central organization of the CPR was brought about by three factors, the first of which was the need to form a large organization to attract foreign, primarily English, capital. The second factor was the desire to reduce overhead costs. In Innis's reading, Canadian policy makers prior to Confederation were well aware of the economic burden that massive investment in a railway network would entail. Maintenance of the railway would involve heavy overhead costs, which could not be dispelled even with attraction of new settlers to the colonies, new settlements, and expansion of agriculture in the province of Canada. Decision makers in the private and public sectors believed that railway expansion was viable only if the network was extended beyond the Canadas to the west. The increased traffic would be sufficient to reduce overhead costs and consequently the economic strain upon Upper and Lower Canada.[68]

The third factor contributing to centralization was the close link between agents of the fur and railway industries and the government-facilitated development of a large centralized railway. Grand Trunk

Railway interests purchased the Hudson's Bay Company – and its jurisdiction over Rupert's Land – in 1863. Confederation followed in 1867. In Innis's reading, it was an instrument used by these agents to attract English capital to facilitate western expansion. The sale of Rupert's Land followed in 1869.[69]

In sum, a network of agents with common aims, and a common economic space under the control of the fur trade, enabled the emergence of a national railway: "The large central organization in the fur trade facilitated the transfer and the organization of the new technique [machine industry in general and Canada's railway in particular] over a wide area."[70] In Innis's reading, Canada's elite shared common beliefs about Canadian economic policy and the appropriate organization for the railway industry, because its members shared a common schema, one that traced its origin to the fur trade. The internal organization of the CPR, he wrote, was in large part determined by final cause:

> The fur trade and its personnel continued to be fundamentally important. The fur trade had not only produced a centralized organization but it had produced a succession of fur traders who were typically self-reliant, energetic, and possessed of keen bargaining ability and high organizing capacity. D.A. Smith . . . was not only an important official in the Hudson's Bay Company, trained in the school of the fur trade, but he was an influential force in the construction and management of the Canadian Pacific Railway which heralded the new industry. The relationship which existed with the opening of western Canada, in which important officials of the Hudson's Bay Company were prominent in the activities of the Bank of Montreal, of the Canadian Pacific Railway, and of the Dominion government, was not accidental.[71]

At the conclusion of his study, however, Innis was careful to emphasize that the internal organization of the Canadian economy in general, and the CPR in particular, was not solely due to the presence of agents and persistent schemas. If Canada was distinguished by large centralized institutions with limited degrees of distributed control, and close collaboration between its government and industries, it was because its economy was embedded in a system characterized by emergent properties and the governance of formal cause, characteristics we would identify today with *complex adaptive systems*. With respect to the former, Innis's most concise and explicit reference to the importance of emergent properties appeared in *Empire and Communication*, a work he published twenty years after the release of *The Fur Trade*: "Concentration on the production of staples for export to more highly industrialized areas in Europe and later in the United States had broad implications for the Canadian economic, political and social structure. Each staple in its turn left its stamp, and the shift to new staples invariably produced periods of crises in which adjustments in the old structure were painfully made and a new pattern created in relation to a new staple."[72]

In the parlance of *complex adaptive systems*, new dissipative structures emerged to enhance the system's capacity to interact with an environment in disequilibrium. That capacity was also enhanced by the governance of formal cause over Canada's economy. The key insight that Innis sought to convey here was that the Canadian economy functioned as an active agent. As such, it routinely altered the identity, internal organization, and arrangement of its constituents in order to heighten its environmental fitness and to maintain its formal integrity. With respect to formal cause, Juarrero observes that the organization of *complex adaptive systems* and autocatalytic sets is "preserved even at the expense of the individual parts that make up its structure at any given moment … The final configuration, a highly pruned and streamlined version of the original, might not even look like the earlier triad ... The ordered environment in which the components of an autocatalytic cycle – or of any complex dynamical system – exists thus selectively (top-down) constrains their behavior and activities ... A component that may be fit in one context may not be in another. Far from being a primary quality, therefore, fitness is a multiply realizable property ... that depends on what occurs elsewhere and previously."[73]

There is a striking parallel between this formulation and Innis's own summary of the staple hypothesis at the end of *The Fur Trade*. Both refer to systems with trajectories determined in part by historically contingent events. Both refer to systems that bifurcate into new arrangements of constituent parts. And both refer to systems capable of incorporating new agents and new realms of activity, while dispensing with sectors that no longer contribute to the fitness of the entire system. Innis writes:

> The trade in staples ... and especially the fur trade, has been responsible for various peculiar tendencies in Canadian development. The maintenance of connections with Europe, at first with France and later with Great Britain, has been a result. The diversity of institutions which has attended this relationship has made for greater elasticity in organization and for greater tolerance among her peoples. This elasticity of institutions facilitated the development of the compromise which evolved in responsible government and the British Empire. Having failed in her own colonial policy England was able to build up an empire in Canada on the remarkable success of French colonial policy. The fur trade permitted the extension of authority and independence across the northern half of the continent. Moreover, the business structure shifted from the elastic organization characteristic of the Northwest Company ... to the more permanent organization from Hudson Bay. The diversity of institutions has made possible the combination of government ownership and private enterprise which has been a further characteristic of Canadian development.[74]

The elements of *complex adaptive systems* and formal cause are all there. By referring to the "extension of authority and independence across the northern half of the continent," "the remarkable success of French colonial policy," and British use of the same to develop responsible government, Innis was emphasizing that the Canadian economy was historically constituted by agents. These agents interacted with each other and with the natural environment. Collectively, agents in Europe and North America selected fur for extraction from the environment, responding to the historical contingencies of European taste and technology and the abundant supply of beaver pelts. The selection was important, in that it was "responsible for various peculiar tendencies in Canadian development." Because the environment in which these agents interacted remained at "the edge of chaos," or at the right mean between "authority and independence," the economy in North America displayed emergent properties in the form of new institutions and schemas.[75]

The purpose of this commercial activity was straightforward; namely, "maintenance of connections with Europe, at first with France and later with Great Britain." By virtue of its interaction with trading partners across the Atlantic and the positive feedback it received in the forms of profit and technology, Canada – and its predecessors – became part of a trading network susceptible to the governance of final and formal cause. Final cause was indicated by the repeated initiatives of Canadian institutions to maintain their trading relationship with Europe, and their frequent resort to a schema of distributed autonomy – a mix of "authority and independence" – to regulate their interaction with the environment.

Formal cause was indicated by the changing organization of the economy and the institutions comprising it. Maintenance of a sustainable relationship with the environment and trading relations with Britain meant, in the parlance of *complex adaptive systems*, that the "ordered environment" of the Canadian economy constrained "the behaviour and activities" of its constituent parts. In the nineteenth century the structure of the fur trade changed. With no new territories available for acquisition, environmental constraints obliged the trade to modify its internal organization to remain profitable, shifting from the distributed system of control characteristic of the Northwest Company to a monopoly, "the more permanent" form of organization favoured by the Hudson's Bay Company.

The constraints of the international economy also prompted change. In this regard, Innis emphasized the importance of the elasticity that characterized Canada's economy. At the institutional level, the tension between centralization and decentralization facilitated self-organization, including the reorganization of the Canadian state. At the national level, it indicated a similar form of distributed control, and the governance of formal cause. The economy, as Innis described it, was an agent, a combination of components akin to a network, one that routinely acquired new components to heighten its fitness and maintain its trading ties with Europe: "The diversity of institutions which has attended this relationship has made for greater elasticity in organization and for greater tolerance among her peoples." In other words, Canada's economic history had followed a path much like the evolution of an autocatalytic set. By virtue of the economy's history – namely its selection of staple products for export – and its receipt of profit and capital from the North Atlantic economy, Innis argued that events occurring, in Juarrero's words, "elsewhere and previously" led to the evolution of an economy with unique characteristics. The capital-intensive nature of staple industries mandated the early selection of the state by institutional networks seeking to acquire capital from abroad.

Given Canada's specialization as a producer of staples, the maintenance of its formal integrity as an economy required continued access to funding. And according to Innis, while the identity of participant institutions changed, one persistent feature of Canada's economic past was the selection and incorporation of the Canadian state in its colonial and dominion guises into new coalitions of institutions, in order to heighten their fitness abroad: "The diversity of institutions has made possible the combination of government ownership and private enterprise which has been a further characteristic of Canadian development."

IV

For Innis, then, the staple hypothesis referred at base to a conception of economic change that reflected the economics he had promoted in his Veblen essay. In his estimation, Canada's economy had been composed of systems that displayed emergent properties and were in turn governed by formal and final cause. This reading also suggests – on a preliminary basis – that Innis's work can be characterized as a methodological and conceptual forerunner of an emerging trend in Atlantic historiography. The verdict is tentative because in *The Fur Trade* the Atlantic Basin is essentially a bit player, a supporting cast member to the play's principal, the Canadian economy. To characterize Innis as a forerunner of Atlantic historiography we need to explore the work in which the Atlantic trade is the primary object of Innis's attention, namely *The Cod Fisheries*.

The reading further suggests that the foil we have been using to read Innis's economic histories, namely the staple theory of development formulated by Mel Watkins, does not reflect the centre-margin dynamic that Innis discussed. The reading is again preliminary because Innis does not tell us a great deal about the centre in *The Fur Trade*. He gives us few specifics about its identity. Is it a unitary actor or does it consist of multiple agents? Neither does he say much about its relative historic success in effecting change. He does tell us, however, that the internal organization of France was affected by the fur trade, and that the French government enjoyed substantial agency in changing the internal organizations of France and New France. He also tells us: "the economic history of Canada has been dominated by the discrepancy between the centre and the margin of civilization."[76]

On balance, Innis does not tell us much. But what he does tell us offers more support for an identification of his writings with an emergent and systemic construct of change than one that is normative. While his description of the French state's reorganization of New France suggests an identification with Watkins, dependency theory, and a normative conception of change, his general propositions regarding Canada's economic history do not. Notice that in his formulation of Canada's relationship with its respective imperial centres after France that Innis does not suggest that their discrepancy in status is due to domination. Rather, he appeals to the economics of increasing returns, the process of cumulative causation that we saw in this chapter and the process that we shall learn more about in the following chapter. As we shall see, reference to the concept of increasing returns will prove extremely useful not only for interpreting Innis's writings on the history of the cod fisheries, but also for understanding his writings on cognitive bias and communication media.

In Innis's account of the fur trade, the initiatives of imperial centres emerge as factors that are relatively peripheral to the evolution and functioning of Canada's economy. While imperial state intervention could reinforce economic trends in place through instruments such as mercantile policy, Innis did not see such actions as determinative. After the institution of free trade in the nineteenth century, Canada's economic relationship with Great Britain remained much as it had been during the mercantile era. As a result of the process of cumulative causation, and formal cause, Canada retained its specialization as an exporter of staples.[77] This reading of Innis's conception of the North Atlantic economy is strengthened by an examination of the writings he devoted to maritime trade and the economic activity that precipitated it – the cod fishery. In *The Cod Fisheries*, Innis would speak at length about the rise and fall of the European empires that circumnavigated the Atlantic, and about the economic processes that facilitated their emergence and hastened their fall. These were the processes that had mediated the relationships of London and Paris with their disparate colonies. And the mediation Innis described took the form of formal and final cause.

3

The Cod Fisheries

In *The Cod Fisheries: The History of an International Economy* (1940), Harold Innis presents a history that is far more ambitious in scope, and far more complex in matter than his study of the fur trade. While he did refer to the importance of the international economy in *The Fur Trade*, his primary concern, as indicated in his subtitle, was the economic history of Canada. In *The Cod Fisheries* he shifted his focus to a different staple, a different ecosystem, and to the history of the North Atlantic economy at large. Innis's purpose was to study the economic histories of Canada's Maritime Provinces, Newfoundland, and New England, territories which in their totality had constituted the economic region that had enabled the North Atlantic economy to function, through its exploitation of the cod fishery and its participation in the carrying trade.

In his respective studies of the fisheries, Innis sought to demonstrate yet again the core proposition of the staple hypothesis; namely, that the structural organization of North America, and to a lesser extent Europe, was the by-product of trade in staples across the North Atlantic.[1] The disparate regions of North America were distinguished by different political, social, and economic structures, all of which resulted from the initiating stage of European economic activity in each region. According to Innis's evolutionary framework, these structures emerged as European agents extracted selected staples from distinct environments. They also persisted over time, or displayed *differential persistence.* Such had been the case in the interior of North America. It was a supposition that Innis would seek to demonstrate again in *The Cod Fisheries*.

And yet, Innis's introduction to *The Cod Fisheries* also revealed a far more fundamental commitment, a desire to describe the dynamics that governed the economic history of the North Atlantic economy. Innis argued that between 1497 and the nineteenth century the structure of the international economy changed, from one regulated by states and monopolistic companies under the mercantile system, to one with thousands of participating agents in a commercial economy.[2] At the same time, the major European powers bordering the Atlantic – Britain, France, Spain, and Portugal – were locked in a contest to establish an economic, and then an imperial, presence in North America. In Innis's estimation, the progression of the former had a direct bearing on the latter: "The problem of markets is a phase in the collapse of empires."[3]

To trace this twofold process, Innis proposed a study of the cod fishery, a choice he justified by noting that the North American fishery was an important arena in "the intensity of the struggle between mercantile systems and empires, and the struggles within mercantile systems."[4] It had also proven historically to be an important stimulant to economic development. Construed as a necessary component of naval defence, European fishing industries received support from the state; they were also an important source of food, a stimulant to trade, and a catalyst for the exchange of specie, an exchange in which Britain and France proved to be the beneficiaries, and Spain and Portugal the losers. In Innis's account, a successful fishery was an essential prerequisite to economic diversification. Economic diversification was a defining attribute of a successful mercantile system. And in the case of North America, a successful mercantile system was – for a time – the basis for a stable imperial regime in North America.

Innis also highlighted the importance of the fishery for a different reason. Its history brought into sharp relief – one sharper than the fur trade – the dynamic of cumulative causation that historically had prompted economic growth and diversification, and equally had prompted imperial decline and collapse. From the standpoint of his long-term commitment to describe the dynamics of economic change, Innis's primary concern in his various accounts of the cod fishery was to learn more about a trading system governed by the economics of increasing returns. He said as much in "The Economic History of the Maritimes," a 1931 article in which he provided a concise overview of the narrative he would later present in *The Cod Fisheries*. In the article's conclusion, he noted that the industrial revolution of the nineteenth century was transforming the characteristics of the North Atlantic economy from those that pertained in the eighteenth century. This was not necessarily a good thing, Innis counselled, since industrialization was limiting ownership of the carrying trade into fewer and fewer hands, a development that potentially might place greater constraints on agents on both sides of the Atlantic engaged in trade. While the future of the international economy could not be predicted, Innis emphasized that a fundamental principle of economic change would prevail – a principle that had governed the economic systems he had studied in the seventeenth and eighteenth centuries, and had received its classic formulation in Adam Smith's *The Wealth of Nations*: "As it is the power of exchanging that gives occasion to the division of labour, so the extent of this division must always be limited by the extent of that power, or in other words, by the extent of the market."[5]

For economists, this formulation has traditionally had a special significance, one that extends beyond the importance of exchange and the onset of division of labour. It is also understood to refer to the process that *induces* division of labour in emerging markets, namely the economics of increasing returns. As Kenneth Arrow, a Nobel Prize–winning economist, notes: "the concept of increasing returns has had a long but uneasy presence in economic analysis. The opening chapters of Adam Smith's *The Wealth of Nations* put great emphasis on increasing returns to explain both specialization and economic growth. Yet the object of study moves quickly to the competitive system ... The English school ... followed the competitive assumption, and quietly dropped Smith's boldly stated proposition that, 'the division of labour is limited by the extent of the market,' division of labour having been shown to lead to increased productivity."[6]

Innis's reference to Adam Smith suggests that, if we are to reach a deeper understanding of *The Cod Fisheries*, we will need to follow three lines of enquiry. To start, we will need to learn more about the concept of increasing returns. What phenomena does this dynamic generate in economic systems? And more to the point, what relationship does it bear with the construct of emergent change generally, and *complex adaptive systems* particularly? We also need to consider briefly whether Innis had access to the concept so conceived and so characterized. The reference to Smith suggests he did. But Innis made no explicit reference to it in his major or minor works. Instead, he opted for Thorstein Veblen's term for recurring change: cumulative causation. We need to establish that both terms point to more or less the same thing. And finally, we need to apply the concept and determine its purchase for interpreting Innis's treatments of the cod fisheries, starting with "The Rise and Fall of the Spanish Fishery in Newfoundland," and concluding with "The Economic History of the Maritimes" and, of course, *The Cod Fisheries*. These readings finally put us in a position to answer the question raised in the preceding chapter: what relationship, if any, does Mel Watkins's theory of normative development have with the writings of Harold Innis? They will also give a basis for establishing Innis's belief in the central importance of positive feedback in economic history and, by extension, the central importance of emergent change and the governance of formal and final cause.

I

For much of the twentieth century, the doctrine of increasing returns was not popular in the field of economics. Despite concerns raised by Innis and a small number of other economists, the majority resisted exploration of the dynamics of market growth and decline because the concept of increasing returns had an important implication: emerging systems can and often do carry within them the potential for more than one outcome.[7] Economists from Veblen's time forward focused instead on the creation of an economics of diminishing returns. They did so to satisfy the discipline's aspiration to meet a basic requirement of science; namely, the capacity to predict the future behaviour of systems within a given domain of study. Accordingly, neo-classical economists began constructing static formulations which assumed that a system under analysis was in a state of equilibrium. The rules governing relations between an economy's constituent parts were seen as fixed, meaning that a system could only proceed to a single outcome, and that future prices of commodities and market share between firms could be determined in advance.[8]

While the assumptions associated with diminishing returns appealed to many scholars, W. Brian Arthur, an economist associated with the Santa Fe Institute in New Mexico, notes that the concept suffers from an important defect: "Such an agreeable picture often does violence to reality."[9] Neo-classical economics does not acknowledge that systems grow and evolve over time; nor does it acknowledge that participating firms can make large, sometimes obscenely large, profits from the market place. Instead, it insists that a system's constituent parts – its participating firms – can only grow so far before environmental conditions impose rising costs or diminishing profits. It further argues that the most a firm can do is to optimize its operations and rest content with the small profits the market provides.[10] To counter this distorted picture, a growing number of economists since the mid-1980s have turned their attention to the economics of increasing returns. The concept now enjoys growing currency in domains ranging from international trade theory and the economics of technology and industrial organization, to economic development.[11]

Much of the credit for this development rests with Arthur, who in the early 1980s contributed to the development of the mathematics necessary to represent economic systems governed by increasing returns. He was instrumental in demonstrating that the characteristics of increasing returns systems can be harmonized with the theory of complex adaptive systems.[12] As such, his explication of the doctrine of increasing returns proves useful, not only for interpreting Innis's narratives devoted to the cod fisheries, but also as a means of bridging Innis's later writings with the theory of complex adaptive systems. In his communication studies, Innis wrote as an economist, using the vocabulary of an economist. A brief overview of the economics of increasing returns will prepare us to reconstruct the dynamics of emergent cultural and cognitive change that he believed governed past and present cultures, and the role he saw communication technology playing in effecting such change.

In Arthur's portrayal of increasing return economics, market activity can be reduced to a conception where agents or products enjoy a measure of success that is self-reinforcing or self-sustaining.[13] The market for operating systems in personal computers is a now classic example of a system governed by increasing returns, one that Arthur repeatedly refers to in his writings. During the 1980s, three products vied for market share, the DOS operating system, CP/M, and Apple's MacIntosh system. While it was unclear at the start of the decade which, if any, system would attain market dominance, Arthur contends that the defining moment occurred shortly after 1980, when IBM concluded a deal with Microsoft to develop an operating system for its PC. Thanks to its introduction of the personal computer, IBM dominated the initial home and business markets for small computers, a development that initiated a process of cumulative causation. Software developers such as Lotus acquired an incentive to develop products using a DOS platform, since more and more of their customers were purchasing computers serviced by DOS. Customers in turn selected DOS since it supported more software, and software companies were subsequently induced to develop a prominent, if not exclusive orientation toward DOS when developing new products. In a clear demonstration of the governance of increasing returns, or positive feedback, Microsoft's operating system emerged as the dominant product of the 1980s.[14]

Markets governed by increasing returns also display a number of other characteristics. A major one is the characteristic emphasized by Adam Smith – division of labour, heightened complexity, or in Arthur's parlance, perpetual novelty. Out-of-equilibrium markets are constantly adapting, constantly seeking to improve their status, and for this reason are constantly seeking newer and more diverse methods to meet the needs and aims of their participants: "Niches are continually created by new markets, new technologies, new behaviours, new institutions. The very act of filling a niche may provide new niches. The result is ongoing, perpetual novelty."[15] In systems governed by increasing returns, Arthur and his collaborators Steven Durlauf and David Lane write, economists are constrained to ask "how new 'things' arise in the world – cognitive things, like 'internal models'; physical things, like 'new technologies,' social things, like new kinds of economic 'units.' And it is clear that if we posit a world of perpetual novelty, then outcomes cannot correspond to steady-state equilibria … The only descriptions that can matter are about transient phenomena – about process and about emergent structures."[16]

Increasing returns markets also display a third characteristic: path dependence, a process whereby a market's selection of a firm or product is in part determined by contingent, historic, events. Envision a scenario in which several firms enter the market and begin competing with one another. A chance encounter with a buyer, the implementation of a new, cost-efficient way to generate a product, or an unexpected order can provide a firm, say Firm A, with an initial edge, enabling it to enjoy the benefit of increasing returns until it enjoys market dominance. Firm B, by contrast, has to endure the misfortune of experiencing increasing returns in reverse: the self-sustaining dynamic will erode the firm's market share.[17]

A fourth feature of systems governed by increasing returns is market lock-in. According to Arthur, once the market selects a firm, that firm generally remains dominant until a firm bearing a new generation of technology emerges to supplant it. American firms learned this lesson the hard way between 1970 and 1987, as they saw their share of the U.S. television and telephone markets plummet in the face of Japanese competitors. While retrieval of market share is not a hopeless proposition, Arthur notes that "the rules of positive feedback imply that it is much harder to recoup a market than to hold on to it in the first place."[18]

Market lock-in occurs in part because some firms enjoy falling unit costs as institution size increases, a characteristic that enables one firm, or a select few, to take advantage of positive feedback from the economy to corner the respective market. The situation in this context is completely different from the scenario that firms face in a diminishing returns market. Firms in an increasing returns market do not have to deal with environmental or other constraints that reduce their profit margin after they pass a certain threshold or scale of activity. In fact, their conditions are the exact reverse. The more they produce, the lower the unit cost, and the higher their profit margin. Arthur again points to Microsoft to illustrate this point. The company enjoyed the effects of lock-in partly because the first copy of Windows cost $50 million to produce, the second $3. Each copy produced and sold thereafter reduced unit cost and raised its profit margin. The company had every incentive to sell as many copies of its operating system as it could. Due to the reinforcement of increasing returns, Microsoft emerged again as a dominant player, locking in the operating system market, and making substantial profits in the process.[19]

Market lock-in also occurs as a result of market effects that can be identified with the governance of formal and final cause. According to Arthur, the high-tech market generally favours the establishment of a market standard in operating systems and computer languages. Having fewer standards is a benefit to the customer, insofar as a small number of standards affords access to a higher quantity of software. It is also of benefit to the producer, insofar as the base of potential customers is widened. In the discipline of economics, the selection of a product by a community of users with a vested interest in uniformity is referred to as a "network effect."[20]

As Arthur describes it, the network effect can be identified with formal and final cause, since a consumer's selection of a product is predicated not only on the basis of personal preference but also on the basis of belonging to a network. The network's community of users favours the selection of a ubiquitous standard in operating systems or software, thanks to a common schema which suggests that the network's behavioural competence will be heightened if it does so. Greater numbers of members will be attracted, more software will be developed to meet their needs, and the formal integrity of the network will be enhanced. With an array of products to serve their needs, network members have no reason to abandon the software or operating system that precipitated the network's emergence in the first place.

The final characteristic of systems governed by increasing returns is that they proceed toward multiple possible outcomes. The outcome selected is determined by contingent events that transpire as the system unfolds. This feature will prove useful (see chapter 5) for understanding Innis's position on the role that communication technology plays in determining a culture's bias toward a given construct of change. In this chapter, however, we concentrate on one consequent of this characteristic highlighted by Arthur; namely, that products selected by the market are not always the best or the most efficient. Arthur points again to the rise of the DOS operating system as an example. Although derided by computer professionals, it nevertheless attained market dominance, despite the availability of the Mac operating system, which was easier to use.[21]

II

Arthur's work, then, presents a construct that demonstrates these characteristics: emergent, self-sustaining growth; systems displaying perpetual novelty and heightened complexity; historical path dependence, or contingency; lock-in, or the dominance of a market by a firm or set of firms; and systems with multiple, potential outcomes, some of which are less than optimal. Innis would have found Arthur's work a powerful expression of these ideas, and would have been intrigued by the way Arthur applied them to explain the dynamics of the software industry and other sectors. But, thanks to his readings of the influential economist Alfred Marshall as well as Veblen, he would not have found them particularly novel. My intention in this section is therefore to demonstrate that Innis received earlier exposure to the term and substance of increasing returns through Marshall.

In addition, my intention in this section is to demonstrate that Marshall's writings on increasing returns can be identified with Veblen's on the dynamics of economic systems. When writing about recurring, self-sustaining change, Innis tended to use two terms: Adam Smith's reference to the division of labour; and Veblen's term "cumulative causation." My reading proceeds on the basis that division of labour, increasing returns, and cumulative causation are all constructs that point to roughly the same thing. But there are scholars, particularly in the Veblen literature, who do not hold to that view, suggesting instead that Veblen understood cumulative causation to be a sequence of mechanical events, each propelled by an instance of efficient cause. Scholars such as Geoffrey Hodgson deny that positive feedback and final cause in the form of teleology played any role in Veblen's understanding of the term. My first task here is therefore to demonstrate that the concepts of increasing returns and cumulative causation point to the same thing, and to suggest that Innis reached the same conclusion, through use of the term "cumulative causation," and through juxtaposition of the term with narratives describing self-reinforcing change. My identification of these terms proceeds with a reading of Marshall and Veblen, and their respective identification of increasing returns and cumulative causation with self-organization and heightened system complexity, contingency, market lock-in, and system exposure to multiple potential outcomes.

Self-Organization and Heightened System Complexity

Innis's autobiography makes clear that he read Marshall's *Principles of Economics* as a graduate student. It is also fair to say that the work made an impression on him, since references to Marshall appear in his Veblen essay and served as a frame of departure for writings as late as the 1940s.[22] That impression was undoubtedly partly negative. Both Innis and Veblen referred to Marshall as an exemplar in the practice of static economics, and to his credit Marshall recognized this characteristic in his own work. "And therefore it is especially needful to remember," he writes, "that economic problems are imperfectly represented when they are treated as problems of statical equilibrium, and not of organic growth. For though the statical treatment alone can give us definiteness and precision of thought, and is therefore a necessary introduction to a more philosophic treatment of society as an organism, it is yet only an introduction."[23]

To build on that introduction, Marshall devoted a portion of his masterwork to describing the conditions associated with organic growth, endogenous change, or, in our parlance, self-organization. In

Book IV of *Principles*, he treats the behaviour of systems governed by diminishing and increasing returns respectively. In the first half, his purpose was to show "how the extra return of raw produce which nature affords to an increased application of capital and labour … tends in the long run to diminish." In the second half, Marshall observed "the other side of the shield," describing how "man's power of productive work increases with the volume of the work that he does."[24] It was a dynamic, he noted, that explained the growth of wealth and a form of growth in which increase in wealth tended "in many ways to make a greater increase more easy than before." Once a firm entered a trajectory governed by increasing returns, its progress, in terms of size, capability, organizational complexity, and acquisition of wealth became self-sustaining: "Every improved process is quickly adopted and made the basis of further improvements; success brings credit and credit brings success; credit and success help to retain old customers and to bring new ones."[25]

Marshall emphasized that increasing returns markets generally settled into a state of equilibrium after a time.[26] He further stressed two points: first, that stability was temporary, as new firms with new practices could emerge to disrupt the status quo,[27] and second, that the price of stability was not diminished complexity. When a market stabilized, and even when it experienced a downturn, the economies and innovations in practice stemming from a phase of self-organizing growth remained. Heightened and persistent complexity was the legacy of every phase of economic growth: "For, when any causal disturbance has caused a great increase in the production of any commodity, and thereby has led to the introduction of extensive economies, these economies are not readily lost. Developments of mechanical appliances, of division of labour and of the means of transport, and improved organization of all kinds, when they have been once obtained are not readily abandoned."[28]

Veblen, for his part, defined cumulative causation as an endogenous form of change – as a process that is properly seen "to be self-continuing or self-propagating and to have no final term."[29] For him, the import of cumulative causation as a disruptive force in economic life was crucial: it suggested that economic systems had evolved, and were continuing to evolve into more complex forms. The static economics of Marshall and others, by contrast, carried the implicit assumption that the process of adaptation and diversification had stopped. They indicated "the conditions of survival to which any innovation is subject, supposing the innovation to have taken place, not the condition of variational growth."[30] Marshall's theorems, said Veblen, treated "the limits which the economic (commonly the pecuniary) interest imposes upon the range of activities to which the other life interests of men incite, rather than theorems as to the manner and degree in which the economic interest creatively shapes the general scheme of life. In great part they formulate the normal inhibitory effect of economic exigencies rather than the cumulative modification and diversification of human activities through the economic interest, by initiating and guiding habits of life and thought."[31] For Veblen, any economics that ultimately failed to recognize the growing complexity of the object that concerned it was simply missing the point and purpose of the discipline: to describe and explain the behaviour of economic systems.

Contingency, Market Lock-in, and System Exposure to Multiple Potential Outcomes

When referring to the historical contingency of increasing-returns markets, Marshall did not use terms like path dependence or lock-in. He referred instead to concepts such as luck and fortune to explain the relative success of one entrepreneur over another, and the resulting dominance of one firm over another. "The future of those who enter" any given occupation, he writes, "cannot be predicted with certainty: some, who start with the least promise, turn out to have great latent ability, and, aided perhaps by good luck, they earn large fortunes; while others, who made a brilliant promise of starting, come to nothing. For the chances of success and failure are to be taken together, much as are the chances of good and bad hauls by a fisherman or of good and bad harvests by a farmer."[32]

In the end, fortune for Marshall counted "for much in business." It could initiate a productive period of growth and expansion for one capable firm. A successful entrepreneur, after showing "his power of turning capital to good account," would soon find himself in a position "to borrow in one way or another almost any amount that he may need. Making good profits he adds to his own capital, and this extra capital of his own is a material security for further borrowings." Fortune could, however, destroy an equally capable firm, through increasing returns operating in reverse: "A very able man may find things going against him; the fact that he is losing money may diminish his power of borrowing. If he is working partly on borrowed capital, it may even make those who have lent it refuse to renew their loans, and may thus cause him to succumb to what would have been but a passing misfortune, if he had been using no capital but his own."[33]

Once fortune rendered its verdict, Marshall pointed to a world much like the one described by Arthur: stronger firms got stronger, to the point that they locked in a market. There was nothing fair about the process. "Continued rivalry" in any given market, Marshall wrote, "is a rule possible only when none of the rivals has its supply governed by the law of increasing return." In markets governed by diminishing returns, nature, the surrounding environment, imposes restraints. Firms seeking to grow reach a point where production costs begin to rise, "and then the others would begin to undersell it." But if one firm, through an innovation, managed to find a new way to create a product, and in so doing managed to circumvent the constraining power of nature, then it would find itself in a position to harvest increasing returns, and "the rivalry would soon cease, for whenever it happened to gain a temporary advantage over its rivals its increased use would lower its supply price and therefore increase its sale – its supply price would then be further lowered, and so on; thus its advantage over its rivals would be continually increased until it had driven them out of the field."[34]

For Marshall, there was nothing elegant or noble about the increasing returns market. In its operation, it was blind. In its execution, it transferred wealth from the weak to the strong. And in its realization, it produced outcomes that were not necessarily optimal. In Appendix H of *Principles*, Marshall warned analysts not to apply the conventional wisdom of mainstream economics to systems governed by increasing returns. There is a tacit assumption, he warned, when considering the oscillations of supply and demand, that "there could be only one position of stable equilibrium in a market." Yet in systems governed by increasing returns, it was important that economists recognize that some systems emerged with "two or more positions of real equilibrium of demand and supply, any one of which is equally consistent with the general circumstances of the market, and any one of which if once reached would be stable, until some great disturbance occurred."[35]

It was also important, Marshall argued, for economists to recognize that in some emerging markets, the first equilibrium point to be reached would be the one stipulating that a given good should be produced in small quantities and sold at a high price. Such a realization offered "a good illustration of the error involved in the doctrine of maximum satisfaction," the doctrine that markets produced the best outcome, "when stated as a universal truth." The same market, in principle, offered "another position of equilibrium corresponding to a larger production and a lower price." It was a much better solution, since it offered equal profit to the producer and a smaller expenditure from the consumer. Unfortunately, Marshall's account also implied that the optimal equilibrium point would be harder to reach.[36]

Veblen's view that cumulative change turned on contingent acts can be retrieved from his criticisms of hedonist psychology and his endorsement of John Elliott Cairnes's economics. Recall from our earlier discussion (chapter 1) that Veblen disavowed hedonist tenets because he believed economic systems were composed of heterogeneous agents who responded to economic stimuli in different ways – ways determined by their social location, their reading of their current situation, and their ambition. The consequent of heterogeneity was the realization that systemic constraints are not mechanical, but are teleological, governed by a third order of causation distinct from human agency and efficient cause.[37] A second consequent of heterogeneity was the conclusion that systems could not be seen to move in a single pre-determined outcome. They gravitated instead to one of multiple potential outcomes: "It follows that an unguided response even to the mere quantitative pecuniary stimuli may take different directions, and so may result in activities of widely differing outcomes." It also followed that human systems might select systems not optimal for the general welfare: "therefore, the outcome of activity set up even by the normal pecuniary stimuli may take a form that may or may not be serviceable to the community."[38]

For Veblen, one manifestation of such an outcome was market lock-in, the emergence of a monopoly in a given market. In Veblen's time, monopolies were of concern to economists, particularly John Bates Clark, who deemed their emergence as an aberration. In the natural scheme of things, Clark argued, economies tended toward *perfect competition*, a state in which no firm could hope to gain dominance over its competitors. To support his stance, Clark offered theoretical constructs that Veblen deemed to be rigorous, perhaps even elegant, but in the end also hopelessly wrong. Put simply, Veblen found that Clark's assumption regarding the competitive nature of markets failed to meet the test of empirical experience, and did not proceed logically from the tenets of Clark's own economic doctrine.

Veblen especially criticized Clark's concept of capital, which in its essential form he understood as physical plant. Such an understanding, Clark believed, was consistent with a market in which market share was stable and ownership of the means of production widely distributed. Veblen rejoined that the essential nature of capital is not physical; it is pecuniary. It is not stable; it flows to whomever the investor deems will bring the best return. And this realization had important consequents. It disrupted the tidy, stable world Clark had created, and brought in "the 'unnatural' phenomena of monopoly as a normal outgrowth of business enterprise."[39]

Veblen also criticized Clark because his economics proceeded from hedonistic principles. The logic of those principles for producers – the maximization of pleasure and the minimization of pain – tended in their fullest extent toward the pursuit and establishment of monopolies, not perfect competition.[40] For Veblen, whether one proceeded from the neat principles of Clark, or from the messier construct of cumulative causation, the cognitive and pecuniary circumstances of modern life both pointed to the persistent potential of market lock-in: monopoly control of markets. And, interestingly, they operated in a market similar to the one described by Marshall – a market in which there were multiple potential equilibria, and in which a monopoly could in principle leverage increasing returns to shift from one point of equilibrium to the next:

> Now, in the theories based on marginal (or "final") utility, value is an expression or measure of "effective utility" – or whatever equivalent term may be preferred. In operating on values, therefore, under the rule of charging what the traffic will bear, the sellers of a monopolised supply, e.g., must operate through the valuations of the buyers; that is to say, they must influence the final utility of the goods or services to such effect that the "total effective utility" of the limited supply to the consumers will be greater than would be the "total effective utility" of a larger supply, which is the point in question. The emphasis falls still more strongly on this illustration of the hedonistic calculus, if it is called to mind that in the common run of such limitations of supply by a monopolistic business management, the management would be able to increase

> the supply at a progressively declining cost beyond the critical point by virtue of the well-known principle of increasing returns from industry.[41]

In the end, then, Thorstein Veblen and Alfred Marshall were exponents of a conceptual landscape very similar to the one described by W. Brian Arthur. Via Arthur, we are exposed to work that translates the construct of the complex adaptive systems into a dynamic describing increasing returns, historical path dependence, and multiple potential market outcomes, features associated with the property of positive feedback. Arthur's work also highlights the role of formal and final cause, through its description of market lock-in. Our survey of Alfred Marshall and Thorstein Veblen indicates that Innis was exposed to most if not all of the concepts highlighted by Arthur. He knew the term "increasing returns," and he knew the phenomena that it described. If his narratives are informed by the concept, some or all of the features described above should be evident in his various treatments of the Atlantic cod fisheries. Let us see if this is so while examining "The Rise and Fall of the Spanish Fishery in Newfoundland."

III

Innis's interest in the Spanish fishery was piqued by its failure. Rich in specie, and in need of fish to supply a palate governed in part by Mediterranean culture and in part by the church, Spain had every incentive to develop a thriving fishing and shipping industry, especially to forestall loss of its specie reserve. In Innis's parlance, Spain was the "reverse side" of Britain's and France's success in the North American fishery.[42] His account in "The Spanish Fishery" begins in 1540. Spain's interest in the region emerged comparatively late in relation to France and England, which had sent expeditions in the first decade of the century. Still, by 1560 Spain had established a considerable presence in the coastal fishery off Newfoundland. Between 1570 and 1580, the industry was at its high point.[43]

Why did Spain fare so poorly? Why did San Sebastian, the main Spanish port concerned with the Newfoundland fishery and international trade, emerge as the poor cousin of Saint-Jean-de-Luz, the port in the neighbouring French province of Labort? Innis's narrative suggests three fundamental reasons: the schema of Spain's fishing industry and government, or final cause; contingent circumstance and the onset of increasing returns; and the emergence of the North Atlantic economy and the governance of formal cause. There is no hint of geographic determinism – no suggestion, for example, that England's proximity to Newfoundland made its dominance in the North Atlantic fishery inevitable.

Innis argued rather that the Spanish fishing industry entered the Newfoundland fishery with a schema that precluded the establishment of a permanent presence along the east coast of North America. With that mindset, the industry also precluded the establishment of settlements and trading networks with Spain, constituents that would have supported a Spanish fishery and shipping industry. Spanish fishermen entered the fishery to meet the demands of their home market, employing methods that had served them in the Irish fishery.[44] Spanish consumers preferred larger fish from the "green fishery," fresh fish shipped to Spain using salt as a preservative agent. The Spanish industry, at least initially, had access to plentiful salt supplies.

Britain by contrast, did not, and was forced to harvest the smaller fish from Newfoundland that were suitable for the "dry fishery." Given the prevailing lack of salt, British fishing vessels had of necessity to dry their catch along the Newfoundland shoreline as a means of preserving it, and therefore had an incentive to construct the necessary infrastructure to support their efforts. With cheap supplies of salt and a market favouring larger fish, the Spanish did not. England's shortage of salt led it to Newfoundland, laying the basis for settlement, trade, and expansion – an expansion precipitated by increasing returns. Spain's preference for large fish and access to cheap salt kept it away. If the Spanish palate had been different, Spain's economic history might also have been different. The contingency of taste had a direct bearing on the trajectory of Spain's economy.[45]

While the Spanish fishing industry did not provide a basis for Spanish expansion into North America, Innis suggests that it might have remained a viable entity if its government had left it alone. The fishery declined in large part because the Spanish government approached the international economy with a schema ill-equipped to ensure the industry's survival. San Sebastian's problems with the fishery were compounded by the state in two ways: by naval impressment and commandeering of fishing vessels – a constant drain on the size of the Spanish shipping fleet; and by economic regulation, which undercut the port's position as a trading centre. As well as making demands on the assets of the fishery, the Spanish navy also undercut the fleet by issuing orders forbidding its departure for Newfoundland without benefit of naval protection, delaying and thereby limiting its access to the fishery. After the Armada, with the navy unable to provide that protection, Spanish ships became increasingly vulnerable to English and French attack. The French could impound Spanish vessels in French ports with little fear of retribution.[46]

For Innis, however, economic regulation proved to be of greater detriment to the Spanish fishery. Regulations instituted in 1567 prohibited foreign ships from carrying goods out of Spanish ports, and by 1577 San Sebastian was forwarding petitions to the capital protesting the strictures on trade. Foreign vessels redirected their trade to Saint-Jean-de-Luz, while small Spanish vessels proceeded to French ports to procure goods. San Sebastian's position was further undercut when a royal tax was imposed on woollen goods.[47] Merchants in Aragon and Navarra sent their products to France to avoid the tax, and foreign vessels were able to take advantage of the altered terms of trade and acquire wool from France as a return cargo. Merchants in San Sebastian and the surrounding province of Guipuzcoa were thereby forced to procure provisions and trade in Saint-Jean-de-Luz, a necessity since the region was unable to produce its own foodstuffs.[48]

Spain's fundamental problem, according to Innis, was its inability to adjust to the demands of an emerging international economy. Vested interests, whether the shipbuilding industry in Renteria, or ports competing with San Sebastian, believed Spain's economic power was sufficiently potent that it could manipulate the international economy to meet Spanish designs. Representations to Madrid by these industries argued that continued use of the 1567 system of regulations would enable Spain to undercut the viability of competing mercantile systems, thereby giving Spain a monopoly over the carrying trade.

Spain's central government, seeing a dichotomy between the country's shipbuilding interests and its carrying interests, consistently ruled in favour of the former. Anxious to retain existing sources of revenue and the integrity of the country's mercantile system, it even responded favourably to Renteria's petition for enhancement of the regulations in 1578, by prohibiting Spaniards from sailing in foreign ships, and foreigners from sailing in Spanish ships.[49] All in all, as Innis saw it, Spain employed a rigid and maladaptive schema in its interaction with the emerging North Atlantic economy: "The effectiveness of political power in checking economic activity was an outstanding feature in the problems of the fishery. The strong political power contributed to the decline of the fishery and suggested a striking contrast to the strength of economic power in England and in New England. The British Empire became possible with the overriding of political power by economic power, but Spain as illustrated in the fishery was limited by the overwhelming strength of political control. The position of Guipuzcoa contrasted strikingly with that of the West Country in England. Elasticity was a characteristic of the northern countries in its fishing and contrasted with the rigidity of central control in Spain."[50]

Conviction that the economy was susceptible to control by one agent – the state – ultimately proved Spain's undoing, and its fishery and carrying trade fell prey to the phenomena of increasing returns, albeit in a way that favoured France: "The effects were cumulative. Shipbuilding in Spain declined with trade in San Sebastian and increased in France with trade in French ports. Moreover, the French in retaliation forbade Spanish ships to load in their harbours and consequently injured Spanish shipping and trade. The cost of shipbuilding was increased with the decline of trade; and cordage, tar, rigging, elm, and supplies for boatbuilding imported from foreigners had increased in cost by one-third. From the standpoint of the government it was pointed out that the royal taxes on wool had declined, provisions for the fleet had increased in price, and ships and seamen were on the decline."[51]

While the Spanish government took steps to reverse the decline of the fishing and carrying trades, its efforts, according to Innis, were neither consistent nor sufficient to dislodge trading patterns already in place. When it did act, the government employed methods poorly suited to the fishing industry. In the 1620s, the authorities in Madrid attempted to revive the Guipuzcoa and Biscay fishing industries. A large company – a monopoly – was proposed, in line with monopolies governing Spain's trade with the East Indies. It proved a failure. Monopolies never fared well in the fishing industry, Innis observed.[52]

Between 1636 and 1640 the government tried to stimulate the industry by reducing taxes and exempting fishing vessels from naval commandeering.[53] These measures were ineffective, however, in the wake of a 1631 salt tax that effectively killed the fishing industry. After the implementation of the tax, the province of Guipuzcoa for the first time since 1540 failed to send fishermen to Newfoundland. The

French industry, by contrast, thrived, given its continued access to cheap salt. Spain's commercial trade and iron industry also collapsed: "Freedom of trade in salt had been the life blood of the provinces."[54]

French Basque and English interests quickly displaced the Spanish fishing industry: "The importance of the fishery as a supply for seamen, as a source for provisions of the poor, and as a basis of trade was no longer in evidence."[55] By Innis's account, a phenomenon akin to economic lock-in had set in: "The fishery had declined too far and the obstacles to its development were too serious for recovery to follow minor measures of this character. Indeed, with the shift of the fishery to Saint-Jean-de-Luz there is considerable evidence to show that capital followed labour and that residents of San Sebastian were engaged in supplying capital to masters of Saint-Jean-de-Luz."[56] The intervention of the San Sebastian capital market in turn prompted the emergence of vested interests whose actions reflected the "network effect" described by Arthur. As Spain's fishing industry declined, a network of agents emerged with an interest in maintaining the dominance of one product – French fish – over another, Spanish fish. Money lenders in San Sebastian, enjoying handsome profits from loans garnering 26 to 28 percent interest on amounts of 100 to 200 ducats, consistently opposed regulations that would harm the French industry: "Vested interests were created which favoured a continuation of the fishery from Saint-Jean-de-Luz and were opposed to measures which threatened its position."[57]

The onset of lock-in also produced a market outcome that was less than optimal. Spain made a final effort to re-ignite its fishery between 1639 and 1642, the effort culminating in a fleet of six ships being sent to Newfoundland in 1643. Its returns were not commensurate with those of the early Spanish fishery. The French, by contrast, "continued to carry out of the country 400,000 ducats of silver and the English to take their profits. Labort with its annual fleet of sixty ships and three thousand seamen had captured the Spanish market. The commandeering of ships and the impressment of sailors was held responsible for the decline ... The small dry and relatively poor quality fish of the English had displaced the excellent fish of the banks caught by the Spanish."[58]

The main text of Innis's article, therefore, presents three characteristics of the economic system described by Arthur: historical path dependence, increasing returns, and lock-in. We have also seen that Spain came out on the short end of these processes, in part because the schemas of its agents – whether the government's or those of Spanish merchants – were ill-equipped for the challenges of the North Atlantic economy. The concluding section of the article can also be aligned with Arthur's economics. There, Innis highlighted what he believed to be the ultimate cause for the decline of the Spanish fishery: formal cause. Its message, however, can come across as equivocal to readers who are unfamiliar with the concept.

Innis began his conclusion by posing a question: which causes were determining as opposed to contributing causes in the decline of the Spanish fishery? Spain's distance from Newfoundland in comparison to England's is cited but dismissed, as it fails to explain Labort's success in France. Other factors, such as the decline of the Spanish navy, and the rise of taxation, which were central in Innis's narrative, are now referred to as "ripples on the surface," rather than "factors determining the main current."[59] Innis's belief in the North Atlantic fishery's susceptibility to multiple outcomes is suggested by his reference to Spain's wood shortage. A healthy fishery, he argued, could have been constructed on ships purchased from elsewhere.[60]

The key factor, Innis concluded, was Guipuzcoa's persistent trade with France and England for provisions, despite encroachments on its ancient trading rights by Spain's central authorities. The province was successful in defending its rights to procure foodstuffs, a demand France and England were happy to fill, given the rising cost of food engendered by Spain's import of specie.

In Innis's account, a trading network emerged in which Spain's behavioural competence was altered by virtue of its participation in an international economy. The resulting internal organization of the Spanish economy, and its trade links abroad, proved persistent, or in current parlance, demonstrated *differential persistence*. The Spanish government proved unable either to halt the export of specie or to stimulate exports of Spanish goods. Its efforts proved futile in the face of regulation imposed by the structure of the North Atlantic economy – that is, by the governance of formal cause: "The persistence and increasing importance of the trade carried by the French Basques and later by England and New England to the northern ports of Spain in Newfoundland cod as well as in provisions and supplies are outstanding factors in that period. It was apparent that powerful forces were tending toward an increase in trade which overwhelmed the relative advantages of Spain in the fishery ... The Newfoundland fishery proved persistent and effective in the transfer of specie to the countries of northern Europe. The importation of gold and silver by Spain raised the prices of commodities; and the relative advantages of the Spanish fishery as compared to the position of Spain as an importer of treasure led to her steady decline in the fishery."[61]

Spain, in essence, specialized. With its economic role constrained by the governance of the North Atlantic economy, and by the schema of its agents, its role was reduced to that of financier and instigator of European economic activity in North America. Its wealth stimulated the "flip side" of French and English activity, with the establishment of New France along the St Lawrence, the establishment of New England along the east coast, and the subsequent bid of those two powers for hegemony over North America. In "The Economic History of the Maritimes" and *The Cod Fishery*, Innis argued that the cod fishery played a major role in ensuring Britain's success over France, and in turn stimulating Britain's own collapse with the advent of the American Revolution. For Innis, both studies would reinforce a lesson he had learned in *The Fur Trade*, and would voice again in his communication studies. The problem of Empire, the problem of imperial survival, was better stated as the problem of increasing returns.

IV

In his two major staple studies, Innis undertook to describe a contest in which Britain and France were the combatants, and for which the prize was hegemony over North America. He also tried to explain why Britain won that contest, and why, with the collapse of the First British Empire, its victory had proven so fleeting. The essence of the matter was simple. The survival of regimes was dependent upon their ability to adapt to the emergent, temporally dependent variant of change he had identified in *The Fur Trade*. Such had been his message then. Such would also be his message in his future communication studies. In the quest for North America, Innis identified economic activity in his two major staple studies as the most important manifestation of that change. Britain adapted. France did not. For Innis, Britain's military victory of necessity had to be grounded on the Empire's economic activity.[62]

Innis also undertook to study the aftermath of the matter. The emergence of European empires in the seventeenth and eighteenth centuries had profoundly transformed the face of North America. In studying the economic histories of the Maritimes, Newfoundland, and New England he endeavoured to renew the argument made in *The Fur Trade*. In all these regions "the continuous and powerful effects of the underlying technique of industry" had had a direct bearing on the types of structures that had emerged, structures governing "the economic, social and political activities of the communities concerned."[63] Economic activity in Central Canada had produced large centralized structures. Innis sought to demonstrate that economic activity on the East Coast had produced decentralized structures. His purpose was to once again to demonstrate the tenets of the staples hypothesis. And while referring to the emergence, culmination, and aftermath of the conflict that structured his histories, he aimed to describe a regime of change characterized by emergence, increasing returns, and formal and final cause.

The Sixteenth Century

The Cod Fisheries begins with the European discovery of North America in 1497, but the thrust of the narrative starts in 1550 with the beginnings of a sustained English presence in the Newfoundland fishery. For Innis, the history of the fishery in the sixteenth century was marked by two significant trends, the first being the rise of England and France as the fishery's major players. While Portugal and Spain both sent fleets in the first half of the century, by 1600 both were overshadowed by their northern competitors.[64] The second trend was the geographic distribution of the respective fisheries, which Innis argued was a result of their specializations. England specialized in dry fish, and rapidly established a major presence along the Avalon peninsula in Newfoundland. The French fleet specialized in fresh fish – the green fishery – and concentrated its activities in the bank fishery, located to the south of Newfoundland. It did not establish a major presence on the island.

This difference was important, argued Innis, because the choices each fishery made in the early phases of English and French expansion had a major impact on each empire's subsequent ability to develop a carrying trade. Initial choices would also determine which empire received the benefit of increasing returns, and subsequent success as an economic and imperial power. In Innis's account, the choices each fishery made were related to their respective environments, their internal organizations, and the governance of formal and final cause. The English fleet entered into the fishery with the disposition to trade, engendered by environmental constraints faced at home. English interest in the Newfoundland fishery was first prompted by Denmark's imposition of licensing fees over the Iceland fishery, England's previous source of supply. The move precipitated a relocation of the centre of the industry from the East Coast to England's West Country, a region with ports closer to Newfoundland, such as Plymouth, Southampton, and Poole. Like the area around the Spanish port of San Sebastian, the West Country was an infertile region dependent on trade, and accordingly it promoted the development of infrastructure across the Atlanatic to process a wide variety of fish prior to shipping it to foreign markets.[65]

The second important constraint, as mentioned, was a shortage of salt. Unlike France and Spain, which had plentiful sources of supply for their fleets, the English industry was forced to procure salt through trade, first with Portugal and then with France. Yet even with a degree of access to supplies of salt, the fishery was forced to rely on alternative forms of preservation. In the Iceland fishery, English fishermen had learned to select fish susceptible to drying into a hard cure, a practice it would continue in Newfoundland. Over the long term, England's constraint worked to its advantage, causing it to specialize in a form of fish highly amenable to trade, and bringing it the benefit of increasing returns. In the sixteenth century, it found a ready market for its product in the Mediterranean. In the seventeenth century, it found a market among European powers sailing in the tropics. Sir David Kirke, who for a period of time held a monopoly over the Newfoundland fishery, would note that no power could send ships to the Indies without the dried fish produced in Newfoundland. The final constraint that promoted trade was the dwindling size of the English domestic market for fish, a development Innis traced to England's shift from Catholicism to Protestantism.[66]

The French, by contrast, foreswore an extensive presence in Newfoundland, and failed to develop a substantial stake in the dry fishery. While the English were aggressive in maintaining their interests, sending large armed ships to harass French and Spanish competitors, the French, according to Innis, had little reason to challenge English claims. Aside from being outgunned, the smaller ships of the French fleet specialized in the green fishery and were in search of larger fish. Consequently, France shifted its fishery from waters adjoining the Avalon peninsula, and its fleets moved either to the north or to the bank fishery south of Newfoundland. Unlike the English, the French had no strong interest in using the fishing fleet as an instrument to promote trade. Consequently, the industry was scattered throughout France, with fishing ports located in the English Channel and the Bay of Biscay, each port servicing markets with disparate tastes. The Paris market in the north preferred large fish; Basque fishermen provided smaller fish for the south of France.[67]

The French fleet's limited inclination to engage in trade was further affected by three factors. It had access to plentiful quantities of salt, and therefore little incentive to develop a specialty in drying fish for trade. Second, the fish it did cure for trade was a poorer product, given the larger size of its catch. Finally, the French industry failed to fully exploit its catch. Its practice was to dispense with the portion of its harvest that did not meet the need of its clientele.[68]

Innis argued that the French fishing industry failed to engage foreign markets in large part because it was embedded in a self-sufficient economy. From the standpoint of the industry and the country as a whole, there was no need, other than specie, to use fish to procure products from abroad. That stance would have a pronounced impact on the subsequent evolution of the fishery and would hamper the French state's later efforts to develop a trading network that would integrate its various colonial possessions: "The self-sufficiency of a continental area contrasted strikingly with the essential demands for trade of an island area. The characteristics of France as a self-sufficient area ... were of fundamental importance to her position as an empire on the Atlantic. A large land area with diversity of resources dependent on wide ranges of climate and other geographical factors tended toward self-sufficiency in contrast with a relatively small island with scarcity of raw materials, an inadequate home market, and essential dependence on trade."[69]

The Seventeenth Century

At base, English fishermen entered the Newfoundland fishery and the seventeenth century with an inclination to engage in intra-imperial and international trade, while the French did not. Nevertheless, in Innis's account, both France and England remained dominant players until the seventeenth century, when a disparity in their fortunes began to appear. Three trends shaped the history of the fishery over the course of this century, he wrote: the struggle by fishing interests to end or prevent monopoly control of the trade; economic diversification; and the emergence of trading networks. England's success in adapting to all three of these trends would give it military and economic dominance in North America by the middle of the eighteenth century.

In Innis's narrative, monopoly company control of North Atlantic trade, which reached its zenith in the sixteenth century, was undercut by the simultaneous emergence of a fishing industry whose operational sphere extended from Europe to Newfoundland, and by the outbreak of hostilities in Europe, particularly the conflict between England and Spain that witnessed England's defeat of the Spanish Armada in 1588. Of the two developments, Innis viewed the emergence of the Newfoundland fishery as the more important, largely because the fishing industry was a trade in which resources could with relative ease be extracted from the environment.[70] Its capital costs were much lower than those for the fur trade. More independent agents were able to participate, and the industry in both England and France enjoyed the support of large capital markets:[71] "In France as in England it demanded the initiative of large numbers carrying on the industry from small vessels. The demands were reflected in aggressive commercialism in contrast with large-scale company organization. It opened a breach in mercantilistic control which was progressively widened."[72]

The onset of conflict with Spain facilitated that breach by interfering with English monopolists' abilities to assert and defend their rights. Despite deteriorating relations with Spain, the English government had accorded monopoly privileges to a select group of English merchants under a new regulatory regime, the Spanish Charter of 1577. In defiance of regulations, fishermen and West Country merchants set up a contraband trading network as early as 1581, linking England, Newfoundland, Spain, and the Mediterranean. For England, the results of the contraband trade were immediate, beneficial, and substantial, including "an abundance of shipping, an outlet for manufactured goods and provisions, a supply of semitropical products and specie, substantial profits, and ideal possibilities for the development of a mercantile policy."[73]

Even monopoly companies were forced to concede that independent commerce with Spain and Brazil had improved England's economic position. Their concession, however, did not preclude the reinstitution of the Spanish Charter of 1577 in 1604, after the cessation of hostilities between the two powers. While trade links were formalized in a treaty between England and Spain that same year, freedom of trade in goods such as cloth, grain, and fish was not extended. It was only after persistent lobbying by West Country merchants that legislation was passed in 1606 granting merchants free access to Spain, Portugal, and France.[74] With some prodding from the fishing industry, England modified its economic policy to reflect newly emergent economic practice: "An expansion of trade because of, and in spite of, both company control and the outbreak of hostilities was largely responsible for a favorable treaty in 1604 ... The failure of company organization to control West Country trade and the West Country fishing industry led to the substitution of regulation which found an extension in the navigation system."[75]

The deregulation of European trade did not end the regulatory challenges faced by the English fishing industry, however. Repeated, and at times successful, attempts were made both by England and by France to organize the Newfoundland and New England fisheries under monopoly control. In the case of England two monopolies were assigned: one to Sir Ferdinando Gorges in 1620, granting him a charter over trade and fishing in New England from the 40th to the 48th degree of latitude; the second to Sir David Kirke in 1637, granting him control over trade in Newfoundland. While English ships were to be given freedom of the fishery, Kirke was given the right to tax foreign vessels, and to impose licensing fees on English ships. According to Innis, Kirke was able to enjoy his monopoly for fourteen years before earning the enmity of the West Country. He made the mistake of asserting his rights too vigorously, thereby offending a powerful lobby. English fishing merchants, by virtue of their concentration in the West Country, had influence in London, and they used it to secure Kirke's recall. As for Gorges, although he was able to restrict English access to the New England fishery, he was unable to stop the region's economic development, which as we shall see was precipitated in part by English fishermen.[76]

The French fishing industry was also the object of several attempts to place its fishing grounds under monopoly control. The main impetus for these initiatives arose from the fur trade. By the sixteenth century, English attacks on French shipping had caused the French fishery to expand to the Gulf of St Lawrence and the Gaspé peninsula. The expansion of the fishery to the Gulf led in turn to trading contacts with local Indians, and the development of the fur trade in these regions.[77] By the end of the century, the fur trade had grown to sufficient size that a monopoly over both the fish and fur industries was granted to the Company of 1599. By 1607, however, Samuel de Champlain reported that Basque and Breton fishermen were violating the company's rights. While Champlain succeeded in his efforts to rationalize the fur trade in 1620, the fishing industry was never brought under control. A final effort was made by the state in 1627, only to dissolve in the 1630s. As Innis saw it, the French fishing industry never proved susceptible to political control, in part because of English competition, and in part because of the internal structure of the fishing industry.[78] Concessions made to French merchants failed, "while in the fur trade monopoly struck deeper root. The atomistic, or small-unit, commercialism of the fishing industry was entrenched in a series of developments."[79] It was a characteristic that enabled the fisheries of both countries to escape control by monopolies imposed by the state: "An industry prosecuted in small vessels subject to limited control, and from European ports scattered over a wide area divided between French and English and between green and dry fishing, conducted on a profit-sharing basis, and selling to different markets was essentially competitive and sharply divisive."[80]

In England's case, trading regulations shifted from a regime employing company control to one governed by the Navigation Acts, which were designed to promote British shipping by mandating that British goods be carried in British vessels. According to Innis, the English also resorted to trade treaties such as the 1604 treaty between England and Spain, and to initiatives of the colonial system designed to use plantations abroad to produce raw products and consumer goods for the English market. By mid-century, Innis suggests, England and France had both reached a point where they accepted the desirability – and inevitability – of adapting their respective mercantile economies to permit their fishing trades to operate relatively unfettered. The North Atlantic, as a result, became populated with agents capable of establishing trading links, legitimate and otherwise, between the Americas, Africa, and Europe. For England, the policy would result in the economic diversification and integration of its empire. France's mercantile policy, by contrast, was less successful, in part because its fishing trade did not wish to enter the carrying trade, and in part because the French government, by committing itself to the fur trade upon assuming the governance of New France, hindered that colony's economic diversification.[81]

With respect to England's colonies, Innis observed that economic diversification emerged in Newfoundland despite the best efforts of West Country merchants and English policy makers to stop it. Initial settlement came from two sources: from fishing vessels that deposited surplus crew prior to returning to Europe, and from plantation companies. The latter were not important contributors to settlement, largely because Newfoundland's topography would not support a thriving agriculture and timber industry. The companies also failed because they did not integrate their efforts with the needs of the fishing industry.[82]

From the standpoint of West Country merchants, the failure of the plantation companies was not an unwelcome development, since they correctly foresaw that settlement would lead to the emergence of an indigenous Newfoundland fishery, which would threaten their interests. Land for drying fish was at a premium, as was the timber necessary to build the infrastructure to support the industry on the island. From the perspective of English merchants, settlers would have an unfair advantage in procuring both resources. Accordingly, to buttress their position English fishing merchants regularly lobbied for and received legislation prohibiting settlement. As late as 1675 an Order in Council was issued affirming a prohibition against settlement and containing provisions to encourage Newfoundland colonists to move elsewhere, particularly to New England.[83]

The prohibitions were never successful, however. As Innis was to reiterate in *The Cod Fisheries*, the fishing industry proved notoriously difficult to regulate via legislation, given the small size of fishing vessels and the relative independence with which fishermen were able to conduct their activities.[84] As matters stood, the interests of individual fishermen ran counter to those of West Country merchants. Ship masters routinely brought crews larger than the minimum complement required to operate the vessel in order to have extra hands while fishing in Newfoundland. They were all too happy to deposit crew members who wished to stay, so as to forgo their transport costs for the return voyage first to Europe, then England. Men were also left behind to safeguard equipment.[85]

As the number of settlers in Newfoundland grew, economic diversification set in. An indigenous fishery and labour market emerged as byeboat keepers – Newfoundlanders who had built their own fishing vessels – began seeking crews to man them. Labour was also required to service the sack ship industry, ships sent to

Newfoundland specifically to purchase fish and convey them to Europe. Both markets, Innis wrote, were supported by masters of fishing vessels who, eager to reduce their transport costs, agreed to carry passengers from Europe to Newfoundland in exchange for a fare.[86]

The fishery also stimulated growth in New England. In 1602 and 1603, reports emerged in Newfoundland and England citing the superior quality of the cod in the Gulf of Maine and New England. The reports prompted not only the presence of the English fishing fleet but also the arrival of settlers transported by the fleet, attracted by the region's possibilities for developing an agricultural base. According to Innis, as settlement progressed, timber and shipbuilding industries were also developed to support the fishery: "The fishery meant a demand for skilled labor, for carpenters, carvers, blacksmiths, and blockmakers, for ships, boats, and provisions; and supplies for a shipbuilding industry such as iron, rope, rigging, sailcloth, planks, and pulleys."[87]

These industries supported the region's indigenous fishery as well as the English fishery. Indeed, according to *The Cod Fisheries*, the New England fishing industry was by the end of the seventeenth century the region's most important player and a formidable competitor to England and France. It was able, for example, to market large Gulf of Maine cod in the lucrative Spanish market of Bilbao as an alternative to the French product. New England also enjoyed the advantage of proximity and year-round access to the region's fishery, enabling its fishermen to employ a wider variety of ships to harvest greater numbers of fish.[88]

While the English government tried to obstruct economic development in Newfoundland, its mercantile policy enabled it to take a more constructive stance toward its other North American possessions, particularly Virginia and the British West Indies. Seeking to minimize imports of Spanish staples and maximize exports of Spanish specie, England deliberately established colonies to produce staples for home markets that until then had been serviced by Spain. As early as 1627, Spanish tobacco was excluded from English markets to protect Virginia's nascent tobacco trade. The colony's success in turn prompted expansion into the Caribbean. Innis relates that England by 1650 had devoted several of its islands to the production of tobacco.[89]

Spain responded to the loss of tobacco markets by turning to the sugar trade. Exports of sugar cane were soon being sent from Spain,

Madeira, the Azores, and Brazil. After the split of Portugal from Spain, however, English ships became an important part of the carrying trade servicing Brazil, obtaining via treaty in 1642 the right to transport most Brazilian goods. Exposure to the lucrative nature of the sugar trade there prompted England to encourage sugar plantations in its colonies in the West Indies. While shipments of sugar arrived in New England from the West Indies as early as 1639, production did not begin in earnest until the 1650s.[90] By mid-century, England had an array of colonies specializing in different commodities, and boasted trading networks linking it with its colonies and Europe: "By 1650 trade was being carried on with Virginia, Barbados, England, Portugal, Spain, Holland and France."[91]

While France, similarly attracted to the sugar market, had established a presence in the West Indies by 1663, it did not enjoy a similar level of commercial activity among its colonies. From the standpoint of mercantile policy this was a serious problem, since its plantation colonies in the West Indies were incapable of producing foodstuffs sufficient to meet their own needs. France could not supply them and as a result its colonies turned to New England for provisions. To rectify this situation, Jean-Baptiste Colbert, Louis XIV's comptroller-general, attempted to establish a trading network linking France's fur, fish, and sugar colonies.

While a few shipments of food were sent from New France in 1670, Colbert's initiative nevertheless failed because, Innis suggests, the French government was working at cross-purposes with itself. Instead of stimulating the economic diversification necessary for trade, upon assuming governance of New France in the 1660s, it instituted economic policies that completely precluded diversification. Like the governing companies before it, the French government tried to manage the colony's economy, channelling development to support the fur trade. That policy hindered the development of an agriculture base and shipping industry and, by the eighteenth century, engendered a degree of inflation that would contribute to the colony's collapse.

The orientation of the French fishing industry further hindered Colbert's efforts to establish trading networks in ways that extended beyond its lack of interest in the carrying trade. New France's position was undercut also by the industry's methods and techniques. Since its vessels required large crews not only for fishing but also for their operation, and since they incurred lower operating costs than their English counterparts, French shipmasters lacked any incentive to leave members of their crew in North America. Once they had visited the Newfoundland fishery, French vessels returned directly to France, unlike English vessels, which routinely detoured to Spain and the Mediterranean before returning to home port. The settlement that might have contributed to the economic development of New France and Acadia was not encouraged.

Colbert's efforts to create networks were finally frustrated by weather. New France was not an ice-free port, and the West Indies were subject to hurricanes from mid-summer to mid-fall. Weather constraints limited the trade between these colonies to a season much shorter than that which New England, with its year-round access to the ocean, enjoyed with the French West Indies.[92]

Innis offers a scenario, then, in which multiple colonies specializing in commodity production are present in the mid-seventeenth century, and multiple agents – those with the capacity to transport goods between settlements along its perimeter – are populating the North Atlantic. Apart from the English fishing industry's historic disposition to trade, how did Innis explain the emergence of trading networks in the seventeenth century? Put simply, he suggested that the English fishing industry – structurally, cognitively, and environmentally – was in a position to benefit from the economics of increasing returns.

With respect to internal organization, W. Brian Arthur notes that the question reduces to one of centralization versus decentralization. An industry governed by diminishing returns requires "not just people to carry out production but people to plan and control it, so it favours a hierarchy of bosses and workers ... Above all it is a world of optimization."[93] It is also a world of centralized control. By contrast, companies governed by increasing returns are more entrepreneurial: "In this milieu, management becomes not production-oriented but mission-oriented." In such an environment, hierarchies dissipate. In order for employees to locate new opportunities, control must be flattened and distributed, and "the deliverers ... need to be organized like commando units in small teams that report directly to the CEO or to the board ... The company's future survival depends upon them."[94]

The orientation of the fishing industry, as Innis described it, mirrored the mission-oriented schema described by Arthur. The reason English fishermen searched for trade, he argued, was that they intuited a basic feature of an increasing returns economy. The more they engaged in fishing and trading, the more the operating costs of the industry's basic unit of production – the fishing vessel – would decrease: "For such cargoes [of lumber and provisions] large numbers of aggressive small owners were ceaselessly in search, either to buy and sell them for profits, or to use them to fill empty holds and cover the costs of outgoing or returning voyagers."[95]

Innis also pointed out that the industry functioned in an environment that did not impose an optimal level of activity on each agent, such as pertains in a diminishing returns economy. In "The Economic History of the Maritimes" he noted that supplies of fish in the fishery were then nearly inexhaustible.[96] The industry was not constrained by limits either in supply or demand: "The geographical background, represented by climate, the salt available, the technique of the industry, and the size and abundance of the fish was a stabilizing factor of supply. In tropical countries, demands for a higher protein content in the diet of the people, the difficulties of cold storage, the rigidity of customs and consumers' preferences, and the dominance of Catholicism were stabilizing factors of demand."[97] In addition to meeting European demand, fish was required to feed European crews heading to the tropics: "The demand for fish was a result of a relatively inelastic demand for specie, and supply responded directly because of the mobility of labor and ships."[98]

By contrast, the French fur trade, hampered as it was by a finite and fluctuating supply of furs, did not emerge as a mechanism for the development of an international carrying trade. With its persistent need to build and maintain infrastructure to support a continental trade, including supply depots, and military fortifications to protect existing sources of supply, production concerns were paramount.[99] Given the industry's perception that settlement would threaten its supply of furs, transport costs were also a constant concern. It was therefore unable to take advantage of passenger fares to reduce operating costs.[100] With such constraints, it is not surprising that, in Innis's account, the industry embraced a structure consistent with an economy governed by diminishing returns: "The Fur trade ... was characterized by centralization of organization whereas the fishing industry has been characterized by decentralization."[101]

In addition to the presence of agents with the structural and cognitive capacity to trade, and the presence of an environment capable of supporting increasing returns, Innis also identified specific commodities as playing a catalytic role in stimulating the emergence of trading networks. In our earlier discussion (chapter 1) we pointed to

Stuart Kauffman's belief that autocatalytic sets emerge in environments populated by catalysts – molecules that promote the combination of molecules and the subsequent emergence of systems that actively interact with their environment.[102] Innis observed that certain commodities such as salt had historically played a similar role, instigating trade, expansion, and subsequent opportunities for further expansion in England's trading networks in the North Atlantic. Salt and dry fish were among the earliest commodities to perform this function:

> England's relative scarcity of salt, her more limited home market, and her concentration of fishing interests in the West Country forced her to depend on areas suited to drying and adjacent to the fishing grounds. She acquired a foothold on Newfoundland for the dry fishery ... By the end of the century England was established on the Avalon Peninsula. The expansion of the markets for light-salted dry fish enabled her to increasing her shipping, her direct trade in fish, and her indirect trade, by using ships released in the long closed season ... Moreover, it meant an expansion of trade, if only because the English fishery depended on solar salt produced in southern continental countries. The demand for cod became a demand for English ships and men. Directly and indirectly the fishing industry hastened the growth of shipping and trade which followed the decline of Spain and Portugal, and the opening of markets beyond the power of Spain to occupy.[103]

As we saw in our consideration of the Spanish fishery, Innis also saw specie as an early catalyst to trade, providing "a sheet anchor for the commercial activity of the Atlantic basin." Anxious to procure specie for its ability to increase "the liquidity and effectiveness of the commercial organization of the countries that received it," England also desired specie to facilitate its trade with India – specie being the only form of payment that country would accept: "The drive for specie in developing trade was evident in the production of commodities of high value and light bulk in the New World ranging from furs to tobacco to sugar."[104]

The combination of willing agents, a conducive environment, and the catalytic commodity of sugar led to the emergence of trading networks in North America, networks that supported England's rise to economic dominance. Innis's account suggests that New England expansion into the West Indies market was initially prompted by the economic diversification the fishing industry facilitated in the first place. New England had industrial and agricultural products that it wanted to sell, and a fishing industry willing not only to ship them but also to develop trade ties for the region: "Through the fishery, trade between tropical and north temperate countries or between areas with an absolute advantage in production was stimulated. Specie was added to the temptation of the advantages provided by sugar and salt ... Capitalizing the advantages of cheap water transport the relatively small unit of the fishing or the trading ship was a powerful driving force for trade. Ships managed by individuals were continuously searching for cargo and seeking out new commodities and channels of trade. Cod was the basis for a strong and flexible economy which demanded and provided a wealth of individual initiative."[105]

Trade between the West Indies and New England had several repercussions. Innis reports that the first was the onset of increasing returns, stimulated by the decline in shipping rates effected by the fishing industry. Unlike the case of New France, where the limitations imposed by the fur trade and the government held the economy in stasis and eventually pushed it into decline, the fishing industry precipitated a second wave of cumulative growth: "The problem represented by ships that lacked either outgoing or return cargoes – bane of the fur trade of New France – was largely solved. Expanding industry and New England trade with the West Indies were aids to further expansion in the fishing industry and trade with the Mediterranean, Europe, and England. The aggressiveness of New England traders in small ships lowered freight rates and contributed to the development of a trading organization."[106]

In response to the initiative of fishing agents, a trading network emerged that served "to knit together the diversities of the empire in North America."[107] The network also began to demonstrate the governance of formal cause by regulating the activities of its constituent parts through positive feedback. According to Innis, as early as 1647 trade had begun to induce West Indian plantations to shift from diversified agriculture to sugar production. A contemporary account provided by Innis noted: "Men are so intent upon planting sugar that they had rather buy foode at very deare rates than produce it by labour, so infinite is the profitt of sugar workes after once accomplished."[108]

While producing high profits, trade also had a tragic consequent. Recall from our discussion of complex adaptive systems that emergent systems will incorporate new constituents from their environment to heighten their formal integrity. The new constituent in this case was slave labour, as demands for cheap labour had arisen by the 1670s. Accordingly, Innis recounts, Africa was incorporated into two trading networks, one linking New England with Africa and the West Indies, the other linking England with the same locales. England sent woollen goods, firearms, and iron to Africa in exchange for slaves, who were shipped to the West Indies. On the return voyage, sugar was conveyed to England. In New England, merchants procured molasses and sugar to make rum, which in turn was shipped to Africa in return for slaves.[109] Participation in the slave trade proved to be profitable for New England, since the West Indies required a cheap source of food to feed its slaves. Increasing returns created a new niche market, which New England was able to fill thanks to the region's expansion of its fishery into Nova Scotia after the Treaty of Utrecht in 1713. With the development of smaller fishing vessels, New England fishermen were able to harvest low-grade fish for shipping to the West Indies.[110]

By the end of the century, then, New England and England had collectively emerged as the beneficiaries of a process initiated by the English fishery at the start of the century, a process comprising the initial stages of economic diversification, the search by agents for trade, the onset of increasing returns, heightened specialization, and additional opportunities to sell fish and trade. They also became the beneficiaries of a final attribute of an increasing returns economy – high profit margins: "The expansion of the New England fishery was chiefly in response to the demands of the British and foreign West Indies. By 1731 this market for oil and refuse fish was held to be bringing sufficient returns to purchase the required rum and molasses, and the salt, provisions, and equipment used in the entire fishery. This left the receipts from the European market as clear profit."[111]

The Eighteenth Century

For Innis, the climax of his narrative occurred in the eighteenth century. The economic trends he had traced from their origins in the sixteenth and seventeenth centuries culminated in two catastrophic events: the collapse of the French Empire in 1763, and the collapse of the First British Empire in 1783, events he wryly noted as being "of special interest to the constitutional historian."[112] For the eighteenth century as for the seventeenth, Innis identified the problem of imperial survival with the problem of increasing returns. Economic growth would support Britain in its competition with France. Economic growth would in turn undercut Britain in its conflict with its colonies. The American Revolution and the institution of a new basis for international North Atlantic trade would be the outcome.

Innis suggests, however, that in the early years of the century New England fishing and carrying interests had little cause for complaint. The region's economy was still enjoying rapid expansion engendered by the sugar trade, and after the British West Indies adopted the plantation system in the 1730s, that expansion received further stimulus. By 1748 large plantation owners had forced most small producers to evacuate to the Dutch West Indies, a rationalization that reduced to 2,551 the white population of Barbados. While doubtless hard on the exiled producers, the move was nevertheless very good for New England, heightening the British West Indies' demand not only for fish, but also for lumber, draft horses, oxen … and slaves. According to Innis, demand for slaves in particular began to skyrocket. On account of the gradual exhaustion of soil in British possessions, greater numbers of hands were required to maintain production levels. In addition to its orders from the British West Indies, New England merchants also enjoyed a growing client base in the French West Indies, islands that were in need of supplies and slaves to expand their production, and, as we have seen, territories unable to procure supplies from France.[113]

Within that emerging trading relationship lay a catalyst for New England's growth. Within it also lay a constituent to assist England in its competition with France. And within it, finally, lay a conflict that would culminate in the American Revolution. According to Innis, British sugar interests, angered by an increase in New England trade with French competitors, pressed London to impose trade restrictions that would restrict American commerce to British possessions. British West Indian planters complained that, since they were forced to bid against French competitors for American goods and services, American trade with the French colonies had caused a reduction in the price of British sugar and raised the price of provisions and shipping. In pressing their case, Innis argued the planters enjoyed a disproportionate influence over the crafting of British legislation, an influence derived from the industry's recent consolidation and the structure of its capital market: "The effectiveness of the short-term credit in commercialism based on the fishing industry was in striking contrast to the limitations of long term credit in the fur trade and in the plantation colonies. Staples demanding long term credit were dependent on capital control in relation to the metropolitan development of Great Britain. Under these conditions the effectiveness of staples interest was evident in political influence and legislation. With dependence on commercialism as in New England the essentially close relationship between the economic and political institutions of the British Empire disappeared."[114]

Pressing for the imposition of a closed market, British sugar interests received it in the form of the Molasses Act of 1733, which forbade the American colonies from importing products from the French West Indies.[115] New England protested the measure, arguing that the new trading regulations robbed the region of a market large to absorb American products. The British West Indies were too small, and were similarly incapable of filling American demands for sugar. But according to Innis, the Molasses Act had little real bearing on the conduct and subsequent growth of New England trade. After the passage of the Navigation Acts in the seventeenth century, New England merchants had routinely engaged in smuggling to escape the strictures of English commercial policy, particularly in Newfoundland where they traded for European goods.[116] In the case of the West Indies, New England merchants simply ignored the restrictions: "With cheaper foreign sugar, and with the difficulties of enforcing the act in an area containing numerous islands, cheap water transportation, and relatively small boats, smuggling increased."[117]

Continued access to French sugar, Innis argued, induced a new cycle of increasing returns. After King George's War (1744–48), New England's trading relationship with the French West Indies deepened. In the years preceding the American Revolution, the limitations of British plantations became all too evident. The British West Indies were able to service only one colony, Rhode Island, and even there British sugar producers only met two thirds of the colony's demands.[118] In order to grow, the American colonies needed French sugar. Through trade, the colonies not only sustained their own growth but also facilitated the onset of increasing returns in the French West Indies, a development that in turn ensured a growing supply of sugar and rum for New England: "The resulting trade became to an increasing extent a basic part of the economic development of the northern colonies. After the war it became even more important, and when the French settled and developed the previously neutral Windward Islands of Dominica, St. Lucia, St. Vincent, and Tobago, this was made easier by exports from the northern colonies."[119]

From the standpoint of the French Empire, however, New England's support of a French colony in the short term would militate France's payment of a very high price in the long term. As Innis characterized it, the British-French rivalry in the eighteenth century was at base a rivalry between economic systems competing for resources. It was this rivalry that mattered. The military conflicts of the mid-eighteenth century merely served to align the continent's political structures with economic structures already in place.[120] Britain's system won because it encouraged, or at least tolerated, interaction between its colonies, and accepted the incorporation of new constituents into its North Atlantic trading networks. By so doing, New England heightened the behavioural competence of its trading network. And by adding the French West Indies, New England increased Britain's competitiveness in the fur trade: "Cheap supplies of molasses as a by-product of sugar and lack of a market for rum and molasses in France were valuable aids to English colonial trade. As for New England, she gained from the colonial policies of France and Great Britain both ... Having French rum, English competition intensified the difficulties of the French fur trade."[121]

France undercut itself by limiting imports of French West Indian rum to protect its brandy industry. In so doing, it was reduced to the position of watching its colonies work at cross-purposes with each other, and witnessing the economic decline of New France. According to Innis, France attempted to limit New England's participation in the fur trade by building military fortifications in the west. That stratagem, however, combined with the government's attempts to manage the colony's economy, created a scenario in which the colony's costs increased while its revenues declined, whereas New England's revenues rose and its costs declined.[122] The government was unable to reverse a cycle that in essence was increasing returns in reverse, and by the time of the Conquest, France had already lost the fundamental contest. Even before the 1763 Treaty of Paris, Britain had gained control of the continent's underlying economic structures.

Innis judged that France failed for two fundamental reasons. First, its agents lacked the disposition, the schema, to trade. In a collective decision akin to a network effect, French fishermen selected the domestic market, and never chose to reverse their decision, despite Colbert's efforts. Final cause precluded the French industry from exploiting the economics of increasing returns and enabling the integration of the French Empire: "The Treaty of Utrecht and Treaty of Paris were milestones in the evolution of economic forces in which the geographical characteristics of an island, with its relative dependence on world trade, and the geographical characteristics of a continent, with its relative dependence on self-sufficiency, had become increasingly important."[123]

In Innis's economic histories, schemas stemmed from the environments in which agents practised. Evolution mattered. The second reason for French failure was the government's persistent efforts to bolster the fur trade in New France, initiatives that hindered economic diversification, and, more specifically, prevented the emergence of an indigenous shipping industry that might have linked France's disparate colonies. It proved a costly mistake. The state's failure to come to grips with the reality of increasing returns led, in Innis's judgment, to the collapse not only of the French Empire but also of the *ancien régime*: "The place of the Crown in New France involved the direct link between trade and public finance and the difficulties which accompanied the inflations after 1700 and 1750. The inability of the French Empire to withstand the inroads of English commercialism led to its breakdown. The collapse of the external empire contributed to the internal breakdown in the French Revolution. France failed to link diverse regions, and England was unable to repress the aggressive integration of diverse regions."[124]

In the case of Britain, Innis argued that the collapse of the First British Empire was occasioned by its inability to contain an increasing returns economy – "the aggressive integration of diverse regions" – within the confines of a mercantile economy. The defeat of France brought to a head a fundamental contradiction in Britain's economic policy. It was simultaneously promoting economic liberalization and commercialism through the Navigation Acts, and economic regulation via the Molasses Act of 1733. The empire's collapse would also highlight the need to reform the basis of trade in the North Atlantic. Just as commercialism had demonstrated the need to shift from company control of North Atlantic trade to mercantilism, it would also demonstrate the state's inability to restrict trans-oceanic trade within prescribed boundaries, and the need for free trade.[125]

Almost immediately after the fall of New France, conflict emerged between Britain and New England. Prior to 1763, the competing needs of Britain's commercial and staple colonies had produced a rough balance in the formulation of British policy. That equilibrium shifted, however, during the peace negotiations leading to the Treaty of Paris. New England's petition for the French sugar colony of Guadeloupe was rejected by Britain, at the behest of the West Indies. After the Treaty of Paris, West Indian sugar interests continued to enjoy a disproportionate influence over the crafting of British legislation. As Innis recounts it, the British government, instead of loosening commercial restraints after the fall of France, began successively to tighten them in a way that favoured its staple colonies in the West Indies and Quebec.[126]

The process began in 1763 when New England merchants responded to an invitation by Guadeloupe's governor-general to re-initiate commercial ties. The resulting trade between New England and the Indies led in turn to the passage of Britain's Sugar Act in 1764, which reinforced the strictures of the Molasses Act prohibiting the colonies' import of foreign sugar cane.[127] The measure provoked alarm throughout New England. Massachusetts governor Francis Bernard claimed that it produced more agitation in his colony than France's capture of Fort William Henry at the start of the French-Indian War. Trade with the French West Indies, Innis noted, had risen to twice the level that had existed when the Molasses Act had been passed in 1733; and in the wake of Britain's acquisition of New France's fur trade, that trade had stimulated another cycle of economic growth.[128] To maintain the benefit of increasing returns, New England needed continued access to French sugar:

> The expansion of colonial and West Indian trade involved competition and an increasing dependence of the colonies on the French West Indies ... In the twenty years between the Treaty of Paris and the Treaty of Versailles the trend of the preceding periods was more marked and reached its ultimate conclusion. British colonial policy encouraged the British West Indies by restrictive legislation, widened the market for New England exports, and increased the necessity of depending on the French West Indies for imports. Encouragement to New England, indirectly by assistance to the West Indies and directly by the encouragement of the fishing industry, increased the disproportion between temperate and trop-

> ical development within the empire. The lack of political elasticity which made possible the control by the sugar planters conflicted with the demands of an expanding economic structure. Rigidity of control based on sugar production clashed with the divisive commercialism of the fishery.[129]

It was a conflict that defied resolution, one that intensified in the years between the Treaty of Paris and the onset of the American Revolution. New England, dependent on continued supplies of sugar to support its expanding trade, continued smuggling, while Britain continued passing legislation designed to restrict American activity, from the Townshend Acts of 1767 and the extension of the East India tea monopoly in 1774 to the Restraining Act of 1775.[130] Britain, writes Innis, failed to realize that it could not contain the increasing returns economy it had spawned. Its regulation of the sugar market within the British Empire had made the commodity highly profitable and had stimulated trade between the British West Indies and New England, a development that stimulated further trade between the American colonies and the French West Indies. Growth in North America promoted growth in the French Caribbean, which prompted further growth in North America. Britain's attempts to restrict American trade led to revolt, revolution, and the subsequent loss of the American colonies. It also led to the belated recognition that North Atlantic trade would have to be organized on a completely new basis: "The activity of commercialism, which played its part in the disappearance of the colonial system but also had been intensified by it, loosened the powerful forces of competition in the Atlantic basin, and made it inevitable that systems of Imperial control should defeat their own ends."[131]

The Nineteenth Century

If the eighteenth century was the climax of Innis's narrative, the nineteenth century was its dénouement, as Britain and its colonies, former and current, adjusted themselves to the economic realities imposed by the collapse of the First British Empire. Having failed to adapt prior to the Revolution, Britain launched a number of political and economic reforms in the nineteenth century, including abolition of the slave trade, abolition of preferences favouring the West Indies, free trade in the form of the Corn Laws, and parliamentary reform.[132] By mid-century, Britain had transformed itself, successfully creating a regime and an economic system capable of functioning within the emergent economic structures that linked it with its colonies, and with trading partners outside the Empire, particularly the United States.

Interestingly, Innis credits the colony of Nova Scotia with providing much of the impetus that led to imperial reform. A significant player in the nineteenth-century North Atlantic economy, Nova Scotia emerges in Innis's narrative as an example of differential persistence. As a colony, Innis suggests, it was inclined to maintain the assertive worldview and the institutional makeup it had learned from New England, attributes reinforced by its own participation in the fishery, and attributes that stood it in good stead in its relationship with London, motivating the colony to lobby for legislation that would protect its interests. Governance in the nineteenth-century British Empire, at least in the white colonies, became steadily more decentralized, in large part thanks to the initiative of Nova Scotia. Innis also suggests that Nova Scotia retained an ability to adapt its institutions. In the face of economic disequilibrium, it self-organized. In the face of an evolving international economy, Nova Scotia made changes that culminated in the advent of responsible government and Confederation.

Following the American Revolution, Nova Scotia became the beneficiary of much of New England's trade within the Empire, particularly with the West Indies. Its economy diversified with the rise of lumber and shipbuilding industries, as well as the development of fishing and agriculture.[133] In the economic order that emerged after the Revolution, Nova Scotia's task became twofold: to enhance its trading interests within Britain's colonial system, and to prevent American incursions into its markets, particularly in the Caribbean and in its fishery. Both of the colony's objectives, Innis writes, were pursued by means of persistent and successful lobbying of the British government.

Nova Scotia's institutions, particularly the Assembly, proved to be vigorous advocates, a stance Innis traced to the colony's ties to New England political culture and to the ties of both regions to the individualistic ethos of the fishing industry. Innis's description in *The Fur Trade* of the history of political and economic institutions of Canada pointed to differential persistence. The fur trade had emerged as a centralized institution, with a behaviour pattern that was transferred to Canada's banks, railways, and government. A similar dynamic,

Innis argued, shaped the behaviour and history of Nova Scotia's institutions: "[Nova Scotia] assumed a position in the forefront of the struggle for control over legislation dealing with the fishery, partly as a result of her ancestral and New England tradition of assertiveness which was in turn based on the fishery, and partly as a result of the inherent peculiarities of her own fishery. Her position was strengthened because the American Revolution made flexibility imperative, and this enabled her to press successfully for modifications in the British commercial system."[134]

While successful in protecting its interests, Nova Scotia suffered a severe setback in 1830 when the United States and Britain concluded a trade agreement giving the Americans permanent access to the West Indies. The agreement precipitated a number of important changes in Nova Scotia, chief among them a drive for greater autonomy within the Empire: "The growth of the nationalism in the colonies was the inevitable accompaniment of the British policy of free trade."[135]

Nova Scotia's demands were precipitated by the need to restructure in the face of an American competitor not bound by Britain's colonial system. Given its loss of the West Indies trade, the province pressed Britain to establish free ports to enable it to establish trading links with new partners. While Britain granted free port status to Halifax and four other ports in 1835, the Nova Scotia Assembly complained two years later that the colony's Legislative Council had degenerated into an advocacy group for Halifax interests. It stood in the way of the expansion of free port status to outlying areas of the colony. Increasingly, Nova Scotians became convinced that their territory's status in the international economy would only be secured by internal political and economic reorganization, the acquisition of responsible government, which Nova Scotia secured in 1839.

The desire for autonomy was precipitated also by Nova Scotia's fishing industry. Its competitiveness had been undercut by duties that raised its costs above those of American competitors, and the Nova Scotia Assembly was prompted to press Britain for powers to repeal differential duties set in Britain, a request that was also granted. Finally, the demand for autonomy was also the result of an increasingly diverse economy, which included agriculture, a sector whose importance had grown as trade with the West Indies declined and trade with Newfoundland increased. In effect, turbulence engendered by the province's immersion in an international economy, and by Nova Scotia's increasingly complex economy, precipitated reform or, in the parlance of complex adaptive systems, self-organization:

> The position of Nova Scotia, made plain by her external policy, was also evident in her internal development. Agriculture and other interests, working through the Assembly, pressed for expenditures on roads and bridges ... Divergence of interests necessitated political adjustment and, in turn, developed the political capacity which became conspicuous in the struggle for responsible government ... The varied character of her resources, her proximity to Prince Edward Island, New Brunswick, and the Gulf of St. Lawrence, and the importance of wooden sailing vessels hastened the growth of various ports, the development of agriculture, the construction of roads, and the expansion of wooden shipbuilding. The centralization of the commercial group at Halifax was offset by the decentralizing tendencies of trade, fishing, and other industries. The inherited influence of New England, evident in Nova Scotia's commercial spirit, was also evident in the province's political development.[136]

Innis's formulation here is striking. Recall that in *The Fur Trade* the tension between centralization and decentralization was a key criterion for Innis enabling the industry, and later the Canadian state, to adapt to changing economic circumstances. Such a formulation also reflects the requisite conditions for emergence in complex adaptive systems. In Innis's narrative, the combination of institutional differential persistence, occasioned by involvement in the fishery and the tension between centre and margin allowed for reform. The bifurcation stimulated by its immersion into the international economy affected not only Nova Scotia's internal economy but also its political and economic links. Confederation, in Innis's narrative, emerges as a form of self-organization, in which turbulence from the outside induces agents to form a network to increase their behavioural competence, thereby heightening the selective advantage of the totality in the environment. Nova Scotia was looking for just such an arrangement to offset American encroachments into its fishery:

> Nova Scotia had early turned to the development of increasingly effective machinery designed to check American encroachments

> on the fishery and on trade. The necessary defensive measures had called for an increasing control over governmental machinery, as had been made plain by the successful struggle of the Assembly against the Council, and by the victory which gave the Assembly control over the customs revenues in the forties. The mechanism had in the end involved a realignment of the British colonial system, cooperation with other provinces, reciprocity, Confederation, and the Treaty of Washington. The success of Nova Scotia, when supported by Canada, coincided with the part played by New England in erecting American tariff barriers. For Newfoundland, the struggle against France, the United States, Nova Scotia, and Canada meant isolation; and for Nova Scotia, the struggle against New England, France, and Newfoundland meant Confederation.[137]

As a colony and as a province, then, Nova Scotia displayed great acumen during the nineteenth century in adapting to the changing conditions of the North Atlantic economy. In *The Cod Fisheries*, Innis portrayed Britain as having demonstrated a similar judiciousness in the sixteenth and seventeenth centuries. In the centuries preceding the American Revolution, Britain had tailored its economic policy to reflect existing economic practice, and did not constrain its agents as France did in New France. As Innis saw it, France had foreclosed the possibility of economic growth and diversification by insisting that its colonial institutions support the fur trade. It could not stimulate increasing returns internally or externally. Despite Colbert's efforts, the French industry proved immune to government entreaties to facilitate commerce between its colonies. By virtue of its history, by virtue of the governance of formal cause, and by virtue of the onset of a network effect, the French industry retained its orientation toward the French domestic market. By the eighteenth century, Britain possessed a trading network with capabilities that the French could not match. France lost the contest for the continent because Britain brought to bear a trading network that incorporated trading partners, including some from the French Empire. By harnessing the capabilities of their various trading networks, the British, in Innis's construct, saw their profits in the fur trade rise, while those of France dwindled. France was reduced to experiencing increasing returns in reverse.

Having finally attained control over North America, *The Cod Fisheries* suggests, the British then abandoned the prudent economic policies that had thus far distinguished them, and instituted policies that sought to channel economic activity instead of simply reflecting it. Seeking to constrain the economic activity of its North American colonies, Britain in turn lost them. For Britain, as for France, the problem of imperial survival was reduced in Innis's narrative to resolution of a much simpler question: how well did each regime manage the onset of increasing returns? In Innis's mind, the answer was not very well. In a contest in which the prize was hegemony over North America, both ultimately lost.

V

Having completed our reading of Innis's four histories, we can now better assess how well they cohere with Mel Watkins's theory of staple development. Here also, the simple answer is, not very well. Innis's writings do suggest that Canada has historically been caught in a "staples trap," as Watkins asserts, but Watkins's appeal to dependency theory to explain Canada's specialization does not cohere with what Innis had to say. It is true that Innis points to France's constraining role in the development of New France, but in analyzing the subsequent development of Canada, he suggests that Canada's specialization in staples was the product of increasing returns and the governance of formal cause. Contrary to the suggestion by Watkins and others, Innis did not see Canada's economy operating under governing rules that differed in their fundamentals from those governing the European centre. As we saw in his history of the Spanish fishery and in *The Fur Trade*, both France and Spain were subjected to the governance of formal cause in his model, and the outcome of that governance was often at variance with what was desired by contemporaries of the time. Spain desired a strong fishery and carrying industry. It got neither.

Innis's writings also suggest a much more complex portrait of the imperial centre than provided by Watkins, whose portraits construe the centre as a single and sovereign actor. But that is not the picture that Innis drew. As we saw in his treatment of the seventeenth century, Innis suggests that Colbert tried to use the French fishery to link France's North American colonies. Because of the industry's adaptation to the French market, however, French fishermen had little incentive to respond to Colbert's encouragement. Formal and final cause precluded the emergence of a French carrying trade, and Colbert was powerless to reverse the network effect already in place. As Innis portrayed it, imperial centres enjoyed neither the unity of identity nor the absolute sovereignty over economic development suggested by Watkins.

Innis does not even suggest that the state proceeded as a unified actor. Despite Colbert's wish to create a commercial economy to unite France's North Atlantic possessions, French policy toward New France hindered the very economic development that would have made commercialism possible. Nor did England have a unified policy. In the seventeenth and eighteenth centuries it alternately desired the security of a mercantile economy and the robust growth of a commercial economy. Britain's failure to realize that it could not have both led in the eighteenth century to the American Revolution.

Watkins's theory also suggests a normative theory of development, but Innis again proposes a different interpretation of Canadian economic history. As William Christian correctly observes, Innis in his staple histories repeatedly emphasized the importance of human purpose in Canada's economic development.[138] Innis stressed two points. First, in trading relationships in which participants were locked into a staples economy, their selection of commodities for trade was in essence a network effect. Staple producers in the West Indies, British North America, and Canada participated because they chose to, because they received positive feedback in the form of profits, and because the imperial centre responded to their needs in the form of capital and legislation. In British possessions, the economic relationship between centre and margin was characterized, as Innis saw it, by interaction, not coercion.

Second, Innis's writings do not suggest that economic development is predetermined by environmental constraints or constraints imposed by extracting commodities from the environment. Rather, the constraints were cultural and numerical. New France's failure to become a commercial economy rested on choices made by the regime and the French fishing industry. The importance of final cause is suggested by the different trajectories of the New French and British North American economies in Innis's narrative. After the collapse of company control in New France, the French government opted for government control instead of commercialism, heightening the colony's dependence on the fur trade, with disastrous results. Britain, by contrast, opted for a commercial economy, which led to economic diversification, the rise of a carrying industry, and trade with the West Indies.

The environment for each economic unit was very similar. Both faced New England as a competitor. Both operated as mercantile systems separate from New England. The point of difference was the way each actor chose to interact with the immediate environment. In the first, New France produced a specialized economy and remained dependent on New England for trade. In the second, Canada produced a diversified economy and competed with New England for trade: "Where the French Empire had failed to link up the fur trade on the St. Lawrence, the fishing industry of the Maritimes, and the sugar plantations of the West Indies, Canada, with an agricultural base on the St. Lawrence was successful."[139]

Canada's economic diversification was not hindered by its extraction of staples. Like any other economic region, Canada's development was limited rather by the number of agents within it, a point Innis underscored by appealing to increasing returns and to Smith's dictum that the power of exchange gives occasion to the division of labour. Innis also emphasized that commercial relations had the power to disrupt centre-margin relations, a contention that differs from that of interpreters such as Daniel Drache, who have appealed to Innis to suggest that trade heightened Canada's dependency. In *The Cod Fisheries*, despite the efforts of interested merchants and state authorities to preserve the status quo, region after region attained economic autonomy from the directives of a neighbouring metropole as a result of a rising population of agents, economic diversification, and trade:

> The industry's intensely competitive nature increased the importance of recognizing and taking advantage of geographical conditions ... As the merchants and fishing ships of the West Country broke the control of the companies in Newfoundland, the merchants and fishermen of New England had an outstanding part in breaking the control of Great Britain in North America. So, too, Nova Scotia became independent of New England; and Newfoundland began to develop along more independent lines and also to develop a trading organization. The influence of the commercialism of the colonies and the Atlantic made itself felt in the breakup of the old empire and in the appearance in 1776 of Adam Smith's *Wealth of Nations*.[140]

In sum, then, Innis presents a picture of economic change based on historical contingency and the actions of multiple agents, not on a single imperial centre. It is also a picture in which systems display emergent properties and the governance of formal and final cause. Given this realization, there are grounds to suggest that, from the standpoint of North Atlantic historiography, Innis can be characterized as a pioneer of concepts that today are enjoying renewed currency among historians in Canada and abroad. While Canadian historians may have legitimate concerns about the execution of his studies, and more specifically may question whether the evidence he provides supports the conclusions he offers, they still have grounds to recommend him. Innis emerges as one of the first economic historians to attempt to understand the history of the North Atlantic economy in terms of emergent properties and the regulation of formal and final cause. As Joel Mokyr points out: "such 'autocatalytic models' which viewed economic history as a disequilibrium process once were shunned by the neoclassical cliometric orthodoxy. Today ... we are getting used to them, and the intellectual gains are substantial."[141] Innis doubtless would have shared Mokyr's sentiments.

With the completion of *The Cod Fisheries*, Innis effectively ended the phase of his career devoted to Canada's economic history. After twenty years of writing about the catastrophes, opportunities, and contingencies of Canada's economic past, a catastrophic event impinged on Innis's and Canada's present; namely, the Second World War. The war dramatically changed the focus of Innis's research in the final decade of his life. Innis shifted his focus away from economic systems to the vastly more daunting subject of culture. Instead of staples, Innis turned his attention to communication technologies. He did so because he believed the regime of change he had studied for the past twenty years would do much to explain why Western culture had collapsed in the first half of the twentieth century. In the process of identifying the constituents of a healthy culture, Innis believed, social scientists had to learn how and where society was governed by the regime of emergent change that he had studied as an economist. In *Political Economy in the Modern State*, he would attempt to persuade his colleagues that cultures were governed by the same regime of emergent change he had witnessed in economic systems. He would further argue that the quantity of information was the control parameter that helped or hindered a society's ability to adapt to its changing environment. Let us see how.

4

Political Economy in the Modern State

In 1946 Innis completed *Political Economy in the Modern State*. The work in many ways was a marked departure for him, both in the form and the content of the study. In contrast to the monograph format that had characterized his economic histories, Innis presented a compilation of articles that he had published in the years prior to and during the Second World War. He would never again return to the monograph format; nor would he submit studies devoted pre-eminently or exclusively to staples. Instead, Innis shifted his focus to a different topic: communication. He would spend his remaining years describing its fundamental role as a help and a hindrance to cultural growth and development.

Characteristically, Innis never set out in explicit terms his reasons for changing his focus. Consequently, scholars have had little choice but to surmise his motives based on his stated intellectual concerns and on his behaviour, given the geopolitical context of the time. The earliest view put forward by colleagues such as Donald Creighton and W.T. Easterbrook was that the shift was a natural outgrowth of his research related to staples. Research into the pulp and paper industries produced an appreciation of the importance of the newspaper industry, and of communication media in general, in stimulating economic, cultural, and social change. In Carl Berger's words, Innis's research contained an "inner logic."[1]

Interpreters since the 1970s, however, have been more disposed to credit the traumatic events associated with the Depression and the Second World War as the precipitating factors. In this line of reasoning, Innis was deeply troubled by the economic orthodoxy that had emerged during the Depression, namely in the writings of John Maynard Keynes. He disagreed with its central premise – championed by colleagues in the social sciences – that society could control the progression of the business cycle through state action, and thereby undo the effects of the Depression. He even more strongly disagreed with the doctrine's presumed outcome, a scenario in which social scientists worked in collaboration with the state. Innis believed it dangerous to have a society in which individuals of intellectual talent tailored their research agendas to the short-term needs of the state. The duty of social scientists as he understood it was to remain in the university, where they would have the freedom to document the long-term economic, social, and cultural trends constraining state and individual activity. Policy makers needed useful intelligence, not fashionable theories.[2]

When he lost this debate, some commentators suggest, it may have been the loss alone, or in combination with the shock of the Second World War, that prompted Innis to begin a study of the historic role played by communication technology, and the historic role played by institutions with a focus on long term change. Carl Berger writes that Innis began his research a month after the Fall of France in 1940. By 1945 he had produced a thousand-page manuscript, the unpublished "History of Communication," which served as the basis for his major communication studies, including the preface and the first seven articles of his first published anthology: *Political Economy in the Modern State.*[3]

In the Innis corpus, there are works that are extensively treated by Innis interpreters, and there are works that are at best lightly treated, or treated not at all. *Political Economy in the Modern State* is one example of the latter category of work.[4] The reason for its comparative neglect can be surmised from a quick survey of its contents. It is a strange book. There is no obvious overarching theme to the collection of articles, save that they all touch in some way on political economy and were all written by Innis. At best, the anthology comes across as an *ad hoc* mixture of old works treating staples and new work on communication technology. And when one examines Innis's earliest forays into communication studies, the essays can come across as empirically thick and conceptually poor, contributions mixing insights from British liberal philosophy – usually written by others – with warnings about the detrimental effects of the printing press. The concepts that distinguished his later communication writings – such as bias and monopoly – are present, but they are also in latent form. They are not defined, and seem to have little bearing on Innis's analysis or on the trajectory of the anthology's narratives. Viewed from the perspective of his later books, *Political Economy* can be perceived as a prototype, an initial attempt at an approach to history that is more successfully applied in *Empire and Communications* and *The Bias of Communication*.

Given the heterogeneous nature of *Political Economy in the Modern State*, such a stance may be understandable, and scholars' neglect of the work may also be understandable. My purpose in this chapter, however, is to argue that the stance is wrong and that the neglect should stop. *Political Economy* is an important work, one that deserves the same prominence as *Empire* and *Bias*, its more widely celebrated counterparts. Why? Consider the significance of this passage from the work, in which Innis presents a remarkable précis of a remarkable view of history: "Machine industry through printing press dispenses with thought or compels it to move in certain channels. The dispersion of thought through the printing industry makes attack on monopoly increasingly difficult. In emphasizing a long-range approach to social phenomena, economic history should contribute to stability. Not only should it supplement political and social history, it should in supplementing them check the tendency in itself and in them to bias and fanaticism."[5]

Innis being Innis, the substance of this passage is condensed, concrete, and in part impenetrable. That being said, some of it, particularly the sections referring to bias and channelled thought, refer to aspects of Innis's thinking that scholars have considered for some time. In this passage, however, Innis mentions a second consequent of communication technology that his interpreters have rarely, if ever, addressed. Here, he is suggesting that cultures have historically been subject not only to the dangers of intellectual stasis but also to the possibility of cultural flux. The implication of this passage is quite important, for it suggests that Innis's communication thought extended beyond the object with which he is typically associated, namely media. Innis was a scholar who thought deeply about a second concept – information – and produced writings that compare favourably with those of important contemporaries, most notably Norbert Wiener. In sum, the ultimate significance of the passage and the book is that they both suggest Innis was an information theorist.

This, to say the least, is not the way Harold Innis is typically characterized by his interpreters. Most summaries of communication theorists' writings portray him as offering three propositions about media: that their material properties engender in individuals and cultures a bias either toward the dimension of space or the dimension of time; that communication technologies, over time, will lock communicants into one bias or another, a state that Innis referred to as the Monopoly of Knowledge; and that cultures, through default or design, can thwart the debilitating effects of media by actively constructing knowledge and continually querying formulations already in circulation, an ethic he referred to as the oral tradition.[6]

Innis' précis however, suggests that he saw a second consequent of communication technology, one that hindered thought, and established the conditions for individual and social fanaticism. Both consequents stemmed from a schema of history in which information emerged as a catalyst for cultural evolution and collapse. Information's significance stemmed not only from its semantics, but also from its physical presence. Through formalisms – forms of representation ranging from words to mathematical notations and literary genres – information gained a concrete and quantitative presence in human culture. And because of its presence and representative function, information circulated, specific dynamics emerged to govern its circulation, and the quantity of words and other formalisms in circulation often accumulated. In principle, circulating information was a useful thing. When the extant quantity passed a certain threshold, however, information, and the dynamics governing its circulation, became dangerous things. In instances of information overload, humans at the individual, social, national, and even species level of organization became dysfunctional. In extreme cases, they stopped functioning altogether and collapsed. In our parlance, Innis saw information as the control parameter that governed emergent cultural change.

The mandate of this chapter, then, is to explore how Innis integrated the concept of information with the construct of emergent change. In earlier chapters, we saw that Innis – through default or design – displayed a penchant for emphasizing one constituent or another of complex systems. In *The Fur Trade* he highlighted the importance of differential persistence; in *The Cod Fisheries* he focused on positive feedback or increasing returns. In *Political Economy* he would stress balance, the edge-of-chaos state that we have seen is the essential precursor to adaptation, complexification, and systemic growth. Through it, Innis would construct a schema of emergent cultural change which he then applied to write a history of the West from Rome to the present. We will explore both in this chapter. Innis would also use the schema as the basis for a jeremiad. Information was a persistent danger to culture, he warned, and unless the West took steps to consider its effects, it would continue its descent into the trauma marked by the First and Second World Wars. Our purpose is to learn why Innis believed the West was in dire straits, and what he believed it must do to remedy the situation. Along the way, we will take brief excursions to examine the concept of information, Norbert Wiener's writings on information dynamics and time series, and Innis's work on cyclonics. They will help us better understand Innis's arguments and prescriptions. And they will underscore his fundamental belief in the importance of emergent change, increasing returns, and the governance of formal and final cause.

I

Establishing His Grounds: Economic Systems as Analogues for Cultural Systems

When Innis began his foray into communication studies, he was faced with a central task: the creation of a schema for cultural change. He had to justify the application of concepts derived from economic history, the domain he knew, to cultural history, the domain he was entering. His purpose was to argue that cultures writ large, and the multiple domains comprising them – politics, religion, commerce, and others – were all complex, hierarchic systems, different in substance, but similar if not identical in kind. For this reason, they were all governed by the same tenet of natural law: the need for distributed control among the system's constituent actors. They were also subject to the same consequent of distributed control: meta-stability. They self-organized into systems that traversed space and extended through time. They moved through time in a cyclic fashion: self-organizing, dissolving, and then re-combining. They were subject to constituents in the environment – control parameters – that prompted dissolution and self-reorganization. And by virtue of their exposure to destabilizing constituents in the environment, they self-regulated through formal cause, altering the functions of their constituent parts during each new phase of self-organization.

To support this argument, Innis began by asserting the systemic nature of economic phenomena and providing a ground to justify his contention that cultural systems should be seen as analogues of economic systems. Not surprisingly, he drew first on the ideas of Adam Smith, whose writings he characterized as "architectonic," not only for economics but also for biology.[7] Quoting Jacob Viner, Innis argued that Smith's *The Wealth of Nations* established that "economic phenomena were manifestations of an underlying order in nature governed by natural forces." This accomplishment "gave to English economics for the first time a definite trend toward logically consistent synthesis of economic relationships, toward 'system building.'" It also gave Smith an opportunity to argue that economic systems were characterized by distributed rather than centralized forms of control, forms of control in which individual and institutional freedom was balanced by the exercise of self-restraint. "The underlying natural order," Viner wrote of Smith's conception of economic systems, "required for its most beneficent operation a system of natural liberty."[8] Smith's construct required liberty. It did not imply license. It did not permit license. Healthy economies and healthy polities required the exercise of institutional and individual restraint, a point Innis emphasized via the writings of Lord Acton: "While 'the doctrine of self-reliance and self-denial, which is the foundation of political economy, was written as legibly in the New Testament as in the *Wealth of Nations*, it was not recognized until our age.' Scotland became 'the land of porridge and political economy.'"[9]

In asserting that economies were systems governed by natural law, Innis laid an initial ground to justify his application of analogical reasoning. He laid a second ground by asserting that there is a biological basis for economic behaviour. He did this largely through his identification of the social sciences with the biological sciences, most particularly in the article "Political Economy in the Modern State," in which he noted the important contributions of Malthus and Darwin "to the science of biology, including economics."[10] Since economic behaviour proceeded from a biological ground, as opposed to a historically specific cultural construction, Innis believed that insights derived from economic behaviour had potential application for understanding the behaviour of systems in other domains of human activity.

With his grounds established, Innis proceeded to his third task, which was to argue that the price system – the shorthand term he used to label emergent, hierarchic economic systems governed by distributed centres of control – should serve as the source analogue, the template, to describe the organization of multiple domains of human society. Thanks to his exposure to Thorstein Veblen's insights on the emergence of value and other writings, Innis saw the significance of the price system as a system of exchange for goods and services whereby the price of a given commodity is not centrally planned but emerges, in principle, from interactions between a distributed network of producers and consumers.[11] Innis acknowledged the often ruthless nature of the free market system. But in a passage in which economic, political, and ecclesiastical hierarchies are presented for comparison and analysis, he argued: "its defects had to be balanced against alternative possibilities. It appears to be the most effective system for introducing freedom and efficiency into hierarchical systems. It has largely avoided the hierarchical limitations of Chinese civilization with its dependence on written examinations, the costs of the ecclesiastical system shown, for example, in celibacy in the Roman Catholic Church, and the dangers of autocracy based on the divine right of kings."[12]

Distributed Control and Self-Organization

While Innis made clear in *Political Economy* that the domains of culture are systems that require a proper balance between freedom and constraint, he did not make explicit the consequent of that balance; namely, the same systems would produce needed adaptation through self-organization. While the point is made implicitly in all the essays devoted to culture, Innis was more forthcoming in a series of letters exchanged with Arthur Cole, a colleague in economic history with whom Innis corresponded regularly during the 1940s, the period in which he wrote his communication studies. The letters are a valuable resource for interpreting Innis's writings. They not only enable us to gain a deeper understanding of Innis's views on emergent change. They also assist us in unearthing the suppositions behind his writings on the formalism of the time series, and his theory of media. What the communication studies render implicit, the Cole correspondence often makes explicit. Accordingly, we will be consulting the series in this chapter and the next.

In March 1945 Innis's correspondence with Cole dealt with the conditions that stimulated the rise of entrepreneurs – a topic Innis believed had significance not only for encouraging economic growth but also for reviving the cultural vitality of the West. Citing works he had recently read by the political economist Achille Loria and the sociologist Nicholas Timasheff, Innis wrote that he was "more and more convinced that we need to know the background which admits of the entrepreneur's emergence and ... the conditions that will admit of his continuance." In that regard, Timasheff's writings were particularly significant for Innis. They suggested that in societies where the constraint of religion and ethics was combined with the freedom of applied force, agents were afforded a stable environment in which to interact, and the emergent properties of law and a functioning economy were the result: "Certainly it would appear that the entrepreneur in the commercial field can only flourish in a society committed to plan and that other types of society are more apt to be dominated by naked force, to use the expression of Bertrand Russell. Political Economy like law seems to emerge when force and ethics overlap (Timasheff) and for that reason the entrepreneur can function only under similar conditions."[13]

Innis would state this point more precisely and clearly in 1952 in a letter to W.T. Easterbrook, a colleague at the Department of Political Economy at the University of Toronto, with whom he corresponded and visited regularly during the last year of his life: "I am not sure that the space time approach is not another way of putting Timasheff's suggestion that law emerges at the point at which force and religion overlap. At this point it would appear that order also appears."[14]

Cultural Systems are Spatio-Temporal Objects that are Meta-Stable

Innis emphasized space and time in his letter to Easterbrook because he believed emergent economic and cultural systems to be spatio-temporal objects. He emphasized in particular the temporal nature of cultural dynamics, in part because he believed that the trajectories of systems through time were non-linear and did not develop along pre-established paths. The dynamics of nature could not be identified with Newtonian mechanics, and as such, in Innis's time were not susceptible to mathematical expression. In his article "On the Economic Significance of Cultural Factors," he noted that the significance of economic history to economics and other disciplines lay "in its concern with long-run trends and its emphasis on training in a search for patterns rather than mathematical formulae."[15] Innis wrote to Cole in October 1941 of his preference for economic studies that stressed "the evolutionary (Spencerian) point of view" because such studies offered "a more solid footing than … the mathematical mechanistic approach."[16]

While emphasizing the importance of time, Innis added in the same letter to Cole that it was important that economic historians not repeat the mistake of social scientists who had grown overly dependent on mathematical formalisms. In so doing, they had privileged the dimension of space and marginalized time. Economic historians were at risk of making the opposite error through their dependence on a different formalism: time series of price data. The object of their concern – economic systems, and by extension cultural systems – had a spatial dimension, and it was important that economic historians keep it in mind: "I have a feeling that geography is important and that it is very easy to forget about it through concentration on prices. We need both if we are to think of a European civilization or at least of the sort that Adam Smith had in mind."[17]

Like Veblen, Innis believed that cultural and economic systems were meta-stable. He believed their trajectory through time should be characterized not as a linear progression but rather as a cycle of growth – temporary stability, disequilibrium, and subsequent re-organization. In "The Newspaper in Economic Development" Innis focused on the need in economics and economic history for "a change in the concept of time," arguing that time could not be "regarded as a straight line but as a series of curves depending on technological advances."[18]

In the article "Political Economy in the Modern State" Innis emphasized his belief that a similar template – a template of catastrophic change – applied to culture. In his mind, the field of political economy took an unfortunate turn after Adam Smith, by shifting its focus from dynamic systems to systems in equilibrium, which were susceptible to mathematical treatment. The emphasis on a single segment of economic phenomena ultimately shifted the discipline's conception of nature – and society – toward the construct of change typified by Marshall's dictum: "'Natura non facit saltum' (Nature never proceeds by leaps)."[19]

Innis countered that civilization was more properly identified with art. In making this allusion, his purpose was to suggest that both were domains of human activity governed by the interplay between choice and constraint. The font of any thriving culture, Innis writes in his article "Political Economy," is behaviour consistent with Calvin's two cardinal rules of human society: self-control as the foundation of virtue, self-sacrifice as the condition of the common weal. Innis's definition of art, obtained from Geoffrey Scott, mirrored the ethic of balance, freedom, and constraint embodied in Calvin's philosophy: "In art, as in life, the chief problem is a right choice in sacrifices. Civilization is the organisation of values."[20]

The problem was also to maintain balance. Innis's identification of civilization with art had an important implication. It suggested that culture was susceptible to cycles of self-organization, collapse, and subsequent self-organization: "Toynbee and students of civilization insist that while 'nature never proceeds by leaps,' civilization proceeds in precisely that fashion. 'All spiritual growth takes place by leaps and bounds, both in the individual and ... in the community' (Burckhardt)."[21] Innis noted in a 1943 letter to Cole his "personal interest in public opinion – particularly the existence of broad plateaus of public opinion and the sharp breaks which occur in it from time to time – a sort of psychological or cultural approach."[22]

Cultural Systems Are Regulated by Control Parameters and Governed by Formal Cause

Culture, therefore, was subject to periods of instability, and then made leaps, displaying emergent properties such as changes in public opinion, before stabilizing once more. Innis's final task in describing cultural dynamics was to account for the basis of cultural meta-stability. In his view, the problem could be reduced to locating the constituent in the environment that affected the terms of interaction – the degree of freedom and constraint – among a system's constituent agents, and between the system and its surrounding environment. It could also be reduced to locating the constituent that was exchanged – the control parameter – a constituent that helped or hindered a system in adapting, balancing its freedom and constraint, and a constituent that was either generated by system participants or acquired from the environment. With respect to interaction, Innis believed that if you altered the terms, you laid the basis for a system's dissolution and its subsequent transformation. And if you did that, you set the stage for the consequent of that transformation: changed behavioural competencies for participating agents in the system. Innis outlined his views on this subject in Section II of "On the Economic Significance of Cultural Factors." There, he provided a condensed history of the North Atlantic economy. And there, he highlighted the features of emergent change that he had identified in *The Cod Fisheries*, including the governance of formal cause.

The focus of his discourse was Britain and its rise to global economic dominance culminating in the nineteenth century. He attributed this rise to three benefits that it had enjoyed: low overhead costs through cheap maritime transport, a developed industrial base, and a potent source of power, coal. By integrating coal with its industrial technique, Britain enhanced and extended its trading network with North America, emerging as an agent specializing in the conversion of raw materials into finished products for export. Select regions in North America emerged as agents specializing in the export of staples such as timber and cotton.[23]

While Britain's trading system was robust, it remained vulnerable to disturbance, typically effected by changes in transport technology arising from the industrial revolution and new sources of energy. Innis greatly stressed this point. New transport systems such as the railway had altered the terms of interaction, and consistently destabilized existing trading patterns by enlarging the spatial extent of the network, lowering overhead costs, and expanding the range of commodities that were exchanged. As the North Atlantic economy went through successive phases of disequilibrium and self-organization, the behavioural competence or specialization of the actors changed.

In addition to developments in transport, a second factor altered the terms of the trade of the nineteenth century: relative advantage. New actors were incorporated into trading networks with new skills that overshadowed those of the system's extant actors and required them in turn to alter their activities. It was a portrait that Innis had also painted in his histories of the cod fisheries. The insertion of a new transport technology into the Atlantic in the form of the fishing boat had led to the emergence of a new trading network – the British North Atlantic economy – to the incorporation of new actors such as the British West Indies, and to the alteration of extant actors, such as Spain. Trade, the relative advantage of a system's actors, and the exercise of formal cause through the distribution of profit, together resulted in the incorporation of the British West Indies as an agricultural colony, and then its transformation into a sugar colony. Trade, formal cause, and relative advantage also transformed Spain from a fishing country into the fishing industry's banker.

In his portrait of Britain's nineteenth-century trading network, Innis referred to the same process, particularly in his description of its evolution in North America. One of Innis's complaints with Frederick Jackson Turner's frontier hypothesis was that it provided an oversimplified rendition of the continent's economic development. In North American economic history, there had never been a single frontier, but rather a succession of frontiers, each with a specialization that reflected existing transport rates and the relative advantage of neighbouring frontiers. The newest frontier generally enjoyed two advantages: new plant and new technique. It was these advantages that precipitated the westward migration of wheat production.[24] Britain was not immune to the disturbances initiated by changes in transport technology and the governance of formal cause. In "On the Economic Significance of Cultural Factors" Innis noted that "England shifted her fields from arable land to pasture."[25]

While the cyclical and self-regulating nature of economic and cultural systems was an important issue, Innis's purpose in *Political Economy* extended beyond providing a description of it. He intended also to outline the conditions that undermined systems, keeping them from self-organizing and adapting to new circumstances. One of the curious features of Section II of "On the Economic Significance of Cultural Factors" is that it juxtaposes two narratives: his account of the British North Atlantic; and an abbreviated history of the West from the collapse of the Roman Empire forward. Innis's purpose is plainly to draw a parallel between the two narratives. In the first, he gives an account of circulating commodities, and the import of new transportation technologies as recurring causes of disturbance. In the second, he brings a narrative of circulating information, and points to a second source of disturbance: new communication technology. From both, we receive an implicit message: the dynamics governing the acquisition and distribution of commodities are the same as those governing the circulation of information. And from the latter, we receive a final message: that information was an important constituent of the history of the West, a constituent that prompted its emergence after the fall of Rome and contributed to its recent collapse. Innis was arguing that information was a cultural parameter that impinged on the meta-stability of cultural systems. It was a factor in history that the reader would do well to learn more about.[26]

II

Excursus I: Innis, Information, and the Dynamics of Information Flow

Before examining Innis's application of this insight to the history of the West, it will be helpful to explore Innis's construct of information and take steps to lift his statement on the dynamics of information from the realm of the implicit to the explicit. To that end, we need a conceptual framework that describes the dynamics of information flow and its systemic consequents. Here, we are fortunate to have the writings of an important contemporary, Norbert Wiener, to assist us. Norbert Wiener was a mathematician based at MIT from 1919 until the early 1960s. He is best known, however, as a founder of the field of cybernetics, a discipline devoted to the study of information, and its impact on control and communication in mechanical and biological systems. His numerous publications on cybernetics in the 1940s and 1950s influenced subsequent research in a wide range of fields, including computing and telecommunications, biology, and psychiatry.[27] He was also an important forerunner of the science of complexity.[28]

For our purposes, Wiener's writings are relevant because of their remarkable similarity to those of Innis.[29] Both argued that the significance of information for any given system was based, in part, on its quantity. And both applied constructs to describe the flow of information and explain the pathologies that emerged from the flow of information. Unlike Innis, however, Wiener provided reasonably clear descriptions of what those constructs were – positive and negative feedback – and the pathologies that emerged from positive feedback: oscillating, uncontrolled behaviour, and, in extreme cases, systemic or cognitive breakdown.

With the cheerful prospect of systemic collapse in mind, let us turn to Innis's construct of information. Information, the philosopher Fred Dretske writes, "has come to be an all-purpose word … with the suggestive power to fulfill a variety of tasks."[30] We can narrow that semantic range somewhat by observing that Innis characterized information in qualitative and quantitative terms. The qualitative approach, in its essence, identifies the word "information" with terms such as content, constructs, and meaning. In the *General Definition of Information* (GDI), for example – a standard in Information Science and more recently the philosophy of computing and information – "information" is formulated as "data + meaning." "Data" refers to distinct patterns or events that are instantiated in matter or energy. "Meaning" refers to formalisms that assist in the perception of data and their integration into larger semantic contexts.[31] A formalism is an instrument for representation. As a term, it refers to representational signs such as words, numbers, graphs, and mathematical notation. It also refers to more complex constructs made up of signs, be they sentences, meters of poetry, genres of literature, analytical constructs, or mathematical models.

Although Innis never specified what he meant by the word "information," his use of the term in *Political Economy* suggests an understanding of its qualitative sense. Information at base was a percept, "the raw data," in Edward Comor's words, "from which knowledge is constructed."[32] The percepts in *Political Economy* that most concerned Innis were those associated with the market economy in the wake of its industrialization in the eighteenth century. In Britain, patterned activity in the form of "the emergence of a complex industrial and trading structure" created an unprecedented demand for commercial intelligence and price data expressed respectively via word and number. Both intelligence and data were critical to agents on the ground. They enabled agents to observe the market, conceive its functions, and influence its future operations: "The rapid and extensive dissemination of information was essential to the effective placing of labour, capital, raw materials and finished products."[33]

While mindful of the qualitative significance of information, Innis was primarily concerned in *Political Economy* with its quantitative impact. For him, that understanding of information suggested that its significance stemmed not only from its semantics but also from its physical presence. Through formalisms, or forms of representation, information gained a concrete and quantitative presence in human culture. And because of its presence and representative function, information circulated, specific dynamics emerged to govern its circulation, and the quantity of words and other formalisms often accumulated, developments that in turn produced devastating consequences.

In the preface to *Political Economy* Innis expressed his concern that communication technology had imposed a heavy price on Western society – an information glut. In recent history the printing press and radio had "enormously increased the difficulties of thought." Both inventions, in conjunction with freedom of expression, had led to "the production of words on an unprecedented scale and ... made them powerless."[34] Words were impotent, Innis argued, because his contemporaries in the 1940s, and those who had preceded him in the nineteenth century, had lost their capacity to construct them into larger wholes, namely constructs that commanded public attention, and were lasting.

In "The Newspaper in Economic Development," the first article of *Political Economy*, Innis argued that the chief culprit for the ruined state of public discourse was the press. Citing Graham Wallas, Innis charged that the press's "emphasis on information and facts" was "destructive of the environment for thought." The press had created an environment in which the public had little "immediate active concern with political considerations." In this context, Innis defined political considerations as a fixed stable frame of reference, a convention, noting John Morley's observation "that literature repudiated conventions while political action has as its very first working principle compliance with conventions: 'All round responsibility for one thing and fuller knowledge of decisive facts makes all the difference.'"[35] In "An Economic Approach to English Literature in the Nineteenth Century," Innis further noted that, aside from impinging on political discourse, the press had created a public lacking the desire and even the capacity to perceive a significant construct. Quoting George Gissing, Innis pointed to a generation of students in the early twentieth century who were "quarter-educated," meaning they were "incapable of sustained attention." Gissing complained of students' preference for Sunday newspapers, which at the time conveyed nothing but "the lightest and frothiest of chit-chatty information – bits of stories, bits of description, bits of scandal, bits of jokes, bits of statistics, bits of foolery. Am I not right?"[36] Mark Pattison, a nineteenth-century British intellectual who strongly influenced Innis, made similar observations. Quoting Pattison in "The University in the Modern Crisis," Innis noted his observation that "there is an organization of thought as well as of labour," an organization he defined as "a scientific formation of mind, a concert of the intellectual faculties." For Pattison, such a concert of the mind could not be obtained when there was a "rapid inculcation of unassimilated information," which "[stupefied] the faculties instead of training them."[37]

Such stupefaction Innis argued resulted from the dynamics of information. To deepen our understanding of them, we should shift at this point to Norbert Wiener's disparate writings on cybernetics, where he said a great deal about the dynamics of information flow, and characterized them respectively as positive and negative feedback. Wiener and his colleagues Arturo Rosenblueth and Julian Bigelow were co-founders of the field of cybernetics, a discipline that drew insights from communication engineering, a field concerned with the design of electric circuits, and control engineering, a field concerned with the creation of regulatory devices to support the proper functioning of tools, including electric circuits.[38]

The chief insight they offered jointly, and Wiener singly in his later writings, was that certain classes of mechanical systems behaved in an analogous fashion to organic systems, particularly in the pathologies they displayed. Under certain circumstances, equipment such as an anti-aircraft battery or a telephone network deviated from its normal behaviour, oscillating wildly from side to side in the case of the battery, crashing completely in the case of the network. In similar circumstances, humans displayed similar pathologies, the oscillation of the battery finding its correlate in a condition called purpose tremor, the collapse of the network finding its analogue in an individual's lapse into insanity.

The reason mechanical and organic systems share pathologies, Wiener argued, is that they also share a need to exchange information with their surrounding environments in order to engage in purposive behaviour. Because of that common dependence, mechanical and organic systems are subject to the dynamics governing circulating information, and to the dangers associated with exposure to too much information. To clarify his point, Wiener appropriated a term from control engineering: feedback. Feedback, in essence, refers to the outcome of a purposive act taken by an agent in its environment. The outcome is first a circular flow of information, extending from the agent to the environment and back again. The information generally refers to two things: the agent's progress in performing an intended act, and the environment's modification or response as a result of the intended act. A second outcome will be action, or more precisely interaction, between the agent and the environment in response to the flow of information.

This interaction will produce one of two effects: it will either reinforce, or regulate and dampen, the initial act of the agent. In the first case, the agent acts, and the environment reacts in a way that supports continuation of the agent's initial act. A self-sustaining process of action and supportive re-action emerges. This process Wiener referred to as positive feedback. One common example of positive feedback noted by Wiener is the unintentional amplification of sound produced by electrical amplifiers, which for our purposes we will characterize as poorly positioned microphones and speakers.[39] At a wedding party, a guest steps up to a microphone to toast the couple. The individual, in connection with the microphone and speakers, forms a system, an agent with the express purpose of amplifying sound. During the toast, the speakers amplify the guest's words so that the audience, the environment, can hear them. The speakers, unfortunately, are too close to the microphone. Their output is inputted into the microphone in addition to the guest's voice. A self-sustaining process emerges: positive feedback. Sound leaves the speakers, enters the microphone, leaves the speakers again, and returns to the microphone. The environment – the members of the wedding party – "supports" the process, initially by positioning the speakers near the microphone and then by doing nothing to hinder the emergence and continuance of positive feedback. The feedback continues – the sound gets louder, shriller, and more unpleasant – until the unfortunate guest stops speaking and covers the microphone, or members of the wedding party move the speakers to prevent speaker-generated sound from reaching the microphone.

In the second case, the environment reacts in a way that induces the agent to modify or cease its initial act in order to realize its initial purpose. This process – of agent adjustment to changing environmental conditions – Wiener and control engineers referred to as negative feedback. For Wiener, the operative behaviour of the governor, or ship-steering engine, was the classic example of negative feedback in action. The purpose of the governor is to steer a ship in the direction specified by the ship's helmsman. In large ships, a governor is an essential instrument since the rudder is too large and too heavy to be manipulated by human power. To fulfill its function while turning a ship, the governor continuously acquires information from the environment to determine the proper orientation of the rudder. It determines the speed and orientation of the ship relative to its assigned heading, and, after the initial act of turning the rudder, alters the angle of the rudder relative to the keel, or spine of the ship, bringing the blade of the rudder closer and closer into alignment with the keel as the ship's bearing gets closer and closer to its assigned heading. As the ship turns, the governor dampens the act of turning. This process of dampening is negative feedback.[40]

For Wiener, the governor and its related control systems based on negative feedback were superior to devices that did not rely on environmental information to determine their subsequent behaviour. At least for the most part. "This negative feedback," he wryly noted in 1954, "has its diseases."[41] In contrast to non-feedback control systems, negative feedback devices were generally more robust. They could adjust themselves to changing quantities of information from the surrounding environment with no visible impairment to their functioning. Wiener argued, however, that there was an upper threshold to the quantity of incoming information that any given control device could accept. If the device crossed that threshold, the process governing its behaviour shifted from negative feedback to positive feedback.[42] The system would lose its capacity to dampen the quantity of incoming information, or check the trajectory of its action, and instead become locked into a recurring pattern of clumsy behaviour: "When these limits are exceeded, the system becomes definitely unstable and goes into oscillations with an amplitude increasing up to the point where the system breaks down."[43]

In his writings, Wiener noted this characteristic in negative feedback devices. It affected not only the governor, but also the control systems associated with devices ranging from anti-aircraft battery and ship's turret to robots. For Wiener, the significance of this trait, and the related dynamics of negative and positive feedback, lay in the light they potentially shed on the functioning of biological systems, including humans. Both mechanical and biological systems were dependent on circulating information. Both employed sensor and effector organs to acquire information, to effect an act or series of acts in the environment, and to monitor their progress in so doing. And both, in the end, might serve as useful analogues to better understand the other, with mechanical systems serving as a template for biological systems, and vice versa. Through such an exercise, Wiener hoped, researchers would gain a deeper understanding of the structure, functioning, and malfunctioning of mechanical and biological systems.[44]

Such was the justification for the field of cybernetics. And such was the basis for the field's initial promise. In large measure, Wiener's work, particularly his 1948 book *Cybernetics*, attracted attention because he and Rosenblueth and Bigelow succeeded in demonstrating the existence of a similar pathology in humans, namely purpose tremor. That commonality in turn suggested the relevance of negative and positive feedback in the functioning and malfunctioning of the nervous system. Purpose tremor is a condition that stems from an injury to the cerebellum. Consider a simple volitional act such as picking up a pencil. A person with purpose tremor will initially appear normal, but when attempting to pick up the pencil, will overshoot the target. In a second attempt, he or she will overreach the pencil yet again. If the person continues, the arm will sink into a pattern of uncontrolled oscillation. The explanation, Wiener hypothesized, was that the cerebellum was not properly dampening the quantity of information returning from the body's sensory organs. As a result, it was triggering muscular responses out of proportion to the task at hand, and muscular tremor was the result.[45]

Wiener further believed that a quantitative approach would also shed light on other pathologies, especially mental disorders. Noting the structural similarities between telephone networks (consisting of chains of relays) and the human brain (consisting of chains of neurons), Wiener argued that telephone networks were robust in their capacity to support ever-increasing quantities of information. Once the information supply passed a certain threshold, however, the entire network broke down.[46] It was entirely possible, Wiener argued, that functional mental disorders emerged in the same way, and that they should be seen "fundamentally as diseases of memory, of the circulating information kept by the brain in active state."[47] Mental disorders were less the result of trauma, disease, and the resulting destruction of tissue, than the result of "the overload of what remains of the nervous system." Hence, humans, with likely "the largest chains of effectively operated neurones [sic]" of all animals, resembled telephone exchanges quite capable of performing complex acts until reaching "the edge of an overload," at which point they would "give way in a serious and catastrophic manner." Once that point was reached, humans "quite suddenly" would "have a form of mental breakdown, very possibly amounting to insanity."[48]

III

These concepts – negative and positive feedback, and the pathologies stemming from circulating information – had their correlates in *Political Economy*. In a history of the West extending from Rome to the mid-twentieth century, Innis presented a narrative in three parts. In the first, the central theme was ascension. In the second, the theme was decline and fall. And in the third, it was recovery and restoration.

In Part One, Innis pointed to Europe's discovery, in the wake of Rome's collapse, of a control mechanism that would enable it to survive and thrive: balance. In Part Two, he would assert a relationship between the control mechanism of balance and the positive feedback flow governing information. Put simply, Innis would assert that the latter undermined the former, and initiated the West's collapse. In Part Three, he would argue that humanity need not be a passive recipient of the information to which it was exposed. For Wiener, negative feedback, in its essence, was a volitional act. Agency was thwarted when an organism was subjected to too much information. Innis reached similar conclusions. In a programmatic statement to colleagues he would argue that measures could be taken to dampen information, and in turn, protect human volition. In Wiener's parlance, steps could be taken to protect the possibility for negative feedback.

Innis's History of the West I: Balance and the Ascension of the West

Rome, for Innis, was a benchmark, an exemplar indicating how and why societies collapsed. The empire fell, he believed, because it had broken a fundamental precept of natural law, the need for balance. Balance for Innis, as we have seen, rested on individuals and institutions finding the right mean between freedom and constraint. At the international, national, institutional, and social levels of human organization, it was a doctrine of distributed control. Power should never be completely centralized, and institutions should find the right mean between centralized and de-centralized forms of control. At the individual level, it was an ethic enjoining self-control, conduct governed by the right balance between freedom and law. In the end, Rome failed because it centralized power to a degree that distinguished it from its ancient imperial counterparts. Church and state were integrated into a single construct, and the economy was regulated by the state.[49] In Innis's reading, economic regulations imposed by Rome's bureaucracy squashed individual autonomy to the point that it proved impossible for a viable economy to emerge, the one thing that would have enabled Rome to sustain itself over the long term. Over time, Rome lost its specie, and what remaining incentives there were to trade. Trade collapsed, and in 410 CE, with the sacking of Rome, so did the empire.[50]

In the ascension phase of his narrative, Innis treats Europe's and then North America's collective response to the mistakes of Rome. The narrative is in essence a tale of ruin and rise, and the realization of the principles that make for a robust society. And not surprisingly, Innis starts with the rise of the church during the medieval era, which he describes as having a twofold significance. First, it legitimized the notion that power should be distributed between institutions. Drawing on Christ's maxim to "Render unto Caesar what is Caesar's," the church put into effect the notion that temporal power should be accorded to the state, and spiritual power to the church.[51] It also introduced the convention that state action in international politics should be constrained, at least in part, by transnational networks. The states for Innis signified the agency in history most responsible for the collective application of force.[52] Transnational networks, by contrast, represented the collective application of restraint, or, in Wiener's terms, negative feedback. The state represented the exercise of volition. Transnational networks, in their turn, protected the potential for volition, through appeal to ethical restraint, economic self-interest, and information regulation.

In *Political Economy*, Innis intermittently referred to "machinery" and "structures." These terms were shorthand, referring typically to systems that defined and regulated the behaviour of their constituent actors. Hence, both terms might refer to the U.S. and Canadian federal systems,[53] the market system,[54] and systems of social relations defined by class.[55] They also referred to international systems composed of national and transnational actors. For Innis, the church was the first transnational institution to emerge after the collapse of Rome. Quoting W.E.H. Lecky, he argued that the Church consolidated "the heterogeneous and anarchical elements" that remained after the fall of Rome, and infused into Christendom a conception of "a bond of unity that is superior to the divisions of nationhood" and "a moral tie ... superior to force."[56] In short, with the rise of the church, the state "was circumscribed in its authority by a force external to its own."[57]

In the end, the Church overplayed its hand. Although initially a force for moderation and scholarship, by the late medieval era it sought to regulate scholarship and thought, provoking in turn the Reformation, the Renaissance, and the Enlightenment, movements of opposition and thought that were supported, in part, by the printing press. With these developments "the vast structure previously centring about religion declined," and with them came "the long struggle for re-organization which began with the breakdown of the control of the church."[58] For Innis, these three movements for reorganization had a double significance. They gave rise to new formulations on balance, formulations that touched on the religious, political, and economic organization of states, and on the behaviour and mental constitution of individuals. And they gave rise to the emergence of new transnational networks to replace the church, networks of individuals and institutions dedicated to promoting international stability and reminding states and citizenries that they had long-term interests to protect.

The Reformation was important in Innis's view because it provided for an even wider distribution of power over morals and religious faith than the church had allowed. Ultimate control over ethics and morals shifted from the state and church to the individual. The Protestant movement articulated the right to freedom of conscience, and ultimately to freedom of assembly with the institution of one's choosing. In terms of balance, it contributed the doctrine of religious liberty and the doctrine of individual integrity, simultaneously inculcating in congregants a respect for freedom and a recognition of the need for restraint. Particularly in the Calvinist and Puritan branches of the movement, as we have seen, Protestantism enforced "two cardinal laws of human society, self-control as the foundation of virtue, [and] self-sacrifice as the condition of the common weal."[59]

To Innis, the significance of this latter formulation on balance was that it engendered the British Enlightenment – the cultural matrix for conservative democracy and classical political economy, the political and economic doctrines that Innis deemed best suited for supporting the emergence of stable, innovative, and culturally vibrant societies. Quoting Ernst Troeltsch, Innis argued that cultures influenced by Calvinism and Puritanism were distinguished by their emphasis on "individualism and by democracy, combined with a strong bias toward authority and a sense of the unchangeable nature of law." This tension between freedom and constraint, centralized and distributed power, made "a conservative democracy possible." In countries influenced by the Lutheran and Catholic churches, by contrast, democracy was "forced into an aggressive and revolutionary attitude."[60]

In Innis's account, conservative democracy emerged because Protestant doctrine emphasizing individual responsibility induced congregants to create forms of ecclesiastical governance in which power was distributed instead of centralized. It further induced a desire, particularly in Britain, to apply the same concept of governance to the political sphere, an application that in turn would distribute power among institutions, classes, and individuals. The process of political reform was not smooth. Innis writes that the central question of British politics in the seventeenth and eighteenth centuries was to what extent power should be centralized. Disagreement on the issue produced the first two civil wars of the English-speaking world. Within Britain, Charles I's efforts to centralize power over parliament resulted in the English Civil War. Within the First British Empire, the efforts of the British Crown and parliament to centralize power over the empire resulted in the American Revolution.[61] The outcome of centuries of religious and political conflict, Innis wrote, was a solution markedly similar to the solution France devised for the fur trade: a political structure characterized by distributed control, with the right mean between centralized and decentralized forms of control. For the United States and Britain the outcome was a "constitution emphasizing balance."[62]

> The revolt of the colonies against the centralizing tendencies of Crown and Parliament brought them face to face with the problem of framing an acceptable central organization in the Constitution. The influence of Milton and Locke, though weakened in England under Walpole and later George III, was reflected in the work of Frederick the Great and Voltaire and carried forward in the philosophy of Jefferson. It favoured decentralization. Hamilton and the federalists favoured centralization. The Declaration of Independence stood in sharp contrast to the Constitution. The compromise of balances in the Crown, Courts, Lords, and Commons in Great Britain emphasized by Blackstone and Montesquieu provided the pattern for checks between sources of power in the President, Congress, and the Supreme Court, and the necessity for appeal to the people.[63]

Several things followed, Innis argued, from the emergence of a conservative political culture composed of multiple institutions that shared power, and multiple individuals dedicated to finding the right balance between volition and self-restraint. One was the emergence of law.[64] By providing an institutional, cultural, and moral basis to restrain a culture's actors, most notably the state, law brought the essential prerequisite for a second development: the emergence of scholarship.[65] Scholarship, in turn, through philosophy and through science, provided the intellectual basis for a third significant development: economic liberty. In the wake of the Renaissance, and in the wake of scientists such as Isaac Newton, scholars began a collective effort to articulate the principles of natural and common law. They further embarked on a collective effort to harmonize human activity, particularly in law and economics, with those principles.[66] One important outcome of that effort was the emergence of classical political economy in Scotland.[67] Calvinist and Puritan doctrine, based on the maxims of self-assertion and self-restraint, and on the dogma of two orders and two sets of rules – one for the natural, the other for the divine – reached one of its highest intellectual expressions in the work of Adam Smith.[68]

The Enlightenment emphasis on balance, in Innis's account, led to the emergence of robust international and national institutions, political and economic actors with the capacity and will to adapt to changing circumstance and institute needed reforms. Innis described these developments in the concluding section of his ascension narrative. At the international level, the Church no longer functioned as the agent for restraint, but other institutions emerged to take its place, most notably commerce: "Weakening of the Church as a device to destroy fanaticism by the invention of printing, the rise of Protestantism, and the emergence of philosophy in the Age of Enlightenment left commerce as the great stabilizer. Its influence was evident in the comparative peace of the nineteenth century."[69]

Innis pointed also to a second constituent of "the delicate machinery for maintaining peace in the last century": transnational networks of policy makers engaged in personal diplomacy. Quoting John Morley, Innis argued that nineteenth-century diplomacy, at its height, had devoted itself to "reconciling interests, soothing jealous susceptibilities, allaying apprehensions, organizing influences, inventing solutions, that the world may move with something like steadiness along the grooves of deep pacific policy, instead of tossing on a viewless sea of violence and passion."[70]

At the national level, the American Revolution was a shock of the first order to Britain. But it also provided the needed impetus for reform – reform that would alter the political, legal, and economic structures of the United Kingdom and enable it to emerge with the United States as a conservative democracy characterized by balance:

"The effects of the contributions of Puritanism to political liberty evident in the revolt of the American colonies, and to economic liberty in the publication of the *Wealth of Nations*, have been described at great length. They compelled the shift from centralization to decentralization in the British Empire."[71]

Thanks to its embrace of decentralization, Britain, like the French fur trade, acquired the needed flexibility to adapt, and became a place where enlightened policy was conceived and then implemented. It pursued economic reform, through repeal of the Navigation Acts; legal reform, via Jeremy Bentham and others; and social reform through William Wilberforce and the abolitionist movement.[72] It was also a land in which critical thought and scholarship flourished. The eighteenth century and the early nineteenth saw the emergence of Smith, Ricardo, and Darwin.[73] It was a culture, Innis believed, that had found the right mean between freedom and constraint – a culture that, in the end, had found balance.

Innis's History of the West II: Information, Increasing Returns, and the Decline and Fall of the West

And then things fell apart. Britain and the United States, and by extension Canada and Europe, were subjected to a rapid influx of information, a development that eroded the intellectual, political, social, and cultural integrity of the Western world. In the phase of his narrative dedicated to decline, Innis pointed to five factors to explain the advent of information overload in the nineteenth century:

- *Demand for Information to Sustain Commercial Activity*. In Innis's narrative, information became an important commodity, particularly in the wake of industrialization. The acquisition of profit and wealth depended on the rapid acquisition and distribution of information.[74]
- *Improvements in Communication Technology*. For Innis, two developments were crucial in his reading of recent history: the convergence of steam and then electric power with the printing press; and the development of new methods for paper production. Both supported the rapid generation and distribution of content.[75]
- *The Emergence of State-funded Compulsory Systems of Education*. Public education systems led to the emergence of a public sphere – a new and important channel for information transmission

that would have important geopolitical and cultural consequences.[76]

- *The Emergence of a Free and Independent Press*. The press was the agent primarily responsible for the information explosion of the nineteenth century. Mid-century, the British press threw off the legal and fiscal constraints that had previously hindered it. Bereft of harsh libel laws and taxes on knowledge, it joined its American counterparts as an institution dedicated to the distribution of knowledge on a commercial basis.[77] That decision initiated the fifth cause of the information glut …
- *The Emergence of a Positive Feedback Process*. By propelling the commercial exchange of information, the press initiated an increasing returns or positive feedback process that encouraged the generation and distribution of ever-increasing quantities of information.

Here, Innis began to address on a deeper level a problem he had first raised at an academic roundtable in 1941. Social scientists who were veterans, he wrote, had "little excuse for forgetting either the lessons of the war or of the peace." The same scholars had no excuse for ignoring the contributions of "Adam Smith and his successors as to the significance of division of labour."[78] The central lesson of the First World War and the following peace, he said, was the press's role in catalyzing the emergence of positive feedback processes, which dramatically increased the quantity of extant information during the nineteenth century. That he had a positive feedback process in mind is indicated first by his reference to Smith's concept of division of labour, which, as we have seen, economists have long identified with the concept of increasing returns. It is also indicated by the substance of his narrative in *Political Economy*. In "The Newspaper in Economic Development," Innis argued that the press's commitment to distribute knowledge on a commercial basis put into effect a process of circular causation that increased distribution and the advertising revenue necessary to sustain it. Quoting Daniel Stuart, founder of the *Morning Post*, Innis noted: "'Advertisements act and react. They attract readers, promote circulation, and circulation attracts advertisements.'"[79]

Aside from tying information distribution to the acquisition of commercial revenue, Innis argued, newspapers further contributed to the information glut by pursuing "measures designed to increase the number of readers and to widen the market."[80] This they accomplished by pressuring governments to build transportation and communication infrastructure. As with the case of advertising, the resulting initiatives set in motion another self-sustaining process akin to increasing returns, one that led to the construction of more infrastructure and the distribution of more information: "The newspaper has been a pioneer in the development of speed in communication and transportation. Extension of railroads and telegraphs brought more rapid transmission of news and wider and faster circulation of newspapers; and newspapers, in turn, demanded further expansion of railroads and telegraph lines."[81] Newspapers in the United States and Britain furthered the impetus for information production by demanding that the state increase the size of their market through the institution of measures for compulsory education. Britain's Education Act of 1870, for example, developed a large public with the ability and desire to read.[82]

The impact of the rapid expansion in circulating information effected by increasing returns – at the social and individual level – was profound. Like Wiener, Innis used insights from his own discipline not only to indicate the presence of positive feedback processes in human culture but also to suggest their dangerous implications for human behaviour and cognition. While Wiener drew on observations of mechanical and organic systems, Innis used his studies of economic systems, and theoretical treatments of business cycles and commodity price variations, to suggest a linkage between social pathologies and the dynamic of increasing returns. For this latter task, Innis also relied on the theoretical works of Thorstein Veblen, particularly writings describing a rapid and violent form of economic change that Innis referred to as "cyclonics."

Excursus II: Innis, Increasing Returns and the Oscillation of Socio-Economic Systems

Innis's dependence on economic theory started with a simple proposition: business cycles are a useful frame of reference for studying human communication and the dynamics of the cultural systems that derive from human interaction. While Innis emphasized in *Political Economy* the contributions that studies of technology and culture could bring to economists' understanding of business cycles, his writings also indicate that a reverse situation could also obtain – that insights from business cycles could be used to better understand cultures and the history of technology. He posited that the respective domains of human activity could be used as analogues to better understand their counterparts.[83] This assertion informed his statement, when reviewing Adam Smith's "architectonic" theory, that political, ecclesiastical, and economic systems were formally and functionally equivalent. It was the also the basis of his interest in the history of human thought, and his observation to Arthur Cole that cultural thought moves in leaps and cycles.

This proposition would also form the basis for a later recommendation in *The Bias of Communication*, namely that social scientists, when studying culture, should apply all the concepts at their disposal, including economic theory. While conceding the danger of argument from analogy, Innis also suggested that scholars have an obligation to apply concepts and test their limits, all the more so because concepts such as the business cycle, its dynamic of increasing returns, and the dynamic's consequent of monopoly, had rarely if ever been applied to the domains of communication and culture: "the neglect of the field of communication in studies of cycles warranted a consideration of the extent to which monopolies of knowledge collapse and extraneous material is lost."[84] In short, the concept of the business cycle would enable scholars to gain a deeper understanding of the cycles of human thought.

Innis's resort to economic theory was also prompted by a second proposition: business cycles do not always proceed smoothly from one iteration to the next. Sometimes they accelerate or fluctuate wildly, and in extreme circumstances collapse. Given that economics and cultures move in cycles, one should also expect, from time to time, to see cultural activity collapse. Innis made this point most strikingly in Section II of "On the Economic Significance of Cultural Factors." It was there that he explicitly created an apposition of two narratives: one referring to the extension of the price system – and the business cycle as he knew it – across the North Atlantic in the sixteenth century; the other referring to the history of the West from the Reformation to the emergence of the printing press. His purpose, as suggested by the transition he makes between the first narrative and the second, was to express an analogy: "The emergence of a complex industrial and trading structure centering about the coal areas of the Anglo-Saxon world assumed not only improvements in transportation but also in communication."[85] This purpose is further suggested by the trajectory of each narrative, and by Innis's assessment of their collective significance. In the first, we read a narrative devoted to the exchange of commodities; in the second, a narrative devoted to the circulation of information. In both, we are told that when the terms of interaction are altered, a disturbance is effected that fundamentally alters the nature of the system in which the object circulates. In the economic system, the change led to the emergence of new regions specializing in new products; in the cultural system, the change prompted the emergence of a new form of governance, democracy, and a new basis for political power, public opinion.

Innis's aim in comparing economic and cultural systems was broader than to suggest that their trajectories were both subject to dissolution and self-organization. He intended also to suggest that both were governed by the same dynamics – increasing returns – and that the potential consequent of that dynamic was the oscillation of the given system and, from time to time, its collapse. His intentions are indicated by his description of the dynamics of economic systems in Section II, and his assessment of the significance of both narratives at the start of Section III. The trajectories of economic systems, Innis writes, are subject to disturbances in "the more or less regular trends" associated with the price system and the business cycle. They are "a result of sudden developments in which costs were lowered, of geographic factors such as access to the great plains and obstruction by mountains, of cyclonic activities such as accompanied the gold rushes around the fringes of the Pacific, and of the development of new sources of power in the opening up of the coal regions of North America."[86]

Here, Innis argues that the trajectories of systems are altered by new forms of interaction brought about by new forms of transport and energy. But he also points to something else: cyclonic activity. As we saw while discussing Innis's assessment of Veblen's writings (chapter 1), Innis saw cyclonics as a particularly violent form of the dynamic that Veblen championed throughout his writings, cumulative causation or increasing returns. At the start of Section III, he specified the consequent of that dynamic, and the significance of the economic and cultural histories he had just presented in Section II: "In all this we can see at least a part of the background of the collapse of Western civilization which begins with the present century."[87]

Finally, Innis's turn to economic theory to explore the social consequents of increasing returns was prompted by his own research into the history of the Klondike gold rush. The patterns of social change described in *Settlement and the Mining Frontier*, his account of that gold rush, precisely match those contained in *Political Economy*. In both, systems emerge that are governed by increasing returns. In both, systems become unstable. And in both, the social psychology of each system's participants changes for the worse, along irrational and nationalistic lines.

For Innis, the Klondike gold rush was significant for two reasons. First, it stimulated the economic boom of the early twentieth century by "the suddenness of the jerk which it gave a continent wallowing in depression." Few events, apart from those on the battlefield, could be said in the twentieth century to have "so profoundly affected the English-speaking people" and to have exercised "so wide an influence in so short a space of time." Second, "this cyclone," as Innis referred to the gold rush, was "a study in economic dynamics." More specifically, it was a form of economic change in which the stages of growth for a given system were compressed into a comparatively short span of time.[88] Economic systems, as Innis understood them, generally evolved through a number of stages, stages that defined:

- *The type of economic activity a given system practised*. In one decade a given region might grow wheat; in a succeeding decade it might raise dairy.
- *The complexity of economic activity*. In the first half of a given century, a given region might host one sector of economic activity, such as agriculture; in the second half, it might host multiple sectors, including
- and service industries.[89]
- *The technique underlying economic activity*. In the initiating phase of an industry, such as gold mining, the primary method for extraction might be manual labour, while in succeeding phases machine extraction might become the dominant method.[90]

Economic systems governed by cyclonics were distinguished by the rapidity with which they went through succeeding phases of economic evolution. Changes that under normal circumstances might have taken decades to realize emerged in as few as five to ten years in a cyclonic system. The reason one economic system became cyclonic while another did not, Innis argued, related to the characteristics of the commodity under extraction. Some commodities, such as gold, by virtue of their high value and their easy mobility, functioned as catalysts for the rapid emergence of new economic systems. Their presence in a given locale enabled them to attract personnel, equipment, and capital at a rate and quantity that less lucrative resources, such as timber, could not draw to other locales.[91] And because they were able to rapidly attract and mobilize large quantities of labour, cyclonic economies stimulated the very process Adam Smith predicted when masses of actors gather and undertake economic activity and exchange: division of labour.

The Klondike gold rush was an exemplar for Innis in this respect. It prompted economic diversification – division of labour – in the form of commercial activity to support the mining industry, and stimulated the emergence of other mining activities, specifically silver and lead.[92] It further stimulated increasing returns – high profits that funded the division of labour, attracted the construction of new transport mechanisms, and introduced novel methods and technologies for extracting gold. These innovations enabled individual and then corporate miners to enter the cumulative causal process described by Veblen, a process that enabled them to extract ever larger quantities of gold more cheaply. Gold's effectiveness in "commanding advanced technique," Innis argued, "increased the production of gold and produced a cumulative tendency."[93] The impact of the economic cyclone was "evident not only in the mobilization characterized by the rush of '98 but also in the enormous returns to the early miners ... The enormous returns available to mature technique led to the emigration of miners at an early date with sacks of gold which found its way into deposits and investments, and possibly to producer's goods and capital equipment in the case of the prudent ... Miners were in a position to emigrate, to remain with their claims, using the gold to introduce new methods of extraction, or to support the activities which characterized the boom of Dawson."[94]

Each change initiated by improvements in transport infrastructure or mining technique reduced costs and stimulated further mining activity. Quoting the Yukon's Gold Commissioner for 1901, Innis noted: "Every reduction in freight rates, every reduction [in] the cost of living in the Yukon Territory makes possible the introduction and operation of a higher class of machinery and cheaper production of gold ... Each change that lessens the cost of production increases the area for profitable working."[95]

The rapid onset of increasing returns had important and often destabilizing consequences for the Yukon and for North America as a whole. One metric that economists use to assess the relative stability of a business cycle is variation in price. When the prices of commodities and other items fluctuate wildly, the system can be said to be in a state of crisis. The economist John Maurice Clark, in a reference to W.C. Mitchell's *Business Cycles*, notes that the definition of a systemic crisis that emerges from Mitchell's work is one in which "business adjustments do not stop at a point of equilibrium, but go on to a point from which a more or less violent reaction is inevitable, and so on without apparent end."[96] Innis knew Mitchell's book. In fact, he identified its substance and significance with Veblen's work on dynamics and prices.[97] It is perhaps not surprising, then, that in describing the flux and division of labour engendered by an increasing returns economy, Innis commented on the fluctuating prices of the Yukon economy: "The transportation system was concerned primarily in 1898 with importation of supplies for the enormous increase in population. [Angelo] Heilprin stated that of the [thirty] passengers on the *Nora* 'the majority were going into the interior to make money through the sale of merchandise' ... Prices fluctuated widely as a result of the season of the year and of numerous unpredictable factors. A general lack of knowledge of the goods on hand made the market unsteady."[98]

In Innis's account, the Yukon's cyclonic economy and increasing returns prompted a second important consequent, acts that by his measures were irrational or promoted dangerous nationalism. In the conclusion of his account of the gold rush, Innis notes: "it is an interesting speculation as to the effects of the Yukon on the feverish activity and the psychology" on Canadian economic policy and North American diplomacy. According to Innis, the gold rush prompted the construction of two transcontinental railway lines, initiatives that he would criticize in a 1938 article as making little economic sense. The Grand Trunk Railway's creation of a rail line to the west, in particular, was a poor decision since its western terminus, Prince Rupert, offered a poor entryway into western Canada, and the line enjoyed no direct connection with the GTR's main network to the east.[99] Innis noted as well that the gold rush also prompted negative nationalism in Canada: "the bitterness which accompanied settlement of the Alaska boundary dispute was a result of the character of the boom."[100]

Innis's History of the West III: Oscillation and the Decline and Fall of the West

The behaviour that emerged from cyclonic systems experiencing increasing returns mirrored the behaviour Innis described in *Political*

Economy for socio-cultural systems experiencing increasing returns. It is important to note here that while Innis was deeply concerned about the present and historical dangers that positive feedback processes posed in the decline phase of his history of the West, he did not see information as an unalloyed evil. In fact, he saw it as a necessary constituent for the effective operation of distributed human systems such as the price system. The key, as he indicated in a passage describing the impact of advertising on the price system, was to find balance, the right mean between too little and too much circulating information: "Decline of advertising and of newspaper size and circulation reduces sensitivity of the price system and accentuates inflexibility and rigidity in depression; increase in advertising, size and circulation accentuates flexibility and elasticity."[101]

Information in the right quantities induced flexibility in distributed systems. Information in excess quantities, by contrast, induced the same instability that Innis had observed in cyclonic systems, and which Wiener had observed in mechanical and organic systems. In his historical narrative, the rapid oscillation in prices that Innis had observed in the Yukon was matched at the societal level by public opinion oscillating from one extreme to another. With the emergence of novel communication technologies, positive feedback processes governing the circulation and dissemination of information, and a literate public, Innis argued, it was worth noting that: "large majorities in political elections accompanied the spread of the newspaper on a large scale in England after the sixties in the last century, and the spread of the radio on this continent. Swings in public opinion are more violent with new inventions in communication, and independent thought is more difficult to sustain."[102]

Like Wiener, Innis observed that systems subjected to rapid influxes of information stimulated by positive feedback became unstable. And like Wiener, Innis further hypothesized, on the basis of his studies of cyclonic systems and the Yukon gold rush, that stresses engendered by information overload might explain the public hysteria and cognitive collapse he believed emerged particularly in Britain and the United States in the late nineteenth and early twentieth centuries. In short, he believed the publics in both countries had been exposed to increasing returns, too much information, and had virtually abandoned reason and gone insane. In his narrative, Innis frequently used words such as "irrational," "fanatic," and "emotional" to describe the public psyche that manifested in both countries in response to the rise of the popular press, a psyche that embraced nationalism and welcomed the prospect of war with Germany. Given the popular mindset he saw, and the heated behaviour he observed in the wake of the Yukon gold rush, the emergence of psychology had a special significance for him. Rhetorically, he asked: "Is the emergence of Freud and the psychologists a result of the spread of irrationalism or an effort to meet the problems of irrationalism?"[103] For Innis, the answer plainly was the former: "The outbreak of irrationality, which in the early part of the twentieth century became evident in the increasing interest in psychology following the steadying effects of commerce in the nineteenth century, is the tragedy of our time. The rationalizing potentialities of the price system and its importance in developing powers of calculation in the individual have failed to prevent a major collapse."[104]

At the individual level of human organization, Innis argued, the massive influx of information triggered by the press undermined individuals' capacity to reason effectively. It was for this reason that Innis voiced his concern that the press and radio had initiated "the production of words on an unprecedented scale and … made them powerless."[105] The British and American publics, Innis said, lost the capacity to translate the percepts contained in words and numbers into formal concepts that expressed the structure and operation of the systems governing political, social, and economic life, and which assisted in their detection. The loss of this capacity, Innis suggested, was due to the loss of the internal balance that was needed to support conservative democracy and individual and collective adaptation to changing circumstance. Humans at all levels of organization – individual, social, and even species – could not withstand the quantities of information being produced by new communication technologies. And for this reason, they could not sustain the internal balance between freedom and restraint enjoined by Calvinism: "It has been argued that man as a biological phenomenon has been unable to sustain the excessive demands of rationalism evident in the mathematics of the price system and of technology."[106]

Rational thought, the product of the balanced culture that had emerged in the eighteenth century, had produced novel communication technologies. Rational thought had in turn produced large quantities of circulating information. And rational thought had produced publics composed of irrational, unreasoning, reactive people. To support his argument, Innis pointed to the decline in culture he perceived to have ensued during the nineteenth century. A vibrant culture had a specific significance for Innis; it indicated the presence of individuals with the requisite balance between freedom and constraint. In the preface to *Political Economy*, Innis, pointing to the detrimental impact of newspapers on cultural growth, argued that: "States are destroyed by ignorance of the most important things in human life, by a profound lack of culture – which, following Plato, is the inability to secure a proper agreement between desire and intellect."[107] Internal balance was essential for the expression of cultural form and the capacity to perceive it. Unfortunately, the press undermined that capacity by generating huge quantities of information, and through it presenting a worldview that stemmed from unchecked excess, a worldview in which all was flux and everything disconnected. The novelist – and journalist – Charles Dickens in this respect was an examplar: "Bagehot commented on his style as reflecting 'the overflow of a copious mind, though not the chastened expression of an harmonious one.' His genius was suited to the delineation of city life since London was like a newspaper: 'Everything is there and everything is disconnected.' This haphazard absence of form encouraged by journalism influenced Thackeray as well as Dickens."[108]

The consequences associated with the individual citizen's loss of internal balance were seen on many levels. First, individuals began to see the world in the same incoherent way that it was being presented to them in the press, and lost the capacity to perceive aesthetic form. They further lost the mental discipline necessary to perceive spatio-temporal pattern, whether in art or a different domain of human society. And perhaps most seriously, with the loss of the capacity for discipline effected by information overload, many in Innis's narrative lost the recognition of any need for balance or discipline, as we saw via his reference to Gissing and Pattison, resting content instead in fragmented bits of knowledge rather than undertaking the work necessary to construct an enduring worldview. Referring to the work of Arnold Bennett, Innis noted "among the defects of the average reader's taste" in the nineteenth century "an absence of all sense of beauty of form."[109] The press had extinguished that sense through its sustained provision of new and different information. Quoting Walter Scott, Innis warned: "'if you are interrupted eternally with these petty avocations the current of the mind is compelled to flow in shallows.'"[110] Constant stimuli, in short, undermined the capacity to pay attention, and with it the capacity to attend to patterns extending across space, and more important, through time: "Improvements in communication have weakened the possibility of sustained thought when it has become most necessary."[111]

The second consequent was the extension of imbalance from the individual to the social, institutional, and international levels of human organization in Europe and North America. As we saw in Innis's account, commercial firms emerged after the invention of the printing press as "the great stabilizer" of power, supplanting the church as the institutions most responsible for checking the power of the state. By default or design, they became the sector of society that reminded state and citizenry that stability mattered, and that relations between states should be mediated by consideration of long-term interests, not short-term emotive concerns shaped by nationalism or other ideologies. However, their success in distributing goods and information, supported by the distributed control inherent in the price system, ultimately sowed the seeds for the disruption of balanced societies in the West and "an enormous extension of power in the modern state."[112]

The commercial sector supported the rise of the state by catalyzing the emergence of a positive feedback dynamic over the West's circulating information. In so doing, it prompted individuals to passively accept each new idea and construct as it emerged, a compulsive practice that Innis derided and characterized as the pursuit of fashion.[113] And at the same time, it also prompted fear in the populations of Britain, the United States, and Canada. Alarmed at the ever-changing nature of its own thinking, and by public discourse in general, the nineteenth-century public transferred its allegiance to the state. To purchase ideological, cultural, and social stability, members of the public consented to the creation of a regime more akin to Rome and the empires of the Near East than to the decentralized polities Innis favoured: "Irrationality introduces fear and the necessity of bureaucracies as at least a protection in continuity against the frequent changes incidental to fashion ... The blight of Oriental despotism which has ever threatened the western world becomes evident in bureaucracy and in turn in militarism. The interest in peace of an intelligent commercial and capitalist society is displaced by the control of the state in bureaucracy, militarism and war."[114]

With the rise of "the totalitarian state," the constraints that had until then maintained balance in societies bounding the North Atlantic fell by the wayside.[115] The first constraint to give way was social. Innis believed stable societies were made up of multiple classes. It was for this reason that he praised Blackstone's and Montesquieu's formulations on the balanced society, mentioned above, composed as they were of Crown, Courts, Lords, and Commons. And it was for this reason that he cited Lord Acton's warning at the beginning of the essay "Political Economy in the Modern State," that "government by the whole people, being the government of the most numerous and powerful class is an evil of the same nature as unmixed monarchy."[116] With the rise of education, the emergence of a free press, and the extension of the franchise in the nineteenth century, such a class – "the public" – emerged.[117] Popular opinion became the basis of political power because the public, through fear generated by instability, through irrational passion generated by circulating information, chose to derive its identity from the nation-state, at the expense of social and transnational sources of identity: "The printing press and new methods of communication have been developed as methods of division rather than cooperation. National and linguistic differences have been accentuated and internationalism weakened. The mechanization of art intensified nationalism."[118]

The second constraint that fell away was institutional. By the latter half of the nineteenth century, nationalism had become such a central feature of public life and policy that it began to interfere with activities – particularly trade – that had earlier been international in scope. Free trade policies instituted in the first half of the nineteenth century were supplanted in the latter half by tariff policies. Significant treaties guaranteeing free trade, such as the Reciprocity Treaty between the United States and Canada, and the Cobden Treaty between the United Kingdom and France, fell by the wayside.[119] For all intents and purposes, states made their own concerns the sole parameter for setting economic and foreign policy and as a result delimited the economic activity of their nationals to the space they controlled. With trade circumscribed by tariff barriers, the commercial sector lost its incentive to concern itself with international affairs, and in turn to regulate the behaviour of the state. In the domains of foreign and economic policy, balance was also lost.

Members of the business community and economic analysts could have protested, claimed Innis, but they did not. Both groups proved as susceptible to the detrimental impact of increasing returns and circulating information as other inhabitants of the nineteenth and twentieth centuries. Participants in the commercial sector accepted the legitimacy of nationalism, and focused on short-term economic opportunities stemming from the installation of tariff barriers: "Following its concentration on the problems of the immediate, commerce has lost its control as a stabilizer of power."[120] Economists, to Innis's chagrin, also accepted nationalism as the organizing principle of economic life. Worse, they displayed the same oscillating, irrational behaviour that Innis had observed in the English electorate during the 1860s and in economic and public actors during the Klondike gold rush. Commenting on the implications of the "Freudian concern with the irrational" in the social sciences, Innis noted "with alarm" the changing fashions in economics: "The breakup of the classical tradition of economics is an indication of the powerful influence of fashions in our times. At one time we are concerned with tariffs, at another with trusts, and still another with money. As newspapers seldom find it to their interest to pursue any subject for more than three or four days, so the economist becomes weary of particular interests or senses that the public is weary of them and changes accordingly. And this paper will be cited as an obsession with the obsession with the immediate. There is a need for a study of economics and insanity supporting that of Durkheim on religion and suicide."[121]

The third constraint to fall was transnational, specifically the informal network of policy makers in Europe's chancelleries and foreign ministries who had engaged in personal diplomacy during the nineteenth century to maintain communication, stability, and in the end, peace. In Innis's account, Europe's diplomacy shifted from the "grooves of deep pacific policy" to the "viewless sea of violence and passion" feared by John Morley, for two reasons. First, the tone of German diplomacy changed, particularly after the ascension of Kaiser Wilhelm II to the throne. Instead of maintaining stability, German diplomats indulged in "veiled menace or tart lecturing."[122] Second, the press chose to exploit personal conflicts between policy makers by featuring them in the news. Public exposure ended the effectiveness of informal diplomacy as an instrument for maintaining peace: "Why has European civilization turned from persuasion to force or from ballots to bullets? ... In the first place the delicate machinery for maintaining peace in the last century has apparently disappeared. The press thrived on personalities and instability followed."[123]

That, to say the least, was putting it mildly. As Innis concluded the decline phase of his narrative, he presented a vision of the North Atlantic international system on the verge of a geopolitical storm. It was not constituted of conservative democracies, but, as he understood it, comprised states more akin in substance to the Nazi totalitarian ideal of *ein Volk, ein Reich, ein Führer.* With one class – publics saturated with information and irrational in orientation; one institution – the state, dedicated to the use of force to resolve international disputes; and one mediator – the press, which presumed to describe the political, social, and economic present for its publics, there remained no systems of checks and balances in Britain, Canada, or the United States to maintain peace, and consequently no constraints to prevent each from sliding repeatedly into war. And so they did. Through the distribution of news, the media brought Innis's narrative to its most dreadful fulfillment: the collapse of the West and the onset of the First World War.[124]

IV

After the war, there was no real, robust recovery in the West. No changes were made to create enduring national and international polities. And no reforms were undertaken to create citizens characterized by a simultaneous commitment to liberty and law. In Innis's narrative, the West limped along, much as it had before the war. The world's subsequent collapse into depression and the Second World War simply confirmed the diagnosis he had made in the decline phase of his narrative: the West was out of balance. The stability of Europe and North America continued to be undermined by information overload and the dynamic of increasing returns. In the recovery and restoration phase of his narrative, Innis presented a programmatic statement indicating how he believed cultural balance and stability could be restored.

Restoration Measure I: Elevation of the University

Innis began his prescription for renewal by urging the university to reassert itself as the institution in the West promoting restraint. It was, after all, a role it had fulfilled before: during the Spanish Inquisition the University of Paris had distinguished itself by preventing the Church from generating the same hysteria in France as it had in Spain with the Inquisition.[125] In Innis's mind, it was time for the institution to distinguish itself again. Because of its traditional commitment to moderation and rational thought, the university stood the best chance of containing the hysteria generated by the press and exploited by the state. In this task, Innis anticipated that scholars in the social sciences and humanities would take a leading role: "The place of the social sciences in Western civilization must be seen in relation to the role of universities. The university has played its greatest role in serving as a stabilizing factor. However inadequately it has played this role in various periods in the history of civilization, it has served as a repository of the reasoning of the ablest minds attracted to it. It has preferred reason to emotion, Voltaire to Rousseau, persuasion to power, ballots to bullets ... It must continue its vital function in checking the dangerous extremes to which all institutions with power are subject. The extreme tendencies of modern civilization shown in the rise of the modern state and in the tyranny of opinion compel universities to resist them."[126]

While the ideal of the social sciences as a force for moderation was compelling in principle, Innis believed that in their current state they were not prepared to assume that role. Quoting Goldwin Smith, Innis noted that "social science if it is to take the place of religion as a conservative force has not yet developed itself or got firm hold of the popular mind."[127] Part of his purpose in making this statement can be determined by considering the context in which it was expressed, namely section IV of "On the Economic Significance of Cultural Factors." There, Innis reiterated his concern that excess information had diminished popular and scholarly thought to the point that both groups had become passive recipients of the ideas to which they were exposed. And there, he emphasized that social science scholars could break the cognitive log-jam in which they were situated by recognizing the fundamental limitations of their respective disciplines. Sociocultural reality was too complex to be characterized using the methods of a single discipline, or expressed using the formalisms of a single discipline.

Restoration Measure II: Information Compression and Visualization

Innis proposed that the social sciences could gain analytical purchase and social stability through the invention of new formalisms, or the appropriation of extant formalisms from neighbouring disciplines. Such acts, he believed, would create conditions conducive for thought by reducing the volume of information circulation in the West.[128] To effect this strategy, Innis argued, invented or appropriated formalisms must first meet the pervasive need for information compression. The task of scholars was to locate forms of representation that communicated essential patterns more quickly and more economically than potential alternatives. Conversely, their task was also to reduce their dependence on formalisms – such as text – that hindered reader perception, enabling them to perceive only fragments of aesthetic, economic, cultural, or social systems.

Innis best expressed his interest in information compression in *Empire and Communications*. There, he presented a narrative of Roman history strikingly similar in content and analysis to his history of the West in *Political Economy*. In the second century BCE, Rome was exposed to a rapid influx of information through its conquest of Greece, its access to papyrus from Egypt, and the emergence of a book trade.[129] That development, Innis suggested, put Rome in jeopardy. It faced the prospect of losing its creative spark and becoming a passive recipient of the ideas to which it was exposed, a danger to which it ultimately succumbed: "Following success in the East, Rome came under the direct influence of Hellenism. 'Captive Greece took captive her proud conqueror' (Horace)."[130] For a time Rome was able to resist the influx of Greek information by retaining its use of Latin prose to support the generation of constructs in scholarship and legal practice, Latin being a much smaller domain of circulating information than its Greek counterpart. Rome also protected itself by adopting shorthand to express and transcribe content. In his discussion of both measures Innis laid great stress on the activities of Cicero, the Roman scholar and statesman.

Innis began his narrative by noting that Roman "opposition to Greek culture" in response to the emergence of Greek influence "favoured an emphasis on Latin prose which had been confined to blunt sentences." In his estimation, "Prose gained fresh power in attempts to meet problems of the Republic," in large measure because it was developed by Latin schools of rhetoric, a development that reached its climax under Cicero.[131] Innis credited Cicero with developing Latin to the point that it became a "philosophical language." He did so by increasing the formal complexity of the language, making it a more flexible instrument that could support rather than constrain thought. More specifically, he made it an instrument that supported the active construction of thought, or the oral tradition. Broken speech was converted into a literary instrument with "concentration and surcharge, magnificent sonority and architectonic sentence building." Written speech became almost the equal of oral speech.[132]

Thanks to this innovation, Cicero was able to undertake activities consistent with those of Innis's account of the Renaissance, Adam Smith in the eighteenth century, and British political and legal reforms in the early nineteenth century. Cicero pointed to the concept of natural law, the need for balance between freedom and constraint, the need to harmonize human activity with natural law, and the need for social reforms. In this task, he was assisted by Greek Stoic philosophy. But Cicero was not a passive recipient of Greek ideas. According to Innis, he creatively applied this philosophy to new circumstances: "Through Cicero ... Stoicism received fresh support in its influence on Roman law. Stoic philosophy brought the ideas of the world state, natural justice, and universal citizenship in an ethical sense, which were independent and superior to the enactment of kings. The conception of natural law brought enlightened criticism to bear on custom, helped to destroy the religious and ceremonial character of law, promoted equality before the law, emphasized the factor of intent, and mitigated unreasoning harshness ... The *jus gentium* began to be conceived as a law common to all mankind and equivalent to the law of nature. 'We are servants of the law in order that we may be free.'"[133]

The creative ferment stemming from Cicero's reforms proved to be short-lived. The pressure stemming from the influx of Greek information proved too strong, and "the effect of writing" became "evident in every phase of cultural life." In culture, the number of written plays in circulation increased. The effect was to diminish the quality of drama, a development that "drove the intelligent from the theatre." In law, jurists ceased their interest in making law consistent with natural law: "Literal interpretation led to neglect of the matter itself. 'The reasons underlying the legal system should not be inquired into, otherwise much that is certain would collapse' (Neratius)."[134]

According to Innis, Cicero and his contemporaries were able to apply one last innovation – information compression in the form of shorthand – to briefly protect Rome's creative spirit: "As the Written Tradition was extended shorthand was introduced to bridge the gap with the Oral Tradition. Cicero dictated to Tiro, a freedman who used shorthand." The innovation worked for a time, but by the first century BCE even that innovation failed. Moves to publish Senate minutes and expedite court proceedings forced lawmakers and jurists to express themselves to a public oriented to receiving unassimilated, fragmented information. The constraint "reinforced the demand for matter-of-fact style in the Senate and brought disaster to the style of Cicero." With the loss of an important tool to support creative thought, Roman life and culture quickly slid into the stance of passivity in relation to knowledge that Innis associated with the Written Tradition.[135]

Information compression was, at least for a time, a useful method to stem the damaging effects of information overload. But how were scholars to apply this insight in the twentieth-century postwar period? Innis answered this question – obliquely – in "On the Economic Significance of Cultural Factors." After stating that social scientists should undertake inter-disciplinary study to demonstrate the warping effects that mathematics had had on the humanities, Innis indicated what he believed economic historians should do in response: "Economic history may provide grappling irons with which to lay hold of areas on the fringe of economics, whether in religion or in art, and with which, in turn, to enrich other subjects, as well as to rescue economics from the present-mindedness which pulverizes other subjects and makes a broad approach almost impossible."[136] This passage, read in conjunction with *The Bias of Communication* and the "History of Communication" provides a basis for suggesting that Innis believed information visualization should serve as the basis for a strategy of information compression. He proposed that researchers in the social sciences and the humanities expand their expressive toolkit beyond text, to include multiple formalisms capable of supporting his two postwar imperatives: information compression and pattern detection.

Primary among these formalisms was information visualization; that is, the translation of data into a visual analogue, such as a two- or three-dimensional graph. Why did Innis consider it important for scholars to more extensively adopt the practice? First, it is based on the realization that not every expressive form is equally adept at transmitting an important pattern latent in data or a primary source. Consider the stock market. There are in principle two ways of following its trajectory, numerically and graphically. At any given point in the day, an investor can access the numerical value of a given stock. However, if the investor's aim is to detect long-term changes in stock value, then a sequential list of prices is of little help. The recipient of the content would have to memorize the information and then mentally abstract some sort of pattern from it. Alternative forms of representation such as the graph, by contrast, demand less cognitive work because they transmit a manageable amount of information for the user to process, and more clearly express the pattern the user needs. An investor can determine at a glance the historical changes in value of a given stock, its rate of growth or decline, and its volatility. In this context, one form of expression – numerical information – is poor at conveying an important pattern; the investor has easy access to fragments of information, but a larger pattern must be abstracted. Graphical information, on the other hand, is optimal, as the viewer can detect the relevant pattern at a glance.

Innis's interest in information visualization can be confirmed by reading passages from the "History of Communication" and *The Bias of Communication* in which he treats the expressive practices of the two domains cited in "On the Economic Significance of Cultural Factors": art and religion. In the domain of art, Innis noted, Italian artists in the fifteenth and sixteenth centuries routinely used multiple forms of representation because of the "general inability to conceive abstract ideas." Information visualization and the use of multiple formalisms helped make difficult ideas accessible and comprehensible to a general populace: "The emblem book was devised by Andreas Alciati early in the sixteenth century ... Poetry, one of the oldest arts, was combined with engraving, one of the newest. 'Emblems reduce intellectual conceptions to sensible images and that which is sensible strikes the memory and is more easily imprinted on it than that which is intellectual' (Bain)."[137]

Multiple formalisms and information visualization also played a crucial role in serving the expressive needs of the Church, particularly in its use of architecture, sculpture, and stained glass. Because of architecture's capacity to vividly express religious truths to a large audience, Innis set great store by Victor Hugo's maxim that "architecture was the great handwriting of the human race."[138] In *The Bias of Communication* he noted: "Stone in architecture and scripture emphasized permanence and durability. In the thirteenth century 'Tout ce que les théologiens, les encyclopédistes, les interprètes de la Bible on dit d'essentiel a été exprimé par la peinture sur verre ou par la sculpture' [Everything essential that theologians, encyclopaedists, Bible interpreters said was expressed through stained glass or sculpture] ... In the Reformation print was used to overwhelm sculpture and architecture as interpreters of scripture."[139]

Innis championed visual forms of representation in part to counteract the pernicious effects of mathematical formalisms on thought and practice in the social sciences and the humanities. He complained of the "superficiality in the mathematical approach" in the social sciences insofar as it failed to capture the complexity of social and cultural phenomena: "This is to recognize that the subject is more difficult than mathematics and to insist that tools must be used, and not described, if interpretation is not to be superseded by antiquarianism." A more important objection to extensive reliance on mathematical formalisms was that they failed to support a fundamental task of the social sciences: pattern detection. They were not designed to express temporal patterns, even the temporal pattern of greatest concern, increasing returns.[140]

In economics, mathematical formulae supported and reinforced economists' inclination to undertake analyses of static systems in equilibrium, analyses that were useful for the present or, at best, for a very limited duration into the future. Not until the early 1980s did economists have the mathematical tools to model increasing returns systems, and that deficiency caused Innis to argue that the social sciences should shed their emerging dependence on mathematics. In addition, because of its specialty, the field of economic history had an important role to play in devising or appropriating formalisms that would support pattern detection and, in turn, cultural adaptation to changing circumstance. The discipline was ideally suited for such a task, he claimed, thanks to "its concern with long-run trends and its emphasis on training in search of patterns rather than mathematical formulae."[141]

Restoration Measure III: Pattern Detection

The cause of spatio-temporal pattern detection required more, however, than the transformation of information, the conversion of content from one formalism into another. It also required, in Innis's view – collocation and interpolation of information across space and through time. Such measures would enable cultures, individuals, and institutions to perceive the systems that defined their activities and constrained them. Eighteenth-century Britain had been ignorant of its systemic context, and pursued policies that in the end cost it the

First British Empire. Innis believed the world could no longer afford a similar degree of ignorance. To support the task of pattern detection, he urged his colleagues to place renewed emphasis on another category of formalism: the series – and, in his economic work, the time series – as a formalism to support expression and analysis.[142] A series is a construct that aggregates content of a particular type or category – qualitative, quantitative, or both – and arranges it into a sequence, as a spatial array, a temporal array, or both. A time series is a more limited construct that arranges quantitative data into a temporal sequence.

Innis championed the series because he believed it to possess a quality that I characterize in this chapter and the next as Innis's principle of number. Like the ancient philosopher Pythagoras, Innis subscribed to a "theory of number" in which number was an underlying "principle of all things: 'Things are numbers.'"[143] Innis so believed because he saw numbers as forms of representation that supported the twin expressive requirements of correspondence and succession. Numbers were instruments of representation that could be used to refer to objects in the real world, distinguish them from their neighbours, and present them in a spatial or temporal sequence. Innis did not believe that forms characterized by the principle of number were always constituted by the formalism of number. The time series supported the twin expressive requirements of correspondence and succession, but so also did the poem. By contrast, Innis held that all forms in this category had a common application: pattern detection. All could be used to establish a relationship between one percept and another: to support the integration of multiple percepts into the construct of a system; and to support the observation of a given system's trajectory through time.

Innis also pressed for the use of series because of their association with statistics and a probabilistic construct of change. These three, used in conjunction, could establish a relationship between one percept and another (correspondence), and the probable future trajectory of a given system (succession). Both for Innis the economic historian and for Innis the communication theorist, these properties were important because they enabled social scientists to map systems and describe their behaviour. From the standpoint of pattern detection, they were also vital because they enabled a researcher to identify the variable – the control parameter – that prompted system dissolution and self-organization.

Innis finally advocated the use of series because they could be used to map and understand systems in which constraints operated locally, not universally. Linear mathematics are unsuitable for such a purpose insofar as they are designed to describe the determinate change imposed on systems governed by universal constraint. Innis was interested in a different category of system: emergent systems, systems such as series, in which constraints operate locally, not universally. They are governed by formal cause, which imposes different constraints on different constituents to preserve and enhance the system's integrity. To explain the operation and constitution of a given system requires the support of a formalism that can differentiate events according to space and time. The mathematics of Innis's time – at least as applied in economics – could not meet these requirements, while series could, and so Innis pressed for their application.

If we are to detect the principle of number, probability, and localized constraint in Innis's writings, we will need to apply a pattern detection measure of our own: we will need to take a final excursion and learn more about time series. It is vital that we do so, or we will miss much that is important in *Political Economy* and Innis's more celebrated communication studies. In this chapter, it will help us to understand Innis's belief that formalisms characterized by the principle of number could be used to map social, cultural, and economic systems. In the next, it will help us to understand the important role that probabilistic change played in Innis's theory of media. Innis has often been accused of being a technological determinist. The charge is without foundation, as a review of time series and probabilistic change will allow us to demonstrate.

This review also enables us to weigh the importance that Innis assigned localized constraint in supporting human communication. The topic is worth considering because of the insights it offers regarding Innis's writings on the oral tradition, a regime of communication he identified with the principle of number and the series. It is also worth pursuing because it provides a basis to identify Innis with another communication theorist from his time, Claude Shannon. Since Innis did not present a detailed justification for the application and interpolation of series, we turn again to the writings of Norbert Wiener, who advocated a similar methodology in his own writings.

Excursus III: Norbert Wiener and the Efficacy of Time Series

In his disparate writings, Wiener defined the time series as a multiple measurement of an object susceptible to numerical representation, "a sequence of quantities recorded in equal intervals of time." For example, if we measure and record the temperature of Ottawa at 6 p.m., and continue the process for the next 365 days, we have a time series. At a fundamental level, Wiener argued, time series are used for the "recording, preservation, transmission and use of information."[144] Use of information in this context, according to Neil Gershenfeld and Andreas Weigend, contemporary specialists on time series, can essentially be reduced to three tasks: forecasting, modelling, and characterizing systems.[145]

Forecasting refers to the generation of predictions regarding the short-term behaviour of a system. *Modelling* refers to a description of the long-term behaviour of a system. For example, the English language is a system; a statement of its phonetic, syntactic, and stylistic rules would constitute a model of its long-term behaviour.[146] Finally, *system characterization* refers to attempts to unearth a system's fundamental properties, where the observer is deprived of *a priori* knowledge about the system. Areas of possible inquiry include the number of degrees of freedom a system enjoys, and its degree of randomness.[147]

Wiener argued that time series should be used for similar purposes, although his statements were less precise. His stated object in studying time series was to devise a "metrical theory of causality," a means to mathematically demonstrate relative degrees of causation – that event *a*, for instance, was more responsible for causing event *b* than event *b* for causing *a*.[148] In the determinate world of Newtonian physics, Wiener argued, the concept of degrees of causation was meaningless. In a system in which the position and momentum of all objects – and the rules governing those objects – are known, "the future of the world can be determined down to the last detail ... Here the whole world at one instant may be regarded as the cause of whatever happens at later instants, and nothing less than the whole world will do as a cause."[149]

The problem with such a conception was that it was not very useful, and flew in the face of experience. A judge trying a murder case was not likely to consider the stars running in their courses a significant cause in the victim's death. By contrast, the fact that the perpetrator chose to drop a brick from the top of Rockefeller Center would be considered important. The basis for Weiner's conclusion sprang not from the single observation that dropping a brick led to a death, but from the realization that in the majority of cases in which a brick had been dropped, someone had died: "The basis of causality is now taken to be statistical and the effectiveness of causality depends upon the fact that certain things happen more often than they do not."[150] The issue of causation is therefore "directly correlated to the notion of probability. If over a large series of cases, under fairly uniform conditions, in nine occurrences where occurrence *a* takes place, it is followed by occurrence *b* in three cases; but in a similar way if out of nine cases where occurrence *a* does not take place occurrence *b* may be expected once, we had better look for occurrence *b* when we see occurrence *a*. Causality is a notion allied to frequency of occurrence."[151]

Wiener further argued that the frequency of occurrence between two events could be established in some cases by resort to the mathematics of statistical mechanics, and to the use of time series. His writings suggest that in making this point he proposed to demonstrate the utility of time series for the purposes of system characterization and prediction. In this sense, his reference to a "metric theory of causation" was unfortunate, since he did not mean to establish that event A "caused" event B in the way we would understand a moving ball to cause a stationary one to move. Rather, he intended to produce a way of demonstrating that event A was related to event B within the context of a larger system, and that time series could be used to demonstrate the characteristics and future behaviour of that system.

To illustrate his point, Wiener began with the proposition that "if we have two series of events in time, when we study each one separately there is a certain amount of information given concerning its future, but its past is determined."[152] Here he briefly touched on some tenets of information theory that require elaboration to follow the remaining portion of his argument. As Alicia Juarrero notes, there is no pattern in nature, no information in a message, without an ordering context to constrain the pattern's components. If there is no constraint, there is no relation between components: "The most random state ... is characterized by events which are both independent and equiprobable."[153] The effect would be akin to randomly typing sets of letters and numbers on a keyboard. The probability of any one character appearing at any time is the same. While the quantity of potential information or message variety is high, the possibility of conveying information is zero.[154]

Accordingly, for actual information content to be present, an ordering process must be present to harness the random components. The generation and transmission of a television signal, for example, requires encryption rules that take the signal away from equiprobability and randomness: television snow. According to Juarrero: "Constraining 'the number of ways in which the various parts of a system can be arranged' ... reduces randomness by altering the equiprobable distribution of signals, thereby enabling potential information to become actual information."[155]

Two orders of constraint may be said to limit and shape systems. One operates in a context-free fashion; it removes the equiprobability of random noise and imposes a probability distribution on the available alternatives. Hence, the constraints imposed by spelling conventions in English lead to letters such as "e" and "s" appearing more often than "z". Knowledge of a system's probability distribution is useful insofar as it enables the observer to differentiate systems. When looking at a document in which the letters "x" and "z" are more plentiful than the letter "a", the observer has a basis for determining the document was not written in English.

Information systems governed solely by universal constraints, however, contain an important drawback: the greater the certainty in message transmission, the greater the reduction in message variety. Taken to its limit, namely 100 percent certainty regarding message transmission, such a scenario in our example would mean the effective transmission of only one letter. The principle is analogous to that which applies in a complex adaptive system. Apply a certain value of the control parameter, and you get flux or noise. Apply a different value and you get stasis or a single message. The attainment of message variety requires the application of an order of constraint that allows users to tread the "'fine line' between constraint and total freedom."[156]

In 1948 Wiener's colleague Claude Shannon made a seminal contribution to communications theory by showing how increased message variety could be reconciled with the goal of noise reduction. In essence, the strategy was to adopt a means of encoding that localized constraint, the means employed in complex adaptive systems, to obtain heightened complexity, the state analogous to increased message variety.[157] Recall that an emergent system can be characterized not only as a network of agents and processes but also as a hierarchy of agents and processes. A system at one level of organization becomes an agent of the next; cells become constituents of organs, organs of organisms.

It is this capacity to localize constraint that enables complex adaptive systems to reach the requisite compromise between entropy and order. While component systems retain their integrity, their capacity to self-organize on multiple levels into ever-larger hierarchies exponentially increases both the potential number of combinations a system can visit, and the behavioural competence of the system.[158] A similar principle applies in language. Spelling, syntax, and grammar rules are akin to self-organizing systems insofar as they make words and letters interdependent. That interdependence, however, means that more words can be created than the twenty-six letters of the alphabet, more sentences than the total number of words in the English language.

The principle of contextual constraint has another important implication: history matters. In the case of sentence generation, the presence of a letter becomes contingent not only on the probability distribution governing the alphabet but also on the sequence of letters and words that precede it. If the letter "q" appears in an English sentence the distribution of possible outcomes is quite narrow. The odds that the next letter will be "u" are high, while the corresponding odds that "q" will appear again are low.[159]

It was this twofold sense of restraint, and the reduced distribution of possible outcomes that restraint imposes, that Wiener referred to when he asserted that a time series contains information about its future. Predictions could be made with time series that were in statistical equilibrium; that is, with series in which the probability distribution of a set of terms in the series "is not changed by moving the entire set bodily forward and backward in time."[160] This requirement corresponds with the concept of context-free constraint. As we saw, English use of the alphabet is governed by a particular probability distribution. The frequency of letter use remains the same, whether in the year 2012 or 2013.

In addition to context-free restraints, however, Wiener also pointed to a second order of constraints, those that were context-specific. The observer, he argued, must first note specific features of the time series that are related to the goal of prediction: "This we term information, and we can define and measure it according to certain rules ... When we know the past of a time series, the distribution of its future is replaced by a narrower distribution which will correspond to a greater amount of information concerning the future. This increase of information may be taken as a measure of its efficacy, of the past in causing the future, and the negative may be taken as an indication of the degree of randomness of the time series."[161]

For Wiener, the goal of prediction was of a piece with the goal of system characterization. He did not take it as given that the past of a particular time series would be the best predictor of its future. In an attempt to assess the future variability of temperatures in Tokyo, for example, the city's past temperatures might provide comparatively little information, indicating a high degree of randomness in the time series. While such a series in isolation was of comparatively little value, if it was viewed in conjunction with another time series, say that for the city of Osaka, it had the potential to explain a great deal. Here, Wiener emphasized two points. First, the principle of the past constraining the future applied not only within time series but also between time series. Second, when two time series are interpolated, we "receive more information concerning the future of each than if we were studying them separately."[162] In other words, the past weather of Tokyo might serve as a more adequate frame of reference for predicting the future weather of Osaka, or vice versa.

The means of evaluating the predictive value of each series was to take a set of temperatures from each city and evaluate their success in predicting the subsequent temperatures of their counterpart. The greater success of Osaka temperatures in constraining the subsequent variability of Tokyo's temperatures could be used as a basis for making three conclusions: that Osaka and Tokyo were affected by the same weather front; that this front moved in an easterly direction; and that Osaka weather could be used to predict Tokyo weather.[163] Using a similar example with reference to North America, Wiener noted: "[Double time series] occasionally make their appearance in engineering applications, but they are most conspicuous in the statistical applications (both economico-sociological and meteorological-geophysical), since in both instances, the relative lead of one time series with respect to another may well give much more information concerning the past of the second than of its own. For example, on account of the general eastward movement of the weather, Chicago weather may well be more important in the forecasting of Boston weather than Boston itself."[164]

Restoration Measure III, Continued: Innis, Interpolation, and Pattern Detection

Innis's methodological writings in *Political Economy*, his practice, and his contemporary correspondence all suggest similar aims to those of Wiener; namely, the use of series to model and characterize systems of interest to the social sciences. The practice of interpolation –of analytic frameworks, formalisms such as series, and data from multiple disciplines – was fundamental to the purpose of pattern detection and, as he would note in 1952, for escaping "from the obsessions of one's own culture."[165] Interpolation forced analysts to look at phenomena they would otherwise not consider. It was also fundamental for discovering relationships between series and histories that were persistent or, in Wiener's words, which displayed frequency of occurrence. Tracing such relationships would enable social scientists to map the spatial extent of systems as well as their constituent regions or components. It would also permit identification of their control parameters and the governance of formal cause.

In "On the Economic Significance of Cultural Factors" Innis argued that the methodology of interpolation necessarily proceeded from the practice of interdisciplinary research. Scholars needed to expand the analytical and expressive instruments in their respective toolkits. In turn, they needed to extend themselves, to accept "the limitations of economic history or of the social sciences or more specifically of one framework of the price system."[166] Such intellectual modesty was necessary, he charged, because scholars were not distinguishing themselves when it came to differentiating the essential from the peripheral while working on a given problem. Historians, for example, were improperly emphasizing politics at the expense of economics. Events such as the American Revolution could not be properly understood if divorced from their economic context. Scholars who focused on specific institutions such as the church or the state were missing important constituents of change, and risked turning the discipline into little more than the handmaid of the powerful: "Economic history can point to the dangers of bias and the necessity for a broader perspective."[167]

But history was not the only discipline at risk. Economic historians, Innis argued, also risked imposing undue biases on their thought, practice, and scholarship by focusing too narrowly on quantitative data relating to prices and interest rates. While useful for detecting economic and social patterns, such studies had little probative value, since they were not juxtaposed with their cultural and technological contexts. Other scholars realized the importance of combining political, pecuniary, and technological approaches, but imposed a national framework on their studies that may or may not have cohered with the economic system under discussion. Historians of technology failed to link their studies with politics or geography.[168] The essence of systems – their spatial extent, their complexity, their behaviour, and their trajectory – would only be captured if scholars applied multiple frameworks and multiple formalisms, including the series.

Innis's methodology of interpolation was likely an extension of his own practice as an economic historian. His correspondence for the period when he was working on the articles associated with *Political Economy* indicates that he was also thinking about the efficacy of time series to support pattern detection. In a letter to Arthur Cole in 1941 Innis revealed that he had already enjoyed a measure of success in employing his methodology in studies of Canada's economic history. Such a "geographic approach" had illuminated the "history of areas in which a given industry remains dominant over a long period – i.e. fur and fish."[169] In his studies of staples and transport systems, Innis had discovered that Canada's economy functioned much like a weather system, insofar as sectors specializing in wheat or other commodities were akin to weather fronts that started in the east and moved west.[170] The factor precipitating change – the control parameter – Innis argued to Cole, was largely the transportation cost. "As technological improvements in transportation emerged the production of geographic areas changed. For example the wheat belt moved steadily west and its place was taken by dairying or some other form of agriculture."[171]

With respect to Canada, then, Innis was able to map the regional patterns defining Canada's economic history, by examining the history and price of commodity production in the country's disparate regions, and juxtaposing those findings with the history of technology and transport rates. He was also able to determine the system's control parameter by detecting a persistent relationship between changes in transport technologies and rates, and subsequent transformations of the Canadian economy. The pattern of change in British and Canadian technological history had proven to be one that had narrowed the probability distribution of Canada's economic future. It engendered a period of economic disequilibrium, self-organization, and change in economic specialization prompted by formal cause, with the newest region of Canada becoming the agent specializing in wheat. Accordingly, Innis was able to characterize Canada's economic history as a "succession of waves of frontiers the character [of] which is largely dependent on transportation rates."[172] He further claimed that if his method were applied to American economic history, a similar result would obtain. He predicted to Cole that "if one could see over a long period changes in transportation rates between Europe or Great Britain to North America and between different parts of North America one would at least have a picture of the succession of production waves which marched across North America."[173]

In short, Innis considered the series to be an essential instrument for the detection of pattern. It was, in turn, an essential instrument for detecting and mapping the behaviour of emergent cultural systems, which were dependent on information to adapt, and which were put into peril and sometimes collapsed from the very thing that enabled them to live, move, and have their being. Innis's purpose in *Political Economy* had been to alert contemporaries to the dangers of information, the dynamics of information, and the communication technologies that gave rise to both. He traced their histories He identified their pathologies. And he proposed countermeasures to mitigate their pernicious and often lethal effects. In his reading of history, the West could no longer afford to be a naïve vessel, a recipient and user of information. In evolutionary terms, it needed to engage in a form of niche construction through the use of information compression, information visualization, and pattern detection. Without these active measures, the West would continue to flail, continue to fight and, in the end, continue to squander its most precious resource: the young.

V

What are the implications of this reading for our understanding of Innis and his thought? It suggests, to start, that *Political Economy* is a far more important work than scholars have traditionally appreciated. It highlights a consequent of communication technology that readings of his more celebrated works have missed: communication technology not only produces cognitive rigidity but it also produces oscillation. In Innis's scheme of history, there is a bias of communication. There is also a flux of communication.

Our reading also suggests that Information, Increasing returns, and Emergent Change were central concepts in Innis's communication thought, as important as the better-known concepts of bias, monopoly of knowledge, and the oral tradition. A realization of this nature should interest Innis scholars because it indicates that Innis meant what he said when he suggested that there was an underlying unity to his work. The bases of that unity were analytical instruments, including business cycle theory and monopoly theory. Our reading has shown that these two instruments were constituents of a worldview that emphasized emergent change and increasing returns. It has also shown that Innis applied these concepts both in his economic studies and in his communication writings. Most Innis scholars assert that Innis's early and late works are of a conceptual piece. This study shares that conclusion. It also deepens it.[174]

With respect to Innis, this review suggests a further implication: that he should be considered an information theorist in his own right. Norbert Wiener is considered to be such a theorist – in part – because of his suggestion that information feedback processes impinge on the behaviour of biological and mechanical systems. Innis made a similar argument, suggesting that information and increasing returns impinged on the behaviour of social systems. His writings were composed in parallel with those of Wiener and, more important, were produced independently of Wiener, with Innis drawing on economics and Wiener on engineering to inform their respective analyses.[175] Innis made a significant intellectual leap on his own. That accomplishment deserves to be recognized, and scholars should do so.

This reading is important finally because it suggests that scholars would profit from keeping Information and Increasing Returns in mind when reading *Empire and Communications* and *The Bias of Communication*. The fruitfulness of such an approach is indicated by comments from Nobel economist Kenneth Arrow. He notes that in the wake of Adam Smith "other analysts in different traditions … saw clearly enough" the significant implication of Division of Labour, or Increasing Returns, namely "the incompatibility of increasing returns and perfect competition, and developed theories of monopoly and oligopoly to explain the economic system implied by increasing returns."[176] It is telling that in "Minerva's Owl," the oft-cited chapter from *Bias*, Innis chose to characterize his intellectual agenda in a way that suggests his intellectual debt to the concept of Increasing Returns. There, his stated purpose was to describe the impact of communication media on "the character of knowledge and to suggest that a monopoly or an oligopoly of knowledge is built up to the point that equilibrium is disturbed."[177] And there, Innis indicated his intent to construct a philosophy of cultural history based on the constructs of emergence and formal and final cause. Again, let us see how.

5

Empire and Communications and *The Bias of Communication*

In May 1948 Harold Innis received one of the singular honours of his long and distinguished career. He was invited to be the featured speaker at Oxford's Beit Lectures, an annual series of talks devoted to a topic in the history of the British Empire. By all rights, the experience should have been one of the highlights of his academic career, but it did not turn out that way. Harold Innis had many fine qualities as a scholar, but even sympathetic critics acknowledged that his lectures could be excruciatingly boring. Hugh Aitken, a former student of his, recalled that the talks at their worst were infuriating, in part because "one was being asked to believe that behind the ambiguity and imprecision there was profound meaning."[1] Canadian audiences generally tolerated the imprecision.[2] The British were less accommodating. Not only had Innis committed the cardinal sin of being boring, but he was also off topic. Instead of giving a lecture devoted to the topics of fur or fish, Innis provided an incoherent rendition of the history of the West. The Oxford audience registered its disapproval with its feet. Some left in the midst of his first lecture; others simply failed to return for the remaining five.[3]

It was not an auspicious debut for the materials that would later constitute his 1950 anthology *Empire and Communications* and serve as a frame of departure for its 1952 successor *The Bias of Communication*. Via an inhospitable and humbling beginning, Innis's most important and controversial contributions made their way into global historiography, and into an initial obscurity they did not deserve. That unfortunate contingency was the by-product of another: the prostate cancer that killed Innis, and removed him from Canadian life and letters in November 1952. With Innis no longer present to promote and explicate his communication writings, the responsibility for his corpus, and its promotion, fell to family and colleagues from the University of Toronto – colleagues who for the most part were inclined to see his economic writings as the essential and enduring feature of his legacy, and colleagues who promoted his writings on fur and fish at the expense of writings that came after 1940. For the remainder of the 1950s, Innis was remembered primarily for his role as a pioneer and leading exponent of the staples hypothesis.[4]

And then came Marshall McLuhan. McLuhan was yet another colleague from the University of Toronto, but one with a style and substance that sharply differentiated him from those who had overseen Innis's legacy to that point. He was not a political economist. He appreciated the force of Innis's writings on media. And in the early 1960s, with the publication of *The Gutenberg Galaxy* and *Understanding Media*, McLuhan brought forward writings that explained – or at least seemed to – the transformation that electronic media, satellites, and computation were effecting on the planet's disparate cultures. As McLuhan garnered worldwide attention, in *The Gutenberg Galaxy* and his succeeding writings, he also brought Innis's two communication anthologies to public attention – frequently, generously, and for the most part accurately. In 1972 McLuhan paid Innis the ultimate compliment of characterizing *The Gutenberg Galaxy* as a footnote to the observations of Innis.[5]

The cumulative effect of McLuhan's promotion of Innis was that scholars realized that the so-called Toronto School of Communication had produced not one media theorist of note, but two. And this time, Innis's writings received a much friendlier reception than they had at Oxford. By the 1970s, William Kuhns had proclaimed Innis to be a post-industrial prophet, while James Carey in an important article differentiated Innis's work from McLuhan's, arguing that it contained a distinct message that should be considered in its own right.[6] By the 1990s, Innis's writings, while never attaining the status or attention of, say, a Marx, a Bakhtin, or a Foucault, had nevertheless succeeded in attracting the attention of thinkers as diverse as John Seely Brown, then-director of Xerox PARC, Gregory Benford, a science fiction writer and physicist, and media critics such as Neil Postman and John Ralston Saul.[7] In 1998 the famed British geographer Sir Peter Hall proclaimed Innis to be "a remarkable intellectual figure, in some ways a 20th-century challenger to Marx."[8] By the end of the twentieth century, Innis's communication writings had recovered from their inauspicious debut at Oxford.

But that newfound respect does not mean that scholars who know Innis, those who have read and interpreted his works, have now reached a point where they can claim a deep understanding of his work. As we saw in the introductory chapter, Charles Acland and William Buxton note "that there is a consensus that he initiated something important, though the consensus-makers may not be sure what."[9] Some responsibility for that ambivalent verdict lies with scholars, many of whom have forwarded readings that either do not accord with what Innis had to say, or are so general or imprecise in their substance that they fail to provide much analytical purchase. The larger burden of responsibility lies, however, with Innis's cryptic pen. The power of his expression was not equal to the penetration of his philosophy. And because the man could not – perhaps even would not – provide a clear expression of the ideas that animated him, Innis ultimately provided in *Empire* and *Bias* a construct of history filled with propositions that seemed plausible in isolation and incommensurable in combination.

The problem Innis bequeathed to his interpreters was not so very different from the one that bedevils modern physics. Physicists work with two fundamental frames of reference – general relativity and quantum mechanics – which cannot be integrated into a single unified theory. Both are powerful and empirically supported. Both – in tandem – satisfy the current intuition that the universe is governed by both contingency and constraint. And both theories – to date – have thwarted physicists' attempts to make the two one. One framework – quantum mechanics – accounts for three of the four fundamental forces governing matter: electromagnetic, strong, and weak forces. The second framework – general relativity – treats the fourth: gravity. Neither has permitted physicists to give theoretical expression to another, perhaps even more fundamental intuition of their discipline, that the universe is a coherent place that can be described in a single, unified framework.

Innis's interpreters have at times wondered if they will ever be in a position to pay his communication writings a similar compliment. His corpus often seems to be more like a fractured landscape than a unified construct, one that resists every effort to integrate its disparate parts. And more important, it seems to resist every effort Innis himself made to create a cosmos out of the empirical chaos that constituted his narratives. The most distressing problem was that Innis offered a reading of history that simultaneously affirmed the importance of human agency and the importance of technological constraint in the history of human thought. That reading, however, never provided a clear sense as to how the latter related to the former. Using the concept of the oral tradition, Innis argued that human expressive instruments could be used to conceive, and then conceive anew. It was a doctrine that suggested that expressive instruments and expressive forms were entities that – when properly applied – could serve to enhance the cognitive flexibility and agency of their users. When it came to the assumption of new forms of thought, Innis argued that it was humans who were in charge. Problems arose for interpreters when Innis introduced two further concepts that seemed to suggest the opposite. Through the concepts of Bias and the monopoly of knowledge, Innis argued – or seemed to – that it was in fact the material properties of technology that determined the limits of human experience, whether a given culture would assume an orientation toward the dimension of time or space.

Needless to say, the three propositions in conjunction continue to pose problems for Innis's interpreters. Northrop Frye, responding to a passage in which Innis asserts that changes in a given culture's communication technology often follow changes in its worldview, was prompted to write: "I do not understand the word 'follow,' as it clearly seems to be Innis' view that changes in communication are involved in, or accompany, or in many cases are even the cause of, historical changes of attention."[10] This problematic feature of Innis's writing was compounded by another: in both studies, Innis seemed to delight in blithely contradicting the generalizations he offered regarding the cognitive impact of media. Consider for example his treatment of papyrus. He believed light media like papyrus prompted a worldview devoted to space, and supported institutions interested in space, such as the state.[11] But in his narrative one finds multiple instances in which papyrus supports institutions and worldviews devoted to time, most notably in his accounts of ancient Egypt, Israel, and Assyria.[12] In his account of ancient Greece, where papyrus and the oral culture co-existed, the narrative shows a shift emphasis in Greece first to space, then time, then space-time, with no apparent shift in the material substrate supporting communication.[13]

Scholars have reacted to these two discrepancies in two ways. Some have been content to focus on Innis's generalizations on media, proclaim him a technological determinist, and then move on.[14] His defenders are loath to accept that verdict. In their minds, Innis had too firm a grasp on the complexity of human history. His mind was original, powerful, and subtle, and it is too much to accept that he would reduce the diversity of the human past down to any one single causal factor. Unfortunately, many of his admirers have sought to resolve the problems posed by his writings in such a way as to diminish the force of his argument. The most common way interpreters have "fixed" the apparent problems in *Empire* and *Bias* is by historicizing Innis's generalizations about media, in effect making physical media and human agency just two of a complex of causes that have historically affected human life and human practice. Via such a reading, the associations Innis drew between media and thought become little more than the product of contingent circumstance, sometimes applying, sometimes not. We are given little if any basis to see how Innis's generalizations retain any interpretive purchase. We are typically not told what manner of relationship – if any – communication technology retains with human thought. And we are not told how such readings can be squared with Innis's insistence that his generalizations were mid-level theories. They were not meant to be seen as universal covering laws. Nor were they meant to be subsumed into concrete descriptions that apply to only one place and one time.[15]

Much of the difficulty attending current interpretation, I suggest, can be attributed to the relationship scholars draw between force and purpose, and to their failure to use a well-defined and well-described model of emergent change to read *Empire* and *Bias*. Typically, interpreters tend to see the relationship between causation and agency as one of *opposition*; the consequent of that assumption is that readings continue to emerge in which media causation is described in terms consistent with linear change and efficient cause.[16] Communication technologies – and other causal factors in history such as the environment – are generally seen as external forces that impress themselves upon the minds and practices of their users or occupants.

The problem with such a reading is that Innis never framed the relation between media causation and human perception and action in those terms. Rather, he posited a relationship of *apposition*, a conclusion derived in large measure from his exposure to the writings of Immanuel Kant. It was Kant's conviction that efficient cause and agent purpose were distinct objects situated in different – and mutually exclusive – systems of knowledge. To one in terms of the other therefore made as little sense as mixing terms from general relativity and quantum mechanics would do now. Kant therefore posited that no antinomy – no incompatibility – existed between the two, and

Innis agreed.[17] Starting from the premise that media bias should not be conceived in terms of efficient cause, Innis in turn crafted a theory of media that derived from human intention and action. He believed the causal factors associated with communication technology to be emergent properties: properties that derive from users' interaction with each other, and with the devices and formalisms at their disposal; and properties that proceed probabilistically, but not inevitably, toward one of multiple potential biases. The purpose of this chapter is to argue that this interpretation is so, and, further, that many of the problems hindering interpretation of *Empire* and *Bias* can be resolved by viewing them through the prism of emergent change. More specifically, this chapter argues that many of the longstanding interpretive problems in the Innis literature can be resolved by reading his narratives through the concepts of increasing returns and formal and final cause.

These claims impose a number of obligations, each of which must be met in their turn. The most pressing and obvious task is to demonstrate that Innis's writings on media can and should be aligned with his doctrine of emergent change. Here, we will consider the analogical argumentation that Innis applied to link his media writings with the theoretical constructs that had informed his economic histories. And here, we will consider Innis's extension of the argument offered in *Political Economy*: that communication technologies can and often do impede the capacity for coherent thought. In that work, he emphasized one consequent of information technology: cognitive flux. In *Empire* and *Bias*, he would explicate a second: cognitive rigidity.

Following that discussion, we examine the historical substance that Innis used to ground his theories of media and cognitive change. In both anthologies, Innis provided grand, sweeping, large-scale and long-scale histories of Egypt, Mesopotamia, Greece, Rome, and the Europe that followed. In each history, he asserted the fundamental importance of the two Kantian *a priori* forms of sensible intuition – space and time – and argued that both were central to the emergence and operation of all domains of human practice.[18] Both ultimately constituted the cognitive and practical frameworks that supported everything from commerce and warfare to politics, theology, philosophy, and more. In addition to their roles in shaping human experience, Innis asserted, the two forms of sensible intuition, hereafter referred to as Kantian forms, were important because they contributed to the regulation of human practice. The form of space contributed a framework to support the creation of institutions and practices devoted to constraint and restraint; and further, it contributed a framework for perceiving and articulating mechanical change. The form of time, by contrast, supported cultural practices devoted to the pursuit of freedom and transformation. Here lay the realm of the ecstatic. And here lay a framework for the perception of emergent change.

Because of their regulating function, Innis maintained, the presence of the two Kantian forms – or biases as he referred to them – was an important measure of cultural health. With them, cultures attained the conceptual equipment needed to perceive changes of consequence in their geopolitical, cultural, and economic environments, and retained the flexibility necessary to adapt. Without them, cultures became dysfunctional and ultimately collapsed. Ancient Greece, he wrote, was an exemplar in this respect. Over the course of its history, it acquired the discipline necessary to support the concurrent reference to space and time. In Innis's parlance, Greece acquired an oligopoly of knowledge and, as a result, it thrived. Our review of Innis's history of the West focuses therefore on his treatment of ancient Greece, in part because it proved such an important case study, and in part because it is there that Innis took the greatest pains to link his object's history with its prevailing conceptions of change.

After reviewing the fundamentals associated with Innis's theories and histories, we will turn to a deeper consideration of our central problem: How did Innis reconcile his belief in human agency, at the individual and collective level, with his belief in media determination? That consideration will start with a detailed look at the oral tradition. In the context of Innis's thought, the oral tradition was a concept. But for the communication scholar it was much more than that: it was a method, an ethic, a way to retain the independence of individuals and groups from the cultural and environmental stimuli that competed for their attention. It supported the need – the necessity – to adapt, to conceive, and then conceive anew. In Innis's eyes, the oral tradition supported human purpose because it presented users with expressive building blocks that could be repurposed to meet new aims and expressive intents. Meaning was not the sole function of some structuring grammar, be it cultural, linguistic, or material. It was also the product of human construction and manipulation of expressive forms governed by context-specific constraints, constraints that derived from formal cause. Human communication was complex both in form and substance, and this realization presented two important implications. It suggested that human expressive instruments could be used to augment the cognitive flexibility of their users. It also suggested that the same instruments could be used to produce high-resolution models of nature and culture, models that increased in complexity and precision over time.

Our final task will be to proceed to an in-depth examination of the precise relationship Innis drew between communication technology and human agents. There, we will discover a theory of media grounded on the Kantian conception of formal purposiveness, or final cause. It was never Innis's intention to posit a linear relationship between the material properties of a given medium and the worldview of the culture it supported. What we will find instead is something that, from the standpoint of the Innis literature, is quite counterintuitive: Innis was not a materialist. He was an idealist, a philosophical orientation that his *Idea File* makes quite clear. We will also find – via an exploration of his correspondence from the 1940s – that Innis was well aware of probabilistic constructs of change, and likely saw the relationship between media properties and human cognition in those terms. And finally, through study of the systemic relationship Innis drew between humans and their instruments for communication, we will find a fitting and final way to demonstrate Innis's commitment to the concept of emergent change and to the governance of formal and final cause.

I

Of all Innis's writings devoted to communication and cultural change, the Introduction to *Empire and Communications* most explicitly presents his ideas. There, he made clear that his interpretive schema stemmed from his earlier work: "In this reference to the problem of attack it will be clear that we have been concerned with the use of certain tools which have proved effective in the interpretation of the economic history of Canada and the British Empire."[19] And there, through reference to those tools, he once again presented a philosophy of history based on emergent change, offering eight propositions touching on media and the historical process. Many, unfortunately, have not received their due attention in the literature. Indeed, most treatments of Innis's communication works have limited their focus to his provocative ideas on communication media, and on the efficacy of the oral tradition in promoting cultural longevity and growth.[20] It is unfortunate that scholars have generally based their readings on such a narrow focus, since Innis never intended such materials to be read in isolation. Let us consider in turn each of Innis's propositions regarding the history of empire.

Proposition One: Polities Aggregate and Disaggregate

Innis used a quotation from James Bryce as the point of departure for his first proposition and for his treatise on the fact of empire. In the history of polities "from the time of Menes down to that of Attila," Bryce writes, "the tendency is generally towards aggregation: and the history of ancient nations shows us, not only an enormous number of petty monarchies and republics swallowed up in the Empire of Rome, but that empire itself far more highly centralized than any preceding one had been."[21] The political unity of Europe collapsed with Rome, however, in the fifth century CE. The continent fractured and remained a patchwork of competing principalities until the thirteenth century, when the trend toward political centralization reasserted itself.

Proposition Two: Empires are Self-Organizing Cultural Systems

When Innis referred to aggregation, he was not referring to empires as aggregates in the sense used in this study; that is, as a conglomeration of independent particles with no relation to each other except that of spatial proximity. He argued rather that empires share a systemic unity by virtue of the interaction of their political, institutional, and individual parts; and that these interactions are supported by communication technologies that Innis believed prompted cycles of self-organization in the life of any given culture. They disrupted extant cultural constructs, and promoted the construction of new domains of thought, new methods for civic life, and new plateaus of public opinion. As we saw in *Political Economy*, Innis believed that cultures grew by leaps. Because communication technologies played such a catalytic role, Innis believed they could serve as a basis for the periodization of history, a point he highlighted by referring to his earlier work on staples. Canada's emphasis on exporting staples to the United States and Britain had had a decisive effect on its economic, political, and social structure. Periodic shifts to different staples introduced periods of heightened disequilibrium, and subsequent self-organization: "Each staple in its turn left its stamp, and the shift to new staples invariably produced periods of crises in which adjustments in the old structure were painfully made and a new pattern created in relation to a new staple."[22]

In *The Bias of Communication*, Innis further confirmed his observations on the relationship between communication technology and cultural self-organization by tying his schema of imperial history to economic theories that described the emergence of monopolies and the progression of the business cycle. In making this link, he suggested the import of increasing returns and final cause in his philosophy of history. It was a link that would prove highly significant for his theory of media. As we saw in chapter 4, Innis suggested that "the neglect of communication in studies of cycles warranted a consideration of the extent to which monopolies of knowledge collapse and extraneous material is lost."[23]

Proposition Three: Enduring Empires Are Balanced Polities

For his third proposition, Innis referred to an argument made both in his staples studies and in *Political Economy in the Modern State*. Empires, as systems, were subject to periods of stress that required adaptation in order to survive. For that adaptation to occur, empires had to maintain a balance between freedom and constraint, the same prerequisite for emergence that applies in any complex adaptive system: "In attempting to understand the basis of these diverse tendencies, we become concerned with the problem of empire, and in particular with factors responsible for the successful operation of 'centrifugal and centripetal forces.'"[24]

Proposition Four: Enduring Empires Manage Their Information Flows

As we saw in *Political Economy*, Innis argued that cultures could only maintain the proper balance between freedom and constraint if they were information-rich but not information-saturated. His fourth proposition, therefore, was that empires could not permit extant information to overwhelm the agents operating within them. A study of successful and unsuccessful empires, he argued, would demonstrate the importance of regulating "the efficiency of communication" as a means to generate "conditions favourable to creative thought."[25]

Proposition Five:
Empires are Governed by Formal Cause

As we saw in *The Cod Fisheries* and *Political Economy*, Innis believed that empires are built on interaction, and that the process of interaction carries a significant price: unintended consequences. When a region is opened to trade and the constraints governing trade – whether in transport or communication – are changed, the region's constitution, its economic structure, becomes more than the product of local design. It begins to reflect the governance of a larger distributed whole, one which assigns each component a specific niche or specialization, incorporates new components to strengthen its formal integrity, and modifies the specialization of existing components if a new agent can perform the task more efficiently. In his staple narratives, Innis had emphasized that trade and systemic governance could prompt economic blowback on the imperial centres that had initiated economic activity. He highlighted the importance of formal cause once again in *Empire and Communications*. And he once again appealed to analogies from his work in economic history – instances of economic blowback prompted by formal cause – to make his point: "Concentration on staple products incidental to the geographic background has involved problems not only in the supply area but also in the demand area, to mention only the effects of specie from Central America on European prices, the effects of the fur trade on France, of wheat production on English agriculture, and of pulp and paper production on public opinion in Anglo-Saxon countries."[26]

Proposition Six:
Enduring Empires Employ the Oral Tradition

In *Empire* and *Bias*, Innis's interest in formal cause extended beyond the operation of large-scale cultural and economic systems. He was also interested in the contribution that context-specific constraints could make to the act of communication, an interest he explored in his treatment of the oral and written traditions. In these works, he introduced his sixth precept: empires survive when their agents adapt prevailing concepts and behaviours to changing circumstance – when, put simply, they follow the oral tradition. Innis referred to this ethic toward knowledge as the oral tradition because it reflected a trait he had observed in oral cultures: they were very good at adapting extant content to meet new needs and generate new understandings, in large measure because they exploited the flexibility of formalisms with context-specific constraints.

Innis *did not* dwell on the oral tradition out of a simple desire to promote speech acts and discourage writing acts. In his framework, it was perfectly possible for a culture governed by the oral tradition, such as ancient Greece, to use written forms of communication to support trade, scholarship, and the conduct of government. Conversely, it was perfectly possible for a culture heavily reliant on speech acts, as Nazi Germany was, to adopt the passive stance toward knowledge which Innis associated with the written tradition. Innis wanted nothing to do with the "mechanical spoken word" that Hitler described in *Mein Kampf*, which had the power to "set sliding the great avalanches of a political and religious nature."[27] The crucial point for Innis was whether the culture and method of communication in question was supporting an agent's active engagement with the ideas and cultural forms in circulation. If both supported the individual's capacity to challenge extant suppositions, then Innis identified them with the oral tradition. Indeed, since the act of writing itself provided a means to deconstruct and make something new, it was an activity he identified with the oral tradition. As he would note in *The Bias of Communication*: "Reading in contrast with writing implies a passive recognition of the power of writing."[28]

Proposition Seven: Empires Are Governed by Final Cause, i: They acquire biases, cognitive states that can be correlated with the physical properties of media

Innis's seventh proposition addressed to communication media is arguably the most celebrated and most debated in the Innis literature. Historically, Innis argued, cultures have shown a tendency to emphasize concerns that relate to the dimensions of space, time, or (in rare instances) space-time. Some cultures, such as ancient Rome, concentrated their energies on problems of governance and law, matters pertaining to the control of space. Other cultures, by contrast, were more disposed to emphasize commercial or religious concerns, matters pertaining to the control of time. In the city-states of Mesopotamia, for example, time and treasure were devoted to the maintenance of the cult, which controlled not only the city's religious life but also its cultural, scientific, and linguistic activity.

For Innis, much of the history of the West could be construed as an effort by cultures and institutions with a bias toward space to come to an accommodation with counterparts retaining a bias toward time. Regimes that failed to reach such an accommodation typically failed to adapt and, in turn, collapsed. The Mesopotamian city-states for example never had more than a modest control over space and routinely proved susceptible to conquest by empires ranging from Egypt to Assyria. In the aftermath of invasion, however, imperial authorities routinely sought accommodation with the city's priestly caste. Rulers who failed to do so ran the risk of civic unrest, as the Babylonian priesthood was not above using its ideological influence over the region's inhabitants to foment rebellion.[29]

The proposition that spiritual and temporal powers have historically clashed was hardly noteworthy. But Innis's claim that a culture's predisposition toward time or space could be correlated with the physical properties of its communication media was a new and ultimately controversial contribution to the historiography of the West. In his essay "The Bias of Communication," Innis argues as follows: "A medium of communication has an important influence on the dissemination of knowledge over space and over time and it becomes necessary to study its characteristics in order to appraise its influence in its cultural setting. According to its characteristics it may be better suited to the dissemination of knowledge over time than over space, particularly if the medium is heavy and durable and not suited to transportation, or to the dissemination of knowledge over space than over time, particularly if the medium is light and easily transported. The relative emphasis on time or space will imply a bias of significance to the culture in which it is embedded."[30]

Media were important, Innis argued, because they placed constraints on human endeavour. If agents employed a heavy, durable medium such as stone or clay it was likely that they would form smaller, decentralized institutions since it would be difficult to convey the communication media over long distances. By contrast, agents using a lighter medium such as papyrus were more likely to form larger centralized institutions capable of controlling sizeable territories.[31] The ultimate importance of a given medium resided, however, in its capacity to channel agent attention to a restricted range of human concerns. Institutions and societies employing durable media were more likely to focus their energies on questions of time, ultimate meaning, and religion, in part because the expense required to instantiate information in them mandated that effort be extended only for activities of the highest significance. By contrast, the cost of transmitting information in papyrus was comparatively low. Cultures employing it and other light media had the luxury of broadening their focus to include other concerns, including law, governance, and philosophy, the problems of space.[32] As we shall see in our final section, Innis identified the phenomenon of media bias, and its consequent, the monopoly of knowledge, with the governance of final cause.

Proposition Eight:
Empires Are Governed by Final Cause, ii:
Empires over time will lock into a given cognitive orientation, or bias. When they do so, they form a monopoly of knowledge

Innis's formulations on cognitive bias provoked controversy because they smacked of technological determinism, a perception that was bolstered by a final concept regarding cultural change offered in "The Bias of Communication." In that essay, Innis argued that the ultimate outcome of agent-medium interaction was not merely the limitation of one's focus to a specific set of concerns; one may have a focus and yet still recognize the existence of phenomena beyond one's domain of concern. Many empires, on the other hand, reached a point at which their agents concluded that their given focus was the only extant focus to be studied. When an agent, in the form of an individual, institution, or society, reached this extreme conclusion, it rigidified into a monopoly of knowledge. Typically, such monopolies formed when a culture shifted from the oral tradition to the written tradition, and concentrated on the acquisition and preservation of existing knowledge as opposed to discovering new knowledge. For Innis, the price of such cognitive rigidity had typically been very high. Cultures that stopped innovating generally became targets for invasion by their neighbours. In the essay "Minerva's Owl" he commented on the effects of a shift from the oral to the written tradition: "An interest in learning assumes a stable society in which organized force is sufficiently powerful to provide sustained protection. Concentration on learning implies a written tradition and introduces monopolistic elements in culture which are followed by rigidities and involve lack of contact with the oral tradition and the vernacular ... 'Most organizations appear as bodies founded for the painless extinction of ideas of the founders' ... This change is accompanied by a weakening of the relations between organized force and the vernacular and collapse in the face of technological change which has taken place in marginal regions which have escaped the influence of a monopoly of knowledge."[33]

II

There may not have been grandeur in this view of history, but there was poetry. For Innis, the metre of history was marked by stasis and oscillation, the recurring wave and feedback loop. It was also marked by the imperative for balance. Balanced societies could muster the creativity needed to perceive the cyclical, emergent flow of history, and recognize their place in it. They could also devise the measures needed for adaptation and survival. Of all the regimes Innis had studied, Greece provided the most explicit confirmation that his generalizations on history, media, and cognitive change had merit. Greece reinforced his view that schemas of change affect all domains of human practice and can be exploited to create innovative cultures that persist. It also supported his belief that a stable present for Europe and North America could be retrieved. For these reasons it makes sense to focus here on Greece when considering the historical grounds Innis used to support his writings on media and history.

Greece, Innis writes, distinguished itself by its routine appeal to constructs of mechanical and emergent change to inform its conduct of "the highest of the political sciences, the science of man." Its history was characterized by efforts to create a polity in which the personal did not do violence to the political, and vice versa. The individual should be permitted to live "with the fullness of life" while fulfilling "his function as a member of the social organism."[34] In his narrative, Greece's quest to balance the social and the local started with one influx of information and ended with another. The first brought Greeks cognitive flexibility. It enabled them to discover on their own that the Kantian forms of space and time were fundamental to human experience and to explore the implications of each for human politics and practice. Information enabled the Greeks to explore the possibility spaces suggested by the bias of space and the bias of time; to experiment, and, in turn, to integrate the fruits of individual and collective experience into the operation of the *polis* and the underlying culture that sustained it. The second influx of information initiated a very different outcome: Greece's decline and collapse. Like the cultures that preceded it and those that succeeded it, Greece lost control of the very things – content, concepts, and information flows – that had made its rise possible in the first place.

Innis's account of Greece begins in the eighth century BCE with the emergence of the city-state, or more properly the family-state, since power was concentrated in the hands of the *Eupatridae*, the Greek nobility. That situation of inequality, aggravated by the fact that existing law was neither written nor posted, but memorized and declared by the *Eupatridae*, presented obvious drawbacks for non-noble Greeks. Popular pressure for change was present almost from the start: "'In the absence of a written code, those who declare and interpret laws may be properly said to make them' (Thirwall)."[35] Social pressure for political change was also prompted by the establishment of colonies between 750 and 670 BCE. The discrepancy in property and civic rights enjoyed by inhabitants of Greece's colonies and original city-states brought questions of governance – questions relating to the control of space – to the fore. Pressure emerged to codify law, and to make it publicly accessible in written form.[36]

A deeper and more fundamental impetus for political reform emerged, however, with the establishment of trading relations with Egypt in 670 BCE. Greece's opening to the Near East afforded access to papyrus and brought with it cultural disequilibrium, as Greece became exposed to increased quantities of information in the form of Egyptian and Mesopotamian ideas, and new forms of literature and poetry. While Greece was not overwhelmed by the influx of information, having limited access to papyrus, the influx was sufficient to prompt questioning of old verities, including those that bolstered the monopoly of the *Eupatridae* on power.[37]

Innis argues that during this period of cultural flux poets began attacking traditional theological concepts while Ionian philosophers generated new ones. One important innovation was the transformation of the nature gods into anthropomorphic deities, each representing a higher function of life. A second innovation was to bring the gods within the constraints of time and space through the philosophy of *eros*. In contrast to the doctrine of the *logos*, which conceived the emergence of form as the by-product of volitional, creative acts by Yahweh or other deities, the Greeks disassociated change from agency and made it a function of a self-sustaining procreative series governed by law: "The Greek view of the relation of men to the gods was mechanical."[38] Quoting Werner Jaeger, Innis noted: "The Logos is a substantialization of an intellectual property or power of God, the creator, who is stationed *outside* the world and brings the world into existence by his own personal fiat. The Greek gods are stationed *inside* the world; they are descended from Heaven and Earth, the two greatest and most exalted parts of the universe; and they are generated acts by the mighty power of Eros, who likewise belongs within the world as an all-engendering primitive force."[39]

In contrast to the Near East, Greece did not have a strongly developed centralized cult with ambitions to regulate Greek public and intellectual life. Consequently, Greek philosophers enjoyed the freedom of tailoring theology to meet the realities of experience: "The Hebrews made philosophy the handmaid of religion and the Greeks subordinated religion to philosophy."[40] One measure of Greek freedom was its capacity to conceive the gods within the rubric of natural law. A second measure was the Ionian philosophers' resort to mathematics for making generalizations, in place of allegory and myth. For Anaximander and other philosophers geometry "was seized upon as the very centre of the true philosophical sort of knowledge. Mathematics was recognized as something which could be reduced to general laws with a scientific content. The Ionians were under the spell of an undissolved relation between man and nature but saw the possibility of establishing an intelligible coherence in the phenomenal world."[41]

The search for intelligibility eventually paid dividends, according to Innis. In 585 BCE Thales of Miletus, building on the Chaldean discovery of the periodic nature of celestial phenomena, correctly predicted the onset of an eclipse.[42] The conceptual advantages of the Ionian philosophers also brought costs, however. As their insights were systematized into the Olympian tradition known as *moria*, a cosmology emerged in which the universe's constituents were seen as discrete components. Instead of emphasizing the secondary properties of phenomena – the "undissolved relation between man and nature" – the Greeks focused on their primary properties. The universe in its totality was an aggregate, governed by a concept of "causality that was static, simultaneous and spatial." Their world was seen as "pluralistic, rationalistic, fatalistic, opposed to otherworldliness, and distributed into spatial provinces."[43]

The Greeks assumed this cost, Innis writes, because they appropriated a category of formalism – geometry – which encouraged them – in part – to see nature and the *polis* in the spatial, fatalistic terms described by *moria*. Geometry was used to "develop a conception of the earth and of the universe" based not on myth but rather on "universal generalizations."[44] Here, Innis's point was similar to one made by Claude Shannon in his theory of information: universal forms of constraint reduce message variety to the point that only one signal can be sent with confidence. Universal constraints do not support the expression, transmission, or perception of message variety via electric signal. For Innis, the same category of constraint in the context of geometry did not support the characterization of diverse cultural and natural objects, or the relations between them. On the contrary, through its "passionate concern for consistency," geometry imposed a "disregard for the data of experience," and in turn produced a conception of the universe devoid of any association with "growth and life."[45] In the end, via *moria* and via geometry, the Greeks produced a worldview not all that different from Newtonian mechanics, with its emphasis on universal law, space, mechanical change, atomism and the primary properties of objects: "The Olympian tradition which assumed fixed limits to the power of gods and men emphasized spatial concepts and in turn geometry. The science of nature dominated by geometry involved a concern with the internal properties of things rather than their relations with other things."[46]

While Greek philosophers were elaborating the philosophy of *moria*, Athenian politicians were simultaneously addressing spatial concerns through constitutional reform. Draco, one of three seminal lawmakers referred to by Innis, began a process of legal reform in 621 BCE that would culminate in the establishment of the democratic city-state in the following century. Draco's contribution was twofold. With the creation of Draco's code, he systematized law and made it a matter of public record. He also loosened the aristocracy's monopoly on power. It was a necessary accommodation. The mountainous topography of Greece made the Athenian army dependent on infantry and forced it to incorporate non-nobles into its ranks.

A noble himself, Draco realized that the stability of Athenian society was threatened by the existence of an army with interests at odds with the ruling class. His solution was to create a second legislative body composed of non-noble *hoplite*, or infantry, as a check to the *Areopagus*, the ruling council composed of the nobility.[47] While Greek society devoted greater attention to spatial relations, the shift was neither sufficient nor complete, according to Innis. The constitution still allocated the lion's share of power to the aristocracy, and Greek law remained saddled with harsh sanctions, including enslavement of debtors with outstanding obligations. It remained, therefore, for Solon, a contemporary of Thales of Miletus, to undertake more fundamental reforms in 594 BCE. During Solon's archonship (the city's executive position) tenets of Ionian philosophy in particular were consciously translated into political practice.

Solon adopted the concept of universal truth suggested by celestial mechanics into a universal conception of justice. Law, Solon argued, should be universally and impartially applied, on the justification that an unremedied injury to the one was a threat to the stability of the whole.[48]

The application of universal justice, however, demanded state mediation of conflict and greater input by the populace in the generation and interpretation of law. Consequently, writes Innis, Solon substantially reduced the range of actions that families could take to seek independent redress for injuries, but augmented the rights of Athenian residents to participate in government. He distributed power, first by removing the nobility's exclusive right to interpret law: "Solon discovered the secret of democracy in 'the constitution of the judicial courts and the whole people' (Bury)." Solon also afforded the city's residents greater access to the city's legislative and executive organs of government, by giving the city's working class a voice on the city's popular assembly, and by removing the nobility's exclusive control of the archonship.[49]

Solon also attended to the needs of space, Innis suggests, by altering policies that were actually or potentially disruptive. He abolished the institution of personal security for debt; there would be no further enslavement based on financial status. He also attempted to forestall friction between the city's commercial class and the nobility by exchanging economic policies that favoured the latter for new ones favouring the former. Insisting on the development of industries such as pottery, Solon forbade the export of natural products except olive oil, a regulation that ran counter to the interests of the ruling class, which had a strong stake in cereal production. That policy, combined with the increased use of metal coins (dating from 700 BCE), stimulated a robust trade in manufactured products.[50]

By Innis's measure, however, Solon's reforms still did not go far enough, for reasons political, philosophical, practical, and theological. Despite his constitutional reforms, "Solon had left the great families too strong," and the regime collapsed in 561 BCE, five years after Solon vacated the archonship.[51] Solon's commercial policies had led to the emergence of the commercial class as a powerful new constituency that was independent, resentful of the aristocracy's pretensions to power, and willing to challenge it. In 561 BCE, Athenian merchants supported Peisistratos' seizure of the government. His coup initiated a fifty-year period in which the city was ruled by tyrants.[52]

Philosophically, Solon's reforms failed because they derived from a construct of change that emphasized a static universe comprising discrete elements. From such a policy one could derive a politics that envisioned factions with competing interests and a state respecting the dignity and integrity of the individual. One could not, however, derive a politics that suggested that factions interact and cooperate to maintain the organic unity and duration of the state: "The philosophy of spatial externality involved discreteness and neglected the importance of continuity."[53] Indeed, the tenets of *moria* and geometry had undercut it. Through its emphasis on periodic change, Ionian philosophy undercut the systemic vision of change provided by myth, and with it the ideological justification for the continuance of the state.[54]

Aside from addressing the need for continuity, Solon's political philosophy was unsatisfactory because it did not account for the temporal experience of merchants operating in a commercial economy based on trade and money. The collapse of Athens suggested the need for a new political philosophy, one which took an interest in a new form of representation – arithmetic – and a new form of intuition: time.[55] The shift in Greek thinking was also prompted by public disaffection with the tenets of Olympian theology. Worshippers, unhappy with a religious tradition in which a practitioner's interaction with the gods was defined as a commercial interaction or bribe to prevent misfortune and garner good fortune, began searching for alternatives that offered interaction and communion with the divine. Many turned to the cult of the mystery god Dionysus and mystic forms of philosophy. According to Innis, while Olympian theology emphasized humanity's discontinuity from the gods, in Dionysian worship, "the characteristic rite was sacramental – an act of communion and reunion with the *daemon*." As a mystic religion it offered the hope of systemic unity, or the "prospect of union with God."[56] Greek philosophical inquiry shifted to concepts emphasizing "time and number (the measure of time) and ... righteousness (*Dike*)."[57]

In addition to an emphasis on time and number, there are other reasons why Innis associated Greek mystical cults and philosophy with systemic change. To start, while the tyrants supported the Dionysian cult in Athens and elsewhere in order to obtain religious sanction for their rule, as an organization it was "not a fixed part of an official state religion" but rather a "trans social organization." It was not bound by political boundaries any more than economic or meteorological systems were. What is more, it embraced a doctrine of emergent change, in part by subscribing to a form of henotheism, and in part by re-embracing the doctrine of the *logos*.[58]

The doctrine of the *logos*, a universal church, communion, and the ecstasy of the spirit were not the only Christian ideas relating to emergent change anticipated by the Dionysian cult. According to Innis the rite also shared the hope of resurrection after death: "As a religion of the life of earth and man, of the life which dies but is perpetually reborn, Dionysian worship had a secret vitality which offset Olympianism with its divine jealousies and the impassable gulf of *moria*."[59] For Innis, the key to much of the vitality associated with Dionysian worship, and with myth in general, lay in its insight that figure emerges from a ground embodying contradictory qualities, be it life and death, freedom and constraint, or space and time. As with complex adaptive systems, forms in mythic constructs of change emerged from the interplay of opposing forces.

> Heraclitus (540–475 [BCE]) emphasized [mythical religions] with its principle of *Dike* or righteousness and contributed to the break-up of concepts of state absolutism. He denied being altogether and regarded all becoming as originating in a war of opposites. "I contemplate the becoming" ... Man was given a place as a completely cosmic being and the claim of wisdom to supremacy was justified by saying that it taught men in speech and action to follow the truth of nature and its divine law. True wisdom was found in language since it was an expression of common wisdom which is in all men and only partly obscured by false opinions. The structure of man's speech was an embodiment of the structure of the world. *Logos* was recorded in speech and *physis* was a

representation of social consciousness. "Do not listen to me but the word and confess that all things are one."[60]

By the closing decade of the sixth century BCE, the Dionysian challenge itself began to face criticism from philosophers for taking its premises too far. The philosophy of Heraclitus, for example, was deemed untenable because it took the extreme position that phenomena enjoyed neither stability nor meta-stability: "The whole was a perpetual flux of change. The cosmos was the dynamics of existence. Being was a perpetual becoming."[61] For the Greeks this position did as much violence to experience as the doctrine of *moria*. And so, the Orphic and Pythagorean movements began the process of reconciling "the static concepts of order and space with the dynamic concepts based on mythical religions."[62] Pythagoras made his contribution to this effort by proposing the use of multiple formalisms. Formalisms that were capable of detecting and expressing static and dynamic patterns. And formalisms that embodied the principles of *correspondence* – "Number was the principle of all things. 'Things are numbers'" – succession – "Moria was replaced by Time and number (the measure of time)" – and *extension* – "From his time there was an intimate association, 'not to say an indissoluble correlation between the theory of numbers and the theory of extension: between arithmetic and geometry.'"[63]

In Innis's reading of Pythagoras, the significance of constructs employing number and geometric formalism was that they could be used "as an aid to the reconstruction of any representation of the conditions involved in nature."[64] Functionally, Pythagoras' reforms, at least as they were characterized by Innis, were similar in principle to those Innis himself had proposed in *Political Economy* and in his correspondence with Arthur Cole. Recall from our discussion in chapter 4 that Innis believed analytic purchase of the socio-economic present and past could be obtained through the use of two formalisms: maps, which derived from geometry and the principle of extension; and time series, which derived from number and the principles of correspondence and succession. Through their use, Innis believed, scholars could generate an integrated economic history of North America, not just case studies of single regions. And through their use, scholars could detect a given culture's location within a given cycle or wave of history. Formalisms adapted to space could only express systems in equilibrium; formalisms adapted to time could only treat systems undergoing emergence. Multiple formalisms, by contrast, permitted the detection of spatio-temporal systems, and their subsequent expression. In the case of economic history, Innis believed that the use of maps and time series would permit the detection of a "succession of production waves."[65] Such was the aspiration of Innis. And such was the contribution of Pythagoras.

The efforts of Pythagoras and other Ionian philosophers to apply rigour and constraint to the dynamic concepts of the Dionysian cult had important consequences for Greek society. In the field of theology, and with the regulation of the cult's ecstasies, the temporal concepts associated with *dike* and the *logos* proved sufficiently palatable to the established Olympian cult to meet acceptance. The transformation was such that by the fourth century BCE Pythagorean doctrine would identify the *logos* with the rational rather than the ecstatic part of the human soul. The recognition of emergent change, however, remained: "Personified reason or the *Logos* as the rational part of the soul with an existence above the daemons had emerged as a second god by 350 [BCE]. An idea of definite conversion or of abiding change in the individual mind had appeared."[66]

In the field of art, an aesthetic emerged emphasizing "the unity of time and space." Prior to Pythagoras, Athenian pottery had been characterized first by geometric patterns (900–700 BCE) and then by narration via a temporal progression of figures. In the sciences, a now familiar metaphor emerged: "Empedocles (490–430 [BCE]), a citizen of a Dorian state, as founder of the Sicilian school of medicine attempted to combine the mystic tradition with Ionian science by emphasizing complexity."[67]

In the field of politics, Cleisthenes, a noble and member of the Athenian *Alcmaeonidae* party, led a revolt in 511 BCE and overthrew the tyrants with military assistance from Sparta. In Innis's account, Cleisthenes came to power with a mandate to establish a constitution that balanced the spatial and temporal concerns of Athens. Prior to the rule of the tyrants, the nobility had exercised too much power, and consequently too much constraint, over Athenian development.[68] During the period of the tyrants, the reverse held true. Athenian society fell into a fifty-year period of heightened disequilibrium: "The tyrants in Athens as in other Greek cities ... emerged between periods dominated by old methods of government and newer powers more closely adapted to economic and social difficulties incidental to problems of spatial organization."[69]

Cleisthenes fulfilled this agenda, according to Innis, through a program designed to end once and for all the *Eupatridae*'s pretensions to power. While Draco had ended the aristocracy's monopoly on the generation of law and Solon had ended its monopoly on its interpretation, Cleisthenes undercut its spiritual power by ending its primacy in Athenian religious life. Much of the nobility's historic hold on the Athenian populace rested on its role in interpreting sacred law, which was based on the city's lunar calendar. Cleisthenes' solution was to replace it with a solar calendar, and to acquire popular support for it by obtaining sanction for the reform from the religious authorities at Delphi.[70] In essence, he usurped control of time, and ended once and for all the nobility's ideological claim to popular allegiance: "The Greeks opposed the raising of gods and religion to an independent position dominating the state and brought to an end the threat of a theocratical and monarchical order."[71]

Cleisthenes consolidated the state's ideological gains with reforms that ended the nobility's control of space: "The family state was broken down and its political and religious claims inherited by the state."[72] He attained this aim first by redrawing the political boundaries inside Athenian territory, creating new units that bore no relation to the historic divisions associated with noble rule. He also undercut the nobility's control of legislation by eliminating the *Areopagus* and creating the Council of 500, a new legislative body. Representation in the new body was allocated on the basis of location, not social status. Power was distributed to the populace, and procedures to mitigate excessive party strife were implemented through resort to ostracism. Through aggressive reform of the spatial and temporal domains of practice in Athens, Cleisthenes laid the basis for a stable polity, a balanced society, and, in turn, a vibrant culture: "A concept of the people in a democratic electoral system based on the territorial principle became the basis of the constitution ... The Greeks seized on the spatial concept as developed by Ionian philosophers and on the temporal concept emphasized by mystical religions to construct a political society which stood the test of resistance to the Persian empire."[73]

In Innis's narrative, however, the Athenian Golden Age lasted only for a brief period during the fifth century BCE. Cleisthenes' reforms brought not only a sense of internal unity to Athens, but also the political acumen necessary to forge an alliance with neighbouring city-states in response to Persia's conquest of Miletus in 494 BCE. The coalition defeated Persia in 478 BCE. The sense of pan-Hellenic unity survived the war, as citizens from neighbouring city-states were permitted to settle in Athens and marry its inhabitants. But the comity was short-lived, and in Innis's opinion the chief reason for the breakdown was the emergence of a second influx of information, a by-product of the growing use of written communication in Greek culture.[74]

The quantity of information circulating in Greek society rose dramatically in the fifth century for reasons both cultural and technical. Prose was construed by the inhabitants of the time as the literary genre of the democratic city-state, and a vibrant literature emerged, although in Innis's opinion its vibrancy was due to its still "very limited book production." Those limitations eventually fell by the wayside, in part because the reduced formal constraints of prose literature made it easier to produce than poetry, and in part because of the emergence of a reading public demanding access to printed works: "In 478 [BCE] Athens had no reading public, but by 430 [BCE] Herodotus found it convenient to turn his recitations into book form." The control parameter of circulating information was also affected by the onset of more efficient writing practices. The direction of Semitic letters in use was reversed, and Greeks began writing from left to right instead of right to left.[75]

The ultimate impact of writing, according to Innis, was that it destroyed "the bond of Greek life." Here, Innis began to point out familiar patterns of decline that he had first identified in *Political Economy*. Greece's information glut, to start, led to the rise of civic nationalism and the corresponding suppression of pan-Hellenic cults, just as the information overload of the nineteenth century had prompted nationalisms and the decline of transnational institutions and practices, such as commerce. In Athens, civic unity was undermined by Pericles' curtailment of the legislature's powers, and the government's disenfranchisement of a substantial portion of the populace. The Delian League, the coalition of city-states dominated by Athens, was split by Athenian efforts to further consolidate its hegemony, and eventually consolidated into two opposing factions, with democratic states following Athens, and oligarchic states following Sparta. The competition of the two blocs for clients eventually precipitated the Peloponnesian War in 431 BCE, which ended with the defeat of Athens in 404 BCE. Sparta enjoyed a brief supremacy, but was itself defeated by the Thebans in 371 BCE. The entire city-state system ended with the rise of Philip of Macedon at the end of the fourth century BCE.[76]

Information overload prompted a second familiar pattern: cultural decline. While Greece experienced a brief resurgence of creativity in the works of Socrates, Plato, and Aristotle, the increasing quantity of written material produced by slave labour, especially after the rise of the Hellenic kingdoms, ultimately resulted in cultural stagnation: "The power of the written word made the Alexandrine age one of 'erudition and criticism,' of specialists rather than poets and scholars. The Alexandrine man was 'a librarian and corrector of proofs and who, pitiable wretch, goes blind from the dust of books and printers' errors' (Nietzche). Collectomania and large libraries accompanied taste and respectability. Aesthetic opinions were crystallized and the dilettante appeared."[77]

With cultural stagnation came an attending trend that Innis also identified in *Political Economy in the Modern State* – a division between elite culture and popular culture.[78] The influx of information subverted the social unity of the city-state, ushering in a division in which the educated subscribed to philosophy, while the populace allied itself with religion, often with faiths from the East: "Communication between those under the influence of philosophy and those under the influence of religions became increasingly difficult. Cultural division facilitated the development of a class structure."[79] Greece's increasing emphasis on the written tradition, Innis charged, ultimately weakened the science and the philosophy that had been its saving grace against Persia, and opened the way for "religions from the East and force from Rome in the West."[80] In the end, Greece declined because it failed to attend to the consequences of written communication. That inattention initially cost it its bearing on the world: its cultural and theological sense of the way things are and must be. Ultimately, it would cost it its independence.

III

Historically, then, in Greece and elsewhere, cognitive bias had afforded important advantages. They had provided a basis to perceive; and they had provided a ground upon which to engage in analogical reasoning and, in turn, to innovate and adapt. But they also had imposed an important cost: the fundamental risk of comfort, comfort with one's assumptions, and comfort with one's circumstances. When cultures such as Greece, Rome, and Egypt became comfortable, Innis believed, they also became passive and, even worse, rigid; they stopped adapting to changing circumstance. The price for that folly was to become one with Nineveh and Tyre.

When considering the trajectory of human history, therefore, it was important for Innis to establish which object truly had had the initiative: the human agent, at the individual and collective level; or the cultural scheme, derived from either space or time. Innis emphasized this concern shortly before he died in a 1952 letter to W.T. Easterbrook: "I am still worried about the problem of intelligence or the ability to get out of the particular rat race that civilization has run into or the possible toleration of a civilization which makes people think sufficiently to at least make possible an escape."[81] The solution Innis came upon for making such an escape was the oral tradition, and in both anthologies he set out to describe its fundamental characteristics. For Innis the communication theorist, the oral tradition was a method, an ethic, a way to see and think differently. It was a philosophy of mind and it had specific things to say about the role language plays in the construction of thought. It was, above all, a statement that thought itself operates according to the principles of formal cause.

Innis began his description of the oral tradition with the proposition that human thought is noise, in essence formless flux. For effective expression to take place, thought must be subjected to constraint, a constraint provided by language: "In the words of [Ernst] Cassirer language transformed the indeterminate into the determinate idea and held it within the sphere of finite dimensions. The spoken word set its seal on and gave definite form to what the mind created and culled away from the total sphere of consciousness ... Herbert Spencer wrote that 'language must be regarded as a hindrance to thought, though the necessary instrument of it.'"[82] Note the similarity here between Innis's formulation and the tenets of information theory listed in the previous chapter. For potential information to become actual information, an ordering process must be imposed. Just as an encryption process is required to translate television noise into an intelligible signal, the structures of language are required to translate mental noise – the total sphere of human consciousness – into an intelligible communication, be it oral or written. For Innis, the relevant structures included more than those associated with the emergent properties of language, such as phonemes and syntax. They also included human-created aesthetic constructs. Genres of expression in poetry and elsewhere could and did play a role in mediating human perception and expression.[83]

To Innis, the structures of language were significant not only because they organized thought but also because they had a bearing on its contents. Popular conceptions of time, for example, were "influenced by language which constrains and fixes prevalent modes of thought."[84] Still, while aesthetic and linguistic structures mediated human perception, they did not totally determine it in the way suggested by postmodern critical theory. Innis's intent was not to announce the death of the human subject.[85] Instead, his purpose was to suggest that the structures of language bore record not only to the regulation of human thought but also to its disruption. The history of language was a record of human innovation, activity that could be charted by distinguishing between the prescribed rules of language and the historical agent's use of the same. His point was similar to that made by the Swiss linguist Ferdinand de Saussure, who differentiated between the formal rules of language, or *langue*, and the individual's use of it, or *parole*.[86] Innis believed that agents were constrained by the rules of language, but were not determined by them. On the contrary, through their use and abuse of language, agents contributed to its evolution over time: "But the speech of the individual continued in a constant struggle with language and brought about constant adjustment. 'The history of language when looked at from the purely grammatical point of view is little other than the history of corruptions' (Lounsbury)."[87]

In the context of the oral tradition, however, the primary significance of structure – be it linguistic or aesthetic – extended beyond its role in patterning human thought and affirming human agency. Rather, it lay in its capacity to support the construction of formalisms and mental constructs that were complex. Innis's understanding of complexity coincides with the contemporary definition of the term; namely, systems composed of components that are coordinated, interconnected, and organized into a complexly differentiated hierarchy.[88] For example, while describing the evolution of the Greek epic poem, Innis noted that: "Nilsson describes the epic style as a conventionalized outcome of a long evolution extending from the thirteenth and twelfth to the ninth and eighth centuries. The great epics were probably developed out of lays constantly retold and amplified. Old ballads were replaced by combinations of a number of episodes into a unity of action. The epic was characterized by extreme complexity and unity."[89]

Innis stressed the issue of complexity in language and formal expression because historically it had had a direct bearing on the capacity of agents and cultures to change their perceptions and consequent performance. When agents had access to complex prose and poetic structures, they obtained a greater array of expressive forms for revising existing schemas, formulating new ones, and exploring their implications. In our discussion of Claude Shannon's information theory and time series, we saw the importance of localized constraint in the emergence of complex adaptive systems and in the construction and transmission of messages. In both cases, the capacity of emergent systems to self-organize into systems, and then into systems of systems, exponentially increases the potential number of combinations a system can visit. Innis held that the same principle applied to language and the construction of thought. The greater the degree of differentiation one found within a given language – the more it comprised a hierarchy of components, systems of components, and systems of systems of components – the greater the capacity of its users to produce models that better approximated their world. In this respect, Innis believed that cultures that actually relied on speech and memory retained a marked advantage, since they continued to use stylistic devices such as rhythm and metre to facilitate memory and thought: "Poetry is significant as a tribute to the oral tradition. Sapir has noted that 'many primitive languages have a formal richness; a latent luxuriance of expression that eclipses anything known to modern civilization.'"[90]

Innis believed that written forms of representation – be they ideographic, pictographic, syllabic, or phonetic – were characterized by differing degrees of complexity, and accordingly afforded differing degrees of flexibility than those found in speech. Writing systems, therefore, also played a role in mediating perception and behaviour.[91] The agent's capacity to retain the creative potential of the oral tradition – to formulate and explore the implications of new concepts – was dependent on the writing system adopted. The closer any system of representation was to the phonetic level of language – the more it was in accord with the formal complexity of the oral tradition – the greater the likelihood that the resulting written documents would emerge as useful models of the objects they purported to represent, models that would support effective adaptation to changes in the cultural, geopolitical, and natural environments. In 1946 Innis noted in his *Idea File* that the alphabet "facilitated development of ideas" and enabled a "closer approximation to reality than crude pictographs or images of organized religion," such as hieroglyphs.[92]

The import of signs was such that it determined an agent's capacity for abstract thought. Innis believed that pictographs and other iconic forms of representation were incapable of producing anything more than rough models of percepts. For this reason cultures employing such signs were incapable of lifting percepts beyond the point of analogy: they could not formulate a general concept. Innis's historical narratives consistently identified hieroglyphics and pictographs with the concrete. In Mesopotamia, for example, before cuneiform symbols were identified with the syllabic level of language, Innis noted: "Concrete pictographs involved an elaborate vocabulary with large numbers of items."[93] The Chinese in his view faced a similar problem with their use of pictographs, one that hindered their capacity to generate an abstract model of time: "It has been argued by Marcel Granet that the Chinese are not equipped to note concepts or to present doctrines discursively. The word does not fix a notion with a definite degree of abstraction or generality but evokes an indefinite complex of particular images. It is completely unsuited to formal precision. Neither time nor space is abstractly conceived; time proceeds by cycles and is round; space is square."[94]

Only cultures identifying signs with syllables and phonemes could generate models of sufficient resolution to permit the abstraction of common patterns from disparate locales. According to Innis, the process of abstraction started as soon as writing was rationalized to the syllabic level in Mesopotamia. "Pictographs and ideograms took on abstract phonetic values, and the study of script became linked to the study of language."[95] New forms of linguistic script heightened Babylon's competence in geometry, enabling it to move from concrete problems of measurement to an abstract conception of Euclidean space. It also enabled the Hebrews to transform their theology from one in which divinities were associated with a concrete activity, to monotheism and a universal ethics.[96]

The Greek alphabet, with its innovation of signs to permit the representation of vowels, enabled Thales of Miletus and other Ionian philosophers to move beyond the Egyptians, who had never managed to go beyond the linkage of percepts to create analogies of limited application. Egyptian geometry, for example, was constrained by its reliance on hieroglyphics, architecture, and other visual forms of representation: "But whereas in Egypt mathematics like ethics and medicine had been developed empirically and stopped short of philosophy, it became to Thales a means of discarding allegory and myth and advancing universal generalizations ... Opposition was evoked in Anaximander (about 611–547 [BCE]), a cartographer, who sought for a more general conception unlimited by qualities. Geometry was used to develop a conception of the earth and of the universe."[97]

While Innis championed individual agency, and saw language and script as tools to support its exercise, he did not see the oral tradition solely as a solitary practice. If it was to reach its potential as a support for creation and adaptation, it had to be a social process, one in which new schemas emerged as a result of interaction with one's peers and the surrounding environment. In 1950 he noted in his *Idea File*: "'Out of frequent and close conversation and much social intercourse a light is of a sudden kindled in the mind, as from a fire that leaps forth, which when once generated keeps itself alive' (Plato)."[98]

While any review of Innis's conception of the oral tradition must make reference to his views on mind, language, complexity, and social interaction, no review would be complete that does not address a fundamental question: why did he believe ancient Greece to be such an effective practitioner of it? Innis provided a threefold answer, one that centred on Greece's environment, its innovations, and its subsequent practice of the oral tradition. Greece was distinguished because it was situated in a technological environment that limited its access to papyrus and a geopolitical environment in which it was distant from Mesopotamia.[99] Those contingencies forestalled its immersion into the written tradition. For a time, it managed to escape the consequences of the information-saturated society described by Albert Schweitzer: "Our spiritual life is disorganized for the over-organization of our external environment leads to the organization of our absence of thought."[100] Unlike the imperia of the Near East, Greece managed to avoid being overwhelmed by the cultural riches of Egypt and Babylon, and accordingly it escaped "the formal patterns of the Orient."[101]

One important innovation that enabled the Greeks to organize their spiritual life and any other feature of life for themselves was, as we have seen, the Greek alphabet. Greece appropriated the Phoenician alphabet in the eighth century BCE and adapted it to Greek needs, in large measure by creating letters that were identified with vowel sounds. Semitic alphabets prior to that point had only identified letters with consonantal sounds, but Innis argued that the Greek alphabet's more precise fit with the phonetic level of language afforded the Greeks a unique advantage.[102] In effect, it gave them more building blocks and hence better models: "They permitted the expression of fine distinctions and light shades of meaning. The Greek language 'responds with happy elasticity to every demand of the Greek intellect ... the earliest work of art created by the spontaneous working of the Greek mind.'"[103]

This innovation – combined with Greece's distance from Egypt and Babylon – laid the basis for another: "the one entirely original literature of Europe." More specifically, Greece generated new poetry such as the epic and lyric, forms rich in internal complexity that were capable of supporting the generation, retention, and distribution of complex cognitive constructs.[104] Greek epics, Innis writes, were in effect systems of components that in modern parlance displayed differential persistence. It was a strategy born as much of necessity as design: "The memory took the place of logical processes in writing and supported an immense burden of vocabulary and grammatical complexity with the help of verse, metre, rhyme, and proverbs. 'Poetry is the chain of the stories' (Arab saying). What was once well said was not to be changed but repeated in the very words of its original author."[105]

The virtue of such a system was its adaptability. The hierarchical nature of poetry allowed not only formulation, but reformulation in response to changing individual and social experience: "Minstrels developed epic poems in hexameter which involved rigidities but permitted elasticities facilitating adaptation to the demands of vernacular speech."[106] Components could be assembled and reassembled, and the semantics of the components adjusted to meet the demands of the new distributed whole. Referring to the oral tradition that preceded the composition of the Hebrew Bible, Innis noted: "The oral as compared with the written transmission of tradition was inherently more consistent and logical in its results because of the constant sifting, refining, and modifying of what did not fit into the tradition. In the cumulative effects of the oral tradition the pieces of an edifice were carried to another site and worked into the structure of a different novel. Fact shifted into legend, legend into myth. Facts worked loose and became detached from their roots in space and time. The story was moulded and remoulded by imagination, passion, prejudice, religious presumption, or aesthetic instinct."[107] In other words, the Bible emerged in a pattern similar to the one we have noted for the autocatalytic set. Just as formal cause regulates the constituent processes of the set, formal cause altered the significance and semantics of the "edifices" that comprised the written version of the Hebrew Bible.

The capacity to purpose and repurpose proved extremely important for Greece, and distinguished its practice of the oral tradition. While the Hebrews used it to support the cause of myth, Greek philosophers used it to articulate a conception of nature governed not by divine caprice but rather by law. The Homeric poems were themselves revisions of earlier myths featuring nature gods and the pervasive influence of magic: "New types of literature reflected the efficiency of the oral tradition in expressing the needs of social change."[108] According to Innis, Homeric literature began the process of humanizing the gods in response to such needs, while later literature sublimated the importance of magic, and emphasized the importance of human ethics. The cumulative effect of these changes was an emphasis on law, and the subsequent separation of science from religion in Greek society: "Anthropomorphism and the absence of magic and limitations on the power of the gods assumed rationalism and the necessity of finding order and coherence in the world. 'The Greek view of the relation of men to the god was mechanical.' Decline of belief in the supernatural led to the explanation of nature in terms of natural causes. With the independent search for truth science was separated from myth. 'By his religion man has been made at home in the world.' The minstrels were followed by the rhapsodists and in turn by the Ionian philosophers. The latter built up where the former pulled down."[109]

Aside from reformulation, Greek use of the oral tradition was also distinguished by its use for interpolation. Greek philosophers used the principle of localized constraint embedded in the oral tradition to revise their constructs of change in the same way that Pythagoras and his followers had used the principle of localized constraint embedded in the principle of number to revise their own. It should come as no surprise, therefore, that Innis identified the two by referring to the time series as a constituent of the oral tradition. As we saw in the previous chapter, Innis argued in *Political Economy in the Modern State* that the juxtaposition of time series and multiple domains of history from the perspective of space offered social scientists valuable insights. Through interpolation of long-term patterns embedded in economic and social data, social scientists could model and characterize the behaviour of social systems. The exercise had a second potential benefit: correction of bias through demonstration that regional and national economies were part of a larger international whole. Time series demonstrated that study of the economy from a purely national perspective was as absurd a proposition as studying meteorology and assuming the weather stopped at the Canadian border.[110]

In his two communication studies, Innis argued that poetry conferred a similar utility on the ancients, particularly in the field of theology: time series and poetry were functionally equivalent. Just as time series referred to phenomena governed by local constraints, poetry referred to chains of stories composed by disparate authors, stories that retained their formal integrity even as they were incorporated into a larger whole. The "temporal order in imagination" in poetry, the process of combining and recombining religious insights, enabled the ancients to overcome religious chauvinism, just as time series in principle could limit or temper economic chauvinism. The Hebrews used it to conceive of a god that transcended borders: "The oral tradition and its relation to poetry implied a concern with time and religion. 'The artist represents *coexistence in space*, the poet *succession in time*' (Lessing at the University of Berlin, 1810). The oral tradition reflected the positive influence of Egypt in the name of Moses, the doctrine that God is the sole creator and the formula from which his name Yahweh is derived, the concept of a single god and the establishment of doctrine based on monotheism, and the recognition of the international, cosmic character of the reigning deity."[111]

In sum, the oral tradition offered the Greeks the means to identify shortcomings in established modes of perception. Through application of the principle of extension and the principle of number, the formalism of the artist and the formalism of the poet, they, through the use of universal and local constraint, achieved the capacity to generate models that provided a better account of observed phenomena. Time series in the form of numeric measurement and poetic component enabled philosophers and theologians to perceive systems that extended beyond national boundaries. The components of poetry enabled Greek philosophers to divorce the study of nature from myth and to identify regularities in natural phenomena.

IV

The oral tradition at base, then, was an assertion of human freedom. It is humans who manipulate structure, not the reverse. It is humans who have the capacity to create information environments that support the construction, interrogation, and reformulation of extant constructs. When Innis's other writings are taken into account, however, it can and should be argued that the oral tradition offers at best a partial defence of human agency, and that Innis knew it. This is clear because Innis pointed to two variants of media: immaterial and material. Immaterial media referred to formalisms, the patterned constructs humans created to express prose, poetry, and mathematical formulae.[112] Material media referred to the substance, the matter, that humans used to instantiate, distribute and store their constructs – everything from papyrus and clay to stone. What the oral tradition offered was a defence against immaterial media, the determinisms, linguistic and otherwise, that scholars have attributed to grammar and other formal structures.

How was Innis able to maintain the possibility of human freedom while simultaneously asserting that the material properties of media could be correlated with a culture's cognitive bias? And how was he able to offer a narrative that in several cases ran counter to the media generalizations he offered? One explanation would be to assert that Innis – like any good historian – made reference to evidence that ran counter to his hypothesis: to show respect for the complexity of history; to argue that the anomalies were not fatal for his hypothesis; and to provide readers the opportunities to determine if they agreed. The argument is plausible. But I suggest that a more compelling argument is that Innis rested his media theory on the concept of final cause and the construct of probabilistic change. If he relied on these expedients, then a case study, say, of papyrus use in conjunction with a cultural bias toward time emerges as an event perfectly consistent with his theory. Space for human agency is retained; and the troubling anomalies removed.

To establish such an argument, however, we will need direction from Innis to assist us for the remainder of this chapter. More specifically, we will need direction to the intellectual contexts from which he drew his ideas on schema change. That direction, I suggest, can be found in his two anthologies, but it also can be located in important complements, most notably primary sources such as the *Idea File* – where Innis drew explicit connections between his media constructs and the economic and philosophic constructs he deemed important – and in the correspondence and minutes of conversations that Innis undertook with colleagues such as Arthur Cole and W.T. Easterbrook. It will also be found in important secondary sources, including the writings of contemporaries such as Ernst Cassirer and B.S. Keirstead, and an important and influential predecessor, Immanuel Kant. These sources – and current writings devoted to the science of complexity and contemporary economics – will prove essential for addressing the four topics necessary for our argument, namely:

- deepening our understanding of the concept of final cause and its consequent: multiple potential outcomes;
- establishing Innis's basis for aligning his theory of media and cognitive change with the concept of final cause: his acceptance of the Kantian concept of formal purposiveness;
- demonstrating his application of formal purposiveness and final cause, and his concurrent provision for multiple outcomes and the exercise of agency;
- and, finally, establishing Innis's understanding that the relationships he drew between human thought and material media were probabilistic in nature.

Final Cause and the Potential for Monopolies or Oligopolies

In chapters 1 and 3, we visited the concept of final cause through the writings of Thorstein Veblen and Alfred Marshall. We also considered its consequent – that emerging systems have more than one endpoint to which they can move – and suggested that Innis was aware of that consequent. Here, we revisit that concept to deepen our understanding of the relationship between final cause and increasing returns on the one hand, and the governance of probabilistic change and the emergence of monopolies and oligopolies on the other. Following the success of Newton's celestial mechanics in the seventeenth century, the concept of final cause fell into disrepute because it suggested that change was not the product of events occurring in time through efficient cause. Instead, it appealed to the pull or agency of a force operating either forward or outside of time. For modern philosophy, it smacked too much of purpose in the form of divine intervention, and was abandoned.[113] Recently, however, the concept has enjoyed a resurgence because it has come to be associated with the process of self-organization, and is now conceived, at least by those with a materialist or naturalist commitment, to operate solely within space and time. In the science of complexity, final cause is identified with the concept of the *attractor*. Self-organizing systems are portrayed as progressing toward a terminus point, a meta-stable state or pattern of behaviour that persists, barring outside influence. This state or pattern of behaviour is the system's *attractor*.

Self-organizing systems are characterized by the presence of multiple potential attractors. Given that the system is governed by a combination of constraint and contingency, environmental constraints limit the number of potential attractors a system can have and can consequently visit. The system is governed by a regime of probabilistic change. When a system self-organizes, any one attractor can be selected. Only one is selected. While the system's constraints make the selection of one attractor more probable than its alternatives, there is no way to predict the system's future trajectory. As the system interacts with the environment, the combination of environmental constraint, contingent circumstance, and the system's history determine which attractor will be selected. The process of self-organization can be seen as the selection and gravitation of a system towards its attractor.[114]

The economics of W. Brian Arthur provides a more concrete expression of the attractor concept, and also affords the advantage of linking it to the concepts of increasing returns and market equilibrium, additions that will prove useful in our review of Innis's writings on media bias. In the discipline of economics, a system has reached its attractor when it reaches equilibrium, whether that equilibrium refers to the spatial distribution of firms from a particular industry among competing regions, or to market share between competing products or technologies. In chapter 3 we saw that economic systems can be governed either by diminishing or increasing returns. Increasing returns are positive feedback mechanisms that determine the market share of competing products. A classic example provided by Arthur is the emergence of the VHS format as the dominant standard of the VCR market. Both VHS and Beta formats started with roughly equal market share, but early small gains in the sales of VHS recorders initiated a process of cumulative causation that resulted in the format gaining a monopoly over the domestic VCR market. Video outlets began stocking more prerecorded VHS tapes than Beta tapes, an action that in turn caused new consumers to opt for VHS players. Since systems governed by increasing returns are characterized by multiple possible outcomes, Arthur argues, the selection of the VHS format was not inevitable. Beta was considered by many experts as the superior product. It could have emerged as the dominant product, had its proponents pursued a different sales strategy and enjoyed better luck.[115]

The distribution of market share in systems governed by increasing returns is not always the all-or-nothing distribution implied by the

VCR market. Arthur notes that systems can also reach points of equilibrium where competing products reach a stable share, or oligopoly, over the market. In a competition between Car A and Car B, for example, Car A might capture 65% to Car B's 35%. Given the same initial conditions but a different history, however, Car B's market share might have reached a 90% share to A's 10%. What is significant, here, however, is that the market can only distribute shares in a finite number of ways. There are only so many attractors that the system can reach. Stated more concretely, a market might divide into shares of 65% to 35%, but never 70% to 30%.[116]

Innis's Appropriation of the Concept of Final Cause via the Kantian Principle of Formal Purposiveness

Arthur's work is important because it raises the possibility that Innis translated the concepts of increasing returns and final cause to his theory of media. Via such a scenario, it makes perfect sense that Innis would have seen cognitive bias as an emergent property of agent-agent and agent-medium interaction, and that he would have seen the selection of bias as a contingent process, with a bias toward space emerging in one context, and toward time in another. And to this point, we have seen evidence in this study that strongly suggests he framed his history of human cognition in precisely these terms:

- We saw the high importance that Innis placed on the concept of increasing returns in his 1941 statement emphasizing Adam Smith's construct: the division of labour;
- We saw, through reference to the writings of Kenneth Arrow in the previous chapter, that economists have understood Smith's construct to refer not only to task differentiation, but to the process prompting task differentiation: increasing returns;
- In our previous chapter, we saw that Innis believed the concept to be applicable to the history of communication, and with it, to the history of human thought;
- Via Arrow and Arthur we have learned that the concepts of increasing returns and final cause are associated and that the two lead to an important, indeterminate consequent in economics: the emergence of monopolies and oligopolies.;
- In chapter 4 and in this chapter we saw Innis's recognition of both consequents of increasing returns. We saw Innis's appeal to

increasing returns through his identification of the history of cognition with business cycle and monopoly theory (See Section I, Proposition Two above). And we saw, through reference to the preface of *The Bias of Communication*, Innis's intention to describe the impact of communication media on "the character of knowledge and to suggest that a monopoly or an oligopoly of knowledge is built up to the point that equilibrium is disturbed."[117]

- And finally, through the writings of Thorstein Veblen and Alfred Marshall, we documented Innis's exposure to the concept of increasing returns and one of its consequents: the emergence of multiple points of equilibria, one of which the system selects as it gravitates towards meta-stability.

What we have not seen is an account that describes why Innis felt it necessary and fitting to frame his histories in these terms. The answer, in essence, is that Innis saw two patterns in the history of human cognition – similarity and variance – which he could not account for using the synthetic principles associated with efficient cause. He believed that cultural constructs and biological forms shared an important feature: similarity. That feature permitted constructs from disparate locales and times to be classified into a hierarchical scheme. Just as biological forms could be classified according to a general trait – a genus – and then classified with greater precision at the subordinate – or species – level, so too could cultural forms. It was a conceptual innovation that permitted him to bring a Greek construct such as the *logos* into association with a British concept such as the division of labour. And it was an innovation that permitted the detection of an important correlation: between the material properties of media on the one hand and the cultural genera of time and space on the other; and an important variation: his agents, individual and social, did not always behave in the manner expected. Sometimes they assumed one bias, while the correlation predicted another. Sometimes they displayed that most wonderful of human penchants: the capacity to be idiosyncratic, to turn on a dime.

Because the synthetic principles associated with efficient cause could not account for the patterns of similarity and variance revealed by his research, Innis searched for a different "logic," one that would provide a new set of synthetic principles and, in turn, justify his belief that human cultural constructs formed a distinct ontology that was subject to classification and study. A detailed study of that logic reveals not only Innis's justification for his domain of study but also the epistemological and metaphysical principles he drew from it. It provides a basis for suggesting that Innis saw schema change as a contingent process, and that he was the exponent of an Idealist interpretation of history.

Innis's appropriation of the logic underlying systems of knowledge based on classification can be illustrated by two extracts from his writings – one referring to Aristotle, the other to Kant – which explicitly address the topic. It can also be shown by taking two further steps, which we will undertake in the next section. The first is to demonstrate that Innis was familiar with the Kant extract as early as 1943 and was therefore in a position to apply its insights to *Empire* and *Bias*. The second is to show that the Kant extract was important to Innis, that he incorporated its logical and epistemological tenets, and the metaphysical tenets associated with it, into his theory of media and cognitive change.

Innis's first reference to a "logic" appears in *Empire and Communications* in a discussion devoted to Aristotelian science. There, he explicitly identifies the classification sciences with final cause and suggests they are governed by a form of change that is neither purely random nor universal: "The biological sciences emphasized classification, which, in the words of Whitehead, stood halfway between the immediate concreteness of the individual theory and the complete abstractions of mathematical notions and involved an emphasis on logic ... As a biologist rather than a physicist he leaned towards final cause."[118] The second reference is contained in a 1951 entry in the *Idea File*, where Innis referred to Immanuel Kant's efforts in the *Critique of Judgment* to assert the autonomy and methodological independence of biology from physics. Kant's purpose was to reconcile a world governed by universal law with a world in which individual agency or purpose existed. Innis noted: "*Critique of Judgement* to prove no antimony between two forms of order ... (1) to refer phenomenon to universal dynamic principle of causality and (2) to regard phenomenon from point of view of purpose and to organize and arrange them accordingly. Kant rejected solutions of both Aristotle and Spinoza – i.e. biology and mathematics. Principle of formal purposiveness and Kant's conclusions as to adaptation of nature to our judgement – in formal purposiveness the logician of Linnaeus' descriptive science."[119]

The material in this second extract is an extremely condensed rendition of a discussion on Kant contained in Ernst Cassirer's *The Problem of Knowledge*. As the extract indicates, Innis was drawn to Cassirer's explication of Kant's efforts to establish the logical foundations of biology. That logic, in Aristotelian biology and the Linnaean biology that Kant knew, rested on the "logic of class concepts," which provided "an indispensable means to the knowledge and scientific description of natural forms."[120] Kant's purpose throughout his career, Cassirer writes, was to locate the *a priori* assumptions adhered to by the various domains of human knowledge. Each discipline adheres to a set of fundamental suppositions that enables it to synthesize individual percepts into a domain that forms the basis of study. In the discipline of physics, phenomena were bound by a logic of relations. Within this variant of logic, "nature" exists as a construct because perception is governed by three synthetic concepts: substance, causality, and reciprocity. Without them, the universe emerges as a chaos, not a cosmos demonstrating order in space and time. They are a necessary prerequisite for experience. From them, all subsequent constructs of nature can be deduced. In the *Critique of Pure Reason*, Kant argued that Newton's *Principia* provided a case study of the "general laws of understanding" in application.[121] The problem, however, was that the suppositions outlined in the *Critique of Pure Reason* could not account for the purposive behaviour of biological organisms. The principles contained in the logic of relations could not account for the fact of self-regulating behaviour demonstrated by living beings. In his *Critique of Judgment*, therefore, Kant made an attempt to establish the autonomy and methodological independence of biology without sacrificing the coherence provided by physics.[122]

The dichotomy between efficient cause and purpose, Cassirer writes, is one that philosophers have attempted to reconcile since the time of Aristotle. Aristotle tried to force a unity by subordinating physics to the principles governing vital phenomena, while Spinoza insisted that all natural phenomena be explained mathematically and mechanically.[123] For Kant, however, the stance of both did violence to reality by erasing the distinction between animate and inanimate matter. Spinoza's formulation, in particular, was no solution because it ignored formal purpose, the self-regulating purposive behaviour characteristics of living organisms: "An organized product of nature is that in which all is reciprocally end and means."[124] Accordingly, in 1790 Kant proposed to establish a complementary set of governing rules for biology, rules that would enable observers to make a "synthesis of rules according to concepts."[125] He proposed to establish a set of synthetic concepts that would complement, not contradict, the universal conditions of natural knowledge identified in the *Critique of Pure Reason*. The problem that Kant faced, Cassirer writes, was finding a means to accomplish his task: "If biology is not to be a 'state within a state,' it must conform to these laws on all points. But how is an 'autonomy' of biology to be attained in this way, a self-legislation that will not appear simply foreign to the principles upon which mathematical physics is founded?"[126]

Kant bridged the divide, according to Cassirer, by declaring purpose and cause to be two separate modes of knowledge: "The *Critique of Judgment* aims to prove that there is no antinomy whatsoever between these two *forms of order* in knowledge. They cannot contradict one another because they relate to problems in distinct fields that must be carefully kept apart." The mode of cause was related to "knowledge of the temporal succession of events." Such events required synthesizing principles entirely different from those required for the mode of purpose, which concerned itself with the structure of living organisms. Such structures were distinguished from their inanimate counterparts because each one formed "a unified self-contained structure," a whole "so formed that it determines the properties of its various parts. Then nature ceases to be an aggregate and becomes a system."[127] In Kant's words: "The principle of purposive combinations and forms in nature is at least, then, one principle more for bringing the appearance under rules, where the laws of mechanistic causality do not suffice."[128] By asserting the incommensurability of the two forms of knowledge, Kant believed he had avoided creating an antinomy between biology and physics. The dichotomy between purpose and cause had no meaning, since his critiques were constructed on separate principles.[129]

With his justification for a distinct discipline and methodology for biology in place, Kant proceeded with his task of unearthing the core suppositions upon which the science of biology then rested. Here he relied on the defining biological work of the eighteenth century to inform his reasoning, the writings of the botanist Carolus Linnaeus. According to Cassirer, Linnaean biology was important because it demonstrated more than any other schema that had preceded it the purchase of the Aristotelian logic of class concepts for organizing biological phenomena. In so doing, it established a domain of knowledge based not on a logic of relation but rather on one of distinction, one in which every individual "was assigned its determinate place in the whole scheme."[130] And in so doing, it provided the clearest, most precise, and most comprehensive classification of biological phenomena ever attempted: "At one stroke the manifold variety of these forms, which were incapable of being seen in any one view, were classified as members according to a regular scheme." Linnaean biology emerged as the exemplar application of the logic of class concepts, and an indispensable tool for biologists.[131]

For Kant, the key challenge was to find a justification for seeing nature in the form of a logical system. The concepts of genus and species were the direct result of a mapping of Aristotle's hierarchical scheme onto natural phenomena. In Kant's estimation, however, no compelling reason, no "transcendental deduction" regarding natural forms had been offered that was comparable to the concepts of substance, causation, and reciprocity in the *Critique of Reason*.[132] The synthetic concepts there do not mandate a universe in which objects or organisms must share some degree of affinity, thereby enabling their classification into larger groupings such as genus and species. One can still speak of a coherent nature governed by efficient cause, a cosmos governed by universal law, but which in other respects discloses an "irreducible diversity in the manifold of its appearances," a cosmos in which "it would be no longer possible to connect particular beings ... as an ascending order." In such a hypothetical universe each "particular ... would have to be described simply by itself."[133]

Such an extreme formulation, writes Cassirer, was an offense to both experience and common sense, and required the construction of a new synthetic concept that Kant referred to as "the principle of formal purposiveness." The principle in essence stated that nature, while governed by universal law, also demonstrated "a thoroughgoing organization" in which forms shared similarities of greater or lesser degree.[134] Kant did not see that principle as a necessary principle underlying the understanding of nature. Rather, it was a principle of the "reflective judgement," a basis for constructing useful heuristics whose validation could only be obtained via interrogation of nature: "Whether or not a perfect classification of natural forms according to class and order, family and genus, is attainable, experience alone can teach us."[135] In Cassirer's reading of Kant, the interrogation of nature involves interaction, a feature of his description that particularly interested Innis. If we see in nature a coherence that matches the form of a logical system, it is because we have made the conscious decision to seek it. According to Cassirer: "The search is not something we are compelled to by the objects; it expresses a peculiar command of the reason. For reason addresses itself to nature, 'to be taught by her, certainly, but not as a pupil who accepts anything that the teacher chooses to say, but rather as a judge invested with the power to require the witness to answer the questions put to him' ... Kant used a note-worthy expression for this interpretation when he spoke of an 'adaptation' of nature to our understanding or to the rules of our faculty of judgment."[136]

Since there was nothing inherent in natural forms that suggested the constitution of the hierarchical scheme of which they were a part, the observer had no option but to construct an ontology: to see if its description could account for known natural forms; and, in turn, to see if its description could account for new forms once they were discovered. And sometimes, nature cooperated, producing new natural forms that aligned with the proffered ontology. To build on this argument, Cassirer drew his readers' attention to a lengthy extract from the *Critique of Judgment*, which he quoted in full. That extract is important because it provides a way to show that Innis understood the principle of formal purposiveness and the consequent "'adaptation' of nature to our understanding" in two ways. First, he understood it to mean an adaptation of nature – or culture – to a proffered ontology. On that basis, he was able to justify his stance as a cultural historian that cultural forms could be described by an ontology composed of two genera – space and time – and that "nature," the cultural objects comprising the human past and present, had adapted itself to that understanding.

Innis also understood the Kantian adaptation of nature in a second sense. Here, he saw cultural phenomena cohering not only with his ontology writ large but also with a single class or *a priori* form within his ontology. In such a scenario, a new medium would arise. It would disrupt the cultural status quo, and create a cognitive space that enabled agents to create new constructs from two classes: space and time. Over time, members of the given culture – through interaction with each other and their surrounding cultural environment – would reach the conclusion that extant phenomena best aligned with constructs from one of the two classes. Further, nature – or culture – was seen to adapt itself to one of the two potential understandings that were available. In Innis's terminology, nature copied art. In our terminology, the given culture gravitated toward one of the two cognitive attractors available to it. For Innis, this was an emergent, indeterminate process, one that resulted from agent-agent, agent-medium, and agent-environment interaction. It was also an inevitable process, one that would lead to a monopoly or oligopoly of knowledge. In this way, Innis was able to suggest that there is an ontology of knowledge, and that ontology sets the bounds through which knowledge is constructed. And in this way, Innis was able to suggest that a given medium can inhabit a given bias in one context, and a different bias in another. Kant writes:

> Any comparison of empirical ideas in order to know empirical laws and accordingly the *specific* forms and, through their comparison with others, the *generically similar* forms in natural objects – all such comparison presupposes this: that in respect to her empirical laws nature has observed a certain economy that to our judgment appears fitting, and an understandable uniformity, and this presupposition as a principle of a priori judgment must precede all comparison.
>
> The reflective judgment thus proceeds with given appearances, in order to bring them under the empirical concepts of certain natural things, not schematically but *technically*, not just mechanically, as it were, as an instrument under the direction of the understanding and the senses but *with art*. The judgment orders the appearance according to the universal, though at the same time indeterminate, principle of a purposive arrangement of nature in a system, as if nature were something favorable to our judgment in the conformity of her particular laws ... to the possibility of experience as a system. Without some such presupposition we cannot hope to find our way in a labyrinth of the multiplicity of separate laws.[137]

Innis's Application of Formal Purposiveness and Final Cause

Through the Kantian concept of formal purposiveness, then, Innis acquired a justification for the study and classification of cultural forms. Nature observed a certain economy, and so too did culture. Both ensured that extant forms gravitated to a finite set of potential configurations; each configuration constituted a point of equilibrium, a point of attraction – or attractor – for the evolution of future forms. Through the logic explicated in Aristotle and Cassirer, we see that the operation of those forms was governed by formal cause and that their stabilization and transformation were governed by final cause. And through the writings of Cassirer and Kant, we see the basis for Innis's belief that there is an ontology of knowledge, and that its perception, confirmation, and extension require creative acts on the part of the observer.

While Innis made reference to these ideas in 1951, the year he published *The Bias of Communication*, there are strong grounds to suggest that he was familiar with the writings of Kant and Cassirer as early as 1943, and was therefore in a position to use them to inform his composition of the articles and lectures comprising *Empire and Communications* and *The Bias of Communication*. In "Political Economy in the Modern State," for example, in rejoinder to Marshall's contention that socio-economic systems should be treated as if they were in equilibrium, Innis replied that similar methodological and conceptual errors had already been made by Aristotle and Spinoza: "The combination of the mathematical and biological fallacies has been challenged by the insistence that civilization is an art."[138] The influence of Kant and Cassirer is further suggested by a 1947 entry in his *Idea File*. There, Innis drew on Cassirer's observation that in Kant there is an "'adaptation' of nature to our faculty of judgment," and on Kant's observation that "the reflective judgment thus proceeds with art." And there, he reduced both formulations to the pithy term, "nature copies art." It was a term he would employ in later *Idea File* entries and publications, and one which he used here to bring Kant's ideas into relation with his own on schema change and communication media: "History does nothing else but repeat itself with dominance of type of thought. Monopoly control over thought and over media implies that nature copies art as nature seen through stigmatic spectacles."[139]

Innis turned to the concepts of formal purposiveness and final cause because he believed the history of human cognition had been driven by a combination of emergent change and individual freedom. He turned to them also because they suggested that a dynamic – such as increasing returns – should be combined with an ontology to explain its increasing complexification over time. The operation of the former on the latter constitutes the core of Innis's histories of cognition, and our purpose here will be to briefly explicate the nature of that relationship, before a review of the evidence which suggests it.

In suggesting that final cause impinged on an ontology constituted by a bias of space and a bias of time, Innis was simply adjusting himself to an architectonic that was established by Adam Smith and consolidated by Charles Darwin. Each identified an ontology: in the case of Smith it was the economy, in the case of Darwin it was natural history. Each in turn identified a dynamic that explained the growing complexification of the environment that concerned them. In Smith's case, the dynamic was increasing returns; in Darwin's, it was of course natural selection. For Smith the outcome was division of labour – more people performing more tasks that were increasingly specialized; for Darwin, the outcome was new species. Innis's intention to emulate Smith and Darwin is indicated by the identification of his histories with monopoly theory and by extension with the ontology of thought and business cycle theory. It is also indicated by his appeal to a dynamic that complexified the ontology underlying thought.

Innis's appeal to a system of knowledge based on classification and a dynamic promoting complexification in turn led to a consideration of the epistemological and metaphysical implications of his ontology. Here, his purpose was to explain two things: novelty and dissemination. How are new cultural forms formulated? And how do they spread? Smith pointed to innovation, while Darwin pointed to mutation. Innis for his part pointed to an individual and collective process of what might best be called realization. Novelty was a problem for Innis. His own research indicated there were instances in history in which societies were locked in monopolies of knowledge, where constructs and artefacts representing only one cognitive bias – that of space, or that of time – were materially at hand. Yet, cultures somehow managed to move beyond the dominance of one bias and visit another, and to begin producing new constructs that derived from that bias. In very rare instances, some managed to attain a situation where they could access both. And the process was not always precipitated by the intervention of a conquering neighbour from the periphery. Some – most notably ancient Greece – managed to move endogenously from one monopoly to another, and to the oligopoly of knowledge as well. The key question was how?

The first prerequisite for change was that equilibrium had to be disturbed. The old order of knowledge had to be disrupted, and the conditions for a new cycle of knowledge created. Such states of disequilibrium, Innis believed, were precipitated by the onset of new communication technologies. Their presence changed "the rate of diffusion, conditions of diffusion" of information.[140] More content could be distributed, and the ways said content could be combined and recombined were accentuated. More important, the disruption permitted a widening of the cognitive potential of the given culture's agents. They were no longer locked in a cognitive monopoly, despite living in an environment of constructs, formalisms, and practices reflecting it. Innis held this belief because the writings of Plato and Immanuel Kant suggested that there are fundamental *a priori* forms governing human perception – particularly human perception of time and space – and that these forms are ultimately situated outside time and space. Innis ultimately grounded his conception of human freedom on the Idealist interpretation of history.

That orientation enabled Innis to devise a conception of knowledge construction and mapping that proceeded via individual realization and social abduction, a scenario in which, in his terms, "nature copied art." That scenario presumed the capacity for "art," the capacity for constructive activity. It also presumed that the ontology comprising space and time would set the bounds for constructive activity. In such a scenario, creative activity meant offering a way to extend the ontology, to create a new sub-category within a category of thought to describe and govern a new domain of activity, or, if you like, a new species of activity. In this way, individual agents "realized" novelty. An *a priori* form, or genera, such as time was brought into relation with a domain of activity such as religion or economics, and a new concept such as division of labour was expressed and brought into association with extant concepts such as the *logos*.

Innis did not believe, however, that the ontology of knowledge was extended at the individual level. That was a social process. At the start of any given knowledge cycle, multiple competing constructs are generated. They originate in the disparate domains of human practice, and reflect the two biases available to human cognition. The "agent" that "chose" from among these competing constructs was the distributed network, or one of the distributed networks that constituted the culture that concerned Innis. Each network in his histories engaged in a process of selection akin to market selection or natural selection; for our purposes we will call it cultural selection. Cultural selection was initiated by dissemination, a positive feedback process akin to increasing returns whereby more and more members adopted the construct until it enjoyed dominance.

The process of cultural selection, Innis believed, was a product of both deliberation and contingency. Social deliberation was supported by abduction, a second stage in the process in which "nature copied art." The individual agent was responsible for the generation of the "art," that is, the cultural constructs deriving from time and space meant to meet the theological, philosophical, political, or other needs arising from the domains in which their author was situated. The social agent – the network or networks comprising a given culture – was responsible for determining via abduction how and when "nature copied art," when nature aligned with the cultural constructs under consideration, when the cultural constructs met the social, cultural, and political needs of the moment. Ultimately, Innis was interested in a scenario where "culture copied art."

Abductive reasoning is distinguished from deduction in that it does not explicate concepts already inherent in an extant, fixed set of principles. It proceeds instead through one or multiple acts of comparison and judgment. The agent applies multiple classifications, constructs, or hypotheses, and determines which among the competitors best explains, describes, or classifies the object or question under consideration.[141] In the case of Innis, the social agent is considering the efficacy of space and time in meeting the social, political, and cultural needs of the moment. Such a scenario presupposes that the social agent – or more accurately its individual members – has the capacity to compare the two classes and judge their respective applicability. They must mentally visit the various categories of the given ontology and determine the construct's "fitness," its degree of correspondence with the task or need at hand. The process of cultural selection occurs via dissemination of competing constructs from space and time, and the convergence, the selection, by the social agent over time on a single class, and the cultural constructs associated with it. This is a deliberate process. But it is also an emergent, historically contingent process. There is no telling ahead of time which of the classes – the points of equilibrium, monopolies of knowledge, attractors, or *a priori* forms respectively known as space and time – it will select. But once that selection is made, only the constructs associated with the given class or monopoly are retained. Those that belong to the competing attractor or monopoly are dispensed with. And the individual and social agent's propensity to consult the *a priori* form at variance with the prevailing monopoly is also dispensed with. It is through this process also that a given medium acquires its bias. It precipitates disequilibrium and the emergence of a new knowledge cycle. Via this historically contingent process, the medium acquires its bias. And via this cycle, a medium such as parchment can acquire a bias of space in one context, and time in another.

We now need to consider whether this construction of the knowledge cycle – and Innis's application of formal purposiveness and final cause – actually coheres with what Innis had to say on the topic? We begin by revisiting two fundamental points: that Innis characterized the history of schema change in cyclical terms, and that he saw the cycle of schema change as analogous in movement and form to that of the business cycle. It was a process that moved between one point of equilibrium – a monopoly or oligopoly – and another. Recall from chapter 4 Innis's insistence in "The Newspaper in Economic Development" that economic history must appropriate "a change in the concept of time." Time, Innis argued, must not be "regarded as a straight line but a series of curves depending on technological advances."[142] Innis's conviction that a similar template applied to culture is indicated by his correspondence with Arthur Cole, and a passage he wrote in "A Plea for Time." As we saw, Innis communicated to Cole in 1943 his "personal interest in public opinion – particularly the existence of broad plateaus of public opinion and the sharp breaks which occur in it from time to time – a sort of psychological or cultural approach."[143] In "A Plea for Time," originally presented as a 1950 lecture to the University of New Brunswick, Innis pointed to the process of schema change during the Great Depression which disrupted the prevailing political-economic wisdom inherited from the nineteenth century. Here, he again pointed to a cyclical process, and here he described the shift from a bias toward time to a bias toward space. Although the status quo of the nineteenth century had worked reasonably well, Innis suggests, things changed radically with the Depression: "limitations progressively increased as evident in business cycles and their destruction of time rigidities. The monopoly of equilibrium was ultimately destroyed in the great depression and gave way to the beginnings of the monopoly of a centralized state. The disappearance of time monopolies facilitated the rapid extension of control by the state and the development of new religions evident in fascism, communism and our way of life."[144]

Each new cycle, Innis writes, is initiated by disruption, a period of disequilibrium prompted by the invention of a new communication technology, and a concurrent shift in the quantity and velocity of information in circulation. The influx of new technology disrupts old orders of thought and creates an open cognitive space in which new constructs can be created and promoted, constructs appealing to space or time. In this phase of the knowledge cycle there is flux. There is potential, potential akin to that found in a television signal. And there is room for agency and creativity, the formulation and application of new constraining principles to support perception, practice, and communication, such as one might apply to create and transmit a television signal. Indeed, for Innis the exercise of creativity was essential, as the prevailing distinctions operating in the given culture were no longer in effect, even those sharply differentiating space and time. In 1946 Innis noted in his *Idea File*: "Patterns in society – development and background of pattern, i.e. religion or philosophy – dependence on rate of diffusion, conditions of diffusion, supported by change in methods of communication – overturn of philosophical and religious patterns or of habits incidental to pattern – breaking down of monopoly position of ideas and emergence of new systems."[145] The following year, again in the *Idea File*, he noted the "problem of change in velocity of time" at the start of a new knowledge cycle, and, in particular, the "difficulty of those operating at one time or tempo suddenly placed in a new tempo – probably a factor in the business cycle. Importance of wiping out differences between space and time as both categories of communication."[146]

Where did this state of flux leave the individual? With extant patterns either no longer available or no longer having purchase, why did Innis believe that agents on the ground were in a position to construct formalisms deriving from space or time? Here we arrive at Innis's appeal to Kant. Innis believed such innovations could take place because he subscribed to Kant's argument that space and time are "pure forms of all sensible intuition, and thereby make possible synthetic *a priori* propositions."[147] Both forms were innate to human consciousness and could be used as the basis for constructive activity. They could not be collectively accessed, however, at any time. When a monopoly of knowledge was in place, Innis believed, a culture's agents were limited to the dominant *a priori* form in place. However, when a state of flux obtained, the two *a priori* forms could, for a time, be accessed as the basis for creative activity.

Our first clue that Innis so believed and so conceived is the first line from "The Problem of Space." There, Innis quoted, or more accurately misquoted, the British scientist James Jeans's 1934 address to the British Association for the Advancement of Science: "Space and Time, and also their space-time product, fall into their places as mere mental frameworks of our own constitution."[148] Two points are worth considering here. The first is that the statement supports the argument that Innis adhered to an ontology of knowledge comprising two categories: space and time. The second is that interpretation of this initiating passage to "The Problem of Space" is not a straightforward matter. Much turns on what Innis meant by the term "constitution." The source materials from which Innis obtained the quotation from Jeans, and the succeeding text in Innis's article both suggest that Innis could have interpreted the word in one of two ways. The word "constitution" can refer to the process of making something; or it can refer to the makeup, the configuration, the underlying state of the agent or object being described. Unfortunately, Francis M. Cornford's "The Invention of Space," the article from which Innis obtained the Jeans quotation, suggests the first definition of "constitution," while Jeans's original address suggests the latter. Cornford resisted the notion of innate conceptions of time and space while Jeans – a well-known Idealist – embraced it.[149]

The problem is compounded when we consider the text that follows Innis's reference to Jeans in "The Problem of Space." There Innis writes: "Gauss held that whereas number was a product of the mind, space had a reality outside the mind whose laws cannot be described a priori. In the history of thought, especially of mathematics, Cassirer remarked, 'at times, the concept of space, at other times, the concept of numbers, took the lead.'"[150] Here Innis puts us in a position where we are confronted with one sentence – Jeans's sentence – which suggests that space and time are *a priori* forms ... or not. We are then confronted with a second sentence – referring to Gauss – which suggests that time is an *a priori* form but space is not. Before he has even completed his first paragraph, Innis has already created a prosaic mess.

Is there a way to move beyond this ambiguous ground and determine Innis's purpose in appropriating the Jeans statement and his connotation of the word "constitution"? I believe there is, and that is to consult the minutes of a conversation W.T. Easterbrook had with Innis shortly before he died. There Innis indicated Kant's influence on his thinking regarding time and space, with Easterbrook reporting that Innis "mentioned Kant's categorical imperatives – space and time – simply accept."[151] Kant did not refer to space and time as categorical imperatives, which are propositions that prompt, or demand, ethical action. Instead, as we have seen, he referred to them as *a priori* forms. Either Innis misspoke, or Easterbrook misreported Innis's words. Either way, Easterbrook's report provides one basis to suggest that Innis understood the term "constitution" and Jeans's statement generally in a Kantian sense; namely, that he believed space and time to be innate, *a priori* forms that structure perception. The purchase of that suggestion is reinforced by a passage that Innis wrote in "A Plea for Time." There, he referred to "the form of mind from Plato to Kant," and suggested that the concept was associated with a construct of change that compared favourably with the mechanistic scheme of change then dominant in the social sciences, a scheme that did not account for history, liberty, or contingency. Subscription to the universal applicability of efficient cause, Innis complained, induced contemporary philosophers to proclaim the form of mind "from Plato to Kant which hallowed existence beyond change" as decadent. The reason for scholarly resistance to the concept of final cause was its suggestion that social and cultural development was ultimately beyond institutional control. Freedom, in this view, lay within the realm of efficient cause. In Innis's mind, however, the social sciences' fixation on mechanical forms of change led to the opposite conclusion: "This contemporary attitude leads to the discouragement of all exercise of the will or the belief in individual power. This sense of power and the instinct for freedom have proved too costly and been replaced by the sham independence of democracy. The political realization of democracy invariably encourages the hypnotist. The behaviourist and the psychological tester have their way. In the words of one of them: 'Great will be our good fortune if the lesson in human engineering which the war has taught us is carried over, directly and effectively, into our civil institutions and activities' (C.S. Yoakum)."[152]

The formulation of new constructs for a new knowledge cycle, then, required the individual's access to *a priori* forms. But Innis also believed that, for creativity to occur, two environmental conditions had to be in place. It is here that he began the alignment of his conception of the knowledge cycle with his overall construct of emergent change. The first condition was human interaction. It was necessary not only for the dissemination of content but also for its emergence in the mind and subsequent formulation. As we saw in our examination of the oral tradition, Innis noted in 1950 that "out of frequent and close conversation and much social intercourse a light is of a sudden kindled in the mind, as from a fire that leaps forth, which when once generated keeps itself alive' (Plato)."[153] The second condition was balance, within the individual, and within the culture in which he or she operates. To recall, in our examination of *Political Economy* we noted Innis's appeal to Calvin's two cardinal rules for society: self-control and self-sacrifice. Quoting Geoffrey Scott, Innis further noted the cultural consequent of self-governance, the emergence of art: "In art, as in life, the chief problem is a right choice in sacrifices. Civilization is the organization of values."[154] We also noted Innis's repeated appeal to the writings of Nicholas Timasheff, who argued that, for cultural forms and practices to emerge, cultures must find the right balance between freedom and constraint. Writing to Easterbrook in 1952, Innis made a corresponding comment: "[I am] not sure that the space time approach is not another way of putting Timasheff's suggestion that law emerges at the point at which force and religion overlap. At this point it would appear that order also appears."[155]

Innis's writings suggest that at the early stages of the knowledge cycle, constructs are potentially derived from both classes of the ontology of knowledge. This is the process of realization. But as the cycle progresses, a process akin to natural or market selection kicks in. The social agent, the distributed network in a given culture, begins a process of cultural selection. It begins gravitating toward one of the two points of equilibrium or attractors available to it: the monopoly of knowledge (space) or the monopoly of knowledge (time). And in so doing, it selects the circulating constructs that are associated with either space or time. The unselected constructs are left behind. This interpretation is suggested by two entries in the *Idea File* which are strongly reminiscent of the concept of increasing returns. The first, inscribed in 1950, indicates that the trajectory of the knowledge cycle is affected by contingent events; the consequent of these contingencies is that the cognitive and practical flexibility of the given culture's agents diminishes over time. Innis writes: "Evolution probably result of sudden development of favourable conditions in early stage and very difficult at later stages when it becomes crystallized i.e. in case of man and change difficult to introduce other than by force. With increasing power of time possibility of sudden rapid adjustment of earlier periods disappeared – resources of world less abundant and available."[156] The point is reinforced by a 1946 entry in the *Idea File*, where Innis notes: "significance of catastrophe or technical development – steady change – population, technology, etc. all point in the same direction."[157]

The process of cultural selection is emergent, he suggests, a process that combines abductive deliberation and contingency. Here, we see a social agent; and we see the agent comparing competing classes of constructs and selecting the class which best meets contemporary needs. The basis for this claim is Innis's use of the trajectory of the business cycle as an analogue for the knowledge cycle. The former consists of an agent – the market – which is a distributed network of consumers. It is governed by a dynamic – increasing returns – which moves the market, and moves it to a point of equilibrium, often a monopoly. That dynamic is propelled by individual decision making on the ground. Initially, each consumer is confronted with an array of products, and different customers opt for different competitors. On the ground, customers begin practising abduction: they compare competing products with their different needs and then select the one that best fits their needs. Over time, the process of individual decision making morphs into a process of collective decision making. A contingent event induces some customers to begin copying the purchasing decisions of their contemporaries. Distributors notice the emerging trend and adjust their inventories accordingly. New consumers notice the same trend, and support the emerging market by purchasing the product now in fashion. A monopoly market emerges, and competing products are left by the wayside. The market selects a product; the social agent abducts one alternative. Innis suggests that a similar process of individual and collective abductive reasoning underlies the selection and dissemination of cultural forms, ideas, and practices. This analogy is indicated by his appeal to monopolies and the business cycle; it is also indicated by his reference to what gets left behind: "resources of the world less abundant and available."[158] As we have seen, Innis also refers to the left-behind residue of creative activity in the preface to *Bias*, where he notes "the neglect of communication in studies of cycles warranted a consideration of the extent to which monopolies of knowledge collapse and extraneous material is lost."[159]

At this juncture, with the dynamic of increasing returns in place, and the process of cultural selection completed, the given culture moves to the selected attractor. Nature begins to copy art. Here, the "indeterminate principle of a purposive arrangement of nature in a system," as Kant refers to it, begins. Here, the adaptation of nature and culture to the constructs of the given culture commences, and extant forms and practices gradually begin to reflect only one bias. And it is here that a given medium acquires its contingent, temporary association with the bias of either space or time. In 1947, as we have seen, Innis recorded in the *Idea File* that "history does nothing else but repeat itself with dominance of type of thought. Monopoly control over thought and over media implies that nature copies art as nature seen through stigmatic spectacles."[160]

Considering the emphasis that has been placed on the material properties of media in the Innis literature, a brief consideration of what Innis is saying here is in order. Note what is the driving force in this description of schema change. It is the emergent, contingent dynamic that is driving the culture toward "monopoly control." That control in turn constrains *both thought and media*. It is not the material properties of media that ultimately determine the bias and monopoly that a culture assumes; rather, it is the process of emergent change and the cognitive attractor – the Kantian form – which the culture selects. It was precisely this process, Innis wrote in a 1951 review essay, that supported the rise of Adam Smith's political economy, and a corresponding architectonic devoted to the bias of time. The review essay is worth considering because it provides a case study of a culture moving to an attractor, and also because it provides further confirmation of Kant's influence on Innis. Innis writes: "In the eighteenth and nineteenth centuries it was possible to develop an architectonic structure to which society could slowly adapt itself, in which nature copied art. The element of time was assumed in the pattern laid down by Adam Smith and the classical economists. Rules were laid down under which society would cooperate."[161]

Innis believed that once a given society had gravitated toward a given monopoly, and had begun to attend to the objects and practices associated with one dimension of human experience, the knowledge cycle was for all intents and purposes complete, until a new medium or an external force disrupted the culture's equilibrium, and the painful process of cultural deconstruction and reconstruction commenced anew. That is all very well, but Innis's description leaves us with two unresolved questions: one is straightforward to address, the other less so. The first question asks where Innis located the attractors that constitute the monopoly of knowledge. The answer should not be assumed. While Innis was plainly influenced by Kant and Idealist constructions of history, it is possible that he might have located the *a priori* forms constituting our perception of space and time within space-time. Some of Innis's contemporaries located the Ideal forms in this world as opposed to a domain that bounds or transcends it, and contemporary philosophers are continuing to formulate versions of Idealism that reject the two-world hypothesis. It is possible that Innis may have done the same.[162]

The evidence we have, however, suggests that Innis did otherwise. We have already seen a negative formulation that indicates that he located his attractors outside space and time: his complaint that contemporary philosophers characterized appeals to "existence beyond change," that is, to Platonic and Kantian forms, as decadent. To that, we can add another. In a 1946 entry in the *Idea File* Innis writes: "Monopoly problem of knowledge – to an important extent based on mediums of communication ... changes in media of enormous significance to civilization as having profound implications to religion, learning, and intellectual capacity and training. Plato's Idea in a sense expressed in monopoly of knowledge."[163] In his communication writings, Innis was not a technological determinist; nor was he a materialist. On the contrary, his characterization of the knowledge cycle, his portraits of the human agent, and his identification of the monopoly of knowledge with the Platonic Idea all suggest he was an exponent of an Idealist interpretation of history.

Innis' appeal to Idealism, however, raises the second question. His writings identify two categories of attractor: the monopoly of knowledge and the oligopoly of knowledge. If the monopoly of knowledge is the category of attractor that is aligned with space and time, the two Kantian forms that concerned Innis, what is the ontological status of the oligopoly of knowledge? Is the attractor it represents an expression of a third, unarticulated, category of *a priori* form, a form called space-time? Or is it something that is derivative, a domain of conception and practice that derives from concurrent access to the two *a priori* forms of space and time, and prior access to just one of the forms, prior to a period of disequilibrium and subsequent synthesis of space and time?

Innis, for his part, seems to have subscribed to the latter view. An oligopoly, by definition, involves the participation of more than one firm in a given market. An oligopoly of knowledge, by extension, suggests the presence of more than one frame of reference, or bias, in a given culture. It constitutes what Innis referred to as a balanced culture. To reach this state, Innis's writings suggest, cultures had to obtain balance at multiple scales of organization. Individuals had to find the right mean between freedom and restraint. Institutions had to find a similar mean, within themselves, and among themselves, to govern "the quantitative pressure" of knowledge, and to permit the emergence of multiple institutions, some with a bias toward space, and others with a bias toward time.[164] Cultures needed to support the acquisition and use of multiple media, to enable their actors to access the *a priori* forms, and to make new constructs that reflected them.

Once these initiating conditions were in place and a subsequent phase of disequilibrium emerged, it became possible for a culture to transform into an oligopoly of knowledge, provided it retained its use of multiple forms of media. In "A Plea for Time," Innis writes: "I have attempted to show elsewhere that in Western civilization a stable society is dependent on an appreciation of a proper balance between the concepts of space and time ... The character of the medium of communication tends to create a bias in civilization favourable to an overemphasis on the time concept or on the space concept and only at rare intervals are the biases offset by the influence of another medium and stability achieved."[165] Once that stability was achieved, cultures would begin to produce the "space-time products" referred to by James Jeans, and in Innis's narrative of ancient Greece. As we have seen, in philosophy Pythagoras produced a methodology for modelling systems based on the principles of number and extension, while in science Empedocles emphasized complexity. In theology, the temporal doctrines of *dike* and *logos* were harmonized with the spatial concepts of the Olympian cult, while in art an aesthetic emerged that converged time and space. And in politics, Cleisthenes crafted a political ideology that fused secular and religious principles and ended once and for all the Athenian nobility's pretensions to a dominant role in public life.

While Innis's account succeeds in demonstrating empirically that some cultures have managed to harmonize spatial and temporal constructs, albeit rarely and fleetingly, his theoretical explanation for that harmonization does pose some problems. Innis's communication histories are distinguished by their integration of Kant and extant economic theories treating monopolies and business cycles. And, within the framework that Innis has created, that integration works to brilliant effect as long as the discussion is limited to cases that describe monopolies. When the discussion shifts to oligopolies of knowledge, however, matters become less clear. And, to his credit, Innis may have recognized that. In the preface to *The Bias of Communication* he notes that he may have extended his economic constructs "too far" and "to undue limits," but adds: "it is a part of the task of the social scientist to test the limits of his tools and to indicate their possibilities."[166] The limit one finds when considering the oligopoly of knowledge is what to make of the point of equilibrium, or attractor. It is equivalent, at least functionally, to the equilibria associated respectively with the monopoly of space and the monopoly of time. But, while one can find a direct equivalence between a Kantian form and a given monopoly in Innis's writing, no equivalent formal underpinning – no *a priori* space-time, if you will – can be found for the oligopoly of knowledge. It may be that Innis believed the Kantian forms somehow merged to form a new point of cognitive gravitation, though how such a process might have worked he does not say; nor does he suggest a precedent in the Kantian or Idealist literature that easily aligns with oligopoly theory. It is more likely that Innis had no idea how the two theoretical traditions could be integrated to explain oligopolies of knowledge, and as a result he determined that he had gone as far as he could in his analysis.

Human Thought, Material Media, and Probabilistic Change

We, however, must press further, and consider one final question before concluding this chapter. I have just presented a picture of a Harold Innis who seems more concerned with the music of the spheres, or at least the music of space-time, than with the matter of communication. How is a Kantian Innis to be reconciled with an Innis who insists that a medium's physical properties can be correlated with a culture's resulting bias? The most straightforward way is to remember that Innis was and remained an economist during the 1940s and 1950s. He was not St Paul. In a perceptive recent essay, William Buxton notes that Innis interpreters have tended to impose an oversimplified framework to describe the trajectory of Innis's career. Before 1940 he was an economist; after 1940 he embarked on the Road to Damascus and became, for whatever reason, a communication theorist. But, as Buxton rightly notes, the pattern of activity underlying Innis's career was in fact far messier.[167] And it would have been even messier had Innis lived past 1952 and continued his work in economics into the 1950s and 1960s.

For our purposes, the issue is important because Innis's correspondence indicates that he remained deeply interested in the economics of the business cycle, to the point that in the early 1950s he considered collaborating with Arthur Cole on a research initiative to be titled the "Time Horizons Project." The correspondence is also relevant here because it establishes Innis's belief that business cycles, and by extension knowledge cycles, were governed by a probabilistic construct of change, a construct that could be established by observation and, in the case of business cycles, by time series and statistics. Under such a regime of change, it is possible for regularity and contingency to coexist. One may observe a global pattern, such as a correlation between the bias of space and light media such as papyrus, and still account for individual anomalies, such as a prophet of Israel using papyrus to support a domain of activity aligned with time. Put differently, if we can establish Innis's exposure to the concept of probabilistic change in conjunction with the business cycle, we have a basis to suggest how he created a construct of history that incorporated both Idealism and contingency on the one hand, and appeals to the material properties of media on the other.

Innis's interest in business cycles and probabilistic change arose from his concern – he would have said obsession – with the dimension of time, and with locating methods to anticipate and adapt to patterns and contingencies as one progressed through time. This interest emerges quite clearly in Innis's communication writings, most notably in "A Plea for Time," where he raised his concern that business and government policy makers were calling upon the social scientist to compile statistics and then "discover patterns or trends which will enable him to predict the future."[168] The difficulty, Innis complained, was that the social sciences did not have the necessary analytical tools to make useful predictions about the future trajectory of the business cycle. True, mathematical formulae were devised, but their utility was suspect for Innis, and at best of use only in the short term. In his estimation, the social sciences were becoming little more than schools of journalism, and suffered from the general malaise plaguing the West, namely neglect of time: "The difficulty of handling the concept of time in economic theory and of developing a reconciliation between the static and dynamic approaches is a reflection of the neglect of the time factor in Western civilization."[169]

Innis's interest in the probabilistic dynamics underpinning business cycles was also evident in the mid-1940s, the period when he was comparing the lectures and essays associated with his first three communication anthologies. Between 1944 and 1947, Innis was in communication with B.S. Keirstead during the composition and publication of Keirstead's *The Theory of Economic Change*. While Innis does not cite Keirstead in either *Empire* or *Bias*, Keirstead's acknowledgment of Innis's assistance during the composition of the work, and Innis's mention of it in later correspondence with Arthur Cole both suggest that Innis had been exposed to a theoretical study of business cycles appealing to probabilistic change in the mid-1940s.[170]

Keirstead's purpose in his study was to explain the behaviour of firms and economic systems in the course of the business cycle. Fundamental to that purpose, he argued, was the derivation of analytic functions that reflected a probabilistic conception of time.[171] Keirstead emphasized the need to appeal to probability theory, since no description of social change could avoid the question of human purpose. While agents, institutions, and markets were constrained in their behaviour by the environment, their future trajectory was not "completely determined by the physical cause, but would be partly influenced ... by human motives responding to the causal physical event."[172] Such motives were governed by the prevailing values or *mores* governing a culture.[173] If an economist had access to these values, Keirstead believed, a simplified model of the future behaviour of a social aggregate could be constructed, and its future inferred on a basis of probability. While such predictions would never be determinate, the field of economics could "claim for them a high degree of probability within the conditions defined by the simplifying assumptions."[174]

Keirstead proposed to translate these insights into a set of functions that would describe the future behaviour of firms during the business cycle. The problem with the existing analytical tools in economics, he argued, was that they rested on the premise that the observed system was in stasis. Market relations governing a firm's cost and subsequent revenues, such as public taste, population size, and capital supply, were seen as operating "out of time." With all factors fixed, it was possible for any given product to derive one function governing the firm's unit cost, and a second governing its revenue. These functions also operated outside time. The two functions could then be traced on a graph, and the firm's equilibrium point determined by examining where the two lines intersected. A firm's future behaviour could be predicted by following this method, since the output prescribed by the equilibrium point was the one production level where a firm could recoup its costs while remaining competitive with peers in a system of perfect competition. Similar principles could be applied to predict the future behaviour of the economy at large.

Or so it was thought. For Keirstead, the method of "comparative statics" – the determination of a firm's or system's potential equilibrium point at any single instance *in time* – had little predictive value for the future behaviour of firms, since they progressed toward their equilibrium points in systems with market relations that changed *over time*. Supply and demand levels changed, thereby altering the conditions of equilibrium. In Keirstead's opinion, the method of "comparative statics" offered at best a means of predicting the short-term behaviour of economic systems. Innis shared this concern.[175] For tools that were useful over the long term, however, what was required was not only a new set of functions but a new conception of change from which to derive those functions. Mechanistic forms of change assumed laws that remained fixed over time. In Keirstead's estimation, market relations evolved over time. And if the market was to be seen as having any coherence at all, it would have to be approached from a probabilistic conception of time. While the specific price and output functions that Keirstead proposed are not relevant for the purposes of this study, the method he proposed for their confirmation is significant here, since it again suggests that Innis had exposure to economic theory relating a probabilistic conception of change to the study of time series: "These price and output functions in time are, or ought to be, capable of measurement, and can be expressed, of course, as functions of one another. I have hoped that statistical inquiry, based on time series, might be able to create mensurable price and cost functions that would correspond to the analytical functions derived here."[176]

Innis also expressed his interest in the relationship between business cycles and probabilistic change in his 1950 correspondence with Cole. In their exchange the two briefly discussed collaborating on a project devoted to the study of "time horizons" of long-lasting firms such as the Hudson's Bay Company. The supposition of both was that successful firms lasted because they retained a schema of time that translated into adaptive behaviour. In the context of these discussions, Innis explicitly raised the possibility that businesses might see greater predictive value for foreseeing future market trends in probability theory than in methods suggested by current economic theory. It was also in the context of these discussions that Innis mentioned Keirstead's work to Cole, suggesting that it and other works "offered the prospect of common ground between theorists and historians" in the field of economics.[177]

The discussion was precipitated in part by Innis's confession in January of his concern "to the point of obsession" with the neglect of time in the social sciences. The field of economics, he said, in particular suffered from its overemphasis on "hedonistic principles" and its corresponding neglect of cultural factors. For Innis, as with Keirstead, a concern with culture implied "an interest in continuity or in the time factor."[178] Such concerns would find a more pronounced expression the following March when Innis delivered his lecture at the University of New Brunswick that would become the basis for "A Plea for Time." The lecture and resulting chapter also provide a basis for suggesting that Innis had the role of human volition and probabilistic change very much in mind when he wrote to Cole. In "A Plea for Time" Innis notes: "The need for a sane and balanced approach to the problem of time in the control of monopolies, and in the whole field of interest theory and in other directions, is evident in the growth of a bureaucracy in a totalitarian state. The static approach to economic theory has been of limited assistance in meeting the problem of time."[179] Innis's intent in this statement is suggested by entries he made in the *Idea File* relating to interest theory. On one level Innis, again like Keirstead, associated the progression of the business cycle with individual volition, noting: "INTEREST RATES – Business fluctuations result of increase or decrease of intensity in belief of possibility of predicting the future – influence of communication."[180] Innis also identified interest theory with a probabilistic conception of change in a 1951 *Idea File* entry: "Problem of time in whole problem of interest theory – development of probability – insurance, etc. – i.e. conflict of pecuniary interest in time and industrial interest in place."[181]

In February 1950 Innis again referred to the themes of volition and probability as he and Cole began discussing the "Time Horizons" project in earnest. Ambitious in scope, the purpose of the project was to study the time perspectives of two or three "economically variant companies" at the various levels of their operation, with the concept of time being defined as "a measure of proper planning," a "directive of thought," and "a measure of action." Such measures were to be applied to evaluate the behaviour of firms from disparate sectors in areas such as acquisition of raw materials, product planning, and maintenance of inventory. Innis's reference to the project in the *Idea File* also contains mention of: "statistical studies over forward orders of machine builders – or inventories or stand-by equipment."[182] While the entry itself does not explicitly state whether participants of the project were themselves supposed to undertake the statistical studies, or were merely to assess the studies undertaken by the subjects of the study, Innis's correspondence with Cole suggests the latter interpretation. Complimenting Cole on "the general hypothesis" for the project, "which you have worked out and which really seems exciting," Innis enquired of Cole "whether it would be possible to obtain from American industries some idea as to how much money they feel should be devoted to forecasting."[183]

Innis further elaborated his interest in forecasting in a 28 February letter to Cole in which he stated his belief that the private sector had "faced and dealt intelligently with the continuity or time problem" in contrast to governments, which he characterized as belonging to "that segment of society which has never considered the problem of continuity and has been essentially transient." For Innis, a central concern for the project would be to determine the duration of the predictions that companies made based on statistics, noting that "it would be interesting to know how far insurance companies feel they can go in using mathematics to forecast the future." Government, in Innis's estimation, held an unhealthy monopoly in the field of prediction, since it based predictions upon the faulty assumptions inherent in comparative statics. And government would remain the primary forecaster of market behaviour until its methods and practices were challenged by the private sector.[184] The two concluded their correspondence on the topic in April, with Innis maintaining his belief in the project's "importance and difficulty."[185]

Through his own statements, then, and in his engagements with Keirstead and Cole, Innis indicated his belief that business cycles were linked with probabilistic change. Do his communication writings provide a basis for suggesting that this analogical reasoning about knowledge cycles extended that far, that he aligned his theory of media with a probabilistic construct of change? The answer is yes, and it is indicated first by the qualified language used in his communication writings on schema change. The emergence of a monopoly of knowledge, he writes, is "to *an important extent* based on mediums of communication (emphasis mine)."[186] Here we see a generality, which, as such, applies some of the time but not all of the time – a formulation fully consistent with a scheme of probabilistic change. Innis expressed a similarly qualified generalization in a discussion on the historic effects of writing, where he noted that "[the] generalizations ... we have just noted must be modified in relation to particular empires." One had to be careful about the unthinking application of generalizations on writing, Innis cautioned, because they hindered "more precise study" and tended "to obscure the differences between civilizations dependent on various media of communication." For this reason, he added, "we shall attempt to suggest the roles of different media with reference to civilizations and to contrast the civilizations."[187] Generalizations were fine, when considering the history of human communication, but one always had to be aware of the specifics of the case.

For Innis, this caveat was particularly true because he was dealing with a domain of knowledge that was governed by the logic of classes and final cause. As we saw in his description of Aristotelian biology, Innis was fully aware that such domains demanded generalizations that stood "half-way between the immediate concreteness of the individual theory and the complete abstractness of mathematical notions."[188] Here, Innis's interest mirrored Kierstead's in the sociophysical event: "there is no *necessity* in individual behaviour ... it is only if you have a sufficient number of individuals that you can assert the group ... [behaves] ... in a specific way," that is in a probabilistic way.[189]

V

In prospect, it is a strange thing to think of Harold Innis as an Idealist. After all, he has arguably done more than any other historian to focus Canadians' attention on the matter of their history and global history. When we think of Innis, we think of fur and fish, stone and papyrus, rivers and telegraphs, not Platonic forms and Kantian critiques. Yet, in retrospect, when one considers those whom Innis identified as instrumental in shaping his work and thought, and his distress at the cognitive damage effected by communication technology, his turn to Idealism emerges as something that is not in the least strange. In the preface to *Bias*, Innis opens with a simple question: "Why do we attend to the things to which we attend?" That question had first been put to Innis while an undergraduate student at McMaster by James Ten Broeke, whom Innis identifies in his autobiography as one of his "most striking teachers." The man and his question evidently made an impression on Innis, for his communication writings are characterized as "reflections stimulated by a consideration of it."[190] What is important here is that Ten Broeke was not simply an undergraduate professor of little note or renown. Leslie Armour and Elizabeth Trott characterize him, on the contrary, as the philosopher "who carried on the Idealist tradition in Canada into the 1930s."[191]

The reference to Ten Broeke suggests that Idealist tenets played a central role in Innis's formation as a student and scholar, and further that they set the terms of reference for his study of communication. That impression is reinforced when one considers Innis's description of Thorstein Veblen, whose writings, along with those of Adam Smith, inspired him to explore the dynamics of emergent change. In his overview of Veblen's career Innis writes that Veblen, because of his background in philosophy, emerges "as the most important economist to come out of America." His philosophy bore little resemblance to those produced by Hegel and Marx; rather, "the roots of his philosophy are to be found in Kantianism." Innis further notes that Veblen's first article was dedicated to Kant's *Critique of Judgement* and that while Veblen, like Darwin, was convinced that the evolution of natural forms had important implications for natural and human history, "he was not convinced of the finality of materialism and mechanism."[192]

Given the stated importance that Innis placed on the questions and writings of both these thinkers, then, it is not surprising that he appropriated Idealism as well as the constructs of emergent and probabilistic change to inform his communication histories. For Innis, history was all about connection: connection precipitated by transport, connection precipitated by *techne*. But the past and present had shown him that communication instruments had repeatedly exacted a price from the cultures that used them. While a stimulant to human creativity and a catalyst for cultural complexity, they had also hindered human cognitive functioning, prompting periods of cultural instability and cultural rigidity. In the twentieth century, they had produced two global wars and, in the West, two attempts at cultural suicide, with a third and final one in near, all too near, prospect. For Innis, the key to survival involved changing a host of practices and constructs, but it could be reduced essentially to a single injunction: pay attention. If the West was to survive, it would have to rededicate itself to protecting the dignity, liberty, and creativity of the individual. Such protection presupposed a fundamental assertion: that humans *could* innovate, even in cultural environments that discouraged creativity in principle, even in cultures that discouraged innovations that ran counter to the prevailing wisdom of the time. For this reason, Innis insisted, Idealism retained its purchase, even as analytic philosophers and other scholars of his generation were rejecting it whole cloth. And for this reason, Innis pressed his colleagues to develop communication practices that protected the autonomy of the individual: practices that compressed information and revealed extant patterns in data; practices that complexified information and supported its expression in new and different combinations. Human creativity could be protected through resort to information visualization and the oral tradition.

Protecting the individual's capacity to be attentive was essential because the self-aware agent is the precursor, the only precursor, of a culture that is vital, one that lives, moves and has its being in an environment of emergent change. Cultures operate in worlds constituted by information flows and positive feedback. These very flows are what break them down and precipitate new cycles of cultural activity, cycles that move probabilistically to a point of equilibrium, a point of cultural stasis. Cultures are the product of final cause. They produce constructs that are governed by formal cause. To continue doing so, to survive and adapt, it is important that agents, individually and collectively, acquire the ethic, the practice of balance. That adaptive activity was what enabled the Greeks to pay attention and in turn to create oligopolies of knowledge – widened domains of attention that enabled them to create enduring cultural constructs and to withstand the threatening storm that was Persia. Only that adaptive activity, Innis writes, will permit the West to withstand the discursive and structural storms of the future, those constituted by emergent change, and the governance of formal and final cause.

6

The Enduring Significance of Harold Adams Innis

In my introduction, somewhat tongue in cheek, I compared Harold Innis to a prophet. It was hard to resist making such a comparison. His writings have the feel of an oracle about them, though skeptics from time to time have charged that they point to nothing more than garbled syntax. In my text it was also hard not to characterize Innis as filling the role of an Isaiah or Jeremiah, and that is what I did from time to time. When reading his works with care, it is hard to avoid the conclusion that he is enjoining us to flee from the wrath to come. And now, in this sixth chapter, I find myself referring back to the same mask and the same metaphor. Harold Innis was a prophet, not because he was obscure, and not because he was hyperbolic, but rather because he produced writings that, in the end, have proven to be prescient. Innis's preoccupation with emergence, with the flows and junctures of history, led him in turn to articulate a number of concerns that have a remarkably contemporary feel to them. When read in conjunction with recent contributions to literatures devoted to social networks, scholarly communication, and the philosophy of Idealism, Innis's writings align well, sometimes surprisingly and specifically well, with the writings and practices of contemporary humanists, scientists, and social scientists. Harold Innis did not originate these ideas. He simply identified them as important. It is instructive and heartening to see that many scholars in the present are now beginning to agree.

SOCIAL NETWORKS

Innis's prescience first becomes evident when we consider his writings in relation to recent social science work devoted to collective decision making. Recall from our surveys of *Political Economy in the Modern State* and Innis's correspondence during the 1940s, that he forwarded the following propositions regarding social dynamics and the impact of information upon them:

- *"Natura non facit saltum."* Nature never proceeds in leaps, but cultures do. Socio-cultural change is catastrophic.
- *Socio-cultural change has a specific morphology*. It is characterized by sharp breaks, as Innis noted to Arthur Cole in 1943, and its rate of change is never constant. If you plot it on a graph it comes across as a series of curves which can be correlated with technological change.
- *Socio-cultural change can and should be correlated with the dynamics of information flow*. Here, Innis had the dynamic of increasing returns, or positive feedback, in mind.
- *Positive feedback can induce system instability, oscillation, and eventually breakdown*. On the ground, individuals contribute to system oscillation by copying their neighbours. Behaviour accordingly becomes unstable on a system-wide level as agents copy one another and collectively adhere to one economic theory, and then another, and vote for one political party, and then another.

Simply put, Innis was asserting that crowds often behave in irrational ways. There was nothing new about this idea when Innis uttered it. Researchers since the time of Goethe have said so, and certainly have said so since the publication of Charles Mackay's *Extraordinary Delusions and the Madness of Crowds* in 1841.[1] What is noteworthy for our purposes is that contemporary researchers studying the economics and sociology of networks are examining afresh the propositions uttered by Innis and others on social dynamics. Duncan Watts, for example, a sociologist interested in the role networks play in supporting the spread of fads, financial bubbles, voting behaviour, and the dissemination of new ideas, notes that emergent behaviours such as these are governed by what sociologists refer to as a *threshold rule*. The rate of adoption of a new behaviour or idea is initially very slow until a given group reaches a critical threshold, or bifurcation point. At the threshold, the rate of adoption increases dramatically, to the point when all or a preponderance of the group will accede to the given idea or behaviour. When this form of decision making is represented on a graph, it is expressed with a morphology similar to the one identified by Innis, as an S-curve, with the initial rate of adoption represented as a nearly horizontal line, the rate of adoption at the critical threshold represented as a nearly vertical line, and the rate of final adoption represented again as a nearly horizontal line.

This pattern appears, Watts and others argue, as a result of a mechanism social scientists refer to as an "information cascade." Information cascades take place because humans can and do behave in ways that contradict long-held assumptions in the social sciences regarding individual conduct. In contrast to rational actor theory, which posits that agents have a perfect knowledge of their working environment, and draw on their own knowledge to respond to environmental challenges, a growing number of social scientists are asserting what most of us intuitively know: we do not have a perfect knowledge of the respective environments in which we live and work. In some circumstances we act in ignorance, because either too little information or too much is at hand. In either case, when we do not know what needs to be done, we follow a longstanding human practice: we look to others for guidance. Stated another way: we copy.[2]

In the recent literature, information cascades are said to emerge because of individual decisions to copy that occur in sequence. Consider the classic example involving Hush Puppies offered by Malcolm Gladwell in his book *The Tipping Point*. In the early 1990s an individual in the East Village of New York decided to wear a new style of shoe, and opted to wear a once-popular but then marginal brand: Hush Puppies. A second person in the village saw it, liked it and decided to follow suit. Two others saw it and bought Hush Puppies, then four, then eight and then more until the village and points beyond reached a critical threshold. An explosion of demand for Hush Puppies emerged in the mid-1990s as individuals, either through preference or a desire to stay current, followed the initial fashion decisions of a few innovators in the East Village. These decisions led to an information cascade – a cumulative series of decisions to copy by an ever-growing number of individuals – and a once-marginal fashion became a fad.[3]

Mimicry is one of the strongest known drivers for human conduct. It is not a uniformly dysfunctional trait. Indeed, when individuals have no knowledge, little knowledge, or too much knowledge at hand, the drive to copy can provide a surprisingly effective basis for good decision making, touching on everything from the decision to purchase a given technology, to the acceptance or rejection of a given political or social value. It was an information cascade, for example, that supported the widespread adoption of the standardized screw in the nineteenth century, an innovation that supported the rise of assembly line production in the twentieth century.[4] Information cascades also prompted the collapse of East Germany in 1989. Over the course of thirteen weeks, citizens in Leipzig gathered every Monday to demonstrate against the abuses perpetrated by the regime's Communist Party. Starting in September and progressing into October, the crowds grew exponentially, forming gatherings initially numbering in the hundreds, then thousands, then tens of thousands, and finally hundreds of thousands. The demonstrations prompted the emergence of similar demonstrations in other East German cities, the resignation of party leader Erich Honecker, the fall of the Berlin Wall in November, and the eventual dissolution of the German Democratic Republic.[5]

While information cascades can prompt individuals to make good decisions, they can also prompt the same persons – en masse – to make surprisingly bad ones. The key problem is that when given individuals submit to a cascade – as Innis indicated in *Political Economy* – they opt to forgo their own values, behavioural norms, knowledge, and capacity for independent research, and choose instead to follow the advice of the crowd. Economic history is replete with examples of people collectively opting to engage in irrational behaviour. The Dutch Tulip bubble of 1634, for example, prompted a wave of speculation on tulip bulbs. Individuals were induced to invest their livelihoods and even their houses, all in the hope of cashing in on the dramatically rising price of tulip bulbs. The frenzy lasted until 1636, when investors suddenly realized that the bulbs held no real value, and the price collapsed to less than a tenth of its highest price. Similar bubbles have emerged in the intervening centuries, including the Plank Road Bubble of the 1840s, the Dot Com Bubble of the 1990s, and, of course, the Housing Bubble of the previous decade.[6] When based on solid knowledge, information cascades can lead to very good decisions. But the combination of positive feedback and easily purchased information can also induce people to abandon their common sense, their virtue and, in the end, their hard-earned substance while making some very stupid decisions, as Innis feared and predicted.

SCHOLARLY COMMUNICATION AND NOVEL EXPRESSIVE FORMS

In our studies of Innis's communication writings, we noted Innis's concern – or more accurately his alarm – at the inability of cultures past and present to adapt to the streams of information to which they were exposed. To put the matter more concretely, human polities showed a distressing tendency to collapse as a result of information overloads. Such had been the fate of Greece. Such was the fate of the West in the twentieth century. Information was implicated in Innis's account of the First and Second World Wars. To remedy the situation, Innis believed, it was important for scholars to expand the expressive toolkit of Western culture, and in particular to undertake two things:

- *Information Visualization*. Innis, through reference to formalisms in art and religion, argued that the essence of concepts and content could be communicated via pictorial means. Such a measure would meet a vital need of the present: information compression.
- *Formalism Integration*. As we saw in our survey of *Political Economy*, and in Innis's correspondence with Arthur Cole, Innis pressed for the use of multiple formalisms, and in particular the convergence of three formalisms: the time series with the map; and – in the case of the Time Horizons Project – the time series with the statistical mathematical equation. Such measures, he believed, would support the tasks of pattern detection and system prediction, and enable contemporaries to detect the emergent systems that defined and constrained human activity.

It is intriguing to see how over the past twenty years multiple scholars from multiple disciplines have reached the same conclusions: to detect significant patterns, to gain traction on new or extant problems, scholars require new, visual methods for expression. And with the advent of increasingly powerful, relatively inexpensive computation and software, many have realized that their respective disciplines are now in a position to invent, appropriate, or disseminate them. This is evident in the numerous recent proclamations of one "turn" or another. One does not have to look very far in literatures devoted to cultural studies, the digital humanities, geography, and even computer science, before finding references to a "visual turn,"[7] an "aesthetic turn,"[8] a "spatial turn,"[9] or a "pictorial turn."[10]

The shift is also evident in the direct statements of scholars themselves. In the social sciences and the humanities, Marguerite Helmers writes: "the previously unquestioned hegemony of verbal text is being challenged by what W.J.T. Mitchell labels the 'pictorial turn' (Picture Theory) – a recognition of the importance and ubiquity of images in the dissemination and reception of information, ideas and opinions ... In the past decade, many scholars have called for collaborative ventures, in essence for disciplining of visual information into a new field."[11] In the humanities specifically, scholars are experimenting with visualization to support applications ranging from historical pedagogy to exploring datasets. In history, the *3D Virtual Buildings Project* uses visual metaphors to illustrate the complex relationship between historical models and the objects they purport to represent.[12] In the digital humanities, Stan Ruecker, Milena Radzikowska, and Stéfan Sinclair note that while Google and similar text-based interfaces are perfectly adequate for searching for specific objects within a collection, searchers seeking to understand the structure of a collection, or the relationships existing between its constituents, are not well supported. "One of our fundamental beliefs," they write, "is that providing the user with a wealth of well-designed visual information is better than attempting to artificially or arbitrarily restrict the amount of information provided" through text supported searches.[13]

Computer scientists, physicists, and mathematicians are also turning to information visualization, again to meet the need for more explicit methods for communicating the relationships prevailing between constituents of information. In the 2003 "Aesthetic Computing Manifesto" published in the journal *Leonardo*, the authors note that while "computer programs and mathematical structures have traditionally been presented in conventional text-based notation," nothing precludes their expression in iconographic terms. Components of code can be represented using metaphors such as boxes or engines, while the flow of data can be represented using analogues such as pipes. The advantage of embracing computer and information visualization, the authors write, is that it will enable the formal structures underlying computer programs and mathematics "to be comprehended and experienced by larger and more diverse populations."[14] The aspiration here is to make computational and mathematical thinking accessible to the many, and the physicist S. James Gates has even gone so far as to suggest that "some mathematicians might dispense with traditional forms of notation altogether. This would herald an enormous shift for human culture."[15]

It might also herald the prospect of enormous intellectual gain. The astronomer Roger Malina suggests that current innovations in content representation may lead to changes "as profound as those produced by the cultural appropriation of technologies of print and perspective underlying the developments now known as humanism."[16] These changes are likely to surface because scholars are extending information visualization beyond the applications that Innis envisaged in two ways, specifically by applying it to support pattern replication and diagrammatic reasoning.

The task of pattern replication stems from the realization that it is one thing to detect an emergent pattern in a complex system, but it is quite another to explain why it arose in the first place. The Anasazi, for example, disappeared in 1300 CE from what is now the Long House Valley in Arizona, after centuries of habitation. Why? The British, in a naval engagement with France and Spain in 1805 just west of Cape Trafalgar decisively defeated both forces. Why? When scholars have considered questions such as these, they traditionally have relied on one of two formalisms to support their reasoning: the logical syllogism (if antecedent *x* holds, then consequent *y* follows ...); or the linear mathematical equation. The difficulty here is that neither formalism is particularly well suited for analyzing socio-cultural systems made up of heterogeneous agents that display discontinuous behaviour. People are different. From the standpoint of the social scientist trying to characterize them, they do not behave. Individually and *en masse*, they display a troubling propensity to turn their behaviour on a dime. Logical syllogisms and linear mathematics are not well suited to dealing with the unpredictability and complexity of social systems because both impose an important assumption: agent homogeneity. To make problems deducible or solvable, scholars produced interpretations that do violence to the complexity of the system under study, and violence to our understanding of the past and present.[17]

To get around the problems posed by conclusions that have pleased few, researchers in multiple disciplines are turning to a new computationally supported formalism known as the agent-based simulation, or ABS.[18] Agent-based simulations are models designed to replicate and analyze the behaviour of physical, biological, and cultural systems. They are composed of the agents, or classes of agents, of the system under study. They also provide a virtual representation of the environment in which the agents act and interact. An "agent" in an ABS can be anything that the analyst chooses to specify, from a microbe to a multinational corporation, and anything in between. The researcher also has the capacity to specify the attributes of individuals within a given class of agent; no assumption of homogeneity is required. Simulations are created by specifying the agents and their rules of behaviour, among themselves and in interaction with the environment. Once these steps have been completed, the simulator activates the program and observes what sorts of patterns emerge.

Patterns emerging in ABS have proven highly significant for scientists, humanists, and social scientists, in large measure because they can and do mirror the patterns observed in real data. Joshua Epstein and Robert Axtell, for example, produced simulations that match – or nearly match – the settlement patterns of the Anasazi across the centuries. By virtue of their simulations, the two argue, with George Gumerman, that the Anasazi evacuation of the Long House Valley can largely be traced to the population's exhaustion of the region's environmental resources.[19] As for the Battle of Trafalgar, Giuseppe Tratteur and Raniero Virgilio produced high-resolution portraits of the battle, portraits that matched the trajectory of the battle, and portraits that correctly identified fourteen of the sixteen ships from the Franco-Spanish fleet that escaped the battle. Their counterfactual simulations and analysis led them to suggest that the central reason for Britain's victory was the quality of its ships and guns. Admiral Nelson's contribution was to provide an optimal strategy, which resulted in minimal losses in life and ships. Other things being equal, however, Britain would still have won, even if Nelson had not been there.[20]

In addition to agent-based modelling, researchers, particularly in mathematics and physics, are revisiting the potential of diagrammatic reasoning to support intellectual exploration and discovery. Here, scholars are turning away from familiar forms of notation – numbers, Greek letters, and the like – and are exploring whether geometric form can produce expressions that have physical meaning and support perception. Put simply, they aspire to see if geometric form will enable researchers to detect interesting things about their objects of study, things that conventional mathematics have either effaced or obscured. Marcus Giaquinto notes that while visual thinking has had a long history in mathematics, its utility has primarily been "psychological, not epistemological ... Thus visual representations have a facilitating role. But that is all, on the prevalent view. They cannot be a resource for discovery, justification, proof, or any other way of adding epistemic value to our mathematical capital – or so it is held."[21]

Giaquinto disagrees with that premise, as does the physicist S. James Gates, as we have seen. Gates's interest in visualization and diagrammatic reasoning stemmed from his work in theoretical physics, and from his attempts to characterize the world of sub-atomic matter, where one is likely to run into strange objects like gluons and even stranger concepts, such as supersymmetry. It is also a world replete with mathematical and conceptual problems that have evaded resolution for the past thirty to forty years, the span of Gates's career. These problems relate, for example, to how physical reality is constituted at the smallest possible scale of physical organization. Is space continuous or is it discrete? They also touch on superstring theory, the construct many physicists believe will support the longed-for integration of quantum mechanics with general relativity. And they touch on information's potential role in the cosmos. Some physicists believe it is the fundamental constituent of the universe. In this view, matter and energy, are derivatives of information, not the reverse.[22]

These are all grand and important questions. But Gates, in his own engagement with a particular subset of them, soon reached the conclusion that traditional mathematics in isolation does not provide the traction necessary to resolve them. In a 2012 interview he noted: "I was consciously looking for an alternative language. A moment ago, you used poetry versus prose. I was kind of looking for a new prose that would allow me to get at these problems in a way that no one had ever thought about before ... We tried to develop this alternative viewpoint to study these properties of the equations. We didn't set out to create a graphical image-based language, but ... mathematics often seems as though it tries to make you tell its story. That's what happened to me. In this study, I was driven to this image-based approach."[23]

The "prose" that Gates and his colleagues developed was a geometric object known as the adinkra. The adinkra is a West African form of iconographic communication. As an analogue, it appealed to the physicists because it is a graphic and economic way to express deep concepts, latent meaning, and wise practices, a property that Gates and his collaborators hoped their prose would share. Their incarnation of the adinkra, however, is a vastly different object from the one produced by West African artists. The physicists' adinkra is an assembly of black and white dots and solid and dotted coloured lines, arranged into combinations that express complex three-, four-, and even higher-dimensional shapes. The objects can be folded and separated. They are important because they can be used to express geometric analogues to classical mathematical equations, such as Maxwell's equations for thermodynamics. They are also important because Gates and his colleagues demonstrated in 2009 that the manipulation of adinkras can mimic the behaviour of mathematical equations. They are important, finally, because adinkra manipulation can induce mathematicians and physicists to perform mathematical equations they had never considered before: in essence, by manipulating the shape, and then following the established methods for converting that operation into mathematical notation.

For Gates, the method proved significant because it produced mathematics that reinforce the theory that information is the fundamental ground of the universe, as physicist John Archibald Wheeler and others have suggested.[24] Gates's work also suggests that the universe operates in a manner analogous to a computer, and contains objects analogous to software. In a 2012 interview about the work referred to above, Gates noted: "[when we] analyzed these objects very carefully we found out that they have attributes of ones and zeros in precisely the same way that computers use ones and zeros to send digital information. And in particular, the kinds of codes we found, which was the most shocking thing for us, is that there's a class of codes that allow your browsers to work in an accurate way. They're called error-correcting codes. We found a role for error-correcting codes in the equations of supersymmetry, and this was just stunning for us."[25]

If Gates is correct, adinkras will have played a major role in integrating two heretofore disparate fields – information theory and theoretical physics – and in so doing, have provided a strong confirmation of the potential gains to be realized through information visualization and diagrammatic reasoning.[26] Innis would have appreciated that, as he doubtless would have appreciated a second trend that has emerged in scholarship today: formalism integration, the use of multiple formalisms to detect patterns in time and space. Here again, there is a case to be made that Innis anticipated a trend that has perhaps found its fullest expression in the development of Geographic Information Systems (GIS), and their subsequent application in the social sciences and history.

Geographic Information Systems are suites of mapmaking and database software that are designed to support the interpolation of attribute with spatial data. Historical Geographers, for example, can use GIS to track migration patterns and the changing ethnic profile of a given neighbourhood over time, by interpolating census data with spatial data from sources such as fire insurance maps. As we saw in our treatments of Innis's communication writings, Innis advocated the same kind of "geographic approach" and integration of formalisms that one finds in GIS today. More specifically, in his writings and correspondence, we pointed to four methodological principles that he believed should be used to detect, describe and analyze economic and cultural systems:

- *Economic and cultural systems should be analyzed from the perspective of time*. Economic history and related social sciences, as Innis noted in *Political Economy*, should search for long-run trends and patterns, not attempt to reduce social phenomena to mathematical formalisms. Such patterns, he noted, could be located in series and time series of data.
- *Economic and cultural systems should be analyzed from the perspective of space*. In his correspondence with Arthur Cole in 1941, Innis advocated a "geographic approach" to economic history, which featured the interpolation of spatial and attribute (price) data. Such an approach had enabled him to trace historical emergent patterns in the fur and fish industries, and the westward migration of the wheat belt in North America in the course of the nineteenth century. It further enabled him to identify transportation networks as the variable that consistently prompted transformations of the continent's economic landscape. When transportation methods changed, the wheat belt shifted west.
- *Statistical Relationships should be drawn between data*. Innis did not explicitly call for the determination of statistical relationships between multiple time series situated in space. As we just saw, however, he did call for an exploration of the relationships between multiple time series from multiple domains from the vantage point of space. As we also saw in Innis's 1950 correspondence with Cole regarding the Time Horizons Project, Innis did indicate an interest in determining statistical relationships within time series from the perspective of time. He believed such studies

would provide commercial firms with a viable means of predicting the future trajectories of their markets. Further, as we saw in our treatments of *Empire and Communications* and *The Bias of Communication*, Innis expressed his belief that phenomena governed by the logic of classes – including economic and cultural systems – were governed by a construct of change consistent with probability theory. Given his interest in establishing relationships between time series, his interest in establishing statistical relationships between data over time, and his belief that emergent systems are governed by a probabilistic conception of change, it is more likely than not that he believed statistical relationships could and should be drawn between data from the standpoints of *both* space and time.

- *Explanation for the emergence and persistence of emergent patterns in cultural and economic systems can and must rest on the interpretation of both quantitative and qualitative data*. While Innis believed that statistical analyses and quantitative data were instruments crucial for the detection of emergent economic and social patterns, he acknowledged that such studies held little analytical value unless the detected patterns were placed in their technical, cultural, and geographical contexts. It was one thing, for example, to detect that wheat patterns in North America moved westward over the course of the nineteenth century, or that the French and English harvested fish in different sectors of the North Atlantic during the sixteenth century. It was quite another to learn that the westward movement was prompted by improvements in transport technology, or that sixteenth-century fishing patterns were determined in part by the French palate and England's need for trade and salt. Such insights could only be purchased, Innis believed, through the interpolation of qualitative and quantitative data.

When Innis's methodological and expressive prescriptions are viewed in conjunction, it is striking how consistent they are with present and emerging approaches in the social sciences. Michael Goodchild, for example, notes that location in the social sciences has traditionally been "just another attribute in a table and not a very important one at that." Other factors, such as education, unemployment or age, seemed far more plausible as variables to explain processes such as crime or social deprivation, and for this reason the social sciences came to view space as a "minor issue and one that these disciplines have often been happy to leave to geographers." Goodchild suggests, however, that the traditional stance of social scientists is beginning to change. As a result of the need to combine insights from multiple disciplines, and thanks to the support of tools and multiple formalisms contained in GIS, many social scientists have gained a renewed respect for the dimension of space as a means of integrating data: "Many social scientists have begun to talk about a 'spatial turn,' a new interest in location, and a new 'spatial social science' that crosses the traditional boundaries between disciplines." Similar interests have emerged in the humanities as well.[27]

Innis's emphasis on integrating formalisms is particularly resonant with methods now being employed in the emergent field of historical GIS. Consider, for example, the following statement from Ian Gregory and Paul Ell, which describes the method they applied to study population change during and after the Great Irish Famine: "Our particular aim has been to make use of all three components of the data: the attribute, the spatial, and the temporal. To handle space, we have used mapping extensively. To handle time, we have used time series graphs. Statistical operations allow all three components to be manipulated in more complex ways than simple mapping."[28]

Apart from mirroring Innis's emphasis on the spatial, temporal, and statistical treatment of data, Gregory and Ell's work on the Irish famine also reflects Innis's emphasis on the need for qualitative data to provide context. The two note that while GIS are very useful in supporting the detection and description of spatio-temporal patterns, analyses based on them cannot "replace or reduce the importance of conventional historical approaches; in fact, they should complement, challenge and enrich them. Without more conventional textual and narrative approaches to history, there is no way of explaining the patterns presented by quantitative, statistical GIS approaches."[29]

As Anne Kelly Knowles notes, the capacity of GIS to support data and formalism integration has in turn led to intellectual gains in domains ranging from environmental and economic history to social history. For example, Geoff Cunfer, in *On the Great Plains*, used GIS to track the land use practices of American farmers over a span of 130 years. In so doing, he challenged a long-held view that the Dust Bowl of the 1930s was the result of poor farming practices. On the contrary, Cunfer argued, American farmers by and large have maintained a sustainable relationship with the environment. The Dust Bowl was an aberration. In the domain of medieval history, Michael McCormick used GIS to challenge the prevailing scholarly opinion on another issue: specifically, the likely date for the re-emergence of the European economy after the collapse of the Roman Empire in the West. In *Origins of the European Economy*, McCormick used GIS to assemble data from multiple fields, ranging from numismatics to diplomatic history, and to argue that a new continental economy emerged around 800 CE, a date that is much earlier than historians have traditionally assumed. Finally, Benjamin Ray used GIS to study the trajectory of the Salem Witch Trial, and in the course of his analysis he noted something interesting: the spatial patterns of the conflict were consistent with those associated with the spread of disease during a pandemic. Epidemiological models may have something to teach historians about what happened in Massachusetts in the seventeenth century.[30]

Thanks to intellectual gains such as these, scholars are now hoping their capacities for data and formalism integration will develop still further, in part because of limitations inherent in GIS. While most off-the-shelf Geographic Information Systems are very good at displaying and analyzing spatial systems, they are not adept at treating the dimension of time.[31] For this reason, some analysts are beginning to suggest that GIS should be converged with agent-based modelling applications.[32] Such an innovation would permit the representation of spatio-temporal systems. It would also enable scholars to go beyond the task of pattern detection toward the goal of pattern replication. Scholars could use such a system to test hypotheses exploring the emergence of systems detected by their GIS software.

Researchers are also exploring new possibilities for data, formalism, and application convergence because of a desire to go beyond the abstract cartographic conventions normally associated with GIS. Stated differently, users of GIS – and beyond them researchers in multiple domains interested in visualization – are seeking greater expressive flexibility.[33] They are looking for applications that will permit the simultaneous representation of multiple systems, systems that are situated at disparate levels of spatial organization ranging from the molecular to the global. And further, they are looking for systems with the capacity to express change at multiple increments of temporal scale, ranging from the nanosecond to the millennium and more.[34]

And finally, scholars are calling for instruments that will permit the multi-modal representation of a given system at a given scale, the capacity to shift between abstract and photo-realistic forms of representation. For example, an anthropologist studying the history of the

Anasazi settlement may require a system that can shift between a representation of the village as an agent-based model – one in which the village is a 2D square and the inhabitants are dots – to a representation situated in a virtual world in which the inhabitants look human, the environment is configured in three dimensions and the village structures appear photo-realistic. The level of abstraction, the level of expressive detail, and the level of resolution incorporated into the model will all depend on the anthropologist's analytical, expressive, and pedagogical need.

A visualization system along the lines described here would require the convergence of multiple software applications. It would also require enormous processing power, power beyond anything found in a contemporary desktop computer or tablet. Despite the challenges, commercial vendors such as ESRI, the creator of ArcGIS, are beginning to design systems that meet at least some of the requirements specified above. Its CityEngine plugin, for example, will enable users of the firm's cartographic software to rapidly generate photo-realistic virtual worlds using procedural methods of 3D object construction. For their part, researchers in literatures ranging from temporal GIS to the digital humanities are beginning to specify their requirements for next generation visualization systems with greater specificity. They are calling for platforms that will converge all or some of the following applications:

- *Google Earth, or an Open-Source Variant*. Google Earth is like a globe, albeit with an important difference. It permits users to view content – whether natural topography or human activity – at multiple levels of spatial organization. In one viewing, a user can observe an entire map of Canada, and then zoom down to view one section of a city such as St Catharines, Ontario. Content can be viewed in multiple formats: cartographic, photographic, and 3D.[35]
- *Geographic Information Systems* (GIS). As noted above, Geographic Information Systems present a suite of tools to support pattern detection in data. A GIS is a spatial database that combines attribute data, such as ethnicity, with spatial data, such as an address.
- *Agent-Based Simulations* (ABS). As also noted above, ABS are designed to simulate the emergence and persistence of complex systems, including social systems. They are emerging as an important complement to GIS.[36]

- *Virtual World Software*. This application and a related application, the game engine, support the creation and dissemination of high-end, photo-realistic 3D and 4D content. Its purpose – generally – is to mimic as closely as possible the appearance of the environment it purports to represent, such as a city block. This requirement includes making provision for environmental features such as lighting and physical laws such as gravity. These environments also permit the annotation of their constituents with such content as text files, 2D graphics, and animations and audio files. Increasingly, virtual worlds are becoming malleable and extensible, meaning that it is becoming possible to change the shape and surface appearance of constituents in real time, without a re-rendering, a re-loading, of the site's 3D content. It is also becoming possible to import a model from a different virtual world into your own.[37]
- *High Performance Computing*. When we speak of modelling social, economic, or military systems, we are considering scenarios in which there are potentially thousands, hundreds of thousands, or even millions of agents. A simulation of a smallpox pandemic in Portland conducted at the Los Alamos National Laboratory, for example, included one million virtual inhabitants.[38] While simulations of this nature are too large to process on desktop computers, they can be run on High Performance Computing (HPC) clusters. High Performance Computing facilities, such as those located at the National Center for Supercomputing Applications in the United States and the Compute Canada network … provide the requisite computational power by networking hundreds and in some cases thousands of processors. The processors work in parallel, and provide sufficient power to simulate complex systems such as galaxies and cells. HPC is a paradigm of computing that by the end of this decade will bring exa-scale levels of computing, and currently provides tera- and peta-scale levels of computing. Tera-scale computing refers to computing clusters that can process one trillion calculations on one trillion bytes of data per second. Exa-scale computing, by extension, will support one quintillion calculations on one quintillion bytes of data per second.[39]

From a certain point of view, this is heady stuff, but it is a scenario that is based on extant or soon-to-be realized technology, and a scenario that is being driven by a very real need: the imperative to cope with Big Data.[40] In multiple research domains, the convergence of computation and the Internet has resulted in a situation where more data are being produced than any individual scholar or team of scholars can process and interpret without the assistance of computation and applications to support visualization and pattern detection. Some variation of the scenario I have described here will be realized once scholars procure the expertise, funding, and computational power to support it. Indeed, some are already trying. As a researcher who advocated the integration of formalisms via the oral tradition, and was dealing with Big Data problems of his own, Harold Innis would doubtless have approved.

IDEALISM

One of Innis's primary objects in his communication writings was to make his colleagues more reflective. He wanted them to think about expressive forms, and why they used them. And he wanted them to consider an even more fundamental question, the one posed by his philosophy professor James Ten Broeke: why do we attend to the things to which we attend? For Innis, much of the answer to that question rested in his belief that all humans possess innate knowledge, the type of knowledge that makes our surroundings intelligible, the type of knowledge that enables us to assume fundamental constructs such as time and space. The sources of that innate knowledge, he held, were the *a priori* forms identified by Plato and Kant. Their way of thinking did much to explain the continuities and transformations of cultural history, and, more important, they provided a basis from which to resist the determinisms then extant in the social sciences, from materialism to technological and environmental determinism. Innis was an Idealist because he had a deep and abiding faith that the human subject was a free agent. We are all subject to forces emanating from our culture and environment. But as far as Innis was concerned, we need not be subsumed by them.

For us in the present, this feature of Innis's thought presents us with a question: did he have a point? Was he right to insist that Idealism remained a viable interpretive framework for understanding the past and present, even if it failed to command widespread assent? I propose that the answer should be a tentative yes. I will not suggest that there is a knockdown argument that supports Idealism and negates its competitors. No such argument exists. What I will suggest, however, is that recent developments in evolutionary biology and physics have made

Idealism more plausible than it was, say, thirty years ago. I will also suggest that, because of these developments, Innis was prescient to insist that Idealism retain a role in our understanding of the here and now, and the then and there.

The field of evolutionary biology is producing work with Idealist implications in response to researchers' growing interest in the phenomenon of convergence in natural history. A convergence, put simply, is the independent emergence of a trait or behaviour in two or more independent evolutionary lines of descent. In the standard view of evolution, this is not supposed to occur: natural history is seen as a contingent process. In a famous passage in the book *Wonderful Life*, the evolutionary biologist Stephen Jay Gould argued that if we, somehow, someway, managed to find a way to rewind the tape of Life, and start it over again, humans would not re-emerge. And there was no reason to assume that some self-aware, intelligent species would emerge either. There were, and there remain, too many contingencies in the evolutionary process. No statements can be made about the probable direction of history. No criteria can be applied to label one trajectory progress and another regress.[41]

Gould's reasoning rested on the fossil evidence from the Cambrian Explosion, material unearthed by a Cambridge expedition to the Burgess Shale in British Columbia in the early 1970s. One member of that expedition was a then young graduate student named Simon Conway Morris. A decade after the publication of Gould's book, Conway Morris published his own work based on the same data, but with very different conclusions. The Cambridge evolutionary biologist argued that the tape of life is not completely characterized by contingency. It in fact contains hundreds if not thousands of examples of convergence.[42] One classic example is the camera eye, which has emerged independently in three separate evolutionary lines, and is found in organisms as diverse as humans and octopi.[43]

For Conway Morris, the fact of convergence presents a number of important implications for our understanding of evolution, the foremost being that, Gould notwithstanding, there is in fact a direction to natural history.[44] The history of life is populated with attractors that have a bearing on the constituents, traits, and behaviours that organisms in a given evolutionary pathway acquired as they became more complex. Natural selection is much more than nature's response to a contingent mutation. In poetic terms, it's "God's search engine."[45] Its purpose is to shift the trajectory of a given evolutionary pathway in the direction specified by the phylogenetic, cognitive, and behavioural attractors already in place. Given this understanding of natural history, Conway Morris believes, contrary to Gould, that if natural history were returned to its starting point, something like humans would emerge again.[46] A second implication of convergence is that if and when complex extra-terrestrial life is discovered, it will not be organized along principles that are completely alien to us. Alien life will likely display constituents and behaviours similar to those found on Earth.[47]

A final implication of convergence is that Idealist principles play a role in natural, and by extension, human history. Conway Morris's appeal to Idealism is based on the observation that humans and certain higher orders of animals, specifically corvids and cetaceans, share many more behavioural traits than is generally realized, including tool making, social play, cooperative hunting, and more significantly, vocalization, in both language and music.[48] Animals have the capacity to learn artificial languages to support intra-specific and inter-specific communication. Their level of learning extends beyond word-object association to include a mastery of semantics and syntax.[49] Some birds are bilingual.[50] In the domain of music, animals have generated music that shares many of the same formal traits as human-generated music.[51]

For Conway Morris, the significance of the cross-species aptitude for linguistic and musical expression is that neither capacity can be reduced to the enviro-cultural or biological constraints in which the given organism finds itself. Linguists have known for some time that an individual's capacity to generate a correct sentence for a given language cannot be reduced to environmental, linguistic stimuli. Such a position has not proven tenable since the 1960s after Noam Chomsky's critique of behavioural linguistics. There, Chomsky drew attention to studies of child language use which pointed to subjects' generation of correct sentence structures to which they had not received prior exposure. For Chomsky, this presented a mystery, and it is one that has tasked linguists ever since. During the process of language acquisition, he writes, there is a "poverty of stimulus" at play. Humans do not receive prior exposure to the syntactic units that they later express.[52]

In the ensuing years, Chomsky's concerns regarding environmental stimuli have received added confirmation via an important discovery: both human and animal languages are constrained by Zipf's Law.

Zipf's Law, the linguist Charles Yang writes, mandates that "the empirical distributions of words follow a curious pattern: relatively few words are used frequently – *very* frequently – while most words occur rarely, with many occurring only once even in large samples of texts. More precisely, the frequency of a word tends to be approximately inversely proportional to its rank in frequency."[53] This inverse power law – first formulated by the Harvard linguist George Kingsley Zipf – has been found to apply in multiple domains ranging from the frequency of earthquakes to the size distribution of firms and cities.[54] It has also been found to apply to larger units of language, including those that touch on syntax and grammar. Scholars have debated the significance of Zipf's findings since the 1950s. Given the discovery that random letter-generating processes can generate corpora that follow Zipf's Law, most linguists have concluded that it has nothing important to say about the operation of language.[55]

However, a recent statistical analysis by Charles Yang of word combinatorics in multiple corpora suggests that it has something *very* important to say about the process of language acquisition. Linguists adhering to the tenets of Construction Grammar posit that language acquisition and generation are governed by the individual's appropriation of "construction-specific" rules or processes from the outside, rules that posit how linguistic form and function should be paired, and how they are subsequently expressed via units such as morphemes, words, idioms, and so on. "Yet the Zipfian distribution of linguistic combinations," Yang writes, ensures "that most 'pairings of form and function' simply will never be heard, never mind stored, and those that do appear may do so with sufficiently low frequency such that no reliable storage and use is possible."[56]

Conway Morris notes that similar Zipf frequency distributions have been located in the communications of bottlenose dolphins and squirrel monkeys.[57] A modified form of Zipf's Law has been discovered in birdsong, and in lab experiments birds have been shown to display an innate ability for species communication (birdsong), even with poverty of stimulus.[58] Conway Morris further notes that attempts to reduce language use and other traits mirroring human intelligence to some extra-linguistic feature of an agent's environment are not likely to bear fruit either. He writes that "primate-like intelligence has emerged in strikingly different contexts. Sitting in trees and laying eggs is one thing, living in an ocean is another, and both contrast with the evolution of the apes in jungle and savannah."[59] The radical dissimilarities in evolutionary niches in which primates and parrots, corvids and cetaceans find themselves all suggest it is unlikely that biologists will locate a common environmental constituent or set of constituents to explain the emergence of language.[60]

Given the difficulties of appealing to environmental stimuli, Noam Chomsky has argued through his conception of generative grammar that the human agent must be the beneficiary of some innate capacity for language. Others – linguists, philosophers, biologists, and cognitive psychologists – have posited a similar concept, universal grammar, and extended its applicability to other species, attempting to tie the innate capacity for communication with the neural architecture of the brain.[61] But here two problems have arisen. Chomsky notes that an assessment of efforts to correlate human language use with neural architecture and activity is "quite easy in this case, because they're almost nonexistent."[62] Conway Morris observes that the problem is compounded by the realization that the neural architectures of cetaceans, primates, and birds are markedly different, and yet "from radically different neural substrates the same type of mind emerges."[63]

The consequent of the lack of a credible environmental or neurological basis for convergent linguistic and other modes of intelligent behaviour is that Conway Morris and other evolutionary biologists are now considering the possibility that Idealism might have something to teach them. The field of biology, Conway Morris notes, "may be much closer to metaphysics than it often cares to acknowledge."[64] If the implication he is drawing from the varying neural architectures of organisms is correct, then mind "is not some sort of epiphenomenon, a simple by-product of chemistry and electrical activity in a squishy organ that happens to be located in the skull."[65] Rather, mind – and more specifically complex intelligence – should be characterized as a real biological property by virtue of its independent emergence on at least three occasions. As such, the mind associated with a given species is subject to evolutionary pressure. Its development is propelled by the mechanism of natural selection, and its development is channelled along an evolutionary landscape populated with attractors. These attractors constitute the destination points of mental evolution, and constitute the intelligences, traits, behaviours, and expressive formalisms that a given species may acquire and express.[66] The evolutionary landscape that Conway Morris is referring to is of course not the physical one in which a given species finds itself. Rather, it is a domain "orthogonal to everyday experience," an adaptive zone that is "an Ideal, a reality both 'out there' but also intimately close, in a 'dimension' discovered by evolution."[67] Expanding on the concept of the adaptive zone proposed by the theologian Edward Oakes, Conway Morris notes that "this line of argument leads inexorably to idealism." If the implications presented by convergence and Oakes's adaptive zone ultimately prove correct, they will suggest that "the existence of mathematics and logic are not accidents of the human condition, culturally and anthropologically constrained, but rather genuine universals."[68]

In the journal *Science*, Patricia Gray and her colleagues have expressed similar thoughts with respect to music, based on the deep and striking similarities shared by human song, whale song, and bird song, including commonalities in rhythmic variations, pitch relationships, and permutations and combinations of notes. There is no intrinsic reason why this should be so. Whales, for example, could easily express nothing more than free-form arrhythmic sounds. Yet the authors find that whales "mix percussive or noisy elements in their songs with relatively pure tones and do so in a ratio similar to that used by humans in Western symphonic music," while the canyon wren's trill "cascades down the musical scale like the opening of Chopin's 'Revolutionary' Etude." These convergences suggest that "though our evolutionary paths have not intersected for 60 million years," music in fact "may predate humans – that rather than being the inventors of music, we are latecomers to the musical scene."[69] In a concluding query, the authors note that "it has been postulated that there is an unproven (and probably unprovable) concept called mathematical Platonism, which supposes that there is a universal mathematics awaiting discovery." Is it possible, they ask, that there is "a universal music awaiting discovery, or is all music just a construct of whatever mind is making it – human, bird, whale? The similarities among human music, bird song, and whale song tempt one to speculate that the Platonic alternative may exist – that there is a universal music awaiting discovery."[70]

Conway Morris's and Gray's speculations are intriguing. Yet their respective references to mathematics raise questions that have long attended Platonic speculations in that field. If there is some metaphorical landscape, some alternate dimension populated by universal forms, where is it? And more to the point, how do we interact with it? During the twentieth century, proponents of Idealism, such as the mathematician Kurt Gödel, were unable to provide plausible answers to the how and where of Platonism, and as a result the concept was marginalized in philosophy and the natural sciences.[71] Here, much turned on what constituted the ground for what was deemed "plausible," and more specifically for the *a priori* assumptions scholars brought to bear to determine how one thing may connect with another.

Those grounds, however, may be changing, courtesy of quantum mechanics. Typically, researchers have adjudicated such questions through the prism of classical mechanics. The consequent of that construction was that one object could not be deemed to be connected to another, unless some transparent connection was seen to bind them. No hidden variables were permitted. Connections had to be seen. They had to be continuous, and they had to be causal. A message between one point and another, for example, had to be mediated by something, such as electro-magnetic media; and its transmission and reception had to be governed by the physics regulating mass and energy. When it comes to human cognition, these rules seemed plausible, and for many remain plausible. Humans, after all, are complex objects and operate at a scale of physical organization that suggests that our communication, and more to the point our thought, should be determined by them.

There is, however, a very different way to think about how two points connect, and that is the method that applies in the sub-atomic realm described by quantum mechanics. There, the rules that are deemed commonsensical about physical objects and their relations no longer apply. An observer can determine the position of a sub-atomic particle, or its velocity, but not both.[72] Objects can and do superposition: they occupy more than one spatial position or state at a given time.[73] And when it comes to interaction, particles can form non-local connections. A non-local connection is one in which no discernible physical bridge – be it a force or medium – is seen to link one particle with another. Particles such as electrons form non-local connections via a process known as quantum entanglement. Once that connection is forged, the two electrons cease acting independently and form a system. The spin of one member of the pair will be instantly mimicked by its counterpart, regardless of the distance separating them.[74]

Albert Einstein was the first to recognize the possibility for quantum entanglement as a consequence of quantum theory, and the finding did not please him. He described the prospect of non-local interaction as "spooky action at a distance."[75] In Einstein's wake, however, the plausibility of non-local interactions between objects situated at multiple spatial scales has become harder to deny, and physicists, astronomers, and philosophers such as Roger Penrose,[76] John Barrow,[77] and James Robert Brown[78] are suggesting that they may constitute the *how* of Idealism. Their line of reasoning proceeds more or less as follows. In 1964 Irish physicist John Bell demonstrated that quantum entanglement was more than a strange artefact of Einstein's math. Through a process of reasoning known as an impossibility theorem, Bell demonstrated that all candidate local explanations for quantum entanglement could not apply, leaving non-locality as the default solution – a chain of reasoning that was empirically supported by Alain Aspect in 1982. Non-local quantum entanglement therefore has a basis in physical reality.[79]

From there, proponents typically point to recent interpretations of quantum physics which suggest that the behaviour of electrons, photons, atoms, and even larger molecules is observer-dependent. Put more succinctly, Eugene Wigner, John von Neumann, and others have suggested that a fundamental connection exists between mind and quantum phenomena. The basis of that position is a classic experiment from physics – the two-slit experiment – in which light is shown to display different properties depending on decisions made by an observer. If the slit is opened, light behaves like a particle; if two slits are opened, light behaves like a wave. The significance of this experiment is that it suggests that light exists in a superposition state – as both a wave and a particle – and that it only resolves to one state or the other when a conscious observer is present to induce and witness that resolution. Von Neumann and others further argued that an unconscious surrogate – such as a robot – will not work as a proxy. Any physical system that is not a conscious agent will instead become entangled with the photon in its superpositioned state. In order for it to resolve to a discrete state – as either a wave, or a particle – matter must be observed.[80]

By virtue of this strange connection, Idealists suggest that quantum phenomena may impinge on the content of thought. They further suggest that such a conclusion is justified by virtue of the detection of quantum phenomena at scales of physical organization larger than the atom. Referring to a 2009 article in the *Proceedings of the National Academy of Sciences*, Bruce Rosenblum and Fred Kuttner note: "'most modern biomolecular scientists view quantum mechanics much as deists view their God; it merely sets the stage for action and then classically understandable, largely deterministic pictures take over.' The paper then comments on a dozen, mostly recent studies denying that mainstream view. These papers report evidence for quantum coherence effects, that is superpositions and entanglements, in biological systems, principally photosynthesis and vision."[81] The cumulative impact of these and other research initiatives, the two write, is that it "makes the apparent display of quantum phenomena in biological systems ever more reasonable."[82]

In principle, then, the concept of non-local communication answers the *how* question of Idealism. As a solution, it is not without its problems, and we will address two below. But it does provide a plausible way of suggesting how *a priori* forms *might* connect with the human agent, and influence the same agent. But what of the *where* question of Idealism? If eternal forms exist, where are they located? Once again, the field of physics provides a potential answer, although this one stems as much from the grander reaches of cosmology as it does from the insights of quantum physics. The short answer that some physicists and philosophers are providing is the Holographic Principle. The Holographic Principle is widely accepted in mathematical physics, and treats the relationship between information and the fabric of space-time.[83]

The principle stemmed from a debate between physicists in response to a single question posed by Stephen Hawking in 1976: what happens to information when it enters a black hole? Hawking's answer then and for some thirty years thereafter was that it ceased to exist. For Leonard Susskind and Gerard t'Hooft, Hawking's main antagonists in what became known as the Black Hole War, the English physicist's answer had to be wrong since it violated a fundamental tenet of physics: information is conserved. Information may be transformed, but it is never lost to the universe. The quantity of information, in other words, remains constant. If Hawking was right, Susskind and t'Hooft argued, then the entire structure of quantum physics would have to be recast.[84]

For our purposes, the Black Hole War is important because of a fundamental discovery that emerged from it. Hawking's question prompted mathematical physicists to model the operation of black holes, and one outcome of that mathematical exploration was the realization that the event horizon of a black hole increases by one Planck length – the smallest unit of spatial length believed to exist – when one bit of information enters into it.[85] From this discovery, Susskind and t'Hooft were able to derive the Holographic Principle which, Susskind writes, asserts "that everything inside a region of space can be described by bits of information restricted to the boundary."[86] Stated differently, it asserts that information is the fundamental ground of the universe from which matter and energy are derived, and that the maximum amount of information that can be associated with a given volume of space is determined by its two-dimensional boundary. Information is constituted in two-dimensional pixels, not three-dimensional vowels, and the maximum number of pixels a given region of space-time will accommodate is determined by its area, not its volume.[87]

The consequent of this realization, Susskind and t'Hooft suggest, is that the three-dimensional environment in which we live is actually a projection of the two-dimensional information situated at the boundary of space-time; hence the Holographic Principle. And where precisely do Susskind and t'Hooft situate this two dimensional boundary? Starting from the tomb of Ulysses S. Grant as a frame of reference, Susskind writes: "we are driven to a mathematical representation involving patterns of pixels dancing across a distant two-dimensional screen and a secret code for translating the scrambled patterns into coherent three-dimensional images. But, of course, there is no screen covered with pixels surrounding every region of space. Grant's coffin is part of Grant's Tomb, which is part of the Solar System, which is contained in a galactic-sized sphere surrounding the Milky Way ... until the entire universe is surrounded. At each level, everything enclosed may be described as a holographic image, but when we go looking for the hologram, it's always out at the next level."[88] The process of reaching for that hologram will continue to larger and larger levels of physical and spatial organization, he writes, "until we come to either the boundary of the universe or infinity."[89] Significantly, Susskind finally notes that "the hologram is quantum mechanical. It flickers and shimmers with the uncertainty of a quantum system, in order that the three-dimensional image have the quantum jitters. We are all made of bits moving in complicated quantum motions, but when we look closely at those bits, we find that they are located out at the furthest boundaries of space."[90]

The worldview that Susskind provides us, then, is one in which immaterial information is prior and the world we perceive is a projection of that information. The Stanford physicist does not specify how such projections occur, but his characterization of the universe's hologram as quantum mechanical suggests that the projections are non-local in nature. Some discontinuous connection exists between the periphery of space-time and the volume of space-time that we perceive and in which we live. Given the characteristics of the Holographic Principle, it is perhaps not surprising that some scientists are suggesting some identification between it and Idealism. The physicist Paolo Zizzi, for example, in her consideration of consciousness in a quantum universe, comments: "as a physicist I feel a kind of reverence for mathematics. Most probably, this leads me to idealize it too much, and all my considerations about mathematics sound quite platonic."[91] Despite that reservation, she presents a model in which the conscious observer operates in a universe that operates like a quantum computer, and is governed by the Holographic Principle. "The outcomes of the overall quantum computation," she writes, "are the universals, the attributes of things in themselves. These universals are partially obtained also by the quantum minds, and are endowed with subjective meaning."[92] Psychologist Mark Germain has also identified Idealism with the Holographic Principle, suggesting that both comport well with Jason Brown's influential neurophilosophy, and more particularly its explication of self, temporal process, and the emergence of moral value.[93]

However, for the conflation of non-locality, the Holographic Principle, and Idealism to stand as an adequate explication of the *how* and *where* of Platonism, there are two problems the philosophy's proponents will eventually have to address. The first is that Einstein's theory of Special Relativity maintains that it is physically impossible to transfer information between two points at a speed faster than light.[94] The cosmos – the theory maintains – is Lorentz invariant.[95] What this means is that the speed of light is constant, regardless of your situation in space or, in physicists' parlance, your inertial frame. It also means that the speed of light constitutes the upper limit of potential velocity for any object travelling from one point to another. It matters little where you are situated or in what direction you are headed. Your inertial frame can be on the ground, on an airplane travelling the speed of sound, or on a spaceship travelling half the speed of light. The speed of light remains constant – 299,792 km/s – even as other constituents of the environment, such as the flow of time, change. Time will pass more slowly, for example, for an occupant of the spaceship than it will for a counterpart on the ground.

There are physicists, however, including John Bell, who have questioned Einstein's suppositions regarding information transfer and the speed of light, largely on account of the phenomenon of quantum entanglement. They suggest that there may be "preferred frames" where speeds exceeding that of light may be attained, affording the possibility of supra-luminal communication.[96] In 1920 Einstein himself recognized the possibility that quantum mechanics might affect the universal applicability of special relativity.[97] More recently, physicists Jean-Daniel Bancal and colleagues have suggested an interesting implication for physicists if a preferred frame cannot be located: "Quantum correlations," they write, must "somehow arise from outside spacetime, in the sense that no story in space and time can describe how they occur."[98]

The second problem for would-be Platonists – particularly those identifying Idealism with quantum mechanics – is a property of quantum entanglement known as the No-Signalling Theorem. Put simply, this theorem states that information transmitted between two points that are entangled is quantum information, not classical information. Quantum information is not discrete. It is in a superpositioned state. To see why this is a problem, consider how communication proceeds at our level of spatial organization with the digital computer. At its most basic level, the computer operates by alternating between two states, which you can label either as "yes" or "no," or "1" or "0." From these two states, it is possible to construct an ever-expanding set of formalisms that support communication and work, and that is precisely what the modern digital computer does. It translates the "1s" and "0s" into software that expresses the formalisms and functions that we require of it.

In a scenario of faster-than-light communication the two alternating states in principle would be attained by manipulation of the directional spin of an electron or photon. The problem is that when a sender transmits a message by quantum entanglement it arrives in a superpositioned state. For the receiver, it is like receiving a message that says "yes" and "no" at the same time. With no prior knowledge of the sender's intentions, the message for all intents and purposes is noise: the receiving partner in the entangled pair expresses the incoming transmission by manifesting directional spins in both directions.[99] Some theoretical physicists such as Shan Gao have expressed the hope that a method will be devised to determine the original sender's signal with high probability, despite the "inherent randomness" associated with quantum information and its collapse to one alternative or another upon receipt, properties that "ruthlessly block the way" to faster-than-light communication.[100]

While physicists debate whether a method of transcending this limit can ever be located, the operating assumption of Idealist philosophers and physicists is that natural selection has already found it. In their eyes, we have the capacity to receive *a priori* forms and non-locally transmitted information because evolution, in the end, has given us the ability to so do. Through this property, we gain access to constraint and, in turn, to the capacity to communicate. And through this property, we gain access to modes of perception that lie outside the resources at hand in our immediate linguistic, cultural, and natural environments. Ideal forms, in short, secure the possibility for novelty, the possibility for choice. Such is the philosophy that scientists like Simon Conway Morris and Roger Penrose are currently trying to promote; and such is the philosophy that Harold Innis sought to promote in his works devoted to communication.

Stating the central point of this chapter in its starkest terms, then: Harold Innis remains known as a significant thinker because he – by the measure of scholarly interests and preoccupations emerging today – was a remarkably prescient thinker. His prescience extended beyond the insight – which he shared with McLuhan – that the act of communication, and the tools designed to support communication, are fundamental constituents of the human past and present, and deserve to be studied in their own right. His writings are important because they anticipated several concerns – concerns topical, practical, and metaphysical – that are now emerging in the humanities, social sciences, and the sciences. One important concern – emergent change – has been the central preoccupation of this book. In the conclusion I propose to briefly revisit Innis's work, early and late, to see how it rested on a construct of history that is markedly similar in substance to a framework now preoccupying researchers across a wide variety of disciplines: the *complex adaptive system*

Conclusion

Harold Innis's career can be characterized as the practice of philosophy by other means. In his studies of Canada's economic history and the history of communication technology, Innis's intent was to explore the nature of social and economic change. And throughout his career, Innis consistently applied a schema of change that is today associated with *complex adaptive systems*. It is this framework that unites his earlier and later work. In his writings, Innis described systems in which economic, political, social, and cognitive structures are emergent properties. They are the by-product of interactions between numerous agents. For such emergence to occur, Innis repeatedly emphasized, agents – whether in the form of members of the public, or economic, political, or cultural institutions – had to operate in an environment in which there was a balance between liberty and constraint. In contemporary terms, such systems had to be operating at the "edge of chaos," a state that could only be obtained through appropriate control of the system's control parameter. As we saw with Stuart Kauffman's genetic switches, the number of connections between genes determined whether the network remained in stasis, or turbulence, or demonstrated emergent behaviour. Innis argued the same point, identifying transportation, institutional governance, and then communication as the key variables of the economic and communication systems he studied. When these variables allowed for the right of distributed decision-making on issues ranging from control over transport facilities to the quantity of circulating information, then self-organization occurred.

Innis also pointed to the phenomenon of differential persistence. Once a system emerges in an environment, it has staying power. It is often incorporated into a larger system as a component, its function determined by the context in which it is embedded. In biological systems, John Holland has identified a three-bone configuration that has found use in contexts as diverse as a fish's gill and a reptile's jaw. Systems displaying differential persistence are also not dependent on the components comprising them for their continued existence. An autocatalytic set, for example, may replace all the components that initially comprised it, and still retain its formal integrity. A standing wave in a stream is not dependent on specific water molecules for its existence. Innis pointed to a similar phenomenon in his studies of change, particularly in his economic histories and his descriptions of the oral tradition.

Finally, this study has illustrated that Innis throughout his career showed an interest in systems governed by formal and final cause, another distinguishing feature of complex adaptive systems. In systems governed by formal cause, the whole is more than the sum of its parts; that is, that the parts self-organize into a system that then regulates the behaviour of its constituent parts. The price of the constraint, however, is worth it, as the capabilities of the system exceed what its agents can do individually. One fascinating trait of such systems is that they display purposive behaviour, or final cause. As this study has emphasized, the two forms of causation are of a piece. Such systems are not passive recipients of matter and energy from the environment, but rather they appropriate resources to maintain their formal integrity. Even simple systems are aided in this task by schemas, models of the environment that enable the system to locate needed resources. Even in simple systems, such schemas are susceptible to change as a result of interaction with the environment. Systems learn. They are also governed by a second dimension of final cause; namely, that emergent systems gravitate toward a fixed state or range of behaviours known as attractors.

Innis expressed many of the core intellectual concerns that would shape his agenda and career in his celebrated defence of Thorstein Veblen, "The Work of Thorstein Veblen." Like Veblen Innis had an ambition to provide a description of economic change that mirrored the course of development in biological organisms, and through Veblen's writings we saw that his description included agent interaction, self-organization, differential persistence, meta-stability, and formal and final cause, the core concepts we identified with complex adaptive systems and emergent change.

In *The Fur Trade*, Innis provided his first treatment of the staples hypothesis, and grounded it on his construct of emergent change. There, he argued that the characteristics of a given region's economic, social, and political structures are directly related to the techniques employed by agents when they first begin extracting resources from the surrounding environment. In the regions that eventually became Canada and the United States, such structures first emerged in the seventeenth century and persisted into the twentieth century. The structure of Canada's economy differed from those of the United States and Britain because its origins were different. The prominent role of the Dominion government in Canada's economic life, and the high degree of centralized control in Canada's economic and transport industries were characteristics that could both be traced to the founding activities of the fur trade.

The narrative of *The Fur Trade* begins with the encounter of European traders with members of the First Nations, and the selection by multiple agents – French and aboriginal, individual and institutional – of fur as the commodity to be extracted from the environment for the purpose of trade. From the start, the trade was subject to periods of heightened disequilibrium that prompted dissolution and self-organization. In the seventeenth century, the industry on the European side appeared first as a free market with multiple competitors. Stress resulting from astute bargaining by aboriginal traders, however, induced Champlain and his colleagues to self-organize into a combination. Subsequent states of disequilibrium in turn forced the French to modify their schema of monopoly. With the onset of war and disease in the 1660s, New France lost its aboriginal suppliers of fur. Subsequent monopolies were forced to send agents into the interior to procure furs, and in so doing, to release control over the terms of trade and transport within North America. Disequilibrium prompted a rescripting of the fur trade's schema, and a new period of self-organization.

Innis's descriptions of Canada's economic history also made repeated reference to the role of formal and final cause. In the case of New France, the market – and by extension formal cause – prompted the French government to heighten the centralization of the colony's religious and agricultural institutions for the purpose of supporting the fur trade. Canada's specialization in staples, according to Innis, resulted from systemic constraints that were the emergent properties of trade, not the dictates of an imperial centre. Final cause was revealed in Innis's insistence on the formative role played by the fur trade on Canada's subsequent economic evolution. Individuals such as Donald Smith applied lessons learned from the fur trade – schemas – in their new roles in the banking, railway, and government sectors of Canada's economy. The outcome of that continuity was differential persistence. The structure of Canada's largest institutions remained highly centralized, with limited degrees of distributed control. In Innis's narrative, Canada's economic and political agents found the right degree of balance – the right degree of distributed control for their environmental and economic circumstances – to support Canada's stability, institutional continuity, and, when necessary, adaptation to changing circumstance.

In his studies of the cod fisheries, Innis turned his attention from Canada's national economy to the international economy of the North Atlantic. Tracing the rise and fall of mercantilism in the British, French, and Spanish empires, Innis focused his attention on the Maritimes and New England, the regions in North America most affected by the Atlantic economy. Reiterating the staples hypothesis, he argued that emergent systems display differential persistence. The persistent political, economic, and social structures of the Atlantic seaboard, he said, could be traced to the initiating stages of European economic activity. The east coast of North America was characterized by institutions in which control was widely distributed, a development that Innis traced to the fishing industry.

He also constructed a narrative in which the economics of increasing returns played a central role. "Increasing returns" is the economic term for positive feedback, the process whereby an emergent system begins channelling the activities of its constituents. In economic systems, agents enter into a self-sustaining process where exchange leads to high profits, growth, and heightened opportunities for further exchange. A second round of exchange leads to still higher profits and opportunities for growth. Adam Smith referred to this process in his famous dictum – of which Innis was well aware – that exchange gives rise to the division of labour, and the extent of that division is determined by the extent of the market.[1] Stated another way, economic systems governed by increasing returns enjoy growth, the continued incorporation of new agents, and a capacity to provide a broader range of services. They become more complex.

Increasing returns held a threefold importance for Innis in his various accounts of the cod fisheries. They explained British and French dominance over the North Atlantic fishery, Britain's victory over France in its bid for hegemony over North America, and the American colonies' economic rationale for revolt against Great Britain in the 1770s. The narrative begins in the sixteenth and seventeenth centuries, when Britain and France, eager to obtain specie from Spain, extended their fishing interests to the coast of Newfoundland. Spain also attempted to create its own fishery, but its efforts were undermined by inept economic regulation, the country's import of specie, and the province of Guipuzcoa's trade with France and then England for foodstuffs. The three factors created a dynamic whereby it became more and more expensive for the Spanish to fish and more and more profitable for the English and French to sell them fish. By the mid-seventeenth century Spain was marginalized from the fishery, and fishing and trade emerged as mechanisms for England and France to obtain Spanish specie.

When he turned to Britain's competition with France, Innis began by referring to a fundamental feature of the North Atlantic economy: it was relatively easy to acquire the capital necessary to procure a fishing vessel. Consequently, the North Atlantic became populated with thousands of agents in a position to conduct international trade. It was the English fishermen, however, who seized the opportunity to engage in commerce. England was a trading country whose geography mandated trade to acquire needed supplies. France, by contrast, was a geographically diverse country that enjoyed a relatively self-sufficient economy. English fishermen were also spurred to trade by the small size of their domestic market and the need for salt as a preservative agent. The industry itself was concentrated in the West Country, where facilities were constructed to sort fish prior to export. The French industry, on the other hand, was dispersed throughout France and enjoyed a domestic market sufficient for its own needs. In short, the English industry, by virtue of its interaction with the home market, was structurally and cognitively predisposed to trade; the French industry was not. Formal and final cause provided England with an advantage as it expanded to Newfoundland.

That advantage, combined with access to a then-inexhaustible resource – cod – laid the groundwork for the emergence of a trading network and an economy of increasing returns. The process was initiated by the English fishing industry's incorporation of growing numbers of people into the North Atlantic economy. Anxious to reduce operating costs, fishermen conveyed settlers to England's North

American colonies, and the introduction of multiple agents there led to exchange and economic diversification. Agriculture, fishing, and shipping industries developed in New England; staples economies in the southern American colonies and the West Indies. By the middle of the seventeenth century, a trading network linking New England with the West Indies had emerged, and with it came the cumulative growth associated with an increasing returns economy. One product of that growth was specialization. High profits – the stimulus of increasing returns and the regulation of formal cause – induced planters to specialize in sugar, and the trading network collectively to incorporate a new constituent – West Africa – into the system to heighten its capabilities: slaves were imported as a source of cheap labour and to produce more sugar. One cycle of profit led to another. The introduction of slaves gave the fishery an opportunity to sell plantation owners low-quality products to feed their captive workforce. Profits from that market niche proved so substantial that it initiated a new round of increasing returns, as shipping costs declined and returns from European trade returned as pure profit. By the eighteenth century, New England serviced a trading network comparable in size to that of Britain.

The emergence and operation of that network ultimately proved fatal for French ambitions in North America. Enjoying robust growth, New England incorporated the French West Indies into its trading system, tapping into its supplies of sugar, molasses, and rum. Colbert, France's comptroller-general, was never able to integrate French colonies into a single trading network; the net effect of that failure was that France's sugar colonies began working at cross-purposes with its fur colony. New England, according to Innis, used West Indian molasses and rum to bolster its position in the fur trade, initiating another round of increasing returns for itself, and a sequence of declining returns for New France. The success of Britain and New England in usurping French sources of fur forced France to construct a series of military fortifications to contain its rivals. That expense, along with dwindling revenues from the trade, destroyed the economic viability of New France. In Innis's narrative, two trading systems competed for resources and the one with superior capabilities won. The conquest merely aligned the continent's political structures with the underlying economic reality of the time.

British hegemony over North America, however, did not bring economic stability. New England's economic growth continued, spurred in part by Britain's takeover of the French fur trade and in part by the region's symbiotic relationship with the French West Indies. New England demand for sugar and molasses continued to rise, and therein lay the problem. Planters in the British West Indies, upset at New England's trade with their French competitors, pressed the British parliament to pass legislation restricting New England's commercial ties to British possessions, a measure realized by the Sugar Act of 1764. The restrictions initiated a conflict that evaded resolution, as New England required quantities of sugar beyond the capacities of the British West Indies to provide. That conflict, combined with additional British legislation restricting American activity, precipitated the American Revolution, and led in turn to the collapse of the First British Empire. Britain's fundamental mistake, according to Innis, was its attempt to regulate a commercial economy governed by increasing returns. That mistake, however, ultimately sparked economic and political reform in Britain, culminating in the dismantling of the mercantile system via the Corn Laws of the 1840s. Free trade in turn prompted disequilibrium and then political and economic reform – self-organization – in Nova Scotia, including responsible government, the colony's participation in the Reciprocity Treaty of 1854, and Confederation.

In 1940 Innis reoriented his focus from economics to the larger, more multi-dimensional problem of culture. While he never explicitly stated his reasons for turning to the study of communication, the likely causes were intellectual concerns generated by the Depression, and the onset of the Second World War. Innis believed the West required a jeremiad, one that would speak truth both to power and the populace. Relying on the same systemic worldview that had informed his studies of the fur trade and the cod fisheries, Innis warned that the West was plagued by a structural problem: it lacked balance. It failed to recognize that culture was governed by a variant of change characterized by self-organization, with constraints resulting from the operation of formal and final cause. Under such conditions, cultural growth and adaptation would only ensue if the West was able to control the variable, the control parameter, which maintained what we would refer to today as the edge-of-chaos balance between cognitive rigidity and flux. That variable was the quantity of circulating information.

Innis's narrative of the history of the West after the collapse of Rome was reduced to a civilizational search for the factors that make for a good society, or, in Innis's parlance, a balanced one. That search led to conceptions of "balance" that rested on institutional checks-and-balances, individual self-discipline, the rule of law, free inquiry, and economic liberty. By the end of the eighteenth century, Innis believed, the principal members of the British Atlantic World had attained those ideals, however imperfectly, however fleetingly. For a time the Second British Empire and the United States were balanced societies. That accomplishment was almost immediately undone, however, by the rise of the commercial press and steam technology in the nineteenth century. These two innovations – the first institutional, the second technological – precipitated an explosion of circulating information in the West.

And here, Innis noticed something important: information flows were governed by the same dynamic as commercial exchange – the dynamic of positive feedback or increasing returns. That dynamic disrupted the balance of the West. With that balance in place, Western polities had displayed the emergent behaviour that Innis associated with healthy cultures, behaviour that led to innovations in politics, economics, and culture. Without that balance, the West began to display the same pathologies that Innis saw in overheated economies such as the Klondike: instability in thought; oscillation in practice; irrationality in politics; and, ultimately, systemic collapse. For Innis, these symptoms found concrete form in the decline of letters and commerce, the collapse of the international system and the scourge of two world wars. Unless steps were taken to perfect the information management practices of Europe and North America, Innis warned, the West could expect more of the same.

To avert that fate, Innis proposed a threefold agenda for the social sciences to facilitate the moral and intellectual regeneration of the West. The first task was for the social sciences to adopt the mantle once assumed by the church and then by commerce; namely, to act as the voice of restraint, the agent working for balance. Philosophically, Innis believed, it was not the mandate of the social sciences to engage in social engineering, but rather to facilitate adaptation by identifying the constraints within which human collectives operated. The British had failed to recognize the significance of increasing returns economics, and the American Revolution had been the result. Innis feared that unless the West gave up its preoccupation with the present, it would repeat the mistakes of the First British Empire.

The second task was to generate new modes of representation that would facilitate public and policymaker recognition of constraint, or pattern in all realms of human activity. Innis feared that members of the reading public were losing the capacity to perceive form. Since the nineteenth century – in his estimation at any rate – literature had lost the sense of aesthetic unity that had tied the disparate parts of the novel together: Dickens's works were little better than journalism. To reverse this trend, Innis appealed to the domains of religion and art for inspiration, and more specifically for their expertise in compressing information and expressing complex ideas in visual form.

Finally, Innis appealed to social scientists to adopt methods that would enable them to model and characterize emergent systems. Such a method, Innis argued, involved more than examining quantitative data. It meant examining the full gamut of human activity – including politics, culture, and technology – and interpolating them from the standpoints of time and space. By following this method of convergence, Innis believed scholars would be able to trace the contours of existing economic and social systems, and in so doing overcome *a priori* biases that hindered scholarly inquiry. Economic or cultural systems were no more constrained by national borders than weather systems. It stood to reason, then, that scholars should not study them from a national perspective. Another virtue of Innis's method was that it enabled him to locate the control parameters that induced periods of cultural and economic disequilibrium prior to self-organization. Innis believed that by juxtaposing the qualitative histories and quantitative time series describing the constituents of economic and cultural systems, he had discovered the two key variables governing societal change: technology and circulating information.

In *Empire and Communications* and *The Bias of Communication* Innis built upon insights initially expressed in *Political Economy in the Modern State*. His primary intent – as indicated by his reference to previous work in economic history – was to demonstrate that the process of cultural change, and by extension the rise and fall of empires, was governed by the dynamics of emergent change. Here, he pointed to the recurring presence of self-organization in imperial history, and the association of communication technology with each cycle of self-organization. That correlation suggested to Innis that communication technology should serve as one basis for the periodization of history. His purpose in the two anthologies was also to reassert the importance of balance – the navigation between centripetal and centrifugal factors – and the importance of information management as a basis for cultural adaptation and evolution.

Ancient Greece was an exemplar for Innis in these two respects. For much of its history it did not enjoy ready access to papyrus, and as a result it was not overwhelmed by the information and ideas of the Near East. Part of the reason it did so well was that it enjoyed an expressive toolkit comprising two media: in addition to papyrus, Greece used the oral tradition. Both technologies provided the Greeks with the tools necessary to manage their information flows, and the means to move endogenously from a monopoly of space to a monopoly of time, and then to an oligopoly of space-time, thereby attaining a state of balance. That adaptive balance, that cognitive flexibility, permitted the Greeks to make impressive contributions in domains ranging from theology to science. It also gave them the acumen, in Innis's mind, to withstand their competitors. Greece prevailed against Persia thanks to its capacity to innovate via the oral tradition.

Innis's final purpose in the two anthologies was to explore the flip side of a problem he had first raised in *Political Economy in the Modern State*. In the earlier work he had examined the first hazardous consequent of communication technology: cognitive flux. In the latter two anthologies, he looked at the second consequent: cognitive rigidity. Innis's purpose was to explore how and why humans became trapped in the constructs of their own devising, and to assert that it was not necessary to remain in that state. Cognitive rigidity could be escaped by consciously recognizing the recurring dangers posed by emergent change. Here Innis would lay heavy stress on individual and social realization of the roles that formal and final cause played in cultural evolution. And here, he would argue that the structuring principles of the former presented one method to counter the dangers posed by the latter. The creative use of expressive instruments could be used, in principle, to overcome the recurring human penchant to stereotype the past, present, and future.

Aside from asserting the possibility for human autonomy, *Empire* and *Bias* were also distinguished by Innis's assertion that there is an ontology to human knowledge, and his description of how human autonomy and creativity worked within it, and in turn, extended it. For Innis, human cultural constructs were marked by their rich diversity. But they also have the mark of similarity, a similarity that permitted their classification into three genera: space, time and space-time. Given that there is an economy, not an infinite diversity, of cultural forms, Innis reached a number of conclusions regarding the process of knowledge construction, conclusions he derived from the writings of Immanuel Kant and Ernst Cassirer. In essence, the process of knowledge construction was emergent, contingent, and regulated by formal and final cause. The concept of efficient cause could not account for the similarities in cultural form that he had observed in his surveys of the past and present. Because final cause was such a central constituent of knowledge production, Innis turned to economics for concepts that would explain how the ontology of knowledge is extended and made more complex. Via this decision, he appropriated business cycle theory, monopoly theory, and, ultimately, the concepts that would distinguish him in the field of communications: media bias and the monopoly of knowledge.

Innis's decision to conceive the history of thought as an ontology made complex by increasing returns presented opportunities and problems for his interpreters. The most immediate gain was that it offered readers a fascinating correlation between the material properties of media and the resulting cognitive bias of the users who appropriated them. Light media such as papyrus generally produced cultures and institutions oriented toward the dimension of space; heavy media, by contrast, encouraged polities or the agents within them to emphasize the dimension of time. Innis further suggested that a bias inherited from a given medium would – over time – become all-encompassing, constituting a monopoly of knowledge.

These ideas, while productive and provocative, also presented problems for Innis scholars, divorced as they were from the intellectual context that gave rise to them. In isolation, they seemed to suggest a form of technological determinism, one which posited a linear relationship between the material substrate of technology and thought. Further, they presented a scenario in which he, apparently blithely, contradicted the generalizations he was seeking to promote. In Innis's narrative, heavy media are from time to time aligned with space, and light media support constructs and institutions devoted to time. A final problem was that Innis's histories never provided a clear sense as to how a culture might move from one bias to another. If an extant monopoly was in place, how did a culture acquire the cognitive resources to think and see differently? We noted that those resources were not always imposed by an actor from the periphery. Some cultures, particularly Greece, managed to change endogenously. We further noted that in the case of Greece its cognitive transformations took place without any change in the material substrate of its communication infrastructure. So, how was it able to shift from one bias to another?

Innis addressed this final question by appealing to an Idealist interpretation of history. As we saw through references to Innis's *Idea File*, the writings of Ernst Cassirer, and the minutes of conversations he had with W.T. Easterbrook, Innis was ultimately a disciple of Immanuel Kant and Plato. He believed that our capacity to reframe the past, present, and future stems from innate, *a priori* intuitions of time and space that we all share. These enable us to see our physical, social, and cultural environments as coherent objects that can be categorized as having a bias toward space, time, or space-time. These enable us to bring constructs such as Newtonian physics into association with Greek philosophies such as *moiria*. Because we have access to structuring principles that differ from those to which we historically have been exposed, we have the capacity to think differently and do differently, particularly in times of stress. If we received our formation in a culture devoted to space, we have within us the capacity to construct a worldview aligned with time.

With respect to Innis's alleged technological determinism, it is a charge without foundation. Innis saw the history of thought in cyclical terms, and each knowledge cycle was governed by the same dynamic as the business cycle: increasing returns and final cause. Drawing on insights from economic theory, as expressed by Alfred Marshall and Thorstein Veblen, Innis recognized that each knowledge cycle, when it emerged, emerged with multiple points of potential equilibria, or attractors, one of which would be selected by the system. These attractors Innis aligned with the *a priori* intuitions described by Kant. He suggested there were points of equilibrium respectively associated with space, time, and space-time. Reasoning from analogy, Innis suggested that the pull of these attractors was so overweening that those caught within them eventually came to see the world only in one way. Just as the dynamic of increasing returns supported the rise of institutional monopolies in emerging markets, it also led to cognitive monopolies in emerging cultures. The only attractor that supported cognitive flexibility was the one supporting the oligopoly of knowledge. It enabled cultures to access insights derived from both space and time. Reasoning again from analogy, Innis concluded that a knowledge cycle's selection of a given bias and equilibrium point was a contingent process. Given that contingency, it was perfectly possible for a given material medium to be affiliated with space in one context, and time in another. Innis believed that it was the attractor associated with a given knowledge cycle that ultimately determined the bias of a given culture, not the material substrate of its communication technology.

In the end, for Innis, the significance of a given medium's physical properties was that they have a statistical, not a linear, relationship with cognitive bias. Light media were *generally* associated with the bias of space, but not always. And heavy media were *generally* affiliated with the bias of time, but again not always. Innis's writings and correspondence provided two grounds to suggest that he conceived the influence of a medium's physical properties in probabilistic terms. His interactions with B.S. Keirstead and Arthur Cole indicate that he thought a great deal about business cycles during the 1940s, not only as a communication theorist but also as an economist. Through Keirstead's writings, Innis was exposed to writings linking the business cycle with statistical change. In his correspondence with Cole on the Time Horizons project, Innis endorsed Keirstead's characterization of the business cycle and stated his interest in studying firms' applications of probability theory to predict their respective futures. Given Innis's construction of the business cycle, it was likely that he reasoned analogically, and would see any relationship in the knowledge cycle, including the relationship between a medium's physical properties and thought, in statistical terms. That supposition was confirmed by a second ground: Innis's own statements on the nature of his generalizations. Innis never intended his writings on media to be seen as general covering laws. Rather, they were properly seen as mid-level generalizations. They occurred with sufficient frequency to command notice. But they were not to be invoked without an accompanying thick description of conditions on the ground.

II

I'd like to conclude this account of one important thinker by referring to the sage advice of another. In his fiction and his prose, Robertson Davies often observed that we rarely come to understand the life and action of another. It was for this reason that he derided the genre of biography, believing that human biography is in large measure governed by masks.[2] When we interact with another, we become men and women of parts: man, woman, professional, lover, friend, partner, even fool. And when we react to others, we categorize them in roles that for reasons fair or foul suit our purposes: sage or pain, friend or foe, and once again, even fool. Davies objected to the genre of biography because it all too often offers a description of pretense, not the person, the parts he or she plays, not the essential qualities that define a life's trajectory and its complexity.

As with biography, so it is with intellectual history. As Tom Cooper and others have noted, scholars have applied multiple masks to describe Innis's life and work, and I venture to say that this study has added still more: prescient thinker, information theorist, and even, in his way, holy fool.[3] By Davies's measure, I have done a dangerous thing, and in conclusion I propose to continue doing a dangerous thing by adding two more masks to account for the enduring significance of Harold Innis. The historian – in the end – has little choice. As Innis himself noted, the scholar generally has access only to one thing: the sediment of human experience.[4] If we are to purchase any coherence from that complexity, we must define, and to define we must apply a mask.

The first mask highlights what most interpreters know but few explicitly say: Harold Innis was a brave thinker. He was not afraid of saying things that ran against the consensus of his colleagues. He was not afraid of applying unfashionable frameworks to support his scholarship. Few scholars then and even fewer now muster the courage to write grand histories on the scale that Innis attempted. And few choose to base their histories on the strikingly original complex of ideas that Innis appropriated for his scholarship. How many researchers would opt to select new objects of study – information and communication media – and incorporate them into a philosophy of history combining business cycle theory and Kantian Idealism?

Innis's exercise of his first mask, however, was tempered by a second: the mask of modest thinker. When you read his prose carefully what comes through is not only its bravery, but its caution. Innis was fully aware that the application of any knowledge construct was, in its way, an act of violence. It may be elegant. It may be powerful. But he believed that neither you, I, nor anyone else should ever give ourselves completely to it. There will always be things the construct misses. There will always be things that it gets wrong. It was for this reason that Innis enjoined his readers to remember that his communication histories were little more than thought experiments. In *The Bias of Communication*, he acknowledged that "I may have extended the theory of monopoly to undue limits," and that "[the] extension of cyclical theory may seem to have been carried too far." But Innis believed it was the duty of the scholar "to test the limits of his tools and to indicate their possibilities."[5] With that mandate came a corresponding responsibility, to respect their limits.

In the end, however, Innis was not Clement Attlee. He was not, as Churchill once said of Attlee, a modest man with much to be modest about. Innis was a profound thinker who knew a great deal about complex systems: how they functioned, how they defined human activity, and how they delimited it. Much of human history, he believed, could be distilled to humanity's efforts to manage the catastrophic and constructive effects of emergent change. In its substance, human history was replete with empires clashing, cultures collapsing, and individuals and institutions creating and managing information flows. It was also filled with human interaction, systems displaying emergent properties, and the governance of formal and final cause. In the end, Innis was a modest thinker, and a brave one. But if there is any mask that is likely to persist, it is this: Harold Adams Innis was a profound thinker who contributed to the twentieth century's growing preoccupation with emergent change.

Notes

INTRODUCTION

1 For personal portraits of Innis, see Anne Innis Dagg, "Memories of My Father," *Queen's Quarterly* 101, 1 (spring 1994): 79–91; and Tom Cooper, "The Unknown Innis," *Journal of Canadian Studies* 12 (winter 1977): 111–18.

2 Marshall McLuhan, "The Later Innis," *Queen's Quarterly* 60 (autumn 1953), 389. Robert Babe remarks: "Innis is not an easy read. Donald Creighton described the style as 'difficult, highly condensed, extremely elliptical, and not infrequently obscure.' Northrop Frye found it 'impenetrable,' at least upon first perusal ... His later works on communication are, if anything, less coherent still. Reviewing *The Bias of Communication* (1951), E.R. Adair berated the author for his 'intellectual shorthand,' complaining that the celebrated political economist 'rarely troubles to put in the words, let alone the phrases, that would show what connection there was in his mind between a sentence and the ones that precede and follow it.' Indeed, Innis' infamous 'History of Communications' awaits publication to this day despite a long line of editorial efforts on the part of luminaries such as Mary Quayle Innis, Northrop Frye, Ian Parker, and William Buxton." Robert Babe, *Canadian Communication Thought: Ten Foundational Writers* (Toronto: University of Toronto Press, 2000), 52.

3 "Review: *Political Economy in the Modern State*," *The Economist* (8 February 1947), 239.

4 Jack Granatstein and Norman Hillmer, "Canadians Who Inspired the World," *Maclean's*, 4 September 2000, 29. In a 1998 survey of the hundred Canadians who inspired the nation in the twentieth century, however, Granatstein and a panel ranked Innis the country's third-most important intellectual: "[he] was no humorist, and his prose style still makes students

shudder. But Innis studied the staple industries – fur, fish, timber and wheat – that had been the mainspring of Canadian development, and his argument that Canada developed because of geography, not despite it, took hold. Examination of the routes followed by trade led him to study the theory of communication, and his ideas piqued Marshall McLuhan's interest and won global acclaim." Granatstein, "Canada's best, they made us think – and laugh," *Maclean's* (1 July 1998), 22. Finally, in its initial issue for the year 2000, the magazine reviewed the best Canadian cultural products of the twentieth century, and deemed Innis's *The Fur Trade* the best non–fiction work of the century, noting "this scholarly 1930 classic about traders and beaver hats accomplished the unlikely task of making Canadian economic history fascinating." "Best of the Century," *Maclean's* (1 January 2000), 241.

5 Judith Stamps, *Unthinking Modernity: Innis, McLuhan and the Frankfurt School* (Montreal and Kingston: McGill-Queen's University Press, 1995), xvii.

6 Charles Acland and William Buxton, "Introduction," in *Harold Innis in the New Century: Reflections and Refractions* (Montreal and Kingston: McGill-Queen's University Press, 1999), 13.

7 Hugh G.J. Aitken, "Myth and Measurement: The Innis Tradition in Economic History," *Journal of Canadian Studies* 12 (winter, 1977), 96.

8 Acland and Buxton, "Introduction," 12.

9 Tom Cooper provides perhaps the best encapsulation of the disparate portraits that now populate the literature: "William Kuhns views Innis within the cluster of twentieth-century 'post-industrial prophets'; James Carey has viewed Innis within the perspective of communications study and the history of technology; Carl Berger has grouped Innis with prominent Canadian historians; Robin Neill has written of Innis the economist; Marshall McLuhan sees Innis as modern parent to the study of effects or 'formal cause'; while his closest colleagues, such as Vincent Bladen and Tom Easterbrook, have seen Innis primarily as they knew him, as a political economist and economic historian, respectively." Cooper, "The Unknown Innis," 114. Judith Stamps notes that until the 1990s Innis's work was not widely viewed in an international context, a stance that worked to the detriment of the literatures devoted to Innis and communication theory: "The lack of extended comparisons may result from the iconic role that Innis and McLuhan have come to play in Canada. It is not a question of inattention. As many know, the two theorists have received considerable attention in Canada. But attention can take insidious forms … In contemporary Canadian studies, as one theorist has noted, Innis is often ritualistically acknowledged and then avoided … Recent texts on communication theory in Canada, useful and informative in their own right, support this judgment as

well. Authors devote space to Innis's and McLuhan's work but carry out their own analyses without appealing to their insights ... For both Innis and McLuhan, the phrase 'technological determinism' had stuck so hard one gets the impression that 'uniquely Canadian' has become a polite phrase for 'uniquely crude' – a theory with a roughly hewn set of concepts that, like the fur trade, is an interesting but odd spin-off of the Pre-Cambrian shield ... Most [critical literatures] look to Europe for theoretical inspiration, and few show awareness of Innis and McLuhan. The time has come to see the two Canadians' work in this broader context and to consider closely what they had to say about the making of the modern world." See Stamps, *Unthinking Modernity*, xiii–xv.

10 Acland and Buxton, "Introduction," 12.

11 Babe, *Canadian Communication Thought*, 41; Stamps, *Unthinking Modernity*, 41.

12 W.T. Easterbrook remarked on this trait in notes he made after a July 1952 visit with Innis: "Innis: July 11/52; mind extremely active – physically, doubtful if holding his own, but still quite strong looking. Talk with Mrs. I.; extraordinary case of a state of mind which envisages nothing but continuing 'just as is' – plans re future etc; unfort letter from Willits, 'sorry to hear you have cancer' – why didn't you tell me – but Harold, you knew this 2 yrs ago – still no change in attitude – my feeling is that death at this stage is so meaningless that simply not accepted as a fact – not a rational matter – no heroics, no act of will, just simply too preposterous to believe – feeling in talking with him that death out of the question – so unreal. Problems for Mrs. I; no thought of making will or any plans re family if death occurs – refusal to take sedatives in spite of pain which begins in evening; ver sever b mid–night– but why take the stuff if getting better, is his attitude. Complained to me of difficulties re walking; doctor baffled, X–ray shows walking impossible, yet walks – and doctor puzzled re attitude, says must know, no attempt to conceal, yet no sign of knowing. The real sufferer, his wife. Problems of 'understanding friends and relatives' – 'must tell him' re nec of final arrangements – concern with his 'religious outlook' – Why Cassidy case so different? C. a romantic, calling in all friends at end, courageous acceptance – no dramatics re Innis and no acceptance yet. Yet strong tendency to reminisce – long talk of early devs in dept (see below) – and writing [his] 'Memoirs' at great rate – his reasoning faculties much too sharp 'not to know,' highly skilled at reading between the lines – but still refusal – euphoria – when does acceptance come, and what then? cancer spreading into hip, no hope, and yet I find myself accepting his attitude as I talk with him." *W.T. Easterbrook Papers*, University of Toronto Archives, B1975-0030/001.

13 Donald Creighton, *Harold Adams Innis: Portrait of a Scholar* (Toronto: University of Toronto Press, 1957), 21–3; Michael Gauvreau, "Baptist religion and the Social Science of Harold Innis," *Canadian Historical Review* 76 (2), 169–71; Harold Innis, *The Bias of Communication* (Toronto: University of Toronto Press, 1995, c. 1951), xxvii. Toward the end of his life, Innis noted in his autobiography of Ten Broeke that he was "one of the most striking teachers" at McMaster:

> The Baptist denomination, like other denominations at that time, was concerned with the pursuit of heresy, and with the expulsion on one or two occasions of members of the staff. But the name of Professor Ten Broeke, as far as I am aware, was never mentioned in this agitation, though he must have been far the most heretical thinker in the university. He opened up the subject of philosophy in such a way as to free those who sought to be free from the conventions of philosophical thought. I remember vividly his arguments with rather fervent evangelical students; never losing his temper but always arguing in the interests of a wider outlook. His books on the subject were primarily concerned with the problem of working out a philosophical basis for theology, when to the orthodox no such problem existed. *Harold Adams Innis Papers,* University of Toronto Archives, B1972-0003/036, File 1: "Autobiography of HAI," 40.

14 Creighton, *Harold Adams Innis*, 31–2.

15 In *Political Economy in the Modern State,* which Innis published in 1946, he pressed his readers to recognize "how prodigal we have been with young life, our most cherished possession, and how careful we must be with that which has been left to us." A major portion of that realization would involve answering a fundamental question: "Why has a century of comparative peace such as prevailed from the end of the Napoleonic wars to the beginning of the last war been followed by the breakdown of Western Civilization? Why has European civilization turned from persuasion to force or from ballots to bullets?" Harold Innis, "The Problems of Rehabilitation," in *Political Economy in the Modern State* (Toronto: Ryerson Press, 1946), 57, 63.

16 Harold Innis, "The Work of Thorstein Veblen," in *Essays in Canadian Economic History* (Toronto: University of Toronto Press, 1956), 24.

17 Harold Innis, *The Fur Trade: An Introduction to Canadian Economic History,* revised edition (Toronto: University of Toronto Press, 1956, c. 1930), 383–6; Harold Innis, *The Cod Fisheries: The History of an International Economy* (Toronto: University of Toronto Press, 1954), 484–6.

18 See Harold Innis, *Political Economy in the Modern State* (Toronto, Ryerson Press, 1946).

19 See Harold Innis, *Empire and Communications* (Oxford: Clarendon Press, 1950); Innis, *The Bias of Communication.*

20 Creighton, *Harold Adams Innis*, 124–46. For a treatment of Innis's work with the Rockefeller Foundation, see Matthew D. Evenden, "Harold Innis, the Arctic Survey, and the Politics of Social Science during the Second World War," *Canadian Historical Review* 79 (1) (1998): 36–68; Eric Havelock, *Harold Innis: A Memoir* (Toronto: Harold Innis Foundation, 1982), 26. Havelock's exact formulation was more understated: "I hazard the opinion that his premature death constituted a minor disaster in the long history of the human understanding," 26. Marshall McLuhan took Havelock to task for this in his introduction to Havelock's memoirs, noting: "I am somewhat dismayed by Havelock's remarks ... [He] is being overly modest." See McLuhan, "The Fecund Interval," Havelock, *Harold Innis*, 10. Despite McLuhan's reservations, it is remarkable, and a measure of Havelock's respect, that a scholar of his stature should undertake such a memorial lecture commemorating Innis in 1978, and then publish the work in 1982. Innis's work generated a similar measure of respect from Northrop Frye, the renowned literary critic from the University of Toronto. In the early 1980s, he led a sadly unsuccessful effort to edit and publish Innis's unpublished *History of Communication*. The introduction he wrote for the effort was later published in Northrop Frye, "Harold Innis: The Strategy of Culture," in *The Eternal Act of Creation: Essays, 1979–1990*, ed. Robert D. Denham (Bloomington and Indianapolis: Indiana University Press, 1993): 154–67.

21 W.T. Easterbrook, "Innis and Economics," *Canadian Journal of Economics and Political Science* 19 (1953), 291.

22 Babe, *Canadian Communication Thought*, 53.

23 Innis, *Political Economy in the Modern State*, 113–15.

24 Vincent di Norcia, "Communications, Time and Power: An Innisian View," *Canadian Journal of Political Science*, 23 (2): 336–41; Vincent di Norcia, "Of Stone Books and Freedom," *Visible Language*, 20 (3) (summer 1986), 347; Paul Heyer, *Communications and History: Theories of Media, Knowledge, and Civilization* (New York: Greenwood Press, 1988), 115; Barrington Nevitt, *The Communication Ecology: Re-presentation versus Replica* (Toronto: Butterworth, 1982), 15; William Melody, "Introduction," in William H. Melody, Liora Salter and Paul Heyer, eds., *Culture, Communication and Dependency* (Norwood, New Jersey: Ablex, 1981), 8; David Crowley, "Harold Innis and the Modern Perspective of Communications," in Melody, Salter, and Heyer, eds., *Culture, Communication, and Dependency*, 236; James W. Carey, "Culture, Geography and Communications: The Work of Harold Innis in an Ameri-

can context," in Melody, Salter, and Heyer, eds., *Culture, Communication, and Dependency*: 79–84; Judith Stamps, "Innis in the Canadian Dialectical Tradition," in *Harold Innis in the New Century: Reflections and Refractions* (Montreal and Kingston: McGill-Queen's University Press, 1999): 48–65; Ian Parker, "Innis, Marx, and the Economics of Communication: A Theoretical Aspect of Canadian Political Economy," in Melody, Salter, and Heyer, eds., *Culture, Communication and Dependency*: 127–43; Ian Parker, "Innis and the Geography of Communications and Empire," *Canadian Geographer*, 37 (4): 353–5; Cole Harris, "Innis on Early Canada," *Canadian Geographer*, 37 (4): 355–7.

25 Parker, "Innis, Marx," 129.

26 Arthur Kroker, *Technology and the Canadian Mind: Innis / McLuhan / Grant* (Montreal: New World Perspectives, 1984); Stamps, *Unthinking Modernity*; Graeme Patterson, *History and Communications: Harold Innis, Marshall McLuhan, and the Interpretation of History* (Toronto: University of Toronto Press, 1990).

27 J. Alexander Watson, *Marginal Man: The Dark Vision of Harold Innis* (Toronto: University of Toronto Press, 2006). For a more sustained criticism of Watson's work, see chapter 4, note 28. Also see John Bonnett, "We're Still Looking: Alexander Watson, Marginal Man, and the Continuing Search for the Hidden Innis," *Canadian Journal of Communication* 33 (4): 721–4.

28 Innis, "The Work of Thorstein Veblen," 17–26.

CHAPTER ONE

1 Philosophers, natural philosophers, and scientists have long been interested in systems that display novel structures and evolve over time. In the latter part of the nineteenth century and the early part of the twentieth, in a span that overlapped the early part of Innis's career, an entire school of philosophy was built on the topic of emergence, and included philosophers such as Conwy Lloyd Morgan, Samuel Alexander, and C.D. Broad. See C. Lloyd Morgan, *Emergent Evolution* (London: Williams and Norgate, 1923); and Samuel Alexander, *Space, Time and Deity* (London: Macmillan, 1927).

There is no evidence, however, that any of these writers had a direct influence on Innis, or any pronounced influence on modern treatments of complexity. With respect to Innis, the influence was at best indirect through the writings of Thorstein Veblen, whom Innis identified as an important influence on his thinking. Veblen scholar Geoffrey Hodgson notes that in the aftermath of a lecture by Conwy Lloyd Morgan in Chicago in 1896, Veblen began work on his major writings in evolutionary economics, a remarkably productive period that would last for twelve years. Hodgson, however, is equivocal on the import of Morgan's lecture. It cannot be established that Veblen attended it, and Morgan's ideas on emergence, Hodgson argues, were at best in their nascent stage. Emergentist philosophers did not fully develop their doctrine until the 1920s.

With respect to present-day complexity researchers, the lack of any strong association with the school of Emergentist philosophy may stem in part from its identification of emergence with constructs of deity and providence. Complexity researcher Joshua Epstein, for example, notes: "I have always been uncomfortable with the vagueness and occasional mysticism surrounding this word." After researching the history of the term and its relation to Emergentist philosophy, Epstein found himself "questioning its adoption altogether." Noting the term's provenance in the work of Alexander, Broad, Morgan, and others, Epstein argued: "the complexity community should be alerted to this history. There is an unmistakable anti-scientific – even deistic – flavor to this movement, which claimed *absolute inexplicability* for emergent phenomena." See Joshua Epstein, *Generative Social Science: Studies in Agent-Based Computational Modeling* (Princeton, New Jersey: Princeton University Press, 2007), 31–2. On the history of Emergentist philosophy, see David Blitz, *Emergent Evolution: Qualitative Novelty and the Levels of Reality* (Boston, Massachusetts: Kluwer Academic Publishers, 1992); Thorstein Veblen's tenuous relationship with Emergentist philosophy is discussed in Geoffrey Hodgson, *The Evolution of Institutional Economics: Agency, Structure and Darwinism in American Institutionalism* (London: Routledge, 2004), 134–42.

2 Floyd Merrell, "Structuralism and Beyond: A Critique of Presuppositions," in John Deely, Brooke Williams, and Felicia E. Kruse, eds., *Frontiers in Semiotics* (Bloomington: Indiana University Press, 1986), 123–4.

3 Ibid., 123–6.

4 Alicia Juarrero, *Dynamics in Action: Intentional Behaviour as a Complex System* (Cambridge, Massachusetts: MIT Press, 1999), 21–3.

5 Merrell, "Structuralism," 124, 126–7.

6 Ibid., 124.

7 Juarrero, *Dynamics*, 22.

8 M. Mitchell Waldrop, *Complexity: The Emerging Science at the Edge of Order and Chaos* (New York: Touchstone Books, 1992), 145.

9 John Holland, *Emergence: From Chaos to Order* (Reading, Massachusetts: Addison-Wesley Publishing Company, 1998), 5–6, 13–14, 225–7; Juarrero, *Dynamics*, 120, 122–3.

10 Holland, *Emergence*, 7, 227; Juarrero, *Dynamics*, 124–5.

11 Waldrop, *Complexity*, 145–6.

12 Juarrero, *Dynamics*, 122–3.
13 Ibid., 122.
14 Holland, *Emergence*, 226.
15 Ibid., 3–4, 225.
16 Juarrero, *Dynamics*, 119.
17 Ibid., 119–20.
18 Ibid., 120.
19 Waldrop, *Complexity*, 106–8.
20 Ibid., 109–12.
21 James Gleick notes, however, that periods of order emerge even after the control parameter has shifted the system into a state of turbulence, or chaos: "Windows of Order Inside Chaos – Even with the simplest equation, the regions of chaos in a bifurcation diagram [of an equation modelling rates of population growth and decline] proves to have an intricate structure ... First, the bifurcation produces periods of 2, 4, 8, 16 ... Then chaos begins, with no regular periods. But then, as the system is driven harder [by the control parameter], windows appear with odd periods. A stable period 3 appears . . . and then the period-doubling begins again: 6, 12, 24." Gleick, *Chaos: Making a New Science* (New York: Penguin Books, 1987), 74; Alicia Juarrero also notes with respect to Bénard Cells: "Increased heat is the order or control parameter that drives the Bénard cells away from equilibrium toward a bifurcation in the case of Bénard cells, moreover, the heat level is altered from the outside. If the amount of heat is reduced, Bénard cells disintegrate, if it is increased further, the water abruptly becomes 'turbulent.' Scientists used to think that turbulence was disorderly; only recently did they discover that the seemingly 'chaotic' behaviour of turbulence is in fact a highly complex form of order." Juarrero, *Dynamics*, 120.
22 Waldrop, *Complexity*, 293.
23 Juarrero, *Dynamics*, 111.
24 Waldrop, *Complexity*, 121–2.
25 Ibid., 123–4.
26 Juarrero, *Dynamics*, 126.
27 Ibid., 127.
28 Waldrop, *Complexity*, 177.
29 Juarrero, *Dynamics*, 127.
30 Harold Innis, "The Work of Thorstein Veblen," in *Essays in Canadian Economic History* (Toronto: University of Toronto Press, 1956), 19. This essay originally appeared in *Southwestern Political and Social Science Quarterly*, 10 (1929): 56–68.
31 Innis, "Thorstein Veblen," 22.

32 Ibid., 25.
33 Ibid., 24.
34 Ibid., 19, 21.
35 Ibid., 22.
36 Ibid.
37 Ibid., 24.
38 Thorstein Veblen, "The Evolution of the Scientific Point of View," in *The Place of Science in Modern Civilization, and other essays* (New York: Russell and Russell, 1961), 37.
39 Innis, "Thorstein Veblen," 25.
40 Ibid., 24.
41 Ibid., 26.
42 Ibid., 26.
43 Ibid., 26 n42.
44 This reading differs from that of other interpreters who suggest that Innis's histories amount to little more than concrete case studies, and that he never intended his theories to be applied to any other locale save Canada. See Robert Babe, *Canadian Communication Thought: Ten Foundational Writers* (Toronto: University of Toronto Press, 2000), 63–4; Carl Berger, *The Writing of Canadian History: Aspects of English-Canadian Historical Writing since 1900*, (Toronto: University of Toronto Press, 1986), 85–94; Cole Harris, "Innis on Early Canada," *Canadian Geographer*, 37 (4): 355–6; Robin Neill, "The Passing of Canadian Economic History," *Journal of Canadian Studies* 12 (winter 1977), 73–6; Daniel Czitrom, *Media and the American Mind: From Morse to McLuhan* (Chapel Hill, North Carolina: University of North Carolina Press, 1982), 150; Trevor Barnes, "Knowing Where You Stand: Harold Innis, Staple Theory, and Local Models," *Canadian Geographer* 37 (4), 357–8. In contrast, I believe Innis's stance is better reflected by William Christian, who wrote in 1977: "Innis treated Canada not as a unique phenomenon, but as a particular one. In the particularity of Canada Innis could see manifestations of universal, or at least general principles." Christian, "Harold Innis as Political Theorist," *Canadian Journal of Political Studies* 10 (1), 21.
45 Innis, "Thorstein Veblen," 26.
46 Thorstein Veblen, "The Preconceptions of Economic Science III," in *The Place of Science in Modern Civilization: And Other Essays* (New York: Russell and Russell, 1961), 148–51.
47 Thorstein Veblen, "The Preconceptions of Economic Science II," in *The Place of Science in Modern Civilization*, 134.
48 Thorstein Veblen, "Why Is Economics Not an Evolutionary Science?" in *The Place of Science in Modern Civilization*, 73–4.

49 Thorstein Veblen, "Professor Clark's Economics," in *The Place of Science in Modern Civilization*, 191.
50 Veblen, "Preconceptions III," 159.
51 Veblen, "Preconceptions III," 150–1.
52 Veblen, "Why is Economics?" 60; Veblen, "Preconceptions I," 84.
53 Thorstein Veblen, "The Evolution of the Scientific Point of View," in *The Place of Science in Modern Civilization*, 37.
54 Veblen, "Why is Economics?" 81.
55 Thorstein Veblen, "The Preconceptions of Economic Science I," in *The Place of Science in Modern Civilization*, 84–5.
56 Ibid., 83.
57 Veblen, "Professor Clark's Economics," 184.
58 Veblen, "Preconceptions I," 82–3.
59 Veblen, "Professor Clark's Economics," 192.
60 Ibid.
61 Geoffrey M. Hodgson, *The Evolution of Institutional Economics: Agency, Structure, and Darwinism in American Institutionalism* (London: Routledge, 2004), 9.
62 Veblen, "Preconceptions III," 151.
63 Ibid.
64 Ibid., 151–2.
65 Ibid., 152.
66 Ibid., 152–3.
67 Ibid., 155–6.
68 Veblen, "Why is Economics?" 74.
69 Ibid., 74–5.
70 Veblen, "Preconceptions II," 132.
71 Ibid., 133–6; Veblen, "Clark's Economics," 203–4.
72 Veblen, "Preconceptions II," 139.
73 Ibid., 129.
74 Ibid., 143–4.
75 Veblen, "Preconceptions III," 168.
76 Ibid., 153.
77 Ibid., 153–4.
78 Ibid., 168.
79 Ibid., 169.
80 Ibid., 169.
81 Veblen, "The Evolution," 38.
82 Veblen, "Why is Economics," 62–3.
83 Veblen, "Preconceptions I," 105.

84 Veblen, "The Evolution," 39.

85 Veblen, "Why is Economics," 77.

86 Veblen, "The Evolution," 39.

87 Veblen provided perhaps his most extensive discussion of his scheme of history, and tentative conclusions on the impact that industrialization would make on modern thought, in *The Theory of the Leisure Class*. See Thorstein Veblen, *The Theory of the Leisure Class: An Economic Study of Institutions* (New York: Modern Library, 1934). Veblen's work was originally published in 1899.

88 Thorstein Veblen, "The Place of Science in Modern Civilization," in *The Place of Science in Modern Civilization*, 26.

89 Veblen, "Preconceptions III," 150.

90 Veblen, "Preconceptions I," 88.

91 Veblen, "The Evolution," 37.

92 Ibid., 37.

93 Veblen, "The Evolution," 54.

94 Veblen, "Preconceptions II," 115.

95 Ibid.

96 Ibid., 115–16.

97 Ibid., 116.

98 Ibid.

99 Veblen, "The Evolution," 37.

100 Ibid., 33.

101 Veblen, "Preconceptions I," 88; Veblen, "Preconceptions II," 115.

102 Veblen, "Preconceptions II," 114.

103 Veblen, "Why is Economics," 68.

104 Ibid., 69.

105 The force of this claim is enhanced when one realizes that most if not all of the features associated with complex adaptive systems have been identified in the Innis literature as significant constituents of his thought.
Interaction and Self-Organization: Paul Heyer, for example, has noted the importance of interacting agents and the consequent formation of pattern in his reading of Innis: "Interplay, formation, and interaction are terms that can be used to describe his view of the historical process." David Crowley has noted that the "causal nexus of change" in Innis's histories are characterized by "the way in which holistically distinct realities arose out of former ones. The task he set for the historian was the mapping of these epochs in terms of the conditions and sequences attending the shift from one form of communication to the other." Judith Stamps has also emphasized a reading of Innis in which interacting agents and contingency figure large, a vision of history describing

a "fluid world beyond the strictures of dualism, a world in whose light one could see history as a process that was simultaneously integrated and decentred." See Paul Heyer, *Communications and History: Theories of Media, Knowledge, and Civilization* (New York: Greenwood Press, 1988), 115; Crowley, "Harold Innis and the Modern Perspective of Communications," in William H. Melody, Liora Salter, and Paul Heyer, eds., *Culture, Communication, and Dependency* (Norwood, New Jersey: Ablex, 1981), 236; Judith Stamps, *Unthinking Modernity: Innis, McLuhan and the Frankfurt School* (Montreal and Kingston: McGill-Queen's University Press, 1995), 18, 56. Vincent di Norcia has also noted the presence of non-linear dynamics in Innis's histories. See di Norcia, "Communications, Time and Power: An Innisian View," *Canadian Journal of Political Science* 23 (2), 348; also see Horace Gray, "Reflections on Innis and Institutional Economics," in Melody, Salter, and Heyer, eds., *Culture, Communication and Dependency*, 101–2; and Meric Gertler, "Harold Innis and the New Industrial Geography," *Canadian Geographer* 37 (4), 361; Marshall McLuhan, "The Later Innis," *Queen's Quarterly* 60 (autumn 1953), 392.

Disequilibrium: Several interpreters have noted the importance of disequilibrium in Innis's constructs of change, particularly those in his economic studies. See Mel Watkins, "The Innis Tradition in Canadian Political Economy," *Canadian Journal of Political and Social Theory* 6 (1–2) (winter/spring 1982), 20; Daniel Drache, "Harold Innis and Canadian Capitalist Development," *Canadian Journal of Political and Social Theory* 6 (1–2): 36–42; Robin Neill. "Rationality and the Information Environment: A Reassessment of the Work of Harold Adams Innis," *Journal of Canadian Studies* 22 (4), 85; Daniel Drache, "Introduction: Celebrating Innis: The Man, the Legacy, and Our Future," in *Staples, Markets and Cultural Change* (Montreal and Kingston: McGill-Queen's University Press, 1995), xxxix.

The Edge of Chaos: Innis's stress on the importance of balance is also a recurring theme in the literature. These interpreters note his insistence on the importance of institutions and cultures maintaining the requisite balance between centralization and decentralization, order and flux. Maintenance of such a mean was an essential precursor to adaptation and change. See Graeme Patterson, *History and Communications: Harold Innis, Marshall McLuhan, the Interpretation of History* (Toronto: University of Toronto Press, 1990), 8; William Melody, "Introduction," in Melody, Salter, and Heyer, eds., *Culture, Communication and Dependency*, 8; Vincent di Norcia, "Of Stone Books and Freedom," in *Visible Language* 20 (3) (Summer 1986), 347; Ian Parker, "Innis, Marx, and the Economics of Communication: A Theoretical Aspect of Canadian Political Economy," in Melody, Salter, and Heyer, eds., *Culture, Communication and Dependency*, 130.

Differential Persistence: Innis commentators have also noted the importance of persistent patterns, or differential persistence, in his histories. Abraham Rotstein, for example, notes that "one of Innis' major propositions, which he asserted often, was the institutional continuity of Canadian economic history." Ian Parker and Ian Angus see similar propositions in Innis's communication studies, particularly in his discussions of persistent mental constructs that governed the worldviews of ancient societies. Parker is taken with Innis's choice of cognitive bias as a framework to study ancient cultures because of "the relatively 'persistent' and 'cumulative' character of 'bias,' its relative temporal invariance." This feature, Parker argues, enables bias to "serve as an analytical focus and an escape from the indeterminancy of the Heraclitean flux." Ian Angus sees similar persistence in Innis's studies of mental constructs associated with the oral tradition. As Angus describes it, Innis outlined a regime of communication in which "the structure of speech in an oral society tends to be additive rather than analytic. In analytic thought, one subordinates the higher category to the lower, and example to the general theory, whereas within orality, one tends to simply add on without any clear pattern of subordination or hierarchy. This key role of memory is extremely important in primary orality, and exerts a formative influence on the whole of societies in which orality is the only, or major, medium of communication. Oral society is homeostatic due to the continuous incorporation of the past into the present. There is no way for that which has really been forgotten to survive. Consequently, oral society orients much of its energy toward not forgetting, towards continuously re-enacting the past in the present ... Originality or creativity does not reside so much in making up new stories but in the quality of its enactment or performance. The oral mind is oriented towards narrative accounts, stories rather than lists." See Abraham Rotstein, "Innis: The Alchemy of Fur and Wheat," *Journal of Canadian Studies*, 12 (winter 1977), 7; Ian Parker, "Harold Innis: Staples, Communications, and the Economics of Capacity, Overhead Costs, Rigidity, and Bias," in Doncan Cameron, ed., *Explorations in Canadian Economic History: Essays in Honour of Irene M. Spry* (Ottawa: University of Ottawa Press, 1985), 91. Ian Angus, "Orality in the twilight of humanism: a critique of the communication theory of Harold Innis," *Continuum: the Australian Journal of Media and Culture* 7 (1) (1993). Available on-line: http://wwwmcc.murdoch.edu.au/ReadingRoom/7.1/Angus.html [15 November 2012].

Formal and Final Cause: Marshall McLuhan and Graeme Patterson have both emphasized the importance of formal cause in Innis's writings, while Robin Neill has suggested that final cause is a defining feature of Innis's economics. Michael Gauvreau has made a similar observation, noting the importance of human purpose in Innis's first major study of a staples industry, *The Fur Trade*: "Human psychology and ability to organize, not the overwhelming influence of Canada's harsh geography or human behavior, dominated *The Fur Trade in Canada*. There was, Innis asserted, a dynamic relationship between geography and human ingenuity." William Christian notes: "The second problem that gave Innis reservations about making settled causal claims was his intense faith in human creativity and the power of thought to transcend circumstances. The first of these aspects is suggested in *The Fur Trade* and *The Cod Fisheries* in his undisguised admiration for the adaptability of the fur traders in the woods beyond the control of their monopolist would-be directors, or the fishermen … frustrating the attempts of parliament and vested interests. A further element here reflects a problem that has teased all would-be determinists. If the medium of communication determined what was thought, how could Innis claim that he had escaped the impact of mechanized print culture in his pleas for time and his biases for the Oral Tradition?" See Marshall McLuhan, "Introduction," in Harold Innis, *The Bias of Communication* (Toronto: University of Toronto Press, 1971), x; Patterson, *History and Communications*, 137; Robin Neill, *A New Theory of Value: The Canadian Economics of H.A. Innis* (Toronto: University of Toronto Press, 1972), 26–7, 123–4; Michael Gauvreau, "Baptist Religion and the Social Science of Harold Innis," *Canadian Historical Review* 76 (2), 187; Christian, "Harold Innis as Political Theorist," 21–42.

CHAPTER TWO

1 Much of the current interest in Atlantic History has been stimulated by the efforts of Bernard Bailyn, particularly his book *Atlantic History: Concept and Contours* (Cambridge, Massachusetts: Harvard University Press, 1995). The most recent survey of Atlantic History, and its constituents such as the Spanish, French and British Atlantics, can be obtained in Jack D. Green and Philip D. Morgan, eds., *Atlantic History: A Critical Appraisal* (Oxford: Oxford University Press, 2009). See especially Philip D. Morgan and Jack D. Green, "Introduction: The Present State of Atlantic History," in *Atlantic History: A Critical Appraisal*: 3–34. The journals *Itinerario*, *Atlantic Studies*, and, more recently, *William and Mary Quarterly* have all featured special issues surveying Atlantic History. See *Itinerario* 20 (1) 1996, the inaugural issue of *Atlantic Studies* 1 (1) 2004, and *William and Mary Quarterly* 3rd Series, 63 (4) (October 2006). See especially Bernard Bailyn, "The Idea of Atlantic History," *Itinerario* 20 (1): 19–44 (1996); William O'Reilly, "Genealogies of Atlantic History," *Atlantic Studies* 1 (1): 66–84; Alison Games, "Beyond the Atlantic: English Globetrotters and Transoceanic Connections," *William and Mary Quarterly*, 3rd Series,

63 (4): 675–92; and Peter A. Coclanis, "Atlantic World or Atlantic/World?" ibid.: 725–42.

Single article treatments touching on the suitability of the Atlantic Ocean as a framework for historical analysis include Ian Steele, "Bernard Bailyn's American Atlantic," *History and Theory*, 46 (1): 48–58; Alison Games, "Atlantic History: Definitions, Challenges and Opportunities," *American Historical Review*, 111 (3): 741–57; Nicholas Canny, "Writing Atlantic History: or, Reconfiguring the History of Colonial British America," *Journal of American History*, 86 (3): 1093–114; Eliga H. Gould, "A Virtual Nation: Greater Britain and the Imperial Legacy of the American Revolution," *American Historical Review* 104 (2): 476–89; and J.G.A. Pocock, "The New British History in Atlantic Perspective: An Antipodean Commentary," *American Historical Review* 104 (2): 490–500.

2 See A.R.M. Lower, *Great Britain's Woodyard; British America and the timber trade, 1763–1867* (Montreal and Kingston: McGill-Queen's University Press, 1973); John Bartlet Brebner, *North Atlantic Triangle: The Interplay of Canada, the United States and Great Britain* (Toronto: Ryerson Press, 1945).

3 William Buxton and Charles Acland, "Harold Innis: A Genealogy of Contesting Portraits," in Charles R. Acland and William J. Buxton, eds., *Harold Innis in the New Century: Reflections and Refractions* (Montreal and Kingston: McGill-Queen's University Press, 1999), 12–13.

4 The need for such an introduction becomes apparent when one considers Innis's marginal presence in the literature as it has emerged over the past fifteen years. While Stephen J. Hornsby argues that "any consideration of the European settlement of North America should begin with the foundational ideas of American historian Frederick Jackson Turner and Canadian political economist Harold Adams Innis," his position is the exception rather than the rule. Most recent surveys of the literature have used Fernand Braudel's *The Mediterranean and the Mediterranean World in the Age of Philip II*, first published in French in 1949, as their point of departure. By contrast, Innis's treatment of the emergence of the North Atlantic economy, *The Cod Fisheries*, was published in 1940, well before Braudel's monograph. See Stephen J. Hornsby, *British Atlantic, American Frontier: Spaces of Power in Early Modern British America* (Hanover, New Hampshire: University Press of New England, 2005), 2; Games, "Definitions, Challenges, and Opportunities," 741; O'Reilly, "Genealogies," 70; Linda Colley, "The Sea Around Us," *New York Review of Books*, 53 (11); Peter A. Coclanis, "*Drang Nach Osten*: Bernard Bailyn, the World-Island, and the Idea of Atlantic History," *Journal of World History* 13 (1): 170; Fernand Braudel, *The Mediterranean and the Mediterranean World in the Age of Philip II*, trans. Sian Reynolds (London:

Collins, 1972); and Harold Adams Innis, *The Cod Fisheries; The History of an International Economy* (New Haven and Toronto: Yale University Press and Ryerson Press, 1940).

Innis's marginal position is indicated not only by the lack of specific reference to his work in the recent literature, but also by citation patterns. While some recent studies devoted to Atlantic History have cited Innis's writings, including contributions by Ian K. Steele, Kenneth J. Banks, and David Hackett Fischer, more have not. Innis's position in the literature has also been damaged by distorted representations of his work. Marc Egnal, in particular, unduly conflates Innis's economic histories with Mel Watkins's staples hypothesis of economic growth, arguing that they have "an odd static quality," and that they also ignore "the impact of culture and long-lived institutions on growth." While these characterizations may fairly represent Watkins's work, they do not apply to Innis. Neither Watkins's nor Egnal's characterizations can stand in the face of a close reading of Innis's works. See Marc Egnal, *New World Economies: The Growth of the Thirteen Colonies and Early Canada* (New York: Oxford University Press, 1998), 6. Aside from Hornsby, recent treatments of Atlantic History that cite Innis include Ian K. Steele, *The English Atlantic, 1675–1740: An Exploration of Communication and Community* (New York: Oxford University Press, 1986); Kenneth J. Banks, *Chasing Empire Across the Sea: Communications and the State in the French Atlantic, 1713–1763* (Montreal and Kingston: McGill-Queen's University Press, 2002); David Hackett Fischer, *Champlain's Dream: The Visionary Adventurer Who Made a New World in Canada* (Toronto: Random House of Canada, 2008); and François Crouzet's and Stanley Engerman's respective contributions in John J. McCusker and Kenneth Morgan, eds., *The Early Modern Atlantic Economy* (Cambridge: Cambridge University Press, 2001). Recent significant works that do not mention Innis include David Armitage and Michael Braddock, eds., *The British Atlantic World, 1500–1800* (New York: Palgrave Macmillan, 2002); John Elliott Huxtable, *Empires of the Atlantic World* (New Haven, Connecticut: Yale University Press, 2007); and Jack P. Greene and Philip D. Morgan, eds., *Atlantic History: A Critical Appraisal* (Oxford: Oxford University Press, 2009).

5 See for example David Hancock, "The British Atlantic World: Co-ordination, Complexity, and the Emergence of an Atlantic Market Economy, 1651–1815," *Itinerario* 23 (2): 107–26. A second version of this paper also appears in Hancock, "Self-Organized Complexity and the Emergence of an Atlantic Market Economy, 1651–1815," in Peter A. Coclanis, ed., *The Atlantic Economy during the Seventeenth and Eighteenth Centuries: Organization, Operation, Practice, And Personnel* (Columbia, South Carolina: University of South Carolina Press, 2005): 30–71.

6 In 1979 W.J. Eccles wrote a harshly critical review of Innis's *The Fur Trade in Canada*, in which he charged that Innis's account was wrong in almost every respect: "The sweeping generalizations and conclusions of this work have been accepted uncritically by too many later historians. Unfortunately, neither his premises, both stated and unstated, his use of historical evidence, nor the conclusions drawn will stand up to close scrutiny and all too many erroneous interpretations of North American history have been made up in consequence ... Innis ... took economic determinism to extremes and grossly exaggerated the role of the fur trade in the history of both North America and Europe." Eccles, "A Belated Review of Harold Adams Innis, *The Fur Trade in Canada*," *Canadian Historical Review* 60 (4), 420. Eccles argued that Innis improperly emphasized the importance of the fur trade to the French economy. In fact, more revenue was generated from plantation colonies in the West Indies. The French maintained their presence in the fur trade as a means to acquire military alliances with the First Nations, an important consideration in its competition with Britain for hegemony over North America. Contrary to Innis, Eccles argued that the internal organization of the French economy was not affected by the fur trade and suffered no material disarrangement after its collapse. Innis's claims that the superiority of British goods, cheaper prices, and Britain's advantageous location in Hudson Bay enabled it to gain supremacy in the fur trade during the eighteenth century, said Eccles, were also incorrect. In fact, the British trade lost market share and was in dire straits in the years before the conquest. Consequently, Innis's claim that New France collapsed because of internal economic stress was also mistaken, according to Eccles. Two years later Eccles's review provoked a rejoinder from Hugh Grant, in which he charged Eccles with offering "a critique of Innis's work without fully understanding it." Innis's purpose in writing *The Fur Trade*, according to Grant, was to demonstrate the trade's "systemic relationship to the broader interests of the European states." In misunderstanding that purpose, said Grant, Eccles had produced a review with a "welter of theoretical conclusions and factual errors." Grant, "One Step Forward, Two Steps Back: Innis, Eccles, and the Canadian Fur Trade," *Canadian Historical Review* 62 (3), 305–6, 313. Eccles responded in the same issue with a spirited defence, accusing Grant of being "determined to demonstrate that Harold A. Innis brought his work *The Fur Trade in Canada* down the mountain engraved on stone tablets." He further charged Grant with failing to do his homework, claiming that his refutations of Eccles's specific points were based on readings from the secondary literature, not on primary research. Eccles, "A Response to Hugh M. Grant on Innis," *Canadian Historical Review* 62 (3), 323.

The response in the literature to this debate has been equivocal. Several scholars have addressed Grant's charge that Eccles failed to see the forest for the trees by rejoining that without trees there can be no forest. John Hutcheson notes that Eccles did "sustain the claim that Innis overemphasized the significance of the fur trade in the North American theatre of the clash between Britain and France ... It is also true that Innis did push his conclusions to extremities, and Grant's reply does not do much to refute Eccles' specific points." See Hutcheson, "Harold Innis and the Unity and Diversity of Confederation," *Journal of Canadian Studies* 17 (4), 71 n7. In 1999 William Buxton and Charles Acland rendered a similar verdict, noting that Grant's defence was "informed more by the championing of general principles of political economic analysis than by claims for the accuracy of Innis' depiction of the fur trade." See Buxton and Acland, "Contesting Portraits," 27 n15. Significantly, Arthur Ray, a historian of the fur trade, wrote a ringing endorsement of the work in an introduction for the 1999 reprint of Innis's *The Fur Trade*. Ray suggested that Innis had in fact been correct on several points of contention, particularly those relating to English success in the fur trade, and concluded that "Innis' great book remains essential reading for the study of Canada." See Ray, "Introduction," in *The Fur Trade in Canada* (Toronto: University of Toronto Press, 1999, c. 1930): xi–xii, xix.

7 See for example Kenneth Buckley, "The Role of Staple Industries in Canada's Economic Development," *Journal of Economic History* 18: 439–50; and Douglas McCalla, "The Ontario Economy in the Long Run," *Ontario History* 90 (2): 97–116.

8 Mel Watkins, "A Staple Theory of Economic Growth," *Canadian Journal of Economics and Political Science* 29 (2) (May 1963): 141–58; Mel Watkins, "The Staple Theory Revisited," *Journal of Canadian Studies*, 12 (5): 83–95; Mel Watkins, "The Innis Tradition in Canadian Political Economy," *Canadian Journal of Political and Social Theory* 6 (1–2): 12–33; Daniel Drache, "Harold Innis and Canadian Capitalist Development," *Canadian Journal of Political and Social Theory* 6 (1–2): 35–60; Hutcheson, "Unity and Diversity," 58; Egnal, *New World Economies*, 4–5.

9 Robin Neill was especially harsh in his criticism, arguing: "Economic history in Canada has been buried and the epitaph chosen has been 'The Staple Theory' ... Its effects on our ability to come to grips with the basic problems of the Canadian economy is already evident ... It is not the staple thesis of the 1930s that has done the damage, but its more recent appearances as a staple theory of economic growth. Over the past twenty years partisan scholars have pressed the thesis into service on every side in the debate over growth ... With the theoretical approach emphasis is placed on making the

facts speak for the theory ... Theoretical revisions of the staple thesis put forward by the proponents of the New Economic History on the one side and the Neo-Marxians, on the other, illustrate the point ... In this version the staple thesis is not a theory of growth. It is a theory of stagnation. It is, nonetheless, a non-historical, normative theory in the same sense as the neoclassical version. And again the proponents assert that the historical facts of the Canadian case have conformed to the norm, or, rather the anti-norm. The same activities of government that were used by North to illustrate the neoclassical theory have been used by Watkins, Naylor and others (e.g., Scheinberg) to show the reactionary character of Canadian governments. Any evidence to the contrary, such as the adoption of the National Policy in 1878, has been reinterpreted to fit the assumed pattern. Again the implications for policy have not had to be spelled out." Neill, "The Passing of Canadian Economic History," *Journal of Canadian Studies* 12 (winter 1977), 73–4. Hugh Aitken has also denied that Innis's writings can be characterized as offering an operational model of development. See Aitken, "Myth and Measurement: The Innis Tradition in Economic History," *Journal of Canadian Studies* 12 (5), 96. Outside the Watkins debate, Vincent di Norcia has also resisted the premise that Innis's philosophy of history can be characterized as progressive. See Vincent di Norcia, "Communications, Time and Power: An Innisian View," *Canadian Journal of Political Science* 23 (2): 350.

10 Aitken, "Myth and Measurement," 96; Cole Harris, "Innis on Early Canada," *Canadian Geographer* 37 (4), 355–7; Robin Neill, "Imperialism and the Staple Theory of Canadian Economic Development: The Historical Perspective," in William H. Melody, Liora Salter, and Paul Heyer, eds., *Culture, Communication and Dependency* (Norwood, New Jersey: Ablex, 1981), 153. Watkins himself conceded in 1977 that his theory "attempted to pull out of more diffuse historical writings, notably by Innis, an explicit theory of economic growth appropriate to Canada and other 'new' countries ... At least in retrospect, its contribution was to give legitimacy to the staples approach ... but this was bought at the high price of constraining the theory to the very limiting paradigm of orthodox economics ... One response to my 1963 paper by Innisians was that it emasculated Innis." Watkins, "The Staple Theory Revisited," 83, 93n4; Carl Berger has noted that Innis's contemporaries also oversimplified his writings, drawing on his work selectively in order to reinforce nationalist themes, particularly the belief that Canada was not an artificial construct but rather rested on a geographic unity demonstrated by the activities of the fur trade. Innis was interpreted as a geographic determinist to reinforce nationalist aims. See Berger, *The Writing of Canadian History: Aspects of English-Canadian Historical Writing since 1900* (Toronto: Uni-

versity of Toronto Press, 1986), 97–102. More recent contributions, however, have drawn the opposite conclusion, noting Innis's appeals to human purpose and culture as important variables in Canada's economic history. See di Norcia, "Communications," 336, 341; Meric Gertler, "Harold Innis and the New Industrial Geography," *Canadian Geographer* 37 (4), 360–3; Grant, "One Step," 320; Horace Gray, "Reflections on Innis and Institutional Economics," in Melody, Salter, and Heyer, eds., *Culture, Communication and Dependency:* 99–110; John Warkentin, "Canada and Its Major Regions: Bouchette, Parkin, Rogers, Innis, Hutchison," *Canadian Geographer* 43 (3), 257.

11 Alexander C. Dow, "Technology, Demand and Canadian Base Metal Markets, 1900–1950," *British Journal of Canadian Studies* 8 (1): 18–41; James Bickerton, "Too Long in Exile: Innis and Maritime Political Economy," in Charles R. Acland and William J. Buxton, eds., *Harold Innis in the New Century: Reflections and Refractions* (Montreal and Kingston: McGill-Queen's University Press, 1999), 237; Ian Angus and Brian Shoesmith, "Dependency/space/policy: an introduction to a dialogue with Harold Innis," *Continuum: The Australian Journal of Media and Culture* 7 (1) (1993), Section II, paragraph 4. Available On-line: http://wwwmcc.murdoch.edu.au/Reading Room/7.1/Angus&S.html [15 November 2012].

As early as 1954, J.M.S. Careless, in his classic article "Frontierism, Metropolitanism, and Canadian History," resisted the notion that Canada or any region of Canada should be classified as a dependent of any imperial centre. He suggested that the Frontier hypothesis, the proposition that Canadian social and cultural characteristics were derivative of settler interaction with the local environment, had run its course in Canadian historiography. In its place, Careless credited Innis and other historians with forwarding the Metropolitan hypothesis, the belief that Canadian development was partly determined by its ties with Europe, primarily Britain. Careless was careful to note, however, that the relationship was characterized by interaction, not domination: "If we reject a frontier determinism we should hardly replace it with a metropolitan determinism." Careless, "Frontierism, Metropolitanism, and Canadian History," *Canadian Historical Review* 35 (1), 19.

12 James W. Carey, "Culture, Geography and Communications: The Work of Harold Innis in an American context," in Melody, Salter, and Heyer, eds., *Culture, Communications and Dependency*, 81. Also see Daniel Drache, "Introduction: Celebrating Innis: The Man, the Legacy, and Our Future," in Drache, ed., *Staples, Markets, and Cultural Change*: xiii–lix.

One reason for the discrepancy in the literature's characterization of Innis – either as a proponent of dependency theory or as a proponent of an ecological construct of economic change – has been the imprecise nature of his prose. A. John Watson notes: "there is still no clear consensus on what Innis and his life's work were about. Everyone agrees that he was an outstanding scholar. But the concern has been with using his work rather than understanding it, with attempts to enlist his authority in posthumous support for this or that point of view. In consequence, he has been variously viewed as an incipient fascist, an anarchist, a radical democrat, an elitist and the forerunner of current Marxist scholarship in Canada. Furthermore, there are passages from his work which seem to support each one of these interpretations." A. John Watson, "Harold Innis and Classical Scholarship," *Journal of Canadian Studies* 12 (winter 1977): 45–61.

A second difficulty has been the lack of a clear analytical focus in the writings of Innis and other proponents of the staples hypothesis. In 1961 Richard Caves and Richard Holton noted: "this interpretation of Canadian development has won almost unanimous acceptance among scholars and the general public as well. True, it is not always clear what is thought to be determined by changes in Canada's staple exports. One infers that, for the early years at least, the usual answer to this question is 'everything.'" Caves and Holton, *The Canadian Economy: Prospects and Retrospect* (Cambridge, Massachusetts: Harvard University Press, 1961), 30.

One unfortunate outcome of the imprecision in the staples literature is that scholars have sometimes identified the Innis tradition as a theory of both dependency and interdependency. Judith Stamps, for example, suggests that Innis's historical writings "offered a dialectical reading of the West as the historical battlefield between imperial and marginal areas. It developed a negative version of that dialectic by emphasizing the contingent rather than the positive aspects of that history and by seeing margins rather than empire as the 'cutting edge' of historical change. In so doing, it described a fluid world beyond the strictures of dualism, a world in whose light one could see history as a process that was simultaneously integrated and decentred." In other words, Stamps saw Innis as describing a relationship characterized by interaction, once control was distributed. The problem, however, is that Stamps also suggests that Innis's histories contain a narrative in which the centre dominates the periphery: "He saw, instead of the happy road to global integration, a vortex – an industrial core with a spatializing momentum that drove it constantly to exploit its surroundings ... He saw, instead of the Enlightenment road to progress, violence – the centrist drive to suppress manufacturing at the margins, the better to colonize them as markets." Stamps, *Unthinking Modernity* (Montreal and Kingston: McGill-Queen's University Press, 1995), 56–7.

In 1959, Hugh Aitken offered a similarly contradictory assessment of the degree of agency that Canada has historically enjoyed in the international economy. On the one hand, Aitken maintained that Canada "has never been the master of its own destiny, as a satellite staple-producing economy, it reflected, and still reflects, in its rate of development the imperatives of more advanced areas." Yet, Aitken also suggested that Canada's growth was linked to endogenous concerns: "Canada today exists as a national economy because its reactions to external pressure have been predominantly positive. That this should be the case was not in any sense necessary or inevitable: it resulted from distinct political and economic decisions. The strategic decisions in the process of economic growth in Canada have historically been such as to promote the creation, integration, and growth of a national economy north of the United States boundary." Hugh G.J. Aitken, "The Changing Structure of the Canadian Economy," in Aitken et al., eds., *The American Economic Impact on Canada* (Durham, North Carolina: Duke University Press, 1959), 3–4; and Aitken, "Myth and Measurement," 96.

13 Harold Innis, *A History of the Canadian Pacific Railway* (Toronto: University of Toronto Press, 1971, c. 1923), xx.

14 Harold Innis, *The Fur Trade in Canada: An Introduction to Canadian Economic History*, revised edition (Toronto: University of Toronto Press, 1956, c. 1930), ix.

15 Alicia Juarrero, *Dynamics in Actions: Intentional Behavior as a Complex System* (Cambridge, Massachusetts: MIT Press, 1999), 105–6.

16 Ibid., 106–7.

17 Ibid., 107.

18 Ernst Cassirer, *The Problem of Knowledge: Philosophy, Science, and History since Hegel*, trans. William H. Woglom and Charles W. Hendel (New Haven: Yale University Press, 1950), 121–2.

19 Juarrero, *Dynamics*, 109.

20 Thorstein Veblen, "Why is Economics Not an Evolutionary Science?" in *The Place of Science in Modern Civilization, and Other Essays* (New York: Russell and Russell, 1961), 74–5.

21 Innis, *Canadian Pacific Railway*, 287.

22 Ibid., 288.

23 Ibid., 289.

24 Ibid., 291.

25 Harold Innis, "Autobiography of Harold Adams Innis," *Harold Adams Innis Papers*, University of Toronto Archives, B1972–0003, Box 36, File 1, 125.

26 Ibid.

27 Harold Innis, "Forest Industries in Canada," *Pacific Affairs* (September 1929):

551–2; Harold Innis, "Pulp and Paper Industries," *Encyclopedia of Canada* (5): 176–85; Harold Innis, "The Lumber Trade in Canada," in *Essays in Canadian Economic History* (Toronto: University of Toronto Press, 1956): 242–51.

28 Harold Innis, "Agriculture," *Encyclopedia of Canada* (1): 16–23; Harold Innis and M.L. Jacobson, "Agriculture and Canadian-American Trade," *Canadian Papers* 3 (6), 17.

29 See Innis, *The Cod Fisheries*, 1940.

30 Harold Innis, *Settlement and the Mining Frontier*, W.A. Mackintosh and W.L.G. Joerg, eds., Canadian Frontiers of Settlement Series, IX (Toronto: Macmillan, 1936).

31 Innis, "Autobiography," 126.

32 A. John Watson, "Marginal Man: Harold Innis' Communication Works in Context" (PhD dissertation in Political Science, University of Toronto, 1981), 193. Also see Alexander John Watson, *Marginal Man: The Dark Vision of Harold Adams Innis* (Toronto: University of Toronto Press, 2006), 118–29.

33 Innis, "Autobiography," 127.

34 Daniel Drache, "Harold Innis and Canadian Capitalist Development," 39. Cited from W.A. MacIntosh, "Economic Factors in Canadian History," in W.T. Easterbrook and M.H. Watkins, eds., *Approaches to Canadian Economic History* (Toronto: McLelland & Stewart, 1967), 15.

35 Innis, *The Fur Trade*, 393.

36 On this point, see Careless, "Frontierism," 1–21.

37 Innis, *The Fur Trade*, 383–4; Careless, "Frontierism," 15; Hutcheson, "Unity and Diversity," 59; Berger, *Writing of Canadian History*, 96–7.

38 Innis, *The Fur Trade*, 383–6.

39 Ibid., 31–3.

40 Ibid., 41–3, 110–14.

41 Ibid., 112.

42 Robin Neill, *A New Theory of Value: The Canadian Economics of H.A. Innis* (Toronto: University of Toronto Press, 1972), 26–7, 123–4.

43 Innis, *The Fur Trade*, 41–2.

44 Ibid., 390–1.

45 Juarrero, *Dynamics*, 109.

46 Innis, *The Fur Trade*, 83. Innis's contentions regarding the impact of the fur trade on the economic organization of France were later to prove highly controversial. See endnote 6 above.

47 Ibid., 38.

48 Ibid., 78–9, 88, 110–11.

49 Ibid., 176.

50 Ibid., 166–9.

51 Ibid., 177.
52 Ibid., 117–18.
53 Ibid., 280.
54 Ibid., 251, 256–7, 279–80.
55 Ibid., 385.
56 Veblen, "Why is Economics?" 71.
57 Ibid., 71–2.
58 Innis, *The Fur Trade*, 393.
59 Ibid., 393–5.
60 Ibid., 395–7.
61 Ibid., 393.
62 Ibid., 396.
63 Ibid., 401.
64 Ibid., 395.
65 Ibid., 396.
66 Ibid., 397.
67 Ibid., 400–1.
68 Ibid., 396.
69 Ibid., 397.
70 Ibid.
71 Ibid.
72 Harold Innis, *Empire and Communications* (Oxford: Clarendon Press, 1950), 5.
73 Juarrero, *Dynamics*, 126.
74 Innis, *The Fur Trade*, 401.
75 This reading is further indicated by Innis's characterization of Nova Scotia politics in 1839. Noting the same tension between authority, in this case the "centralization of the commercial group at Halifax," and independence, "the decentralizing tendencies of trade, fishing, and other industries," Innis argued that the outcome of the specific conflict over the colony's tariff policies was a shift to responsible government: "The convergence of different racial, religious, and economic groups, together with the Imperial influence that was likewise concentrated in Halifax as a naval centre, contributed to the 'intellectual awakening of Nova Scotia' and to that balancing of interests which made her the cradle of responsible government in the 'Second Empire.'" Innis, *The Cod Fisheries*, 489.
76 Innis, *The Fur Trade*, 385.
77 Ibid.

CHAPTER THREE

1 Harold Innis, *The Cod Fisheries: The History of an International Economy* (Toronto: Ryerson Press, 1940), ix.

2 See chapter 4 of Innis, *The Cod Fisheries*: 52–94.

3 Ibid., xi.

4 Ibid., x.

5 Harold Innis, "An Introduction to the Economic History of the Maritimes, Including Newfoundland, and New England," in Mary Q. Innis, ed., *Essays in Canadian Economic History* (Toronto: University of Toronto Press, 1962, c. 1956), 42.

6 Kenneth Arrow, "Foreword," in W. Brian Arthur, *Increasing Returns and Path Dependence in the Economy* (Ann Arbor: University of Michigan Press, 1994), ix.

7 In Canada, Innis's influence waned rapidly after he died. In the discipline of economics most economists embraced the tenets of neo-classical economics propounded by American economists such as Milton Friedman at the University of Chicago. By the 1970s most Canadian economic historians had also foresworn Innis's political economy in favour of the "new economic history," a second American intellectual import, and one with a strong orientation toward quantitative history. See Mel Watkins, "The Innis Tradition in Canadian Political Economy," *Canadian Journal of Political and Social Theory* 6 (1–2) (spring 1982): 13–17. For more general assessments of Innis's influence in Canadian historiography, see William Westfall, "The Ambivalent Verdict: Harold Innis and Canadian History," in *Culture, Communication and Dependency: The Tradition of H.A. Innis* (Norwood, New Jersey: Ablex Publishing Corporation, 1982), 37–51; and Carl Berger, *The Writing of Canadian History: Aspects of English-Canadian Historical Writing since 1900*, second edition (Toronto: University of Toronto Press, 1986), 85–111; 187–207.

8 W. Brian Arthur, "Positive Feedbacks in the Economy," at *Santa Fe Institute Website*, p. 5. Available on-line: http://tuvalu.santafe.edu/~wbarthur/Papers/SciAm_Article.pdf [12 November 2012. The article is also available in print version. See Arthur, "Positive Feedbacks in the Economy," *Scientific American* 262 (February 1990), 92–9.

9 Arthur, "Positive Feedback," 1.

10 By way of example, Arthur points to the case of a coffee plantation. Its place in such a market is fixed by a combination of environmental and systemic constraints that set a threshold on the plantation's expansion. In a market populated by numerous competitors, the plantation only has so much land

at its disposal. Other choice lands have already been occupied by neighbouring plantations. Within the lands at its disposal, the plantation can only expand so far to attain its maximum profit. If it passes this threshold, it will eventually begin incorporating land less suitable for cultivation, and expenses will rise at a rate more rapid than revenue, reducing the plantation's profit margin and its chances of gaining the maximum profit from the resources at its disposal. In such a scenario, the plantation experiences diminishing returns, and there is no breaking out of the discipline set by the system's constraints. The plantation does not enjoy the luxury of raising prices to restore its profit margins. Its competitors sell an equivalent product, and there are enough of them that the plantation will simply lose business if it raises prices. In such a market, the plantation is characterized as being in *perfect competition* with its counterparts. It does not enjoy a predominant share of the market, nor can it ever aspire to attain it. And given that it operates in a market with a large number of competitors, the price it charges for coffee will never exceed its costs except by a minimal amount. Its profit margins will always be small. See W. Brian Arthur, "Increasing Returns and the New World of Business," at *Santa Fe Institute Website,* pp. 2–3. Available on-line: http://tuvalu.santafe.edu/~wbarthur/Papers/HBR.pdf [12 November 2012].

The same article appears in print in Arthur, "Increasing Returns and the New World of Business," *Harvard Business Review* 74 (4): 100–11.

11 W. Brian Arthur, "Preface," at *Santa Fe Institute Website,* p. 2. Available on-line: http://www.santafe.edu/~wbarthur/Papers/Pdf_files/Preface.pdf [12 November 2012].

The same article appears in print version. See Arthur, "Preface," in *Increasing Returns and Path Dependence in the Economy* (Ann Arbor: University of Michigan Press, 1994).

12 For a general overview of Arthur's work see H. Mitchell Waldrop, *Complexity: The Emerging Science at the Edge of Order and Chaos* (New York: Touchstone, 1992): 15–51. In addition to applying the concept of increasing returns to systems with competing firms and technologies, Arthur has also applied it to questions relevant to spatial economics, including industry location patterns, and the development of urban systems. See Arthur, "Urban Systems and Historical Path Dependence," in *Increasing Returns*: 99–110; and Arthur, "Industry Location Patterns and the Importance of History," in *Increasing Returns*: 49–67.

13 Arthur, "Preface," 3.

14 Arthur, "Increasing Returns," 2–3.

15 W. Brian Arthur, Steven Durlauf, and David A. Lane, "Introduction: Process

and Emergence in the Economy," in W. Brian Arthur, Steven Durlauf, and David A. Lane, eds., *The Economy As an Evolving Complex System II* (Reading, Massachusetts: Addison-Wesley, 1997), 4; Also see W. Brian Arthur, "Out-of-Equilibrium Economics and Agent-Based Modeling," in K. Judd and L. Tesfatsion, eds., *Handbook of Computational Economics, Volume 2: Agent-Based Computational Economics* (New York: Elsevier-North Holland, 2006), 1557.

16 Arthur, Durlauf, and Lane, "Introduction," 6.

17 Arthur, "Positive Feedback," 5.

18 Ibid., 8.

19 Arthur, "Increasing Returns," 3–4.

20 Ibid., 3. For more on network effects, see chapter 2 of Stephen E. Margolis and Stanley J. Liebowitz, *Winners, Losers and Microsoft: Competition and Antitrust in High Technology* (Oakland, California: Independent Institute, 1999).

21 Arthur, "Increasing Returns," 3. Economists often refer to this characteristic as the QWERTY effect, in reference to the standard keyboard found on most English language typewriters and keyboards. With reference to typing speed it is not the most efficient keyboard design, but it has persisted due to widespread customer use. See Arthur, "Positive Feedback," 9.

22 See Alfred Marshall, *Principles of Economics*, 8th edition (London: Macmillan and Co., Ltd. 1920, c. 1890). Available on-line at *Library of Economics and Liberty Website*: http://www.econlib.org/library/Marshall/marP.html [12 November 2012]. Innis mentioned reading Marshall as a graduate student in his unpublished 1952 autobiography, and referenced the work three times in the communication essays of *Political Economy in the Modern State*. See Harold Innis, "The Autobiography of Harold Adams Innis," *University of Toronto Archives*, B1972-0003. Series 17, Box 36, File 1, p. 80; Harold Innis, "An Economic Approach to English Literature in the Nineteenth Century," in *Political Economy in the Modern State* (Toronto: Ryerson Press, 1946), 53; and Harold Innis, "Political Economy in the Modern State," in *Political Economy in the Modern State* (Toronto: Ryerson Press, 1946), 118, 127.

23 Marshall, *Principles of Economics*, V.XII.16. Available on-line at: http://www.econlib.org/library/Marshall/marP39.html [12 November 2012].

24 Marshall, *Principles of Economics*, IV.XIII.1. Available on-line at: http://www.econlib.org/library/Marshall/marP27.html [12 November 2012].

25 Marshall, *Principles of Economics*, IV.XIII.3. Available on-line at: http://www.econlib.org/library/Marshall/marP27.html [12 November 2012].

26 Marshall, *Principles of Economics*, App.H.4. Available on-line at: http://www.econlib.org/library/Marshall/marP63.html [12 November 2012].

27 Marshall, *Principles*, IV.XI.16 Available on-line at: http://www.econlib.org/library/Marshall/marP25.html [12 November 2012].

28 Marshall, *Principles of Economics*, App.H.9. Available on-line at: http://www.econlib.org/library/Marshall/marP63.html [12 November 2012].

29 Thorstein Veblen, "The Evolution of the Scientific Point of View," in *The Place of Science in Modern Civilization, and other essays* (New York: Russell and Russell, 1961), 37.

30 Thorstein Veblen, "The Preconceptions of Economic Science III," in *The Place of Science in Modern Civilization*, 177.

31 Veblen, "Preconceptions III," 177.

32 Marshall, *Principles of Economics*, VI.V.23 Available on-line at: http://www.econlib.org/library/Marshall/marP47.html [12 November 2012].

33 Marshall, *Principles of Economics*, IV.XII.47 Available on-line at: http://www.econlib.org/library/Marshall/marP26.html [12 November 2012].

34 Marshall, *Principles of Economics*, V.VI.25, fn. 63. Available on-line at: http://www.econlib.org/library/Marshall/marP33.html [12 November 2012].

35 Marshall, *Principles of Economics*, App.H.5. Available on-line at: http://www.econlib.org/library/Marshall/marP63.html [12 November 2012].

36 Marshall, *Principles of Economics*, V.XIII.22, fn. 126. Available on-line at: http://www.econlib.org/library/Marshall/marP40.html [12 November 2012].

37 Veblen and Cairnes both believed that the assumption of human agency mandated the corresponding assumption that system constraints are an emergent property deriving from human decision-making on the ground. System constraints could never be seen as static. At best they were meta-stable. When they adapted, they moved, and they were governed by a form of causation entirely different from efficient cause. "The concept of dispassionate cumulative causation," Veblen writes, "has often and effectively been helped out by the notion that there is in all this some sort of meliorative trend that exercises a constraining guidance over the course of causes and effects." [See Thorstein Veblen, "Why is Economics Not an Evolutionary Science?" in *The Place of Science in Modern Civilization*, 64].

That meliorative trend, he wrote in a reading and endorsement of Smith's concept of the Invisible Hand, is of an entirely different order than efficient cause. There is a third order of causation: "another element of continuity besides that of brute cause and effect present in the step-by-step process whereby the natural course of things reaches its final term." The presence of a third element supporting the continuity and given trajectory of a system, in addition to human action and efficient cause, was indicated by the possibility of diverting a system from progression toward its given, optimal end. The construction of "the natural course of things" in Smith's doctrine did not mean the necessary course of things. If Smith had meant the latter "no divergence of events from the natural or legitimate course of things would be possible." [See Veblen, "Why is Economics," 64; Thorstein Veblen, "The Preconceptions of Economic Science II," in *The Place of Science in Modern Civilization*, 115–16].

The presence of a third element – teleology – was also indicated by the capacity of systems to recover their initial heading if disrupted by human volition, an act of nature, or both. By contrast, in systems governed by efficient cause the cessation of aberrant actions would "not leave the outcome the same as if no interference had taken place. This recuperative power of nature is of an extra-mechanical character. The continuity of sequence by force of which the natural course of things prevails is, therefore, not of the nature of cause and effect, since it bridges intervals and interruptions not in the causal sequence." [See Veblen, "Preconceptions II," 116].

38 Thorstein Veblen, "The Preconceptions of Economic Science III," in *The Place of Science in Modern Civilization*, 153–4.

39 Thorstein Veblen, "Professor Clark's Economics," in *The Place of Science in Modern Civilization*, 197.

40 Ibid., 213.

41 Ibid., 215–16.

42 Harold Innis, "The Rise and Fall of the Spanish Fishery in Newfoundland," in *Essays in Canadian Economic History* (Toronto: University of Toronto Press, 1962, c. 1956), 58.

43 Ibid., 44–6.

44 Ibid., 44.

45 Ibid.

46 Ibid., 45, 47, 52, 53.

47 Ibid., 46.

48 Ibid., 46–7.

49 Ibid., 48–9.

50 Ibid., 50–1.

51 Ibid., 47.

52 Ibid., 55.

53 Ibid., 56.

54 Ibid., 55.

55 Ibid., 56.

56 Ibid., 57–8.

57 Ibid., 58.

58 Ibid., 57.

59 Ibid., 60.

60 Ibid.
61 Ibid.
62 Innis, "Autobiography of Harold Adams Innis," 39–40.
63 Innis, "Economic History of the Maritimes," 39.
64 Innis, *Cod Fisheries*, 11–52.
65 Ibid., 32, 49, 177.
66 Innis, "Economic History of the Maritimes," 31; Innis, *Cod Fisheries*, 51–2.
67 Innis, *Cod Fisheries*, 46–7, 49, 50, 81, and 136.
68 Ibid., 130.
69 Innis, "Economic History of the Maritimes," 31.
70 Innis, *Cod Fisheries*, 39, 91.
71 Ibid., 34, 41–2.
72 Ibid., 42.
73 Ibid., 52.
74 Innis, "Economic History of the Maritimes," 61; and Innis, *Cod Fisheries*, 65.
75 Innis, *Cod Fisheries*, 35, 66.
76 Ibid., 67–8, 73–6, 81, 93–4.
77 Ibid., 90–1.
78 Innis, *The Fur Trade*, 31–3; and Innis, *Cod Fisheries*, 81–92.
79 Innis, *Cod Fisheries*, 49, 500.
80 Ibid., 94.
81 Ibid., 91–2, 505.
82 Ibid., 70; and Innis, "Economic History of the Maritimes," 32.
83 Innis, *Cod Fisheries*, 97–102.
84 Ibid., 165.
85 Ibid., 53, 100–1.
86 Ibid., 137.
87 Ibid., 133.
88 Innis, *Cod Fisheries*, 90, 117, 118, 133, 137; Innis, "Economic History of the Maritimes," 32.
89 Innis, *Cod Fisheries*, 78, 501.
90 Ibid., 78–9, 114.
91 Ibid., 79, 114.
92 Ibid., 120–31, 505.
93 Arthur, "Increasing Returns," 5.
94 Ibid., 5.
95 Innis, *Cod Fisheries*, 175.
96 Innis, "Economic History of the Maritimes," 29.
97 Innis, *Cod Fisheries*, 485–6.

98 Ibid., 503.
99 Ibid.
100 Ibid., 175.
101 Innis, "Economic History of the Maritimes," 28.
102 See Waldrop, *Complexity*, 121–4.
103 Innis, *Cod Fisheries*, 51.
104 Ibid., 500–1.
105 Innis, "Economic History of the Maritimes," 40.
106 Innis, *Cod Fisheries*, 174–5.
107 Ibid., 137.
108 Ibid., 78.
109 Ibid., 115, 118.
110 Ibid., 115, 117.
111 Ibid., 161.
112 Innis, "Economic History of the Maritimes," 34.
113 Innis, *Cod Fisheries*, 161–4.
114 Ibid., 213.
115 Ibid., 164.
116 Ibid., 114.
117 Ibid., 165.
118 Ibid., 201, 210–11.
119 Ibid., 165, 201.
120 Harold Innis, "Autobiography of Harold Adams Innis," 39–40.
121 Innis, *Cod Fisheries*, 174, 176.
122 Ibid., 176, 505. Also see Innis, *The Fur Trade*, 78–9, 88, 110–11.
123 Innis, *Cod Fisheries*, 178–9.
124 Ibid., 505–6.
125 Ibid., 504.
126 Ibid., 202.
127 Ibid.
128 Ibid., 203, 504.
129 Ibid., 201, 210–11.
130 Ibid., 205–6.
131 Ibid., 502.
132 Ibid., 504.
133 Ibid., 230.
134 Ibid., 373.
135 Ibid., 489.
136 Ibid., 284, 489.
137 Ibid., 372–3.

138 William Christian, "Harold Innis as Political Theorist," in *Canadian Journal of Political Science* 10 (1): 30.
139 Innis, *Cod Fisheries*, 504.
140 Ibid., 212.
141 Joel Mokyr, "Review: Jared Diamond, *Guns, Germs and Steel: The Fates of Human Societies*" at *EH.Net*, para. 3. Available On-line: http://eh.net/book_reviews/guns-germs-and-steel-fates-human-societies [12 November 2012].

CHAPTER FOUR

1 Donald Creighton, *Harold Adams Innis: Portrait of a Scholar* (Toronto: University of Toronto Press, 1957), 111–12; W.T. Easterbrook, "Innis and Economics," *Canadian Journal of Economics and Political Science* 19 (1953): 292; Carl Berger, *The Writing of Canadian History: Aspects of English-Canadian Historical Writing since 1900*, second edition (Toronto: University of Toronto Press, 1986), 188.
2 J. Alexander Watson argues that Innis's shift to communication may have been prompted by the departure of his junior colleague, Irene Biss, to marry Graham Spry in 1938. In Watson's account, Innis collaborated closely with Biss in the mid-1930s. He confided in her, and may have fallen in love with her. He was opposed to her engagement, and was deeply hurt when she finally did marry, in large measure because Spry represented the very sort of public activism by scholars that Innis opposed. He severed all contacts with her and never spoke to her again. Spry founded the *Canadian Radio League*, which mobilized public support behind the concept of a public broadcasting system and ultimately resulted in the founding of the Canadian Broadcasting Corporation. Watson argues that it is no coincidence that Innis turned his attention to communication after he and Biss ended their working relationship.

Watson's argument is interesting, but I do not find it a compelling explanation for Innis's shift to communications. The first problem is that Watson's evidence on the nature of the Innis-Biss relationship, as he himself notes, is circumstantial. Clearly the relationship was important to him. But any inference that it, singly, or in conjunction with other factors, prompted the shift, is at best speculative. Second, Innis had other motives, intellectual and emotional, to make the shift, motives that I believe were more important. To start, as we shall see in this chapter, Innis believed that factors other than price signals influenced the behaviour of economic, and by extension cultural systems. Information was an important constituent of economic and cultural life, one to which economists had not rendered due attention. The communication studies were the result. Second, as any cursory reading of the preface of *Political Economy in the Modern State* will show, Innis, as a veteran of the First World War, was deeply affected by the advent of the Second World War. As far as he was concerned, the West had crashed twice over the span of three decades, and he proposed to find out why, through the study of communication technologies. On Watson's argument see J. Alexander Watson, *Marginal Man: The Dark Vision of Harold Innis* (Toronto: University of Toronto Press, 2006), 194–7.

3 See Doug Owram, *The Government Generation: Canadian Intellectuals and the State, 1900–1945* (Toronto: University of Toronto Press, 1986), 166, 213, 268; A. John Watson, "Marginal Man: Harold Innis's Communication Works in Context" (PhD dissertation, University of Toronto, 1981), 310; Philip Massolin, "Academic Modernization and the Decline of Higher Learning: The University Question in the later Scholarship of Harold Innis," *Canadian Journal of Communication* 23 (1): 45–64, (winter 1998); Berger, *Canadian History*, 187–8; Ian Angus, "Orality in the twilight of humanism: a critique of the communication theory of Harold Innis," in *Continuum: The Australian Journal of Media and Culture* 7 (1) 1993, Par. 12; available on-line: http://wwwmcc.murdoch.edu.au/ReadingRoom/7.1/Angus.html [13 November 2012].

4 Robert Babe, "Review, *Harold Innis* by Paul Heyer," *Canadian Journal of Communication* 29 (2) (2004), 230.

5 Harold Innis, "On the Economic Significance of Cultural Factors," in *Political Economy in the Modern State* (Toronto: Ryerson Press, 1946), 100.

6 See for example Charles Acland and William Buxton, "Introduction: A Genealogy of Contesting Portraits," in C. Acland and W. Buxton, eds., *Harold Innis in the New Century: Reflections and Refractions* (Montreal and Kingston: McGill-Queen's University Press, 1999): 3–28; Robert Babe. *Canadian Communication Thought: Ten Foundational Writers* (Toronto: University of Toronto Press, 2000); Watson, *Marginal Man*, 2006.

7 Harold Innis, "Political Economy in the Modern State," in *Political Economy in the Modern State*, 115.

8 Ibid., 114.

9 Ibid.

10 Ibid., 116.

11 Thorstein Veblen, "The Preconceptions of Economic Science III," in *The Place of Science in Modern Civilization, and other essays* (New York: Russell and Russell, 1961), 169. Also see Paul Trescott, *The Logic of the Price System* (New York: McGraw-Hill, 1970): 15–22.

12 Harold Innis, "Preface," in *Political Economy in the Modern State*, ix.

13 Harold Innis to Arthur Cole, 19 March 1945, *Harold Innis Papers*, University

of Toronto Archives, B1972-0025, Box 11, File 1. With respect to the entrepreneur, Innis wrote to Cole: "I have a feeling that this is a subject of fundamental significance to Western civilization and that we had not raised the question as to why the American entrepreneur occupied a crucial position ... I suspect that the entrepreneur approach touches every phase of American cultural activity and is appreciated by very few of those concerned with it other than by way of contempt." See Harold Innis to Arthur Cole, no date – probably 1945, *Harold Innis Papers*, University of Toronto Archives, B1972-0025, Box 11, File 1.

14 Harold Innis to W.T. Easterbrook, no date – probably 1952, *Easterbrook Papers,* University of Toronto Archives, B1975-0030/001.

15 Harold Innis, "On the Economic Significance of Cultural Factors," in *Political Economy in the Modern State*, 100.

16 Harold Innis to Arthur Cole, 21 October 1941, *Harold Innis Papers*, University of Toronto Archives, B72-0025, Box 11, File 1.

17 Harold Innis to Arthur Cole, 31 October 1941, *Harold Innis Papers*, ibid.

18 Harold Innis, "The Newspaper in Economic Development," in *Political Economy in the Modern State*, 34.

19 Innis, "Political Economy," 127.

20 Ibid. Cited from Geoffrey Scott, *The Architecture of Humanism* (London, 1926), 163.

21 Innis, "Political Economy," 127.

22 Harold Innis to Arthur Cole, 2 April 1943, *Harold Innis Papers*, University of Toronto Archives, B72-0025, Box 11, File 1.

23 Innis, "Cultural Factors," 89.

24 Harold Innis to Arthur Cole, 31 October 1941, *Harold Innis Papers*, University of Toronto Archives, B72-0025, Box 11, File 1.

25 Innis, "Cultural Factors," 89.

26 Ibid., 88–94.

27 Flo Conway and Jim Siegelman, *Dark Hero of the Information Age: In Search of Norbert Wiener, the Father of Cybernetics* (New York: Basic Books, 2005), 193.

28 Ibid., 184–90; M. Mitchell Waldrop, *Complexity: The Emerging Science at the Edge of Order and Chaos* (New York: Touchstone Books, 1992), 287.

29 It is remarkable that these two bodies of work have often been mentioned in conjunction, but never subjected to a sustained reading. Innis and Marshall McLuhan were founders of the Toronto School of Communication, while a similar school containing researchers from MIT and elsewhere emerged as a result of Wiener's writings. Associates of both Innis and Wiener recognized that common ideas were emerging from both schools,

yet interpreters in the intervening years have never taken the opportunity to subject the writings of Innis and Wiener to a sustained comparison.

Examples of communication researchers referring to opposite numbers at MIT or Toronto include Karl Deutsch, who reviewed Innis's *The Bias of Communication* in 1952. Marshall McLuhan and Innis indicated their knowledge of Deutsch's work, and, in turn, that of Wiener in correspondence undertaken in 1951. See Karl Deutsch, "Review: *The Bias of Communication* by Harold A. Innis," *Canadian Journal of Economics and Political Science* 18 (3) (August 1952): 388–90; Harold Innis to Marshall McLuhan, 26 February 1951, 14 March 1951, *Harold Innis Papers*, University of Toronto Archives, B1972-0003, Box 5, Folder 18, "Correspondence with M. McLuhan, H.J. Cody, G.M. Weir, and A.L. MacDonald. [1939–1952]."

The impact of Wiener's writings on McLuhan was much more extensive than it was for Innis. In much of the literature, McLuhan is generally characterized as being critical of Wiener's writings from his initial exposure to them. See for example, William Buxton, "Harold Innis' 'French Inflection': Origins, Themes and Implications of his 1951 Address at le Collège de France," *Canadian Journal of Communication* 29 (2) (2004), 179.

McLuhan's own correspondence, and recent contributions to the McLuhan literature, suggest, however, that his stance may have been more complex. In March 1951, two weeks after writing a letter to Innis criticizing Deutsch's and Wiener's approach to communication studies, McLuhan initiated a correspondence with Wiener, pointing to commonalities between Wiener's conceptions of feedback circuits and poetic constructs in literature. The following month, Wiener replied thanking McLuhan for his correspondence and his favourable comments on his two books on cybernetics. He also replied that while care needed to be exercised in the application of any analogy, he did not view McLuhan's suggestion "as by any means necessarily absurd," and expressed the hope that the two of them would soon meet in order to exchange ideas. Whether McLuhan took up Wiener's invitation is unclear. If he did, there is no indication of it in the Wiener papers at MIT. McLuhan did write the following November, however, complaining that researchers in economics and sociology at the University of Toronto failed to appreciate the use of "discontinuity as a technique of explanation," as expressed in his book *The Mechanical Bride*, and asked Wiener for his comment. It was a curious letter, and if Wiener did respond to it, a copy does not survive in his records. See H.M. McLuhan to Norbert Wiener, 28 March 1951, Toronto. File 135, Box 9, *Norbert Wiener Papers*, MIT Archives; Norbert Wiener to H.M. McLuhan, 17 April 1951, Paris. Folder 136, Box 9, *Norbert Wiener Papers*, MIT Archives; and H.M. McLuhan to Norbert Wiener, November 10, 1951, Toronto. Folder 143, Box 10, *Norbert Wiener Papers*, MIT Archives.

Further, McLuhan scholar Donald Theall, a former student of McLuhan's, notes that in 1950 he observed that "McLuhan could almost instantaneously intuit the relevance of Norbert Wiener's and C.E. Shannon and Warren Weaver's ideas about cybernetics and systems theory in the light of modernist art, literature, poetics, aesthetic theory and cultural production ... He quickly rejected [Wiener's] mathematical theory of communication, but the impact of the world examined in Wiener's *The Human Use of Human Beings* (1950) had a profound effect on McLuhan ... His fascination with cybernetics increased the year following our first meeting when he encountered Jurgen Reusch and Gregory Bateson's *Communication: The Social Matrix of Psychiatry*, which I had urged him to read." Fred Ward notes that Reusch and Bateson argued that the self as "the subject of psychiatry was enmeshed in and largely shaped by a complex web of information exchange. In keeping with Wiener's cybernetics, they viewed social life as a system of communication and the individual as both a key element within that system and a system in his or her own right." See Donald Theall, *The Virtual Marshall McLuhan* (Montreal and Kingston: McGill-Queen's University Press, 2001), 30; Fred Turner, *From Counterculture to Cyberculture* (Toronto: University of Toronto Press, 2006), 52–3.

One work that is a partial exception to my characterization of scholarly neglect is William Kuhns's *The Post-Industrial Prophets: Interpretations of Technology*. In this work, which contains chapters devoted to the writings of Innis and Wiener respectively, Kuhns notes that Innis "attempted reading history through forms rather than content, through information flow and control rather than political heroes, wars, and trade. He is often closer in his thought to the cybernetic interpretation of Norbert Wiener ... than to the awesome tradition of historians and philosophers from whom he draws such an array of data." See Kuhns, *Post-Industrial Prophets* (New York: Weybright and Talley, 1971), 143. Unfortunately, Kuhns never chose to provide a sustained comparative reading to support this perceptive argument, save for briefly noting that both authors were interested in systems governed by information flows that maintained homeostasis, a state of equilibrium with their surrounding environments controlled by negative feedback. Kuhns's reading differs from this study insofar as it does not reference *Political Economy in the Modern State*, does not reference Innis' interest in positive feedback or increasing returns, and does not mention Innis's common concern with Wiener on the pathologies that emerged in systems governed by positive feedback. My thanks to Paul Heyer for referring me to Kuhns's important study.

30 Fred Dretske, *Knowledge and the Flow of Information* (Cambridge, Massachusetts: MIT Press, 1981), ix.

31 Luciano Floridi, "Semantic Conceptions of Information," in Edward N. Zalta, ed., *The Stanford Encyclopedia of Philosophy* (Spring 2007 Edition), 2007. Available on-line: http://plato.stanford.edu/archives/spr2007/entries/information-semantic [13 November 2012].

32 Edward Comor, "When More is Less: Time, Space and Knowledge in Information Societies," in Robin Mansell, Rohan Samarajiva and Amy Mahan, eds., *Networking Knowledge for Information Societies: Institutions & Intervention* (Delft, The Netherlands: University of Delft Press), 240.

33 Innis, "Preface," ix; Innis, "The Newspaper," 3; Innis, "Cultural Factors," 89.

34 Innis, "Preface," vii.

35 Innis, "The Newspaper," 19, 30.

36 Harold Innis, "An Economic Approach to English Literature in the Nineteenth Century," in *Political Economy in the Modern State* (Toronto: Ryerson Press, 1946), 46 n21.

37 Harold Innis, "The University in the Modern Crisis," in *Political Economy in the Modern State* (Toronto: Ryerson Press, 1946), 76–7.

38 Arturo Rosenblueth, Norbert Wiener, and J. Garcia Ramos. 1985, "Muscular Clonus: Cybernetics and Physiology," in P. Masani, ed., *Norbert Wiener: Collected Works,* Volume IV (Cambridge, Massachusetts: MIT Press), 488.

39 Arturo Rosenblueth, Norbert Wiener, and Julian Bigelow, "Behavior, Purpose and Teleology," *Philosophy of Science* 10 (1), 19.

40 Rosenblueth, Wiener, and Garcia Ramos, "Muscular Clonus," 488–90.

41 Norbert Wiener, "Men, Machines and the World About," in Masani, ed., *Norbert Wiener Collected Works,* 794.

42 Wiener, "Men, Machines," 794.

43 Rosenblueth, Wiener and Garcia Ramos, "Muscular Clonus," 490.

44 Norbert Wiener, *I am a Mathematician: The Latter Life of a Prodigy* (Cambridge, Massachusetts: MIT Press, 1964): 244, 253; Norbert Wiener, "Cybernetics," in Masani, ed., *Norbert Wiener Collected Works*, 791–2.

45 Norbert Wiener, "Cybernetics: The Word Describes a New Field of Study Shared by Many Sciences," in Masani, ed., *Norbert Wiener Collected Works*: 784; Norbert Wiener, *Cybernetics: or Control and Communication in the Animal and the Machine* (Cambridge, Massachusetts: MIT Press, 1948), 95–6.

46 Wiener, "Cybernetics: The Word Describes a New Field of Study," 787–8.

47 Ibid., 786.

48 Ibid., 788.

49 Innis, "Political Economy," 103.

50 Harold Innis, "The Written Tradition and the Roman Empire," in *Empire and Communications* (Oxford: Clarendon Press, 1950), 129–30.
51 Innis, "Political Economy," 104.
52 Innis, "Preface," xiv; Innis, "The University," 77–8; Innis, "Political Economy," 136.
53 Innis, "Preface," x; Innis, "The Newspaper," 11.
54 Innis, "The Newspaper," 34; Innis, "Cultural Factors," 89.
55 Innis, "The Newspaper," 11, 33; Innis, "Economic Approach," 54.
56 Innis, "Political Economy," 105.
57 Ibid., 104.
58 Innis, "Preface," xiv; Innis, "Cultural Factors," 90.
59 Innis, "Political Economy," 105.
60 Innis, "The University," 79–80, cited from Ernst Troeltsch, *The Social Teaching of the Christian Churches* (George Allen & Unwin, 1931), 619; Innis, "Political Economy," 145.
61 Innis, "Political Economy," 105–7.
62 Ibid., 131.
63 Ibid., 108–9.
64 Innis, "Cultural Factors," 95.
65 Innis, "Political Economy," 138.
66 Innis, "Preface," xvi.
67 Innis, "Political Economy," 113.
68 Ibid., 106, 114.
69 Innis, "Cultural Factors," 97.
70 Harold Innis, "The Problems of Rehabilitation," in *Political Economy in the Modern State* (Toronto: Ryerson Press, 1946), 57.
71 Innis, "Political Economy," 117.
72 Ibid., 116–17.
73 Innis, "Preface," xii; Innis, "Political Economy, 143–4.
74 Innis, "Cultural Factors," 89; Innis, "The Newspaper," 3; Innis, "Preface," ix.
75 Innis, "Cultural Factors," 89; Innis, "Political Economy," 134; Innis, "The Newspaper," 12.
76 Innis, "Cultural Factors," 89–90; Innis, "Economic Approach," 45.
77 Innis, "The Newspaper," 3–8, 12–15, 27–34; Innis, "Economic Approach," 37.
78 Harold Innis, "Comment: Social Sciences in the Post-War World," *Canadian Historical Review* 22 (2), 118.
79 Innis, "The Newspaper," 4.
80 Ibid., 17.
81 Ibid., 32.
82 Ibid., 17–18.

83 Innis, "The Newspaper," 34; Innis, "Cultural Factors," 83–7.
84 Innis, "Preface," in *The Bias of Communication* (Toronto: University of Toronto Press, 1995, c. 1951), xxvii.
85 Innis, "Cultural Factors," 89.
86 Ibid.
87 Ibid., 94.
88 Arthur Lower and Harold Innis, *Settlement and the Forest Frontier in Eastern Canada / Settlement and the Mining Frontier* (Toronto: Macmillan, 1936): 183, 257.
89 Innis, "Cultural Factors," 88–9; Harold Innis to Arthur Cole, 31 October 1941, *Harold Innis Papers*, University of Toronto Archives, B72-0025, Box 11, File 1.
90 Lower and Innis, *Settlement and the Forest Frontier*, 252, 261.
91 Ibid., 257, 260–1.
92 Ibid., 258, 265.
93 Ibid., 258.
94 Ibid., 257.
95 Ibid., 217.
96 John Maurice Clark, "Business Acceleration and the Law of Demand: A Technical Factor in Economic Cycles," *Journal of Political Economy* 25 (3), 217.
97 Harold Innis, "The Work of Thorstein Veblen," in Mary Q. Innis, ed., *Essays in Canadian Economic History* (Toronto: University of Toronto Press, 1956), 19.
98 Lower and Innis, *Settlement and the Forest Frontier*, 194.
99 Harold Innis, "Transportation in the Canadian Economy," in Mary Q. Innis, ed., *Essays in Canadian Economic History*, 226.
100 Lower and Innis, *Settlement and the Forest Frontier*, 269.
101 Innis, "The Newspaper," 34.
102 Innis, "Preface," vii.
103 Innis, "Cultural Factors," 99.
104 Ibid., 98–9.
105 Innis, "Preface," vii.
106 Innis, "Cultural Factors," 99.
107 Innis, "Preface," x.
108 Innis, "Economic Approach," 42.
109 Ibid., 51.
110 Innis, "The Newspaper," 30.
111 Innis, "The Preface," xiv.
112 Innis, "Political Economy," 136.

113 Harold Innis, "A Plea for the University Tradition," in *Political Economy in the Modern State*: 64–5.
114 Innis, "The University," 77–8.
115 Ibid.
116 Innis, "Political Economy," 103.
117 Innis, "The Newspaper," 17; Innis, "Political Economy," 120–30.
118 Innis, "Cultural Factors," 99–100.
119 Innis, "Political Economy," 135.
120 Innis, "Cultural Factors," 99–100.
121 Ibid., 95–6.
122 Innis, "Problems," 57.
123 Ibid., 57.
124 Innis, "Cultural Factors," 94; Innis, "The Newspaper," 22; Innis, "Problems," 58.
125 Innis, "Political Economy," 141.
126 Ibid.
127 Innis, "Cultural Factors," 101.
128 Ibid., 101–2.
129 Innis, "The Written Tradition," 115, 118–19.
130 Ibid., 115.
131 Ibid., 116–17.
132 Ibid., 117.
133 Ibid., 117–18.
134 Ibid., 119–20.
135 Ibid., 120.
136 Innis, "Cultural Factors," 101.
137 Harold Innis, "Chapter 6: Printing in the Sixteenth Century," in "History of Communication," *Harold Innis Papers*, University of Toronto Archives, B1972-003, Box 17, pp. 35–6, 38. Innis's source for the quotation on the import of emblems is not clear. He cites an author named Bain, but I was unable to locate an author with the surname Bain using this quotation in a text search using tools such as Google Books. The original source for this quote, however, is not the author Innis cites but rather Francis Bacon, who was treating the qualities of emblems in a defence of emblematic literature. See Elbert Nevins Sebring Thompson, *Literary Bypaths of the Renaissance* (Freeport, New York: Books for Libraries Press, 1968, c. 1924), 32. Cited from Francis Bacon, *De Augmentis Scientarium*, Book 5, Chapter 5.
138 Innis, "Cultural Factors," 91.
139 Harold Innis, "The Problem of Space," in *The Bias of Communication*, 126, 128. Innis's source on the importance of sculpture and stained glass is the

preface of Emile Mâle's "*L'art religieux du* XIIIe *siècle en France: étude sur l'iconographie du moyen age et sur ses sources d'inspiration,* 3ème éd., rev. et augm (Paris: Libr. A. Colin, 1910).

140 Innis, "Cultural Factors," 100–1.

141 Ibid., 100.

142 Robin Neill observes of Innis that he "sought explanation in history and time series, not in theoretical argument." See Robin Neill, "Economic Historiography in the 1950s: The Saskatchewan School," *Journal of Canadian Studies* 34 (3), 254.

143 Harold Innis, "The Oral Tradition and Greek Civilization," in *Empire and Communications*, 88.

144 Wiener, *Cybernetics*, 61.

145 Neil A. Gershenfeld and Andreas S. Weigend, "The Future of Time Series: Learning and Understanding," in A.S. Weigend and N.A. Gershenfeld, eds., *Time Series Prediction: Forecasting the Future and Understanding the Past* (Reading Massachusetts: Addison-Wesley, 1994), 2.

146 Alicia Juarrero, *Dynamics in Action: Intentional Behaviour as a Complex System* (Cambridge, Massachusetts: MIT Press, 1999), 138.

147 Gershenfeld and Weigend, "The Future," 2.

148 Norbert Wiener, "My Connection with Cybernetics," in Mesani, ed., *Norbert Wiener: Collected Works with Commentaries*, 120.

149 Norbert Wiener, "Measure and Probability," *Norbert Wiener Papers*, MIT Archives, MC22, Box 31D, Folder 799, p. 3

150 Norbert Wiener, "Causality and Information," *Norbert Wiener Papers*, MIT Archives, MC22, Box 29C, Folder 687, pp. 1–3.

151 Norbert Wiener, "Measure and Probability," 6.

152 Wiener, "My Connection," 14.

153 Juarrero, *Dynamics*, 134.

154 Ibid.

155 Ibid.

156 Ibid., 136.

157 Ibid.

158 Ibid., 122–3.

159 Ibid., 136–8.

160 Wiener, "Measure and Probability," 9.

161 Ibid.

162 Wiener, "My Connection," 120.

163 Wiener, "Measure and Probability," 9–10.

164 Norbert Wiener, "The Extrapolation, Interpolation, and Smoothing of Stationary Time Series: With Engineering Applications." *Norbert Wiener Papers*,

MIT Press, MC22, Box 28A, Folder 561A, p. 37. Wiener published this manuscript in 1949. Also see the conclusion of Chapter 1 in *Extrapolation, Interpolation, and Smoothing of Stationary Time Series: With Engineering Applications* (Cambridge, Massachusetts: MIT Press, 1966, c. 1949).

165 Harold Innis to W.T. Easterbrook, 7 June 1952, *Easterbrook Papers*, University of Toronto Archives, B1975-0030/001.

166 Innis, "Cultural Factors," 83.

167 Ibid., 84–5.

168 Ibid., 86–7.

169 Harold Innis to Arthur Cole, 31 October 1941, *Harold Innis Papers*, University of Toronto Archives, B72-0025, Box 11, File 1.

170 On this point, see Robin Neill, *A New Theory of Value: The Canadian Economics of H.A. Innis* (Toronto: University of Toronto Press, 1972): 50–61. Also see Harold Innis, "The Penetrative Powers of the Price System," in *Political Economy in the Modern State*, 166.

171 Harold Innis to Arthur Cole, 31 October 1941, *Harold Innis Papers*, University of Toronto Archives, B72-0025, Box 11, File 1.

172 Harold Innis to Arthur Cole, 31 October 1941, *Harold Innis Papers*, ibid.

173 Ibid.

174 While most scholars agree that the two periods of Innis's writing are linked, there is little consensus as to how. Various interpreters have prioritized one Innisian concept or another and pressed for its acceptance as the bridge that unites the whole. Several studies have suggested the parallel rests in Innis's interest in the material properties of media and staples. Innis, it is held, believed the physical properties of both were instrumental in producing either large institutions with an interest in controlling space, or smaller-scale institutions preoccupied with the problems of time. See Daniel Czitrom, *Media and the American Mind: From Morse to McLuhan* (Chapel Hill, North Carolina: University of North Carolina Press, 1982), 149, 155; Graeme Patterson, *History and Communications: Harold Innis, Marshall McLuhan and the Interpretation of History* (Toronto: University of Toronto Press, 1990): 3; Trevor Barnes, "Knowing Where You Stand: Harold Innis, Staple Theory, and Local Models," *Canadian Geographer* 37 (4): 357–9; Barrington Nevitt, *The Communication Ecology: Re-presentation versus Replica* (Toronto: Butterworth, 1982), 15.

Other commentators have emphasized Innis's interest in cognitive bias and monopolies, the underlying forces responsible for the emergence and collapse of empires, factors mediating centre-periphery relations, and Innis's liberalisms. See William J. Buxton, "Harold Innis' Excavation of Modernity: The Newspaper Industry, Industry, Communications, and the Decline of

Public Life," *Canadian Journal of Communication* 23 (2) 1998. Available on-line: http://www.cjc-online.ca/index.php/journal/article/view/1047/953 Par. 8. [13 November 2012]; Judith Stamps, *Unthinking Modernity: Innis, McLuhan and the Frankfurt School* (Montreal and Kingston: McGill-Queen's University Press, 1995), 70; Mel Watkins, "The Innis Tradition in Canadian Political Economy," *Canadian Journal of Political and Social Theory* 6 (1–2), 16. spring/winter 1982; Ian Angus, "Orality in the twilight of humanism: a critique of the communication theory of Harold Innis," *Continuum: The Australian Journal of Media and Culture* 7 (1) (1993). Available on-line: http://wwwmcc.murdoch.edu.au/ReadingRoom/7.1/Angus.html Para. 11–17. [13 November 2012]; Leslie Pal, "Scholarship and the Later Innis," *Journal of Canadian Studies* 12 (winter 1977), 32.

As we saw in the Introduction, scholars have not found these diverse interpretations to be a cause for celebration. In fact, as William Buxton and Charles Acland note, the reaction has been just the opposite: bewilderment. Paul Heyer has declared Innis's intentions with respect to this question and others as forever beyond recall. See William Buxton and Charles Acland, "Harold Innis: A Genealogy of Contesting Portraits," in Charles R. Acland and William J. Buxton, eds., *Harold Innis in the New Century: Reflections and Refractions* (Montreal and Kingston: McGill-Queen's University Press, 1999), 12; Paul Heyer, *Communications and History: Theories of Media, Knowledge and Civilization* (New York: Greenwood Press, 1988), 117.

175 See note 29 above.

176 Kenneth Arrow, "Foreword," in W. Brian Arthur, *Increasing Returns and Path Dependence in the Economy* (Ann Arbor: University of Michigan Press, 1994), ix.

177 Harold Innis, "Minerva's Owl," in *The Bias of Communication*, 3–4.

CHAPTER FIVE

1 Hugh G.J. Aitken, "Myth and Measurement: The Innis Tradition in Economic History," *Journal of Canadian Studies* 12 (winter 1977), 96.

2 Donald Creighton reports that Innis in his 1947 presidential address to the *Royal Society of Canada* remained "unhappily conscious of his prolixity." To compensate, he read his "whole, detailed, highly condensed argument" in a "hurried and unemphatic fashion. Many in his audience were puzzled or bewildered." The address, "Minerva's Owl," became the first chapter of Innis's 1952 study, *The Bias of Communication*. See Donald Creighton, *Harold Adams Innis: Portrait of a Scholar* (Toronto: University of Toronto Press, 1957), 126.

3 Robert Babe, *Canadian Communication Thought: Ten Foundational Writers* (Toronto: University of Toronto Press, 2000), 54.

4 William J. Buxton and Charles R. Acland, "Harold Innis: A Genealogy of Contesting Portraits," in Charles R. Acland and William Buxton, eds., Introduction to *Harold Innis in the New Century: Reflections and Refractions* (Montreal and Kingston: McGill-Queen's University Press, 1999), 6–9.

5 Marshall McLuhan, "Foreword," in Harold Innis, *The Bias of Communication* (Toronto: University of Toronto, 1972), ix.

6 William Kuhns, *The Post-Industrial Prophets: Interpretations of Technology* (New York: Weybright and Talley, 1971); James W. Carey, "Harold Innis and Marshall McLuhan," *Antioch Review* (spring 1967): 5–39.

7 John Seely Brown and Paul Duguid, *The Social Life of Information* (Cambridge, Massachusetts: *Harvard Business Review Press,* 2000), 30, 200; Gregory Benford, *Deep Time: How Humanity Communicates across Millennia* (New York: Avon Books, 1999), 209–10; Neil Postman, *Technopoly: The Surrender of Culture to Technology* (New York: Knopf, 1992), 9, 19–20; John Ralston Saul, *The Doubter's Companion* (New York: Free Press, 1994), 262, 292, 331; John Ralston Saul, *The Unconscious Civilization* (New York: Simon and Schuster, 1995), 55.

8 Sir Peter Hall, *Cities in Civilization* (New York: Pantheon Books, 1998), 506.

9 Buxton and Acland, "Genealogy," 12.

10 Northrop Frye, "Harold Innis: The Strategy of Culture," in Robert D. Denham, ed., *The Eternal Act of Creation: Essays, 1979–1990* (Bloomington and Indianapolis: Indiana University Press, 1993), 155.

11 Harold Innis, "The Bias of Communication," in *The Bias of Communication* (Toronto: University of Toronto Press, 1995), 33.

12 Harold Innis, "The Problem of Space," in *The Bias of Communication*: 95; Harold Innis, "Minerva's Owl," in *The Bias of Communication*, 6; Innis, "Bias," 39; Harold Innis, "Babylonia," in *Empire and Communications* in *Empire and Communications* (Oxford, Clarendon Press, 1950), 45–8.

13 Harold Innis, "The Oral Tradition and Greek Civilization," in *Empire and Communications*: 64–100.

14 Judith Stamps notes that "Innis has been read as a mechanist so often that the point is worth repeating. Innis never offered a determinist version of history based on certain media or binary sets of oppositional media." See Judith Stamps, *Unthinking Modernity: Innis, McLuhan, and the Frankfurt School* (Montreal and Kingston: McGill-Queen's University Press, 1995), 67. Two contemporary characterizations of Innis as a technological determinist include Daniel Czitrom, *Media and the American Mind: From Morse to McLuhan* (Chapel Hill, North Carolina: University of North Carolina Press,

1982), 156; and Robert Cox, "Civilizations: Encounters and Transformations," *Studies in Political Economy: A Socialist Review* 47 (summer 1995), 156.

15 For recent historicist readings of Innis, see Ronald J. Deibert, "Between Essentialism and Constructivism: Harold Innis and World Order Transformations," in Rita Watson and Menahem Blondheim, eds., *The Toronto School of Communication Theory: Interpretations, Extensions, Applications* (Toronto and Jerusalem: University of Toronto Press and Hebrew University Magnes Press, 2008): 29–52; Menahem Blondheim, "'The Significance of Communication' According to Harold Innis," in Watson and Blondheim, eds., *Toronto School of Communication Theory*: 53–81; Paul Frosh, "The Bias of Bias: Innis, Lessig and the Problem of Space," in Watson and Blondheim, eds., *Toronto School of Communication Theory*: 147–69; Xiaoquan Zhao, "Revitalizing Time: An Innisian Perspective on the Internet," in Watson and Blondheim, eds., *Toronto School of Communication Theory*: 199–214.

16 This is a problem that has undercut the force of some recent interpretations of Innis that have tied his theory of media to constructs of ecological change. I should say at the start that these readings have made a valuable contribution to our understanding of Innis through their insistence that Innis's philosophy of history was not mono-causal. Instead, they argue persuasively that Innis's communication writings offer a construct of cultural history that is complex and multi-causal, and leaves room for human agency.

Some appeals to ecological change can be criticized, however, for their lack of conceptual and analytical precision, particularly in the conception of change they associate with Innis's theory of media. Judith Stamps, for example, through her emphasis on negative dialectics, suggests the importance of agent interaction and systemic change in Innis's thought. Vincent di Norcia has also suggested that Innis's purpose was to study systems governed by an indeterminate form of change. Cultures, as Innis drew them, were social ecologies. The problem, however, is that both authors have also provided readings suggesting efficient cause. Stamps identifies Innis's theory of media with a geological conception of history, referring to technology as a causal layer that supplemented his studies of geography, economics, and politics. The metaphor suggests an aggregation of forces, not a system. Di Norcia also appeals to a reading of Innis in which competing historical forces and institutions operate not in unity with agents, but independently of them. That independence, combined with a narrative in which institutions worked at cross-purposes with each other, leads di Norcia to suggest that in Innis's histories human freedom emerges by virtue of conflict. Freedom emerges not because of constraint but in spite of it. The diffuse picture is unfortunate because it is not clear whether the two authors are aligning media with a conception of efficient cause or formal and final cause. See Judith Stamps, *Unthinking Modernity*, 67; Vincent di Norcia, "Of Stone Books and Freedom," *Visible Language* 20 (3), 354–7.

For works identifying Innis with an ecological construction of change see the Introduction, note 24. Also see Ronald J. Deibert, "Harold Innis and the Empire of Speed," *Review of International Studies* 25 (2): 273–89. 1999; Ian Parker, "Harold Innis as a Canadian Geographer," *Canadian Geographer*, 32 (1) (March 1988): 63–9; and Trevor Barnes, "Knowing Where You Stand: Harold Innis, Staple Theory, and Local Models," *Canadian Geographer*, 37 (4) (1993): 357–9; and Limor Shifman and Menahem Blondheim, "From the Spider to the Web: Innis' Ecological Approach to the Evolution of Communication Technologies," in Watson and Blondheim, eds., *Toronto School of Communication Theory*: 337–60.

17 Ernst Cassirer, *The Problem of Knowledge: Philosophy, Science, and History since Hegel*, trans. William H. Woglom and Charles W. Hendel (New Haven: Yale University Press, 1950), 121–2, 125–6. Whether Innis should have accepted Kant's reasoning is of course debatable. Alicia Juarrero argues that Kant in essence begged the question of the relationship between force and purpose by emphasizing the synthetic principles underlying each. As for Kant, he believed the perceived discrepancy between the two represented either a failure of reason or a limitation in human capacity to perceive. It was possible that natural phenomena were governed by principles extending beyond "the sensible," the segment of phenomena that humans can perceive, and that resolution could only be reached in the "supersensible," making the project in principle beyond human grasp. Nature may not be susceptible to encapsulation in a single human formulation. See Alicia Juarrero, *Dynamics in Action: Intentional Behavior as a Complex System* (Cambridge, Massachusetts: MIT Press, 1999), 47.

18 For Kant's description of the Transcendental Aesthetic generally, and his discussion of "the pure form of sensible intuitions" particularly, see Immanuel Kant, *Critique of Pure Reason*, A21-A22/B35-36.

19 Innis, "Introduction," *Empire and Communications* (Oxford: Clarendon Press, 1950), 5–6.

20 William Buxton complains that Innis scholars in their attempts to unearth "clearly articulated claims and propositions" from *Empire and Communications* and *The Bias of Communication* have limited themselves to "key sections from these works as the basis for generating claims about the meaning of Innis' work." The emphasis by interpreters on Innis's statements regarding the space-binding or time-binding properties of media has hin-

dered their appreciation of a crucial element in his narrative; namely, "how the printing complex – in varying ways and through multiple guises – has been implicated in the onslaught of modernity." See William Buxton, "Harold Innis' Excavation of Modernity: The Newspaper Industry, Communications, and the Decline of Public Life," *Canadian Journal of Communication*, 23 (2) (1998). Available On-line: http://www.cjc–online.ca/index.php/journal/article/viewArticle/1047/953 [14 November 2012].

21 Innis, "Introduction," 6.
22 Ibid., 5.
23 Innis, "Preface," in *The Bias of Communication*, xvii.
24 Innis, "Introduction," 6–7.
25 Ibid., 10–11.
26 Ibid., 5.
27 Ibid., 8, fn1.
28 Innis, "Minerva's Owl," 4.
29 Innis, "Introduction," 7; Harold Innis, "Babylonia," in *Empire and Communications*, 30–63.
30 Innis, "Bias of Communication," 33.
31 Innis, "Introduction," 7.
32 Innis, "Bias," 34.
33 Innis, "Minerva's Owl," 4.
34 Harold Innis, "The Oral Tradition and Greek Civilization," in *Empire and Communications*, 81.
35 Innis, "Oral," 81–2.
36 Innis, "Oral," 83; and Innis, "Bias," 42.
37 Innis, "Bias," 42; Innis, "Oral," 76, 80–1; and "Innis, "Minerva's Owl," 7.
38 Innis, "Oral," 76.
39 Ibid., 77. Cited from Werner Jaeger, *The Theology of the Early Greek Philosophers* (Oxford: Oxford University Press, 1947), 16.
40 Innis, "Oral," 80.
41 Harold Innis, "The Problem of Space," in *The Bias of Communication*, 110; and Innis, "Oral," 78.
42 Innis, "Bias," 42.
43 Innis, "Oral," 78–9. Also see Innis, "Space," 111–12.
44 Innis, "Oral," 78.
45 Innis, "Space," 110; Innis, "Oral," 92.
46 Innis, "Bias," 42.
47 Innis, "Oral," 82; Innis, "Bias," 41–2; Innis, "Minerva's Owl," 7; and Innis, "Space," 106–7.

48 Innis, "Oral," 83–4; Innis, "Bias," 42; and Innis, "Space," 107.
49 Innis, "Oral," 83, 85; and Innis, "Bias," 42.
50 Innis, "Oral," 86; Innis, "Minerva's Owl," 8; Innis, "Space," 107; and Innis, "Bias," 42.
51 Innis, "Space," 107.
52 Innis, "Oral," 86; and Innis, "Bias," 42.
53 Innis, "Bias," 42.
54 Innis, "Oral," 86.
55 Innis, "Bias," 42.
56 Innis, "Oral," 87.
57 Ibid., 86–7.
58 Ibid., 87.
59 Ibid., 87.
60 Ibid., 91–2.
61 Innis, "Space," 111.
62 Innis, "Oral," 91.
63 Innis, "Oral," 86, 88; Innis, "Space," 111.
64 Innis, "Oral," 88.
65 Harold Innis to Arthur H. Cole, 31 October 1941, *Harold Adams Innis Papers*, University of Toronto Archives, B1972-0025, Box 11, File 1.
66 Harold Innis, "The Written Tradition and the Roman Empire," in *Empire and Communications*, 110.
67 Innis, "Oral," 92.
68 Innis, "Space," 107.
69 Ibid.
70 Innis, "Space," 107.
71 Innis, "Oral," 90.
72 Ibid.
73 Ibid.
74 Ibid., 91.
75 Ibid., 96–7.
76 Ibid., 98–100; and "Innis, "Space," 43–4.
77 Innis, "Roman Empire," 110, 112–13.
78 The emergence of a cultural divide between the elite and popular classes of a given culture as a result of information overload is a recurring theme in Innis's history of the West. In "An Economic Approach to English Literature," Innis argues that popular and elite culture split with the rise of the newspaper and the invention of the steam-driven printing press. As we saw in our last chapter, Innis suggested that a similar pattern occurred in Rome during the time of Cicero. The influx of information from Greece under-

mined the integrity and originality of Roman legal scholarship and Roman theatre. Innis's argument here presents a striking contradiction in his assessment of the impact of information overload on human societies. On the one hand, information overload seems to create political unity, with people shedding class and transnational constructs of identity in favour of the civil identity derived from the state. On the other hand, information gluts prompt a division in cultural preferences, with popular classes embracing different cultural products and religious options than their counterparts in the elite intellectual and civil strata for the given culture. Innis does not explain why communication technology prompts unity on the one hand, and division on the other. See Harold Innis, "An Economic Approach to English Literature," in *Political Economy in the Modern State* (Toronto: Ryerson Press, 1946), 42, 51–2; Innis, "Roman Empire," 115–20.

79 Innis, "Roman Empire," 115.

80 Ibid.

81 Harold Innis to W.T. Easterbrook, 11 May 1952, *Harold Adams Innis Papers*, University of Toronto Archives, B72-0025, Box 11, File 6.

82 Innis, "Introduction," 9.

83 Innis, "Oral," 70.

84 Innis, "Time," 62.

85 The French philosopher Jacques Derrida, a leading proponent of postmodernism, has by contrast proclaimed the death of the subject. He argues that the self "is inscribed in language, is a 'function' of language, becomes a speaking subject only by making its speech conform – even in so-called creation, or in so-called transgression – to the system of the rules of language as a system of differences." See Jacques Derrida, "*Différance*," in Peggy Kamuf, ed., *A Derrida Reader: Between the Blinds* (New York: Columbia University Press, 1991), 67. This section originally appeared in Derrida's *Margins of Philosophy*, trans. Alan Bass (Chicago: University of Chicago Press, 1982). See also Briankle G. Chang, "Deconstructing Communication: Derrida and the (Im)possibility of Communication," *History of European Ideas*, 9 (3), 564; Peter Munz, "How Nietzsche's Ideas about Language Came to be Transformed into Derrida's Ideology of Deconstruction," *Australian Journal of Politics and History* 40 (Special Edition): 57–71, 1994; Georg Iggers, *Historiography in the Twentieth Century* (London: Wesleyan University Press, 1997): 118–33.

86 William L. Reese, *Dictionary of Philosophy and Religion*, new and enlarged edition (Atlantic Highlands, New Jersey: Humanities Press, 1996, c. 1980), 680.

87 Innis, "Introduction," 9.

88 Juarrero, *Dynamics*, 122–3.
89 Innis, "Oral," 72.
90 Innis, "Introduction," 8–9.
91 Innis's argument is not dissimilar to the effect of software packages mentioned in chapter 2, where it was noted that users form systems with their tools, and their behavioural competence is changed by virtue of their interaction with the software.
92 Harold Innis, *The Idea File of Harold Adams Innis*, edited by William Christian (Toronto: University of Toronto Press, 1980), 53.
93 Innis, "Babylonia," 32.
94 Innis, "Time," 62. In this case, Innis was too trusting of his sources. His portrayal of Chinese conceptions of time fails to take into account the *I Ching*, or Chinese book of changes, which contains a conception of emergent change arising from the opposing forces of *yin* and *yang* which Innis surely would have found congenial. See Reese, *Dictionary of Philosophy and Religion*, 84.
95 Innis, "Babylonia," 32.
96 Ibid., 32–3, 40–1, 53–4, and 62.
97 Innis, "Oral," 78. See also Innis, "Babylonia," 52–3.
98 Innis, *Idea File*, 192.
99 Innis, "Bias," 41.
100 Innis, "Time," 86.
101 Innis, "Minerva's Owl," 7–8; and Innis, "Oral," 70.
102 Innis, "Minerva's Owl," 71; Innis, "Oral," 71. In "The Bias of Communication" Innis places the introduction of writing in the seventh century BCE. See Innis, "Bias," 41.
103 Innis, "Oral," 71.
104 Innis, "Minerva's Owl," 9.
105 Innis, "Space," 105.
106 Innis, "Oral," 71.
107 Innis, "Space," 102.
108 Innis, "Oral," 76.
109 Ibid., 76–7. Quotations cited from M.P. Nilsson, *A History of Greek Religion* (Oxford, Clarendon Press, 1925), 179.
110 Harold A. Innis and Jan O.M. Broek, "Geography and Nationalism: A Discussion," *Geographical Review*, 35 (2) (April 1945), 302.
111 Innis, "Space," 102–3, 106.
112 Innis, "Oral," 70, 80.
113 Alicia Juarrero, *Dynamics in Actions: Intentional Behavior as a Complex System* (Cambridge, Massachusetts: MIT Press, 1999): 21–3, 128.

114 Juarrero, *Dynamics in Actions*, 152–8.

115 W. Brian Arthur, "Positive Feedbacks in the Economy," in *Increasing Returns and Path Dependence in the Economy* (Ann Arbor: University of Michigan Press, 1994), 2. Also see W. Brian Arthur, "Industry Location Patterns and the Importance of History," in *Increasing Returns and Path Dependence in the Economy*: 49–68.

116 W. Brian Arthur, "Preface," in *Increasing Returns and Path Dependence in the Economy*: xii; M. Mitchell Waldrop, *Complexity: The Emerging Science at the Edge of Order and Chaos* (New York: Touchstone, 1992): 45–6; Arthur, "Industry Location," 54–5; W. Brian Arthur, "Competing Technologies, Increasing returns and Lock-in by Historical Events," *Economic Journal*, 99 (1989): 106–31.

117 Innis, "Minerva's Owl," 3–4.

118 Harold Innis, "The Written Tradition and the Roman Empire," in *Empire and Communications* (Oxford: Clarendon Press, 1950), 111.

119 Innis, *Idea File*, 249–50.

120 Ernst Cassirer, *The Problem of Knowledge: Philosophy, Science, and History since Hegel*, Trans. William H. Woglom and Charles W. Hendel (New Haven: Yale University Press, 1950), 124.

121 Cassirer, *Problem of Knowledge*, 118–25.

122 Ibid., 118, 125.

123 Ibid., 122–3.

124 Ibid., 120, cited from Kant, *Kritik der Urteilskraft*, edited by K. Rosenkranz, "I. Kants Sämmtliche Werke," Teil IV, 65, S. (Leipzig, L. Voss, 1838), 260.

125 Cassirer, *Problem of Knowledge*, 121.

126 Ibid., 120.

127 Ibid., 121.

128 Ibid., 122.

129 Ibid., 121–2, 125–6. According to Juarrero, by emphasizing synthetic principles Kant essentially avoided the question of reconciling cause and purpose. In Kant's view, the discrepancy represented either a failure of reason or a limitation in human capacity to perceive. It was possible that natural phenomena were governed by principles extending beyond "the sensible," the segment of phenomena humans can perceive, and that resolution could only be reached in the "supersensible," making the project in principle beyond human grasp. Nature may not be susceptible to encapsulation in a single human formulation. See Juarrero, *Dynamics*, 47.

130 Cassirer, *Problem of Knowledge*, 124.

131 Ibid.

132 Ibid., 124–5.

133 Ibid., 125.
134 Ibid.
135 Ibid., 126.
136 Ibid.
137 Ibid., 126–7.
138 Harold Innis, "Political Economy in the Modern State," in *Proceedings of the American Philosophical Society* 87 (4), 334. The proceedings indicate that Innis presented the paper upon which "Political Economy" is based in November 1943. The article, and hence the quotation, of course, was also published in the anthology of the same name. See Harold Innis, "Political Economy in the Modern State," in *Political Economy in the Modern State* (Toronto: Ryerson Press, 1946), 127.
139 Innis, *Idea File*, 102.
140 Ibid., 34.
141 Treatments describing abductive reasoning include Douglas Walton, *Abductive Reasoning* (Tuscaloosa, Alabama: University of Alabama Press, 2004) and John R. Josephson and Susan G. Josephson, eds. *Abductive Inference: Computation, Philosophy, Technology* (Cambridge: Cambridge University Press, 1994).
142 Harold Innis, "The Newspaper in Economic Development," in *Political Economy in the Modern State*, 34.
143 Harold Innis to Arthur Cole, 2 April 1943, *Harold Innis Papers*, University of Toronto Archives, B72-0025, Box 11, File 1.
144 Innis, "Time," 88.
145 Innis, *Idea File*, 34.
146 Ibid., 130.
147 Immanuel Kant, *Critique of Pure Reason*, A39/B56, translated and edited by Paul Geyer and Allen W. Wood (Cambridge: Cambridge University Press, 1998), 166.
148 In the original Jeans address, and the F.M. Cornford essay from which Innis obtained the quotation, the final word of the sentence is "construction," not "constitution." See Innis, "Space," 92; F.M. Cornford, "The Invention of Space," in *Essays in Honour of Gilbert Murray* (London: George Allen Unwin, 1936), 216; and James Jeans, "James Jeans addresses the British Association in 1934." Available on-line: http://www–history.mcs.st–and.ac.uk/Extras/BA_1934_J1.html [13 March 2012].
149 In "The Invention of Space," Cornford treats ancient conceptions of space and argues that Greek formulations of geometric space did not derive from common sense and were "not implicit in the mind of the Homeric or pre-

Homeric Greek." Constructs of space were not discovered, they were invented, he suggests. Commenting on Jeans, Cornford argued that "the steel structure of the universe," or pre-Einsteinian conceptions of space and time turn out to be "less like steel than india-rubber and the india-rubber itself exists only as an arbitrary figment of the human brain." See Cornford, "Invention," 216, 218.

If one examines Jeans's address directly, however, one finds statements that suggest humans access *a priori* forms – including space and time – which shape their cognition of the surrounding environment. Consider, for example, the force of these two sentences, which follow the one Cornford cited, and are part of the same paragraph: "They [space and time] are of course very important frameworks, being nothing less than the frameworks along which our minds receive their whole knowledge of the outer world ... Thus space and time are of preponderating importance to our minds as the media through which the messages from the outer world enter the 'gateways of knowledge,' our senses, and in terms of which they are classified." Toward the end of his address, Jeans made his philosophical stance even more explicit by claiming that modern physics had moved beyond "the forbidding materialism of the Victorian scientist. His objective and material universe is proved to consist of little more than constructs of our own minds. To this extent, then, modern physics has moved in the direction of philosophic idealism." See James Jeans, "James Jeans addresses the British Association in 1934." Available on-line: http://www-history.mcs.st-and.ac.uk/Extras/BA_1934_J1.html [13 March 2012]; and James Jeans, "James Jeans addresses the British Association in 1934, Part 2." Available on-line: http://www-history.mcs.st-and.ac.uk/Extras/BA_1934_J2.html [13 March 2012]

If Innis's citation practices served as the sole basis for determining the connotation he assigned the term "constitution," then preference would have to be given to Francis Cornford's definition. Innis cited "The Invention of Space" more than once in his communication anthologies, and also referred to other works written by the same author. By contrast, none of Innis's four communication works contain any independent additional references to the writings of James Jeans. Innis's citations provide no basis for suggesting he had seen any portion of Jeans's address apart from the material quoted by Cornford. Cornford did not quote the statements by Jeans that I have noted above.

Still, I believe there are substantial reasons to suggest that Innis understood the quotation he used in the manner Jeans intended, and not in the manner that Cornford used it. To start, Jeans was a well-known popularizer of scientific concepts in the 1930s, filling a role similar to that played by Richard Dawkins and Brian Greene today. He was also known for championing an Idealist reading of the new physics. Innis was well versed in the philosophy and science of his time, and it does not seem credible that he would have interpreted Jeans in any other way. It would be akin to reading a passage from Richard Dawkins today and concluding he was an advocate of creation science. Second, as Alexander John Watson has shown in *Marginal Man*, Innis had the disturbing habit of taking a quote from a source and ascribing to it a significance at variance with what the original author intended. (See Alexander John Watson, *Marginal Man: The Dark Vision of Harold Innis* [Toronto: University of Toronto Press, 2006]). It is not implausible, therefore, that he ascribed a different meaning to Jeans's quotation than the one provided by Cornford. Finally, as I show later in this chapter, the most compelling reason to suggest that Innis understood Jeans's statement in Idealist terms is Innis's acknowledgement in a conversation with W.T. Easterbrook that he accepted Immanuel Kant's definition of time and space as *a priori* forms.

150 Innis, "Space," 92

151 W.T. Easterbrook, Notes on Conversations with Harold Innis, 3 July 1952, *W.T. Easterbrook Papers*, University of Toronto Archives, B1975-0030, Box 1.

152 Innis, "Time," 90.

153 Innis, *Idea File*, 192.

154 Innis, "Political Economy," 127, cited from Geoffrey Scott, *The Architecture of Humanism* (London: Methuen, 1926), 163.

155 Harold Innis to W.T. Easterbrook, no date – probably 1952, *Easterbrook Papers,* University of Toronto Archives, B1975-0030/001.

156 Innis, *Idea File*, 191.

157 Ibid., 51.

158 Ibid., 191.

159 Innis, "Preface," xxvii.

160 Innis, *Idea File*, 102.

161 Harold Innis, "Review article: 'Sub Specie Temporis,'" *Canadian Journal of Economics and Political Science* 17 (1951), 553–7.

162 On this point, see the Introduction of Jeremy Dunham, Iain Hamilton Grant, and Sean Watson, *Idealism: The History of a Philosophy* (Montreal and Kingston: McGill-Queen's University Press, 2011).

163 Innis, *Idea File*, 99.

164 Harold Innis, "A Critical Review," in *The Bias of Communication* (Toronto: University of Toronto Press, 1995), 191.

165 Innis, "Time," 64.
166 Harold Innis, "Preface," xxvii.
167 William Buxton, "North by Northwest: Harold Innis and the 'Advancement of Knowledge of the Canadian North,'" in *Harold Innis and the North: Appraisals and Contestations* (Montreal and Kingston: McGill-Queen's University Press, forthcoming).
168 Innis, "Time," 86.
169 Ibid.
170 See B.S Keirstead, *The Theory of Economic Change* (Toronto: Macmillan of Canada, 1948), v, 267.
171 Ibid., 38–49, 253.
172 Ibid., 24.
173 Ibid., 28.
174 Ibid., 26.
175 Ibid., 38–49, 253; Innis, "Time," 86, 89.
176 Keirstead, *Economic Change*, 253, n10.
177 Harold Innis to Arthur Cole, no date (internal evidence in the letter suggests it was written after 19 February 1950), *Harold Innis Papers*, University of Toronto Archives, B72-0025, Box 11, File 1.
178 Harold Innis to Arthur Cole, 9 January 1950 and 20 January 1950, *Harold Innis Papers*, University of Toronto Archives, B72-0025, Box 11, File 1.
179 Innis, "Time," 75.
180 Harold Innis, "Idea File. Microfilm copy for private circulation. Preface by S.D. Clark," *Harold Innis Papers*, University of Toronto Archives, B72-0003, Box 14, File 1. Page 159.
181 Innis, *The Idea File*, 246.
182 Ibid., 191–2.
183 Harold Innis to Arthur Cole, 4 February 1950, *Harold Innis Papers*, University of Toronto Archives, B72-0025, Box 11, File 1.
184 Harold Innis to Arthur Cole, 28 February 1950, *Harold Innis Papers*, University of Toronto Archives, B1972-0025, Box 11, File 1.
185 Harold Innis to Arthur Cole, 24 April 1950, *Harold Innis Papers*, University of Toronto Archives, B72-0025, Box 11, File 1.
186 Innis, *Idea File*, 99.
187 Innis, "Introduction," 12–13.
188 Innis, "Roman Empire," 111.
189 Kierstead, *Economic Change*, 22.
190 Innis, "Preface," xxvii; Harold Innis, "Memoir of Harold Adams Innis: Covering the Years 1894–1922," *Canadian Journal of Communications*. 29 (2), S-26.

191 Leslie Armour and Elizabeth Trott, *The Faces of Reason: An Essay on Philosophy and Culture in English Canada 1850-1950* (Waterloo, Ontario: Wilfrid Laurier University Press, 1981), 354.

192 Harold Innis, "The Work of Thorstein Veblen," in Mary Quayle Innis, ed., *Essays in Canadian Economic History* (Toronto: University of Toronto Press, 1956), 18–19.

CHAPTER SIX

1 Mikhail Bakthin, *Rabelais and His World*, translated by Hélène Iswolsky (Cambridge, Massachusetts: MIT Press, 1968), 254–6; Charles Mackay, *Extraordinary Delusions and the Madness of Crowds* (New York: Harmony Books, 1980).

2 Duncan Watts, *Six Degrees: The Science of a Connected Age* (New York: W.W. Norton and Company, 2003): 195–219; James Surowiecki, *The Wisdom of Crowds* (New York: Anchor Books, 2004): 40–65; Sushil Bikhchandani, David Hirshleifer, and Ivo Welch, "A Theory of Fads, Fashion, Custom, and Cultural Change as Information Cascades," *Journal of Political Economy* 100 (5): 992–1026.

3 Malcolm Gladwell, *The Tipping Point* (Boston: Little Brown and Company, 2000).

4 Surowiecki, *Wisdom of Crowds*, 56–7.

5 Watts, *Six Degrees*, 204–5.

6 Ibid., 196–8; Surowiecki, *Wisdom of Crowds*, 53–5.

7 References to the visual turn in the social sciences include G. Rose, *Visual Methodologies* (London, Sage, 2001); G. Rose, "On the need to ask how, exactly, is geography 'visual'?" *Antipode* 35 (2): 212–21; John E. Thornes, "The Visual Turn and Geography," *Antipode* 36 (5): 787–94; and Anna Grimshaw and Amanda Ravetz, eds. *Visualizing Anthropology* (Bristol, UK: Intellect Books, 2005). For considerations of the visual turn from the standpoint of archival and information studies see Joan M. Schwartz, "Negotiating the Visual Turn: New Perspectives on Images and Archives," *American Archivist* 67 (1), (spring–summer 2004): 107–22.; and Stan Ruecker, Milena Radzikowska, and Stéfan Sinclair, *Visual Interface Design for Digital Cultural Heritage* (Farnham, UK: Ashgate, 2011). A mathematical consideration of the visual turn can be found in Marcus Giaquinto, *Visual Thinking in Mathematics* (Oxford, UK: Oxford University Press, 2011).

8 Reference to the aesthetic turn has been particularly pronounced in computer science generally and the field of human-computer interaction in particular. See L.E. Udsen and A.H. Jorgensen, "The aesthetic turn: unravelling

recent aesthetic approaches to human-computer interaction," *Digital Creativity* 16 (4) (2005): 205–16; Roger F. Malina, "A Forty-Year Perspective on Aesthetic Computing in the Leonardo Journal," in Paul Fishwick, ed., *Aesthetic Computing* (Cambridge, Massachusetts: MIT Press, 2006): 62–71; Neora Berger Shem-Shaul, et al., "Aesthetic Computing Manifesto," *Leonardo* 36 (4), (August 2003), 255..

9 See for example Barney Warf and Santa Arias, eds., *The Spatial Turn: Interdisciplinary Perspectives* (Oxford: Routledge, 2009); Simon Gunn, "The Spatial Turn: Changing Histories of Space and Place," in Simon Gunn and Robert J. Morris, eds., *Identities in Space: Contested Terrains in the Western City since 1850* (Aldershot, UK: Ashgate, 2001): 1–14; Jesper Falkheimer and Andre Jansson, eds., *Geographies of Communication: The Spatial Turn in Media Studies* (Göteborg, Sweden: Nordicom, 2006); and Diarmid A. Finnegan, "The Spatial Turn: Geographical Approaches in the History of Science," *Journal of the History of Biology* 41 (2) (2008): 369–88.

10 See W.J.T. Mitchell, "The Pictorial Turn," *ArtForum* 30 (7): 89–94. See also W.J.T. Mitchell, *Picture Theory* (Chicago: University of Chicago Press, 1995); and Neal Curtis, ed., *The Pictorial Turn* (Oxford: Routledge, 2010).

11 Cited in Richard Chalfen. "Looking Two Ways: Mapping the Social Scientific Study of Visual Culture," in *The SAGE Handbook of Visual Research Methods* (London, Sage Publications, 2011), 41. Helmers's comments were made as part of a call for publications by Parlor Press for a series of publications titled Visual Rhetoric. See http://www.parlorpress.com/visualrhetoric.html [30 September 2012].

12 See http://www.brocku.ca/3DVirtualBuildings [30 September 2012]. For an overview of the aims and pedagogy of *The 3D Virtual Buildings Project*, see John Bonnett, "New Technologies, New Formalisms for Historians: *The 3D Virtual Buildings Project*." In *Literary and Linguistic Computing* 19, 3 (September 2004): 273–87.; and John Bonnett, "Following in Rabelais' Footsteps: Immersive History and the 3D Virtual Buildings Project," *Journal of the American Association for History and Computing* 6 (2) (September 2003). Available on-line at: http://quod.lib.umich.edu/j/jahc/3310410.0006.202?rgn=main;view=fulltext [30 September 2012]. Other historians who have considered the potential of visualization to contribute to the field of history include Mark Moss and David Staley. See Moss, *Toward the Visualization of History: The Past as Image* (Lanham, Maryland: Rowman and Littlefield, 2008); and Staley, *Computers, Visualization, and History: How New Technology Will Transform Our Understanding of the Past* (Armonk, New York: M.E. Sharpe, 2003).

13 Ruecker, Radzikowska, and Sinclair, *Visual Interface Design for Digital Cultural Heritage*, 3.

14 Berger Shem-Shaul et al. "Aesthetic Computing Manifesto," 255.

15 "Transcript for Uncovering the Codes for Reality, March 1, 2012," at *On Being with Krista Tippett Website*. Available on-line at: http://www.onbeing.org/program/uncovering–codes–reality/transcript/1458#main_content [30 September 2012].

16 Malina, "A Forty-Year Perspective on Aesthetic Computing," 62.

17 Fred Weinstein offers an astute overview of the problems that agent heterogeneity and discontinuous behaviour have posed for twentieth-century social science theory. See Weinstein, "Psychohistory and the Crisis of the Social Sciences," *History and Theory* 34 (December 1995): 299–319. For a discussion of the problems that traditional formalisms have posed for reasoning about social dynamics, see J. Stephen Lansing, "'Artificial Societies' and the Social Sciences," *Artificial Life* 8 (2002): 272–92.

18 A good introductory, multi-disciplinary account of agent-based modeling can be found in Jonathan Rauch, "Seeing around Corners," *Atlantic Monthly*, April 2002: 35–48. More scholarly treatments include Joshua Epstein, *Generative Social Science: Studies in Agent-Based Computational Modeling* (Princeton, New Jersey: Princeton University Press, 2006); and Joshua Epstein and Robert Axtell, *Growing Artificial Societies: Social Science from the Bottom Up* (Washington, DC: Brookings Institute, 1996). Another volume featuring the work of multiple scholars, and multiple disciplines extending beyond economics, is Leigh Tesfatsion and Kenneth Judd, eds., *Handbook of Computational Economics, Volume 2: Agent-Based Computational Economics* (Boston: Elsevier, 2006).

19 Rauch, "Seeing Around Corners," 45–6; Robert L. Axtell et al., "Population Growth and Collapse in a Multiagent Model of the Kayenta Anasazi in Long House Valley," *Proceedings of the National Academy of Sciences of the United States of America*, vol. 99, supplement 3 (14 May 2002): 7275–9.

20 G. Trautteur and R. Virgilio, "An agent-based computational model for the Battle of Trafalgar: a comparison between analytical and simulative methods of research," in *Enabling Technologies: Infrastructure for Collaborative Enterprises, 2003.* WET ICE *2003. Proceedings. Twelfth* IEEE *International Workshops*, 9–11 June 2003: 377–82.

21 Giaquinto, *Visual Thinking in Mathematics*, 1.

22 See S. James Gates. "Symbols of Power," *Physics World* 23 (6): 34–9; Michael Moyer, "Is Space Digital?" *Scientific American*, February 2012: 30–7; Jacob D. Bekenstein, "Information in the Holographic Universe," *Scientific American*, August 2003: 58–66. Brian Greene provides an accessible introduction to the world of Superstring theory in *The Elegant Universe: Superstrings, Hidden*

Dimensions, and the Quest for the Ultimate Theory (New York: Vintage Books, 2000).

23 "Transcript for Uncovering the Codes for Reality," *On Being with Krista Tippett Website*.

24 Wheeler is often used as a frame of departure for discussions of digital physics, physics based on the supposition that everything derives from information, in large measure because of his famous aphorism: "It from Bit." See John Archibald Wheeler, "Information, physics, quantum: The search for links," in W. Zurek, ed., *Complexity, Entropy, and the Physics of Information* (Redwood City, California: Addison-Wesley, 1990): 3–28.

25 "Transcript for Uncovering the Codes for Reality," http://www.onbeing.org/program/uncovering-codes-reality/transcript/1458#main_content [30 September 2012].

26 Gates, "Symbols of Power," 39.

27 Michael Goodchild, "Social Sciences: Interest in GIS Grows," *ArcNews* 26 (1) (spring 2004): 1, 3. Available on-line at: http://www.esri.com/news/arcnews/spring04articles/social-sciences.html [29 September 2012]. In the humanities, scholars have also expressed an interest in GIS, and the use of its software to explore their topics using space as a frame of reference. See David J. Bodenhamer, John Corrigan, and Trevor M. Harris, eds., *The Spatial Humanities: GIS and the Future of Humanities Scholarship* (Bloomington, Indiana: Indiana University Press, 2010).

28 Ian Gregory and Paul Ell, "Analyzing spatiotemporal change by use of National Historical Geographical Information Systems: Population Change during and after the Great Irish Famine," *Historical Methods* 38 (4), 166.

29 Gregory and Ell, "Analyzing spatiotemporal change," 166.

30 Anne Kelly Knowles, "GIS and History," in Anne Kelly Knowles, ed., *Placing History: How Maps, Spatial Data, and GIS are Changing Historical Scholarship* (Redlands, California: ESTI Press, 2008): 1–26; Geoff Cunfer, *On the Great Plains: Agriculture and Environment* (College Station, Texas: A&M University Press, 2005); Michael McCormick, *Origins of the European economy : Communications and Commerce, A.D. 300–900* (Cambridge, UK: Cambridge University Press, 2001); Benjamin C. Ray, "'The horrid calamity which, plague-like, spread': Understanding the Salem witch trials as a Social Epidemic." Unpublished Paper. Available on-line at: http://pages.shanti.virginia.edu/2010_02_MDST3703/files/2010/02/Microsoft-Word-Salem.pdf [6 September 2012].

31 Ian Gregory, "Exploiting Time and Space: A Challenge for GIS in the Digital Humanities," in David J. Bodenhamer, John Corrigan, and Trevor M. Harris,

eds., *The Spatial Humanities: GIS and the Future of Humanities Scholarship* (Bloomington, Indiana: Indiana University Press, 2010): 59.

32 May Yuan and Kathleen Hornsby, *Computation and Visualization for Understanding Dynamics in Geographic Domains*. (Boca Raton, Florida: CRC Press, 2008): 10; David A. Bennett and Wenwu Tang, "Mobile, Aware, Intelligent Agents (MAIA)." In Kathleen Stewart Hornsby and May Yuan, eds., *Understanding Dynamics of Geographic Domains* (Boca Raton, Florida: CRC Press, 2008): 171–86.

33 John Corrigan, "Qualitative GIS and Emergent Semantics," in Bodenhamer, Corrigan, and Harris, eds., *The Spatial Humanities*, 82–3.

34 See, for example, Gary Lock, "Representations of Space and Place in the Humanities," in Bodenhamer, Corrigan and Harris, eds., *The Spatial Humanities*, 92–3.

35 May Yuan, "Mapping Text," in Bodenhamer, Corrigan and Harris, eds., *The Spatial Humanities*, 116–17; Trevor M. Harris, L. Jesse Rouse, and Susan Bergeron, "The Geospatial Semantic Web, Pareto GIS, and the Humanities," in Bodenhamer, Corrigan and Harris, eds., *The Spatial Humanities*, 124–42.

36 Lock, "Representations of Space and Place in the Humanities," 97.

37 The convergence of GIS and virtual worlds is being encouraged, in part, by the interest of spatial humanists in "deep mapping." The *deep map*, David Bodenhamer writes, is "an avant-garde technique first urged by the Situationist International in 1950s France. Popularized by author William Least Heat-Moon in *PrairyErth (a deep map)*, the approach 'attempts to record and represent the grain and patina of place through juxtapositions and interpenetrations of the historical and the contemporary, the political and the poetic, the discursive and the sensual' ... In its methods deep mapping conflates oral testimony, anthology, memoir, biography, images, natural history and everything you might event want to say about a place, resulting in an eclectic work akin to eighteenth- and early nineteenth-century gazetteers and travel accounts. Its best form results in a subtle and multilayered view of a small area of the earth." The "rapid convergence of GIS and other technologies, especially multimedia and gaming tools," Bodenhamer continues, "suggests that we are not far from the point when it will be possible to construct deep maps and landscapes of culture for any place where people leave records of their experiences." See David J. Bodenhamer, "The Potential of Spatial Humanities," in Bodenhamer, Corrigan, and Harris, eds., *The Spatial Humanities*, 26–8. Also see Lock, "Representations of Space and Place in the Humanities," 97–101; and Trevor M. Harris, John Corrigan and David J. Bodenhamer, "Challenges for the Spatial Humanities," in Bodenhamer, Corrigan, and Harris, eds., *The Spatial Humanities*, 171.

38 Chris L. Barrett, Stephen G. Eubank, and James P. Smith, "If Smallpox Strikes Portland ... " *Scientific American* 292 (3): 54–61.

39 For a brief introduction to High Performance Computing, see John Bonnett, Geoffrey Rockwell, and Kyle Kuchmey, "High Performance Computing in the Arts and Humanities," at: SHARCNET – *Shared Hierarchical Academic Research Computing Network Website*. Available on-line at: http://www.sharcnet.ca/Documents/HHPC/hpcdh.html [1 October 2012] (Posted September 2008); A recent call for humanities and social science researchers to use HPC in conjunction with agent-based modelling and virtual world software can be found in John Bonnett, "High–Performance Computing: An Agenda for the Social Sciences and the Humanities in Canada," *Digital Studies* 1 (2). 2009. Available on-line at: http://www.digitalstudies.org/ojs/index.php/digital_studies/article/view/168/211 [1 October 2012].

40 Big Data has traditionally been a concern of researchers in the sciences, although scholars in the social sciences and humanities are starting to incorporate it into their research through funding initiatives such as *The Digging into Data Challenge*. For a recent overview of its implications for research infrastructure and scholarly communication, see Tony Hay, Stewart Tansley, and Kristin Tolle, eds. *The Fourth Paradigm: Data-Intensive Scientific Discovery* (Redmond, Washington: Microsoft Research, 2009).

41 Stephen Jay Gould, *Wonderful Life: The Burgess Shale and the Nature of History* (New York: W.W. Norton, 1989), 23–52.

42 Simon Conway Morris, *The Crucible of Creation: The Burgess Shale and the Rise of Animals* (Oxford: Oxford University Press, 1998).

43 Simon Conway Morris, "Evolution and Convergence: Some Wider Considerations," in *The Deep Structure of Biology: Is Convergence Sufficiently Ubiquitous to Give a Directional Signal?* (West Conshohocken, Pennsylvania: Templeton Foundation Press, 2008): 54; Nicola S. Clayton and Nathan J. Emery, "Canny Corvids and Political Primates: A Case," in Conway Morris, ed., *The Deep Structure of Biology*: 130.

44 The most comprehensive exposition of Conway Morris's argument can be found in Simon Conway Morris, *Life's Solution: Inevitable Humans in a Lonely Universe* (Cambridge: Cambridge University Press, 2003). In his article "Evolution and Convergence," Conway Morris writes: "It seems, therefore, that the study of evolution, and especially of evolutionary convergence, will provide us with the outline of a 'map.' In some ways, it will be a strange sort of cartography because the map shows mostly the evolutionary destinations. How you get to a particular destination, say, humanoid intelligence, is distinctly less important than the end result. If, as I argue, evolution has

some fundamental predictabilities, then is not the vocabulary of surprise associated with the documentation of evolutionary convergence in itself all the more surprising? Almost invariably the words tend toward adjectives of stupefaction: *astonishing, astounding, remarkable, striking*, even *uncanny* and *stunning*, are all stock-in-trade responses. As I have pointed out elsewhere, although pronounced by loyal Darwinians, these exclamations seem to reveal a sense of unease. This, I conjecture, is at the least reflecting a hesitancy as to evolution's having a degree of directionality and, perhaps in the more alert investigator, their worst fears of the reemergence of a telos." See Conway Morris, "Evolution and Convergence," 50.

45 See Simon Conway Morris, "Darwin was right. Up to a point," *The Guardian*, 12 (February 2009). Available on-line at: http://www.guardian.co.uk/global/2009/feb/12/simon–conway–morris–darwin [3 October 2012]. Conway Morris writes: "Convergence is, in my opinion, not only deeply fascinating but, curiously, it is as often overlooked. More importantly, it hints at the existence of a deeper structure to biology. It helps us to delineate a metaphorical map across which evolution must navigate. In this sense the Darwinian mechanisms and the organic substrate we call life are really a search engine to discover particular solutions, including intelligence and—risky thought—perhaps deeper realities?" Simon Conway Morris, "Aliens Like Us?" *Astronomy and Geophysics* 46 (4): 26.

46 On this point Conway Morris writes: "Is science apparently running out of things to do simply because scientists hardly know how to tackle the yet-deeper problems that have been revealed? ... At least in the area of biology, one senses that not only have we hardly started, but the simple fact of evolution does little to explain the sheer complexity, fine balance, and potential of living systems. My sense, therefore, is that evolutionary convergence is, at the least, a straw in the wind, pointing to a deeper pattern of biological organization. Metaphorically, does not the ubiquity of convergence point to a map of life, a rugged landscape of almost entirely inaccessible regions that are threaded through by silver roads of vitality?" See Simon Conway Morris, "Introduction," in *The Deep Structure of Biology*, ix.

47 See Conway Morris, "Aliens Like Us?" and Simon Conway Morris, "Predicting what extra-terrestrials will be like: and preparing for the worst," *Philosophical Transactions. Series A, Mathematical, Physical, and Engineering Sciences* 369 (1936): 555–71.

48 Conway Morris, "Evolution and Convergence," 48.

49 Conway Morris, *Life's Solution*, 252–3.

50 Conway Morris notes: "The realization that there are important parallels between birdsong and human speech include, for example, second language

acquisition [or bilingualism] (see I.M. Pepperberg and D.M. Neapolitan in *Ethology* 77 [1988]: 150–68), and evidence for cultural transmission (see R.B. Payne et al. in *Behaviour* 77 [1981]: 199–221)." Conway Morris, *Life's Solution*, 412 n175.

51 With respect to the formal traits of birdsong, Conway Morris notes: "we tend to regard bird mimics as simply amusing, and their songs as only incidentally beautiful and in reality vocal expressions of territorial demarcation and the urgent priorities of mate attraction. Perhaps so, but it transpires that in reality there are under-appreciated similarities between our vocalizations and those of the birds, both in terms of songs and musical output (and even drumming with a stick) and neurology. Thus, with respect to song, both birds and humans share such features as 'interval inversion, simple harmonic relations, and retention of melody with change of key,' while our 'simple melodic canon ... is reminiscent of the matched countersinging of many bird species." Conway Morris, *Life's Solution*, 225–6. Conway Morris's quotations are from Allison Droupe and Patricia Kuhl, "Birdsong and human speech: Common themes and mechanisms," *Annual Review of Neuroscience* 22 (1999): 567–631.

52 Martin A. Nowak, Natalia L. Komarov, and Partha Niyogi write: "Language consists of words and rules. The finite ensemble of memorized words is called the mental lexicon, whereas the set of rules is called the mental grammar of a person. Grammar is the computational system … that is essential for creating the infinite expressibility of human language. Children acquire their mental grammar spontaneously and without formal training. Children of the same speech community reliably learn the same grammar. Exactly how the mental grammar comes into a child's mind is a puzzle. Children have to deduce the rules of their native language from sample sentences they receive from their parents and others. This information is insufficient for uniquely determining the underlying grammatical principles. Linguists call this phenomenon the "poverty of stimulus" or the "paradox of language acquisition." The proposed solution is universal grammar.

Universal grammar consists of (i) a mechanism to generate a search space for all candidate mental grammars and (ii) a learning procedure that specifies how to evaluate the sample sentences. Universal grammar is not learned but is required for language learning. It is innate." See Martin A. Nowak, Natalia L. Komarov, and Partha Niyogi, "Evolution of Universal Grammar," *Science* 291 (5501), 114. Also see Noam Chomsky, *Aspects of the Theory of Syntax* (Cambridge, Massachusetts: MIT Press, 1965).

53 Charles Yang, "Who's Afraid of George Kingsley Zipf?" Unpublished Paper. Department of Linguistics & Computer Science. University of Pennsylva-

nia, 4; Available on-line at: http://www.ling.upenn.edu/~ycharles/papers/zipf new.pdf [9 October 2012].

54 A good accessible introduction to Zipf's Law, and description of the domains to which it has been applied, can be found in Rauch, "Seeing Around Corners," 40–2.

55 Yang, "George Kingsley Zipf," 5.

56 Ibid., 13–14, 18.

57 Conway Morris, *Life's Solution*, 422n140; Conway Morris's treatment here is partly based on Brenda McCowan, Laurance R. Doyle, and Sean F. Hanser, "Using Information Theory to Assess the Diversity, Complexity, and Development of Communicative Repertoires," *Journal of Comparative Psychology* 116 (2): 166–72. Also see Simon Conway Morris, "The Boyle Lecture 2005: Darwin's Compass: How Evolution Discovers the Song of Creation," *Faith Magazine*, November-December 2005. Available on-line at: http://www.faith.org.uk/publications/Magazines/Nov05/Nov05DarwinsCom pass.html [9 October 2012].

58 Experiments undertaken by Allison Doupe and Patricia Kuhl suggest that birds, even with poverty of stimulus, display a capacity to "innately recognize their own species song. This recognition is presumed to underlie much of the innate predisposition to learn conspecific song evident in the tutoring experiments. Thus, both humans and birds start out perceptually prepared for specific vocal learning." See Doupe and Kuhl, "Birdsong and Human Speech," *Annual Review of Neuroscience* 22 (1999): 582–3. Examples of references to a modified version of Zipf's Law – one which employs a device known as a "Mandelbrot fit" – while studying animal communication includes Todd M. Freeberg and Jeffrey R. Lucas, "Information Theoretical Approaches to Chick-a-dee Calls of Carolina Chickadees (*Poecile carolinensis*)," *Journal of Comparative Psychology* 126 (1) (2012): 68–81; and J.P. Hailman and M.S. Ficken, "Combinatorial animal communication with computable syntax: 'chick-a-dee' calling qualifies as 'language' by structural linguistics," *Animal Behaviour* 34 (1899–1901); and Elodie Briefer et al., "Are bird song complexity and song sharing shaped by habitat structure? An information theory and statistical approach," *Journal of Theoretical Biology* 262 (1) (2010): 151–64. Also see B. McCowan et al., "The appropriate use of Zipf's law in animal communication studies," *Animal Behaviour* 69 (2005): F1–F7.

59 Conway Morris, "Darwin's Compass."

60 Conway Morris, *Life's Solution*, 422n136.

61 Nowak, Komarov, and Niyogi, "Evolution of Universal Grammar," 115. For his part, Chomsky is sceptical that the study of language and mind will be

easily integrated into studies of the brain, or that language acquisition and use will someday, some way, be reduced to the neural architecture of the brain. In an important 1995 essay, "Language and Nature," Chomsky complained that scholars too readily assume that the study of language will be unified, and subsumed, by neuroscience: "We don't know how eventual unification might proceed in this case, or if we have hit upon the right categories to seek to unify, or even if the question falls within our cognitive reach. We have no warrant simply to assume that mental properties are to be reduced to 'neural network properties,' to take a typical claim (Patricia Churchland 1994). Similar pronouncements have often proven false in other domains and are without any particular scientific merit in this case." See Noam Chomsky, "Language and Nature," *Mind* 104 (413), 2. Despite recent advances in neuroscience, Chomsky's position on the relationship between neuroscience and linguistics has not changed. For a more recent statement of his position, see the text associated with note 62 below.

62 Noam Chomsky, *The Science of Language: Interviews with James McGilvray* (Cambridge: Cambridge University Press, 2012), 67.

63 Conway Morris, "Darwin's Compass."

64 Conway Morris, "Evolution and Convergence," 61.

65 Conway Morris, "Darwin's Compass."

66 Conway Morris, "Introduction," ix; Conway Morris, "Evolution and Convergence," 50.

67 Conway Morris, "Darwin's Compass."

68 Conway Morris, "Evolution and Convergence," 60.

69 Patricia Gray et al. "The Nature of Music and the Music of Nature," *Science*, 291 (5501) (2001), 52.

70 Ibid., 54.

71 In 1947 Gödel famously declared that mathematical intuition should be considered on a par with human senses that can track the external environment. He writes: "Despite their remoteness from sense experience, we do have something like a perception also of the objects of set theory, as is seen from the fact that the axioms force themselves upon us as being true. I don't see any reason why we should have any less confidence in this kind of perception, i.e., in mathematical intuition, than in sense perception ... The set-theoretic paradoxes are hardly any more troublesome for mathematics than deceptions of the senses are for physics." Cited from James Robert Brown, *Platonism, Naturalism, and Mathematical Knowledge* (New York: Routledge, 2012), 61. For recent treatments on the intersection between Idealist philosophy and mathematics see Brown, *Platonism, Naturalism, and Mathematical Knowledge*; John D. Barrow, *Pi in the Sky: Counting, Thinking,*

and Being (Oxford: Clarendon Press, 1992); and Mario Livio, *Is God a Mathematician?* (New York: Simon and Schuster, 2009).

72 Nick Herbert, *Quantum Reality: Beyond the New Physics – An Excursion into Metaphysics and the Meaning of Reality* (New York: Anchor Books, 1985), 46–7.

73 Seth Lloyd, *Programming the Universe: A Quantum Computer Scientist Takes on the Cosmos* (New York: Vintage Books, 2006), 100–11.

74 Ibid., 117–19.

75 Ibid., 119–21.

76 Roger Penrose, *The Emperor's New Mind: Concerning Computers, Minds, and the Laws of Physics* (Oxford: Oxford University Press, 1989); Roger Penrose, *Shadows of the Mind: A Search for the Missing Science of Consciousness* (Oxford: Oxford University Press, 1994).

77 Barrow, *Pi in the Sky*. See especially 278–9.

78 Brown, *Platonism, Naturalism, and Mathematical Knowledge*.

79 Herbert, *Quantum Reality*, 211–31.

80 Bruce Rosenblum and Fred Kuttner, *Quantum Enigma: Physics Encounters Consciousness*. Second Edition (Oxford: Oxford University Press, 2011): 87–100; 237–56.

81 Ibid., 199. The authors are quoting Peter G. Wolynes, "Some quantum weirdness in physiology," *PNAS* 106 (41): 17247.

82 Rosenblum and Kuttner, *Quantum Enigma*, 196.

83 Leonard Susskind, *The Black Hole War: My Battle with Stephen Hawking to Make the World Safe for Quantum Mechanics* (New York: Little, Brown and Company, 2008), 301; For introductions to the Holographic Principle, see Jacob D. Bekenstein, "Information in the Holographic Universe," *Scientific American* (August 2003): 58–65; and R. Buosso, "The Holographic Principle," *Reviews in Modern Physics* 74 (2002): 825–74.

84 Susskind, *The Black Hole War*, 8–9.

85 Ibid., 154, 269, 335.

86 Ibid., 298.

87 Ibid., 295–306.

88 Ibid., 300–1.

89 Ibid., 300.

90 Ibid., 305.

91 Paola Zizzi, "Consciousness and Logic in a Quantum-Computing Universe," in Jack A. Tuszynski, ed., *The Emerging Physics of Consciousness* (New York: Springer, 2006), 477.

92 Ibid., 457.

93 Mark Germaine, "Process Psychology, Neurology, and the Science and Philosophy of Mind," *Acta Neuropsychologica* 5 (1/2): 8–20.

94 David Z. Albert and Rivka Galchen, "A Quantum Threat to Special Relativity," *Scientific American* 300 (3): 32–9.

95 See chapter 5 of Shan Gao, *Quantum, Relativity, Consciousness and Beyond* (Seattle: Amazon Kindle Direct Publishing, 2011); and Shan Gao, *Quantum Motion: Unveiling the Mysterious Quantum World* (Bury St Edmonds, UK: Arima Publishing, 2006): 133–45.

96 See section "Where to Find It?" chapter 8 of Shan Gao, *Quantum, Relativity, Consciousness and Beyond.* Gao cites John Bell, "Quantum Field Theory without Observers," *Physics Reports* 137 (1986): 49–54.

97 Shan Gao writes: "We stress that the absolute validity of the principle of relativity must be limited due to the existence of [a] preferred Lorentz frame. The principle of relativity does not hold true for the collapse process of the wave function. It should be mentioned that Einstein, the founder of special relativity, also realized the possible limitation of the principle of relativity. He thought, 'As long as one was convinced that all natural phenomena were capable of representation with the help of classical mechanics, there was no need to doubt the validity of this principle of relativity. But in view of the more recent development of electrodynamics and optics, it became more and more evident that classical mechanics affords an insufficient foundation for the physical description of all natural phenomena. At this juncture the question of the validity of the principle of relativity became ripe for discussion, and it did not appear impossible that the answer to this question might be in the negative.'" See Shan Gao, *Quantum, Relativity, Consciousness and Beyond,* chapter 7, section, "The incompatibility problem and absolute frame." Gao's quotation of Einstein is from chapter 5 of Albert Einstein, *Relativity: The Special and General Theory*, translated by Robert W. Larson (New York: Henry Holt, 1920). Available on-line at: http://www.bartleby.com/173/5.html [18 October 2012].

98 Jean-Daniel Bancal et al., "Quantum nonlocality based on finite-speed causal influences leads to superluminal signaling," at *ArXiv e-prints database*. arXiv:1110.3795. Publication date 10/2011. Available on-line at: http://arxiv.org/abs/1110.3795 [13 October 2012].

99 See chapter 5 of Seth Lloyd, *Programming the Universe* (New York: Alfred Knopf, 2006).

100 See chapter 8, section "Further Discussions," of Shan Gao, *Quantum, Relativity, Consciousness and Beyond.*

CONCLUSION

1 Harold Innis, "An Introduction to the Economic History of the Maritimes, Including Newfoundland, and New England," in *Essays in Canadian Economic History*, edited by Mary Q. Innis (Toronto: University of Toronto Press, 1962, c. 1956), 42.

2 K.P. Stitch, "The Leaven of Wine and Spirits in the Fiction of Robertson Davies," in *Robertson Davies: A Mingling of Contrarities* (Ottawa: University of Ottawa Press, 2001), 75.

3 See Tom Cooper, "The Unknown Innis," *Journal of Canadian Studies*, 12 (winter 1977), 114. By "fool," I mean the sort of fool described by Mikhail Bakhtin in *Rabelais and his World*. Bakhtin characterized holy fools as outsiders who juxtapose observations from different domains of human experience to produce laughter and to force their audience to confront ideas that they are often unwilling to face, due to fear, or pride. The holy fool could be a devastatingly effective literary device to express ideas about society, culture, and the social construction of nature that could not be expressed in other venues and other genres. See Bakhtin, *Rabelais and his World*, translated by Hélène Iswolsky (Cambridge, Massachusetts: MIT Press, 1968).

4 Harold Innis, "The Role of Intelligence: Some Further Notes," *Canadian Journal of Economics and Political Science* 1 (2), 283.

5 Harold Innis, "Preface," in *The Bias of Communication* (Toronto: University of Toronto Press, 1951), xxvii.

Index